AF608138

RALLY *the* SCATTERED BELIEVERS

RELIGION IN
NORTH AMERICA

Catherine L. Albanese
and Stephen J. Stein, *editors*

RALLY *the* SCATTERED BELIEVERS

NORTHERN NEW ENGLAND'S RELIGIOUS GEOGRAPHY

SHELBY M. BALIK

Indiana University Press
Bloomington and Indianapolis

This book is a publication of

INDIANA UNIVERSITY PRESS
Office of Scholarly Publishing
Herman B Wells Library 350
1320 East 10th Street
Bloomington, Indiana 47405 USA

iupress.indiana.edu

Telephone orders 800-842-6796
Fax orders 812-855-7931

♾ The paper used in this publication meets the minimum requirements of the American National Standard for Information Sciences—Permanence of Paper for Printed Library Materials, ANSI Z39.48–1992.

Manufactured in the United States of America

Library of Congress Cataloging-in-Publication Data

Balik, Shelby M.
Rally the scattered believers : northern New England's religious geography / Shelby M. Balik.
pages cm. — (Religion in North America)
Includes bibliographical references and index.
ISBN 978-0-253-01210-4 (cloth) — ISBN 978-0-253-01213-5 (ebook)
1. New England—Church history. 2. Ecclesiastical geography—New England. 3. Religion and geography—New England. I. Title.
BR530.B35 2014
277.4'081—dc23

2013043182

1 2 3 4 5 19 18 17 16 15 14

To Bill, Carly, and Peter,
with much love.

Contents

Foreword

SHELBY M. BALIK's new book showcases movement, travel, and the scatteredness that comes with them. Scattered believers, we can guess, have a more stressful time than those who stay in one place. That reality provides an important clue to the importance of her work for American religious studies. Balik uses a spatial-studies approach to assess religious change in northern New England (Vermont, New Hampshire, and Maine) in the years following the Revolution and into the early national period. The region was isolated by the standards of the time, and within this vast and challenging arena, two religious systems competed. The first, Congregationalism, followed the town-church model of lower New England. Here, residency meant orthodoxy, and doctrinal aberrations were frequently overlooked to preserve geographical unity. The second, a cadre of movements, ranging from Baptist to Methodist to Universalist to Freewill Baptist, embraced itinerancy, with the piety promoted by the Second Great Awakening as its major calling card. As the two models interacted, argues Balik, a new physical and spiritual topography emerged, a "crazy quilt of faiths sewn together by threads of exchange, competition, and debate."

Balik brings to her subject theoretical perspectives gleaned from the spatial-studies work of scholars such as Edward Linenthal, David Chidester, Belden Lane, and Amy DeRogatis. In her own application, however, Balik moves spatial studies into a new and more complex terrain. Most such studies focus on existing landscapes or on built environments considered as (at least temporary) fixed structures. By contrast, Balik follows movement across space, emphasizing fluidity and change. The geographical hinterland brought travel and migration to be sure. But, even for those who remained in towns, it also brought inexorable change. Mission societies undercut town churches and re-formed Congregationalism to fit an itinerant landscape.

In narrating what happened as the two models of itinerancy and fixed location met, Balik is at pains to show that the story is not a simple one of Congregationalist decline. Instead, she suggests a more complex set of transformations in which each model in some ways imitated the other and ended in an identifiably different form from its shape at the beginning of the period. Town churches faced the migration of their congregants and consequent instability as well as a lack of ministers. As time passed, they employed visiting ministers and cooperated with new networking mission societies that made them look increasingly like itinerants. In their turn, itinerants moved into new definitions of community that brought emergent religious groups into collaboration with one another on a multi-denominational basis and also into settled parishes. Piety continued to abound among them, intensely familial and also denominational. As Balik tells the story, the only part of itinerancy that died was itinerancy itself—an ironic twist, to be sure, to the earlier announcement of a traveling Zion.

As Balik unfolds this narrative, she makes impressive use of available evidence and provides helpful charts and summaries. With her focus on the distinctly understudied northern New England region in a relatively circumscribed time period, she brings significant new material to the attention of specialists in the post-Revolutionary and early national eras. But her story should not be read as simply one that fills a gap in post-colonial religious historiography. Rather, with its attention to how competing cultural forms negotiated their differences in a time of change, her work gives readers not only historical but also sociological insight. In short, she exposes difficult processes of cultural coping that anticipate the way religion would be worked out in much of the new United States. As she explores these processes in one specific area, Balik underscores the unlikely combination of tradition and innovation. This north country was truly a place of paradox—expanding outward with a new and ecumenically open pluralism at the same time that it narrowed with the restricted vision of intense and beleaguered religious groups.

So *Rally the Scattered Believers* signals a metaphorical and spiritual journey, an inner expedition, if you will, that historical actors were compelled to undertake. That said, the irony of the end of itinerancy in the emergence of a new order takes on additional meaning. Spatial studies become not merely a scrutiny of topography. They look beneath the surface of maps and movements to discover a geography that is distinctly interior and *moral* (to borrow a phrase from Amy DeRogatis). Traveled landscapes, in Shelby M. Balik's book, are inner as well as outer. Scattering affects the heart.

Catherine L. Albanese
Stephen J. Stein
Series Editors

Acknowledgments

If it takes a village to raise a child, then it takes a metropolis to write a book. This one has been in the works for some dozen years, which means I owe quite a lot of thanks to quite a lot of people. I am delighted, at last, to make good on those debts.

This book is, in large part, a product of other people's great teaching. Teachers rarely get enough credit, and the fruits of their labor often do not become apparent until decades after the fact. So, as long as I have this forum for giving thanks, I am going to use it to recognize the teachers who worked so hard on my behalf. Long (*long*) ago, Karen Armstrong and Elyse Eisner taught me to love writing. Susan Turner-Jones and Joannie Parker challenged me to write better. Leni Wildflower and Kevin O'Malley showed me a much bigger world than I had known and nudged me out into it. Timothy Harris and the late Jack Thomas taught me to write like a historian. Howard Chudacoff taught me to think like one. More importantly, he got me wondering (whether he knew it or not) if I should try thinking like a historian for a living.

The teachers to whom I owe the most are my graduate school professors. In seminars with Steve Kantrowitz and the late Paul Boyer, I read books and asked questions that led me to my research topic. Bill Cronon inspired me to think about landscapes in ways that have carried into this book, and Ron Numbers and Bill Reese helped advance the project by posing thoughtful and challenging questions. The late Jeanne Boydston's keen intellect sharpened my thinking from the very first seminar I took with her, and her feedback helped me pinpoint my argument as I whittled down a behemoth of a manuscript. Even more importantly, Jeanne provided the best model I can imagine of an unfailingly incisive but always generous-minded and humane scholar. I wish I had thanked her for that while I had the chance. And I owe especially profound thanks to Charles Cohen. During my years at Wisconsin, he spilled vats of red ink on my papers and chapters in an effort to turn me into a more precise thinker and writer. If I have argued my points and defined my terms clearly in these pages, it's very much to his credit (and if I haven't, the blame is all my own). Since I finished at Wisconsin, Chuck has offered patient and steadfast support, despite a few twists and turns that left my professional future very much in question. I hope this book offers reassurance that his faith in me was well-founded.

Devising a research topic is one thing. Carrying it out is quite another, and my project—which led me to twenty libraries scattered throughout nine states—posed major financial and logistical challenges. It would have been impossible without the support I received from the American Antiquarian Society, the Graduate Student Council and History Department at the University of Wisconsin–Madison, the National Society of the Colonial Dames in the State of Wisconsin, the New England Regional Fellowship Consortium, the Louisville Institute, and the School of Letters, Arts, and Sciences at Metropolitan State University of Denver. To this list, I should add another, less direct source of financial aid: the relatives, friends, and friends-of-friends who hosted me during my research travels. Sara Fazio and Lindsey Baden, Joe Hall and Melissa Sundell, Wendy and Bruce Hazard, Ronnie and Frank Maslan, and Kari and Andy Rieser all offered spare rooms (or, in the Hazards' case, a cabin in the Maine woods—where, very appropriately, a previous resident had inscribed biblical verses all around the property). Their hospitality and generosity saved me from debt, loneliness, and dicey motels.

During these research trips and in the years since, I have benefited from the assistance of archivists, librarians, and others who helped me navigate their repositories, suggested sources that I might never have found on my own, and helped me secure copyright permissions. I gratefully acknowledge Joanne Chaison, John Hench, Marie Lamoureaux, and Caroline Sloat at the American Antiquarian Society; Nancy Blostein, Betsy Dunbar, and Jan Ballard at the American Baptist Historical Society; Frances O'Donnell at the Andover-Harvard Theological Library; Dawn Piscitello at the Boston University Theological Library; Harold Worthley and Jessica Steytler at the Congregational Library and Archives; Nancy Milnor and Barbara Austin at the Connecticut Historical Society; Bill Barry, Nick Noyes, Stephanie Philbrick, and Dani Fazio at the Maine Historical Society; Cherylinne Pina and Conrad Wright at the Massachusetts Historical Society; Bill Copeley, D. B. Garvin, and David Smolen at the New Hampshire Historical Society; Suzanne Douglas and Eva Garcelon-Hart at the Henry Sheldon Museum; Paul Carnahan and Marjorie Strong at the Vermont Historical Society; Gregory Sanford and Kathy Watters at the Vermont State Archives; and Michael Edmonds and Laura Hemming at the Wisconsin Historical Society. Thanks as well to the staffs at the Auraria Library in Denver, the Massachusetts Archives, the Maine State Archives, the Milner Library at Illinois State University, the New Hampshire Division of Archives and Records Management, the New Hampshire State Library, the Phillips Library, and the University of Vermont Special Collections. It would have been simply impossible to manage my research without them.

I am also grateful to colleagues who have given of their time and expertise to help me improve this book. Jim Drake generously (and voluntarily!) read the whole manuscript and gave insightful feedback. Tom Altherr, Kate Carté Engel, Monys Hagen, Laresh Jayasanker, Kim Klimek, Steve Leonard, Andrea

Maestrejuan, Laura McCall, John Monnett, and Amy Wood all read sections and offered wise and much-appreciated suggestions. Linda Smith Rhoads and Caroline Sloat, in their capacities as editors of articles drawn from this project (along with the anonymous reviewers of those articles), helped me sharpen my points and prose in ways that ultimately benefited the book. Colleagues on H-Net lists chimed in with insights that have saved me from error and ignorance. I also appreciate the feedback I received at conferences and seminars where I presented parts of this research. In particular, the 2003–2004 Fellows at the American Antiquarian Society, the 2004–2005 Fellows at the Massachusetts Historical Society, the participants in the 2006 Louisville Winter Seminar, my fellow FREACs in the Front Range Early American Consortium, and participants in the Metro Unpublished Papers and Extended Thesis Seminar (MUPPETS) have offered suggestions that launched me forward or set me straight at different stages of this project.

As a first-time author, I've been lucky to find steady hands and level heads to guide me through the steps to publication. It was by pure serendipity that a friend of a friend put me in touch with Mark Cook, who created beautiful maps that enhance the book more than I thought possible. I am also extremely fortunate that my book found a home at Indiana University Press. Series editors Catherine Albanese and Stephen Stein each read the manuscript closely, and their advice for improving it was spot-on. I thank them for both their insight and their commitment to this project. Dee Mortensen has shepherded the book through the editorial process with patience, encouragement, and good humor. Sarah Jacobi has been ready with quick answers to my steady stream of questions on permissions, manuscript preparation, and the like. Margaret Hogan was my good friend long before she took this book on as its copyeditor. Now that she has tamed my unwieldy prose and caught my blundering mistakes, I owe her a great professional debt on top of countless personal ones. Angela Burton and Nancy Lightfoot made the whole operation run smoothly, and IUP's production team made the book look great. It has been my privilege to work with all of them.

An undertaking of this scale requires much solitary work. But it also depends on collaboration, conversation, and moral support. I am grateful to colleagues who have offered sounding boards, suggestions, and much-needed perspective (and, perhaps most importantly, distraction from the book). At the University of Wisconsin–Madison, my extended cohort of early Americanists—including James Carrott, Sarah Costello, Spencer Fluhman, Joe Hall, Rob Harper, Maggie Hogan, Eric Morser, Monica Najar, and Hannah Nyala West—provided intellectual and social camaraderie, along with a few truly regrettable film showings. From Madison to Normal to Denver, I am lucky to have enjoyed the company and collegiality of friends who have listened to my ramblings, shared their wisdom, and talked me down from very tall trees. Rather than include a long list of names that would inevitably leave someone out, I'll just say this: you know who you are, and I thank you. Along the way, Sandy Heitzkey, Jim Schlender, Donna Potempa, Sharon Roehling, and the late Judy Cochran have protected me from my own ineptitude by helping me navigate various bureaucracies. And I have many times been the lucky beneficiary of those who stood ready to give me a hand up when I needed it. Pamela Laird, Myra Rich, Jonathan Sassi, Beth Barton Schweiger, and Susan Schulten have all offered critical support at pivotal moments in my career, for which I am sincerely grateful.

I suspect I am not alone among academics when I say that of all the people listed in these pages, my family knows me the best but my work the least. It is to their credit that they have been so supportive through an incomprehensibly long journey. My parents, Allen and Barbara Balik, started me off on a lifetime of learning by filling our home with conversation and my shelves with books. They, along with Randy and Noelle Balik, Ruth and Peter Philpott, Kathy Philpott Costa, and Amauri Costa, have offered unconditional encouragement despite my rudely typing away at this manuscript during family visits. I appreciate their moral support and their enthusiasm for my work, and especially their habit of asking about my career path in very delicately phrased questions so as not to induce panic attacks. I thank them for their faith that it would all work out somehow. And guess what? It has worked out, indeed.

My children, Carly and Peter, have contributed precisely nothing to the book but have made up for that by bringing untold joy into our lives. Among my greatest delights as a parent has been watching my children learn, and their exuberant sense of discovery has added new layers of meaning to my world. Growing up with two academics as parents, they cannot remember a time without two books in progress in our house, for which we surely owe them an apology (and probably therapy). I admit there have been too many times when I've had to choose writing over storybook-reading, crayfish-catching, or snowman-building. They have weathered the neglect with good cheer and resourcefulness. We've asked much patience of them, but I do recall an evening around the dinner table when they told us they were proud of us for writing books. Carly and Peter, we're proud of you, too.

My husband, Bill Philpott, has read so many drafts and helped me untangle so many logical and writerly knots that every page of this book bears his imprint. Thank goodness for that. He is my in-house editor, closest colleague, and greatest inspiration as a writer and teacher. Beyond any of these things, he is a true partner, and my dearest and most beloved friend. For all of this and more, I thank him.

A Note on Places

The names of towns, counties, rivers, and other landmarks have changed over time. I have attempted to respect the historic names while also making references to those places recognizable to modern readers. Accordingly, I have used modern spellings in my prose but have left the older spellings stand in primary quotes. Similarly, the maps in this book are intended to evoke northern New England as its early republican inhabitants would have understood the region. Place names and locations reflect the maps of that era as accurately as possible, using historic names and spellings. Rivers, lakes, and mountain ranges are drawn as they appear on early maps, which were created with older cartographic techniques, even though these natural features might look different on modern maps.

RALLY *the* SCATTERED BELIEVERS

Introduction

Churching the Northern Wilds

ON ONE POINT layfolk and clergy agreed: there were quite a lot of people, but precious little religion, in New England's northern reaches. New migrants coursed through outlying settlements during the early decades of the new republic, rushing past the abandoned farms and ramshackle cottages that earlier travelers had left in their wakes. Witnesses wrote of towns "fast filling up with inhabitants" who came "from different places [and brought] with them different customs," and outposts so congested that "mountaineers . . . are crowding up the cliffs after one another, and planting their log huts where . . . bears would never think of inhabiting."[1] The relentless mobility was disconcerting to many who experienced it; despite the influx, one settler reported feeling "as much alone . . . as if I was ten thousand miles from any inhabitants."[2] Neighbors were everywhere, but communities were hard to come by.

Such erratic settlement made for difficult church-gathering. Poor towns with transient occupants could not support thriving congregations, but many of these same settlers nonetheless wanted contact with ministers and churches. Sensing an opportunity, all manner of clergy followed migrants into the hinterland, hoping to stake claims to religious territory before competitors could make deep inroads. Congregationalists, who considered northern New England an extension of their home turf in Connecticut and Massachusetts, were annoyed by what they saw as their rivals' audacity. Missionary William Miller complained of spiritual chaos in Vermont, wrought by Methodists, Universalists, "corrupt Baptists," and "nothingarians" who seemed to have flooded "this Northern World."[3] But such grumbling could not stop the upstarts' explosive growth. So Congregationalists, too, jumped into the fray. The General Association of Connecticut, a Congregationalist body, declared that "as new settlements are rapidly forming in the wilderness, the work is daily growing more extensive, laborious, and important."[4] Their adversaries agreed. As the clergy—and the laity they courted—pursued the

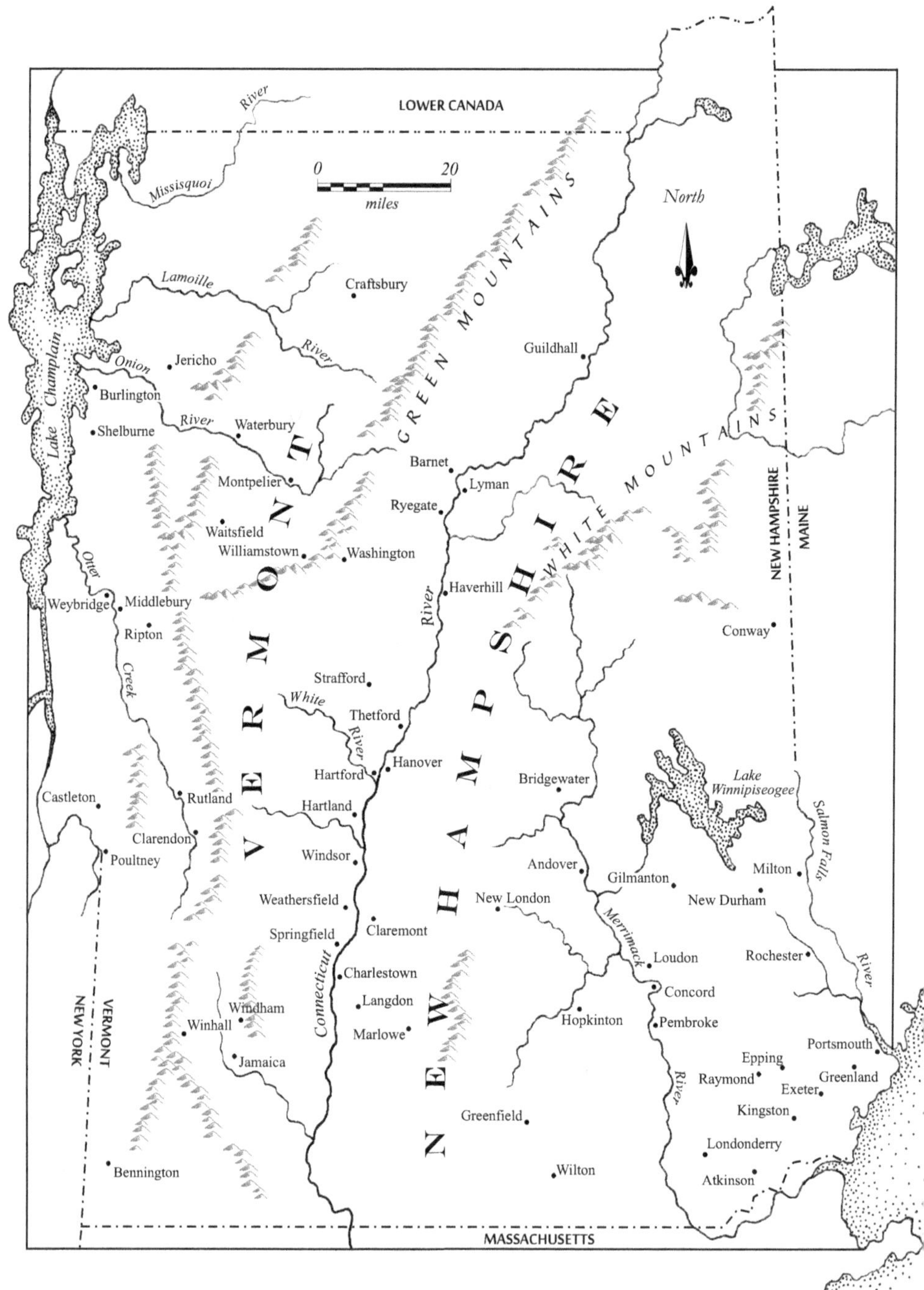

Maps 0.1 and 0.2. Vermont, New Hampshire, and Maine, ca. 1780–1830. Although some county lines in each state changed over the early nineteenth century, the towns—most of which had been chartered during the colonial period—remained more or less the same. (Note: the map of Vermont and New Hampshire is not drawn to the same scale as that of Maine.) *Maps by Mark Cook.*

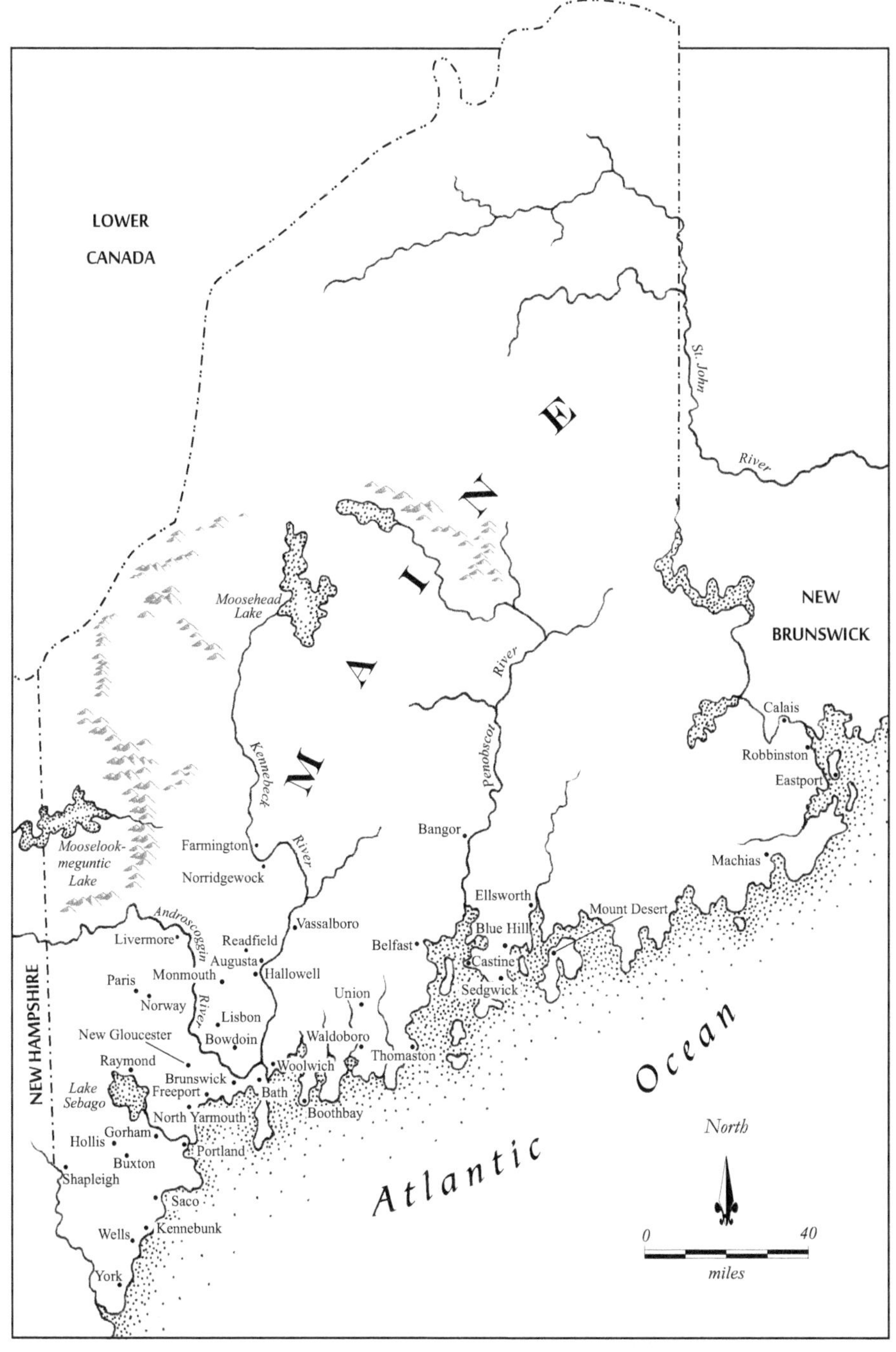
LOWER
CANADA
M A I N E
St. John
River
NEW
BRUNSWICK
Moosehead
Lake
River
Penobscot
Kennebeck
River
Calais
Robbinston
Eastport
Mooselook-
meguntic
Lake
Farmington
Norridgewock
Bangor
Machias
Ellsworth
Mount Desert
Androscoggin
Vassalboro
Blue Hill
Livermore
Readfield
Belfast
Augusta
Castine
Monmouth
Hallowell
Paris
Sedgwick
Norway
River
Union
Lisbon
New Gloucester
Bowdoin
Waldoboro
Thomaston
NEW HAMPSHIRE
Raymond
Woolwich
Brunswick
Lake
Sebago
Freeport
Bath
North Yarmouth
Boothbay
Ocean
Gorham
Hollis
Portland
Buxton
Atlantic
North
Shapleigh
Saco
Kennebunk
Wells
0
40
miles
York

work of conversion and church-building, they laid the groundwork for a new religious world.

How did this world take shape? To answer this question, this book considers how ministers and laypeople remapped northern New England's *religious geography:* the many ways in which denominations and churchgoers organized their communities spatially. Religious geography unfolded in two different dimensions: physical space—the actual and relative locations of institutions, clergy, and layfolk—and spiritual space—the ways clergy and laity arranged their relationships to give shape to religious communities. Migrants and settlers, families and churches, seekers and preachers all transformed the region's religious culture by extending spiritual ties across the physical landscapes on which they lived.

Americans have a long history of molding their spiritual practices and experiences to their notions of space and using religious ritual to recast their physical environments.[5] The first generation of Puritans worked to create "gardens in the wilderness" by clearing evil and sin (as well as trees, brush, and overgrowth) from their settlements, spreading out farmscapes where forests once stood. In eighteenth-century Virginia, elegant Anglican churches superimposed gentility onto a landscape once dotted with rundown shacks, allowing elites to display their social graces as they led processions to worship. Nineteenth-century migrants from New England to Ohio modeled new settlements after the towns they had left behind, hoping that duplicate town plans would foster the same pious sensibilities. And in Kentucky and points west, Methodists used camp meetings to tame their own frontier surroundings by infusing religious ritual with the Victorian propriety to which they aspired.[6] In all of these places, churchgoers and clergy fashioned landscapes that paralleled their spiritual worlds. More than merely reflecting or illustrating religious values, they created spaces that embodied their spirituality in physical form.

In northern New England, too, institutions, ministers, and worshipers mapped their environment to make it conform to their spiritual ideals. The northern frontier was the backdrop for two competing religious geographies: the town-church and itinerant systems. The town church (historically linked to the Congregationalist establishment) conceived of its religious community as organically rooted in a particular place, and it joined believers and nonbelievers in a common spiritual endeavor with their minister. Neighbors who occupied coterminous civil and religious spaces invested in each other's spiritual fates and shared covenant duties. The Congregationalist system, also known as the New England Way, had originated with New England's first Puritan settlers. They founded churches that shared boundaries with towns, each keeping all the town's residents under its watch, even though only baptized and converted Christians enjoyed the privileges of full membership. Under the New England Way, each town church was an independent polity, a covenanted society of believers and their clergy who united to improve the community's spiritual and moral well-being. Although Congregationalists modified the New England Way over the ensuing 150 years, the town-church model remained in place, as did its religious geography. The church consisted of a web of relationships based on mutual duty, its participants bound to each other and facing the pulpit together.

Adherents to the itinerant system, on the other hand, did not plant spiritual roots in specific physical places. Instead, scattered Methodists, Universalists, and regular and Freewill Baptists forged religious ties that transcended town borders. Although these denominations differed on doctrinal points, they shared, to varying degrees, a hierarchical and centralized administrative style that enforced uniformity in doctrine, discipline, and practice over a broad region. Each denomination offered a crowded calendar of annual, quarterly, and monthly meetings that brought presiding elders together with local preachers and itinerants (and sometimes laity) in gatherings that rotated among towns, counties, and states. Beneath these layers of meetings lay local bodies—churches, classes, and conferences—that were linked to each other and to their denominations through a far-reaching itinerant network. Under this plan, religious bonds among scattered believers superseded the ties between individual congregations and their towns. Rather than looking inward to their communities, members of local churches looked outward to other congregations with whom they shared common doctrines and rituals.[7]

These two geographies collided as Maine, New Hampshire, and Vermont grew more crowded in the decades following the American Revolution. Although southern New England was a mature society by then, northern New England was very much a place in progress. There were a few older, well-established towns, but much of the region was lightly settled, highly mobile, and lacking signs of permanence such as roads, schools, churches, or market centers. The earliest English migrants to the region had been mostly Congregationalists from Massachusetts and Connecticut who plotted out settlements in the northern seaports in the seventeenth century. A slow trickle of settlers followed throughout the eighteenth century, concentrating in coastal areas and major river valleys and scattering lightly around the hinterland in between. They brought a straightforward template for organizing religious communities: the New England town church. But when these migrants tried to overlay this blueprint on the northern landscape, they found that the region's topography confounded efforts to gather churches. Mountains and ravines carved up parishes; narrow gorges walled in tiny settlements, leaving impoverished inhabitants unable to support ministers; and thin, rocky soil forced would-be farmers into lives of perpetual migration, untethered to communities and congregations. And soon they faced another obstacle: dissenters streamed into the area and challenged this fragile parish system. The Baptists, whose numbers had started to grow before the American Revolution, posed the earliest threat. Beginning in the 1780s, waves of Methodists, Universalists, Freewill Baptists, and others began to disrupt the town-church geography by crossing parish lines to worship, refusing to pay ministerial taxes, and creating rival institutions that reached into the backcountry.

If the old town-church system would not work, then what would? Faced with this quandary, northern New Englanders redesigned their religious world to fit the place where they found themselves. By the 1830s, the region's physical landscape of religion looked very different than it had decades earlier. The clergy and laity had erased parish boundaries, created new fixtures of church governance that extended beyond town lines to manage networks of believers, and in the process dismantled the old town-church establishment. Just as importantly, the region's *spiritual* landscape had shifted. No longer did one's town define one's religious community. Instead, believers sought each other out through correspondence and print, and they relied on traveling preachers for leadership, forging fluid bonds of faith that befitted a geographically fluid population. What had taken shape in northern New England was a new religious landscape for a new evangelical age.

Just as northern New Englanders altered their religious landscapes, so too did their encounters with physical landscapes frame their religious experiences. Accordingly, this book treats geography not just as a spiritual or theoretical construct but as a tangible fact of everyday life. To understand how geography intertwined with people's spiritual experiences, we must enter those people's physical spaces. Today, if you were to venture up the highest peaks and into the most remote hinterlands of Vermont, New Hampshire, or Maine, you would find ruins of stone walls, a couple of feet high, threading through forests and lining even the craggiest paths. They resemble the same kinds of stone walls that remain ubiquitous throughout southern New England, once marking property lines in town centers and pastures. The walls in northern New England's mountains likewise marked people's homes and farms. Quite far from any town, on hillsides where long-ago paths might have accommodated horses but not wagons—that is where people *lived.* But recognizing this fact raises more questions than it answers. If settlers made their homes in these unforgiving landscapes, how did they forge community? How did they form neighborhoods? How did they get to town and church? People who lived near town centers understandably felt invested in the meetinghouses and ministers their taxes supported. But what about these mountaintop settlers, and the clergy who ministered to them? How did the physical spaces they occupied inform their spiritual experiences and inclinations? This book answers those questions by considering how layfolk and clergy created religious communities and institutions in these challenging places.

Religious change advanced through northern New England at a halting and uneven pace, over equally uneven landscapes. A town situated on a flat river plain or harbor, with access to roads, might have boasted one or two churches, perhaps a settled minister, and hosted a steady stream of itinerants passing through. But a settlement secluded in a gorge nearby might have gone months or years without seeing a pastor or holding communion. And the region's mountainous and wooded northern tier comprised a patchwork of uninhabited townships and parishes, which existed only on maps and in official records, the relics of older charters and land grants. Different kinds of religious communities materialized at different times in different places, depending on a town's stage of settlement, the presence or absence of missionaries and itinerant ministers, and the economic or demographic stability that facilitated or precluded church-building. The book thus casts a wide net over northern New England, because the flow of people and ideas between more cosmopolitan towns and remote settlements was crucial to the regional dynamics of expansion and exchange.

With its mix of wilderness, pastoral, and maritime landscapes, northern New England was a proving ground for Congregationalists, Universalists, regular and Freewill Baptists, and Methodists, all of whom created far-reaching spiritual networks that linked churchly outposts. They did so despite an impoverished and transient population unable to support clergy, and despite persistent challenges from both rival groups and the unchurched. To be sure, members of other denominations and practitioners of other belief systems—Quakers, Shakers, Presbyterians, Catholics, the Christian Connection, and Native Americans—crossed paths with the layfolk and ministers who fill these pages. But the groups at the center of this study saw themselves in competition and conversation with each other, vying for pieces of the same spiritual ground. Others were more peripheral to that conversation, either because they positioned themselves as outsiders (Shakers), concentrated locally rather than spreading widely (Presbyterians and Episcopalians), or had not reached significant numbers by the 1820s (Catholics). The denominations featured here understood themselves as both collaborators and competitors in a common enterprise. Together, willingly or not, they drove new patterns of religious organization that marked a dramatic shift in the region's religious culture.

The way they succeeded in northern New England forces us to rethink a familiar story—the story of how evangelicalism reshaped America's religious landscape during the early republic. Many historians have written about the Second Great Awakening, a period of widespread revivalism between the 1790s and the 1830s that gave rise to new denominations, more radical theologies, and a network of missionary and benevolence organizations that sought to deliver the gospel to the unconverted. These scholars have often stressed the populist and democratic nature of these revivals. Upstart religious movements swept cities, middle-class enclaves, and the backcountry, attracting followers with camp meetings and revivals and preaching a language of personal spiritual empowerment. In doing so, the narrative continues, they drew popular support away from established churches and forced them into decline. It is certainly true that evangelicals of the early republic churched unprecedented numbers of converts. In that sense, the Second Great Awakening played a key role in the rise of American religious pluralism in the nineteenth century, along with the evangelical sensibility that came to dominate (and still dominates) American Protestantism.[8] But the new movements' *popular* appeal did not necessarily make them *populist,* and the fact that they offered an alternative to established churches did not necessarily convince all churchgoers to accept that choice.

To suggest that Congregationalism withered in the face of an evangelical challenge implies that there was a cohesive evangelical challenge in the first place. There was not. Groups like the Methodists and Freewill Baptists undeniably struck emotional chords with their converts, but they were neither especially democratic nor especially united across denominational lines. Once a believer joined an evangelical church, she submitted to disciplinary and doctrinal authority that stretched from her local congregation to regional or national conferences and erected spiritual walls to protect believers from more corrupting religious and secular influences. Some groups, like the Methodists, rejected almost any lay leadership and were in that sense *less* democratic than their Congregationalist counterparts. Moreover, no consistent style or doctrine connected the dissenters. The Baptists agreed with the Congregationalists on more doctrinal points than they did with the Methodists, who often found themselves at odds with both groups. The Universalists were not evangelical in theology or sensibility, but they shared a governing style with the Freewill Baptists and Methodists and saw themselves in spiritual conversation and competition with the other denominations that figure into this book. And the Congregationalists expanded right along with their rivals. Their own gains—far beyond what they managed as the established church in an unchurched frontier—call into question the argument that they failed to match their competitors' populist approach. Indeed, northern New England's history shows that the religious transformation of the early nineteenth century depended not on the advent of democratic theology or a united assault on established churches, but rather on the ways all of the region's denominations—the Congregationalists and the upstarts—negotiated new physical and spiritual ground.

The big story of religious life in early republican New England is not one of populist ascension or Congregationalist declension but of the unfurling of a far more complex religious culture across a widening landscape. The town-church and itinerant systems battled over doctrinal and stylistic differences, but (more significantly) they also clashed over their incompatible systems for mapping out religious communities. Scholars of spatial studies have shown the many ways in which people have vested their environments with religious meaning, constructing sacred space through shared (and often contested) rituals.[9] These scholars have tended to conceive of religious space in terms of fixed features of built and natural landscapes. To be sure, so did the early American faithful, who sought divine presence in churches, forests, and fields. But this book suggests that we consider sacred space not only in terms of fixed places and landmarks but also in terms of movement across landscapes. Northern New England's religious culture came less from where people worshiped, or even how they did, than from the communities that coalesced and converged as people moved through physical space, and the institutions that stretched out to meet them. It was this elasticity, born of migration and expansion, that gave shape to the region's spiritual character and transformed its religious geography.

To explore this transformation, this book considers church, state, and settlement in northern New England. In other words, it examines how the northern frontier's ecclesiastical, political, and social contexts created a new religious landscape. The ecclesiastical underpinnings of northern New England's religious culture underwent a dramatic transformation during the early republic.[10] The principal movements of the Second Great Awakening covered new ground, literally, through an institutional expansion. They created centralized hierarchies to administer disparate churches, established publishing concerns to raise funds and reach new audiences, and sent itinerants into remote areas to gather new congregations. In doing so, they cemented a new style of American religious organization.[11] It was the geographic sweep of these new institutions, more than any social or political implications of their doctrines, that wreaked havoc on town-church communities.

As denominations expanded their administrative operations, they also rearranged sacred space. Under the town-church model, parishes, each (ideally) anchored by a meetinghouse at its spiritual and physical center, had segmented the landscape. Meetinghouses served civil and religious functions, but they assumed greater religious significance during the early republic when churchgoers built more expensive, permanent, and increasingly elaborate structures that marked the space as sacred. As the architectural centers of their towns, Congregationalist meetinghouses provided focal points of religious activity and visible symbols of a religious community's covenant.[12] But the itinerant denominations overlaid this very ordered landscape with their own religious geography. Lacking ties to particular places, they occupied more ephemeral spiritual spaces. Their churchgoers met in schoolhouses, courthouses, borrowed or shared meetinghouses, private homes, forests, groves, or fields. In these settings, anyone—church member or not, town resident or not—could join the congregation. Whereas the town meetinghouses symbolized stability and permanency, the itinerant groups' sacred spaces suggested fluidity. So did their patterns of movement across the land. Quarterly meetings, conferences, and revivals created temporary gathering points in the hinterland, where believers came together from distant towns and drifted away again after the meeting had concluded. In between meetings, itinerant preachers connected far-flung laity and clergy through visits and correspondence. The ecclesiastical transformation of the northern frontier had implications far beyond religious diversity. The new and old denominations that wrestled for control over towns and churches altered the very idea of church membership and its relationship to physical place.

So did the severing of church-state ties. Just as the Great Awakening transformed the region's ecclesiastical landscape, disestablishment altered the politics of religion. Historian Nathan O. Hatch asserts that debates over establishment and dissent faded in the United States after 1800, by which point religious taxation had ended in most states.[13] But such was not the case in New England, where debates over establishment raged on as states reconsidered and then dissolved constitutional church-state ties. Few disputed the right of conscience. Instead, the discourse of religious toleration focused on how to preserve moral order should the states abandon their traditional roles as buttresses for religious authority.[14] Vermont, New Hampshire, and Maine all eventually ended compulsory religious taxation, but that move alone did not inaugurate a new era of religious liberty or end the states' intervention in religious life. The separation of church and state progressed in a contested struggle that took decades to resolve.

The politics of disestablishment in northern New England largely reflected tensions between the clergy and other supporters of the Standing Order, who sought to protect town churches, and dissenters, whose religious communities transcended town borders. Each state's establishment was rooted in the town-church geography, and debates over religious liberty focused more on the town-church system itself—especially the state's authority to compel towns to support ministers—than on broad issues of religious toleration. Even after these states ended compulsory religious support, the legacy of establishment continued to favor Congregationalists and heighten tensions among towns, churches, and churchgoers. The upstart movements expanded not because of disestablishment but rather in spite of a persistent town-church legacy.

Just as churches and states laid out fluid spiritual landscapes, churchgoers occupied fluid spiritual worlds. Looking beyond churchly institutions affords a fuller picture of a religious culture in which the clergy were often absent. Accordingly, the social context ranks along with the ecclesiastical and political arenas as the third major underpinning of northern New England's religious geography.[15] Lay religious culture existed in tension with, but not necessarily in revolt against, denominational cultures. The laity, both faithful and unchurched, acted as exhorters, lay leaders, and consumers in an active spiritual marketplace. Religious pluralism and disestablishment gave people more choices, yielding more flexible religious identities and behaviors and altering the lay-clergy relationship. Layfolk sustained religious communities, with or without the clergy's help, through quasi-institutional bodies like conferences and prayer societies, and through lay institutions like class meetings. The unchurched, too, dabbled in all of these activities, thereby supporting a religious culture that, in many ways, rejected them. At the same time, the faithful engaged in secular pursuits like drinking alcohol and attending dances, and they attended worship sporadically, if at all. All told, the laity claimed authority to accept faith or reject it, to change affiliations, or to devise doctrines of their own making.

Much of the laity understood the religious geography of the northern frontier in ways that both overlapped and competed with the maps that states and churches tried to impose. Instead of thinking about their spiritual landscape as patchworks of local churches or webs of disparate congregations connected through itinerancy, laypeople plotted out concentric circles that surrounded the self, the family, the town, and the region. They experienced religious life in private prayer, public worship, and reading and writing. They joined wider social and spiritual networks in which regional migration patterns scattered friends and relations, even as correspondence and an expansive print culture united them.[16] The laity did not wholly reject institutional geographies. But by charting their own spiritual maps, they collaborated with denominations and the states to create the northern frontier's religious culture.

Congregationalists who watched their rivals and the laity dismantle old spiritual boundaries feared their own demise—until they began to use their rivals' tactics to their own advantage. To be sure, the itinerant system gradually supplanted town churches as the dominant means of religious expansion in northern New England. Camp meetings and other revivals blurred parish boundaries. Itinerants, circuit riders, and missionaries crossed paths in the northern hinterlands. Usually in competition, but often in collaboration, they sought to revive the faithful, build churches, enforce moral order, and guide congregations. Although Congregationalists still hoped to plant permanent churches of their own, many of the denomination's ministers adopted itinerant circuits, traveling about to tend to distant flocks, all the while relying on lay societies to maintain worship in the clergy's absence. The Congregationalists' embrace of itinerancy reflected a new approach to church-founding and evangelism, echoing the patterns other denominations had introduced. And they succeeded in ways they would surely not have predicted at the outset. The missionary enterprise kept Congregationalism afloat and even helped extend its reach, just as evangelical competitors tried to lure its adherents away. Missionaries spent the early decades of the nineteenth century gathering churches and filling them with parishioners at a feverish pace. But—under the authority of missionary societies and depending on the efforts of traveling missionaries—these Congregationalists did so by embracing the itinerant plan and sacrificing the town-church tradition.

With the decline of the town-church system came a geographic transformation of religious life. Old religious boundaries dissolved and new ones emerged. Under the new itinerant system, the laity and clergy located sacred space for themselves. Everyday structures like schoolhouses or homes might contain an ephemeral spirituality when they housed congregations; fields and woods might take on a transcendent quality when they provided the setting for revivals or conversions. Sacred space could be tightly bound, as when a single believer retreated to a private room for secret prayer, or nearly boundless, as when two faraway correspondents spilled the depths of their souls into letters. By rearranging religious geographies, the denominations and churchgoers of northern New England found sacred meaning in a vast landscape.

In doing so, northern New England's laity and clergy reinvented the notion of religious community. Congregations and families gathered and scattered at a dizzying pace, so people glued religious communities together by reading, writing, and itinerancy, which allowed them to find their spiritual bearings and overcome isolation. Print and correspondence networks, along with travel to preach and visit, inspired reflection and lifted the spirits; they also strengthened northern New England's social and religious foundations as the region's peripatetic laity expanded webs of friendship and kinship. The printed word has been crucial in forming what Benedict Anderson has called "imagined communities" in which governments, the press, and citizens have mingled in wide-ranging social and political spheres by engaging each other in print.[17] By affording them access to a larger and richer spiritual forum than most believers would have found within their own neighborhoods, reading, writing, and mobility fostered similar virtual communities—religious ones—on the New England frontier, where tangible communities gathered slowly. In this crowded, contentious virtual space, believers and nonbelievers, clergy and laity, neighbors and strangers mingled, argued, and persuaded or alienated one another without ever setting foot in the same church—or even the same town.

Northern New England's clergy and layfolk situated religious experiences, identities, and communities within a new physical and spiritual topography. Its principal denominations, their followers, and the unchurched engaged in a decades-long conversation about the nature of religious liberty, spiritual community, and pluralism. The clergy and laity alike carried on doctrinal debates, created intersecting itinerant networks, attended one another's meetings—both as critics and as guests—and competed for (and often shared) churchgoers and meetinghouses. In the process, they reoriented northern New England's religious life around a new and distinctive Protestant evangelical culture.

Although northern New England's spiritual world remained rooted in its own context, the ways in which that region's denominations and communities coalesced had implications for patterns of religious expansion throughout the rapidly growing nation. By using centralized hierarchies, denominations could cover large territories as they planted churches. By emphasizing denominational identity instead of town residence as the standard of membership, religious communities moved away from the parish system and toward a new style of organization that worked for a mobile society. Swept up in the change, the clergy and laity alike wove themselves into intricate fabric of spiritual life in northern New England: a crazy quilt of faiths sewn together by threads of exchange, competition, and debate.

1 No Schism in the Body

The Town Church in Crisis

William Jenks, the Congregationalist minister of Bath, Maine, surveyed his town's religious climate with some distress in 1810. When he had arrived from Cambridge, Massachusetts, four years earlier, he had found a unified town eager to settle a minister. But over the next few years, Bath's residents split off into three churches—two Congregationalist and one Baptist—and the Methodists threatened to add a fourth. Troubled by the splintering of Bath's churchgoers, Jenks devised a "plan of union." His solution: the Baptists, like the Congregationalists, should offer communion to any converted believer but still retain the "peculiarities" of their own practices. That way, Jenks thought, they could enjoy liberty of conscience without opening a "schism in the body," or a rift in the town's spiritual unity. Never mind that open communion violated Baptist doctrine—Jenks's main goal was not to promote diversity or toleration but to preserve the town as a godly unit, in keeping with Congregationalist town-church tradition. If churchgoers did not assemble together regularly for worship, at least they could mingle for the Lord's Supper so as to keep Bath's religious community intact. "A reciprocity of Christian love," Jenks proposed, "could tend to close the breach which now separates *chief friends*."[1]

Jenks's plan, which never came to fruition, sought to reconcile two competing models of religious community. The first—Jenks's preference—was the Congregationalist town church, which placed the town's residents under a single church's watch and persisted in New England well into the nineteenth century. The second, which the Baptists and other dissenters favored, was the itinerant model, which attracted churchgoers based on shared doctrine rather than neighborhood. As the anchor of the local religious community, the town church bore almost all responsibility for discipline, religious instruction, and its own financial support. Relatives and neighbors gathered in church regularly, under the steady guidance of one minister, and kept watch over each other's spiritual and moral well-being. This system depended on towns that were both financially secure and socially stable enough to construct meetinghouses, support ministers, and fund religious education. But more importantly, the town-church ideal also assumed that churchgoers would embrace a corporate mindset that tied individual piety to the fate of the community. According to this cooperative vision, neighbors chose to join a religious community rather than pursue individual desires to opt out, thereby sustaining the town church morally and spiritually.[2]

The religious geography of the town church, in its ideal form, conceived of each church as an organic religious entity rooted in a particular place and visually oriented around a meetinghouse. This physical layout reflected its spiritual landscape, in which believers and non-believers arranged themselves in inward-looking circles around the town minister. Neighbors who shared spiritual and physical space could police each other and enforce moral standards, thereby extending the church's reach through (but not beyond) the town. The town church, then, was both a spiritual construct and a concrete, tangible place that could not exist without the families, neighborhoods, and buildings within its bounds. But the town church was never as stable in northern New England as the ideal suggested it should be. Scattered settlement, transience, and poverty prevented many towns from settling ministers and gathering churches, even when settlers hoped to do so. Town churches developed nonetheless, but with fragile physical and spiritual boundaries. When these boundaries gave way to the combined pressures of disestablishment, sectarianism, and divisions within Congregationalism itself, many feared for the town church's survival. As a church's borders became increasingly permeable, the ideal of a stable town church became increasingly untenable. In northern New England's ever-shifting religious landscape, Congregationalists grappled with the question of how to reshape their boundaries so they might ultimately preserve their communities.

At the core of the town-church tradition lay the town itself: a geographic entity with physical borders that contained the church and its members and excluded outsiders. Accordingly, the physical geography of the town church reinforced both the town lines that bound the community together and the space within, where a spiritual community took root. The equation of town and church dated to early American Puritanism, when New England colonists devised a state-church system in which overlapping town, church, and household authorities supported the religious community and reinforced doctrine and moral discipline. According to the New England Way, which embodied this confluence of town and church, the community of neighbors sustained the community of believers—and, ideally, the two were one and the same.[3] As the Congregationalist establishment persisted into the early republic, town churches remained deeply rooted in their physical landscapes and architectural layouts, and their religious practices reinforced these connections between physical and spiritual space.

According to the town-church ideal, geographic proximity nurtured spiritual unity; the town itself was important because it provided visible boundaries between insiders and outsiders. Only by sharing sacred and secular spaces could members of the town church truly know each other's hearts and bolster each other's piety. Although outsiders sometimes participated, their status was clearly secondary to that of the local members. Such was the case when out-of-town church members tried to usurp control of the Congregational Church in Hanover, New Hampshire, in 1805. The Hanover church had long welcomed members from towns across the river in Vermont. Not only did these border towns lack churches, but Hanover churchgoers relied on outside membership for funding. But a factional dispute erupted over which minister to hire: many of the Vermonters supported one candidate, and the local Hanover churchgoers (who comprised a minority of the church membership) favored another. The locals argued that town rule—not majority rule—should guide church policy. Accordingly, the committee of the Hanover church asked the Vermonters why local residents should "resign to you the Temple that we have built for the worship of our God," leaving the meetinghouse to interlopers while locals went "as sheep without a shepherd, seeking places [to] worship among strangers."[4] The Hanover residents' concerns were paramount; whatever the church majority wished, the town's first priority was to maintain the boundaries of its own spiritual community.

When residence defined membership in a particular community, a person had no need (and could even find it damaging) to seek religious sustenance elsewhere. After the Wilton (New Hampshire) Congregational Church lost members over a doctrinal dispute, the church committee declared that "the separation from the church of members residing in the same place . . . we look upon as highly schismatic and irregular."[5] Even after these members reorganized as the Second Congregational Church of Wilton, the original church refused to recognize their departure. Similarly, Thomas Merrill, the pastor at the Middlebury (Vermont) Congregational Church, argued that a church should not permit a member "living near the meeting house" to worship elsewhere, regardless of whether the member in question preferred the minister at the second church. "To grant such a request," Merrill argued, would be tantamount to "splitting up Christians." He added that "there is something if not scismatic yet extremely disagreeable in having one of the same faith . . . drive away from the meetinghouse" every Sabbath morning to attend a different church.[6] For Merrill, the town's geographic boundaries and organic bonds trumped the tug of conscience that might draw a churchgoer to a more distant congregation.

This rule also applied to those who adopted new faiths. Town churches rarely considered sectarian preference grounds to permit a parishioner to seek another church. Joel Winch, a Vermonter who had been raised a Congregationalist but embraced Methodism as a young adult, asked his town church to dismiss him to a nearby Methodist church in 1802. The congregation refused, arguing that Winch was bound to obey his covenant to the town church as long as he believed it to be a true Christian church. After several votes in which the church refused to dismiss or expel him, Winch finally walked out, declaring that he "determined to stand fast in the liberty whare in Christ had made me free."[7] The Cumberland (Maine) Association also resisted losing church members due to sectarian differences. In 1824, the association advised one of its ministers to discipline a Universalist, not for doctrinal error but for skipping regular worship instead. "The belief in Universalism as the alleged cause of that neglect," they declared, was "not a justification of the delinquence."[8] The association assumed that all townspeople would support the church and attend worship, whatever their spiritual bent. Neighborly bonds tied churchgoers together in a united community.

As sectarian competition intensified through the early nineteenth century, town churches and societies guarded their institutions' geographic integrity with ever-greater vigilance. With an eye toward preserving the church's financial base and spiritual bedrock, leaders fiercely defended their parishes from infringement and objected when churchgoers asked to withdraw. When some members of the Congregational church in Greenfield, New Hampshire, sought to form their own Presbyterian church in 1822, the church refused to allow them to leave. An outside council supported the church's stance, insisting that such an exodus "would be hostile to the best interest of this people." But the conflict persisted; the Presbyterians repeatedly asked to withdraw, to no avail. Church leaders argued in 1825 that "two churches . . . would greatly strengthen division among the people . . . and thus prevent the future united and harmonious enjoyment of gospel privileges, and the means of grace." They finally agreed, however, to dismiss members who wished to transfer to Presbyterian churches in other towns. Because the compromise allowed the Presbyterians to join other congregations rather than visibly disrupt their own religious community, the Greenfield Congregationalists found the solution more palatable.[9] By tolerating departures only on the condition that they not yield another church in their town, local leaders acknowledged dissent but maintained the primacy and integrity of the town-church geography.

Many features of the town-church ideal focused not on teaching a uniform orthodoxy but rather on creating ways to join Christian neighbors in shared rituals and institutions. Ritual reinforced the town church's physical geography because the town itself provided the stage on which believers and observers acted out their spiritual relationships. The most important ritual was the Lord's Supper, or communion, which featured preaching and prayer along with the actual sacrament.[10] Churches usually hosted quarterly communions, but since this was one of the few rituals that depended on a minister's presence, remote settlements often did without for years at a time. Although the Lord's Supper itself took place during one service, the communion season typically lasted several days. After a series of preparatory meetings, members gathered to witness or participate in the sacrament. The ritual reinforced the religious landscape of the town church: the minister presided over the ceremony in which members old and new assumed prominent roles as they took communion. Those who were not members, whether hopeful converts or other churchgoers, might have joined in preparatory prayer but could only watch the communion ritual.

Sacramental seasons became town gatherings that dramatized Christian fellowship and the unity of all believers. Consequently, town churches looked askance at the separate communion seasons that some other churches held. The Congregational Church in Wilmington, Vermont, disciplined several members who, in 1806, joined a church that "refuses fellowship and communion with us thus depriving us of their watch . . . and refusing ours over them."[11] Clergy often tried—sometimes successfully—to convince dissenters to join their communions. When Stephen Peabody of Atkinson, New Hampshire, sought his congregation's approval to let a Baptist woman commune with them, they allowed it.[12] Congregationalist missionary Samuel Goddard similarly invited the Methodists in Lyman, New Hampshire, to unite with the rest of the town for the Lord's Supper.[13] And in Bath, William Jenks repeatedly reissued his invitation to "all who love our Lord Jesus Christ, of whatever denomination of professed [Christians], and who are in regular standing in their respective Chh's to partake" in the Lord's Supper.[14] Most Baptists in Bath, as elsewhere, declined.

But many dissenters preferred open communion, and they sometimes broke with their own churches and joined the Congregationalists for that reason alone. A Bangor, Maine, churchgoer was excommunicated from her Baptist church solely because she preferred to commune with the town. In all other respects, she favored Baptist doctrine, but the Congregationalist church received her anyway.[15] Like many other town churches, the Bangor Congregationalists hoped that open communion would strengthen the bonds of common faith and transcend denominational idiosyncrasies. To be sure, not every Congregationalist agreed with this principle; many preferred not to seek the fellowship of Baptists and other religious rivals. But most Congregationalist town churches, and especially their ministers, hoped to maintain the integrity of the geographic churchly community, however spiritually divided it may have become.

The point of open communion was to sustain the town as a united core of believers who invested in each other's spiritual welfare because they shared physical space as neighbors. Town churches sought other ways to accommodate a range of beliefs, thereby giving churchgoers fewer reasons to leave. Many drew up flexible covenants and confessions of faith, which contained broad principles of Protestant Christianity rather than specific Calvinist doctrines like predestination. The constitution of the Church and Society of Bridgewater, New Hampshire, declared that its purpose was "not to regard any Denomination in preference to another neither Sectary or Perswasion," but rather to ensure that "each denomination Shall injoy as equall priviledges as our several sentiments will admit of."[16] Similarly, one of William Jenks's colleagues advised him to "make as few articles in the profession as essential to belief as you can." By taking this approach, town churches hoped to attract and maintain a large local membership.[17]

Alternatively, many churches allowed new members to write their own statements, as long as these pledges did not include elements that Congregationalists considered un-Christian (like tenets of Universalism). It was exactly this kind of policy that led to the split in Wilton, New Hampshire. When the church allowed new members to compose their own confessions of faith in 1822, many congregants protested, arguing that such a policy would raise the risk of introducing "not 'one faith,' but many, and those contrary and opposite one another." But the church leadership responded that most doctrinal differences were mere distractions that clouded the essential truths of Christianity. "Certainly it must be offensive to the great Head of the church," they lamented, "to erect these interpretations into a fence to debar Christ's disciples from the ordinances."[18] The Wilton committee valued neighborly unity over doctrinal purity, so that "none may have occasion to say that our religion is a religion of strife and debate."[19]

To be sure, town-church defenders had the luxuries of power and precedent on their side. Most longstanding town churches were Congregationalist, and the tendency to wax indignant about defections masked bitterness over losing support, not to mention jealousy toward new churches. Nonetheless, the principle of a community bound by spiritual, civil, and geographic ties was deeply embedded in Congregationalism. Whether unanimity was historically coerced or genuine, the visible signs of its deterioration distressed those who embraced the ideal.

The town church's physical landscape was cemented not just in religious organization and ritual but also in the structures of churches themselves. The demarcation of churches as sacred spaces was a relatively recent development among Congregationalists. Early Puritans did not distinguish the meetinghouse in such a way. Their doctrine did not require a consecrated building for worship; the "church" referred to the communicants rather than the physical structure in which they gathered, which commonly doubled as a town hall.[20] But during the early eighteenth century, southern New England's congregations replaced simple and often dilapidated meetinghouses with more permanent and conspicuous structures that emphasized their religious functions with such embellishments as elaborate pews and pulpits, steeples, bells, and detailed woodwork.[21] New England meetinghouses still were not consecrated, and many continued to serve civil purposes (particularly in smaller towns and parishes). But these structures increasingly featured elements that clearly marked the space within as sacred.[22] And their growing presence in northern New England's built landscape anchored the town-church ideal in the physical geography.

In northern New England, this church-building boom did not begin until after the American Revolution, when dramatic population growth created the need for new places for worship. Ephraim Abbot, on a missionary tour of Maine in 1812, noted that the towns of Robbinston and Calais had recently built meetinghouses, and that similar projects were underway in Machias and Eastport (though the latter project stalled during the War of 1812 due to a shortage of funds and was never completed). During the same period, congregations also erected churches in Alna, Gorham, Norridgewock, Waterford, and elsewhere.[23] New Hampshire and Vermont saw similar patterns. Beginning in the 1780s, the Vermont towns of Bennington, Guildhall, Marlboro, Pomfret, Ryegate, Thetford, and Weathersfield all commenced work on their meetinghouses.[24] In New Hampshire, Deering, Dublin, Exeter, Milton, and Stoddard also began to build churches.[25] All of these towns financed church-building with tax assessments or lotteries.

Towns generally located meetinghouses near their commercial centers, where political, economic, social, and religious activity intersected. Although meetinghouse locations often changed due to political maneuvering and negotiation, once settled they in turn determined the best locations for roads, taverns, markets, and other gathering places.[26] As of 1800, only a handful of northern New England towns devoted separate structures to religious worship and town government.[27] For most, meetinghouse construction fulfilled both religious and civil aims, as in Guildhall, Vermont, where inhabitants stated their need for a "convenient House for Public Worship [and] any business of a Public nature."[28] In such towns, new meetinghouses stood as the focal point of spiritual and civil activity. The post-Revolutionary flurry of church-building, then, carried with it a dual significance. On the one hand, increasingly elaborate meetinghouses reflected a common perception that congregations required dedicated spaces fit for worship. But at the same time, the comingling of civil and spiritual functions within these spaces symbolized these towns' intertwined political and spiritual realms.

Even when towns used their meetinghouses for public business, they devoted greater attention to delineating the space within from the profane world that lay outside the church's doors. That world contained not only sectarian rivals and the unchurched but also a vast wilderness that seemed to defy efforts at settlement and town planning. Increasingly elaborate and carefully planned churches stood in stark contrast to the wilderness setting. Typical was the Williamstown, Vermont, church, which designed its door with geometric simplicity and mathematical proportions (see fig. 1.1). Neoclassical architectural features

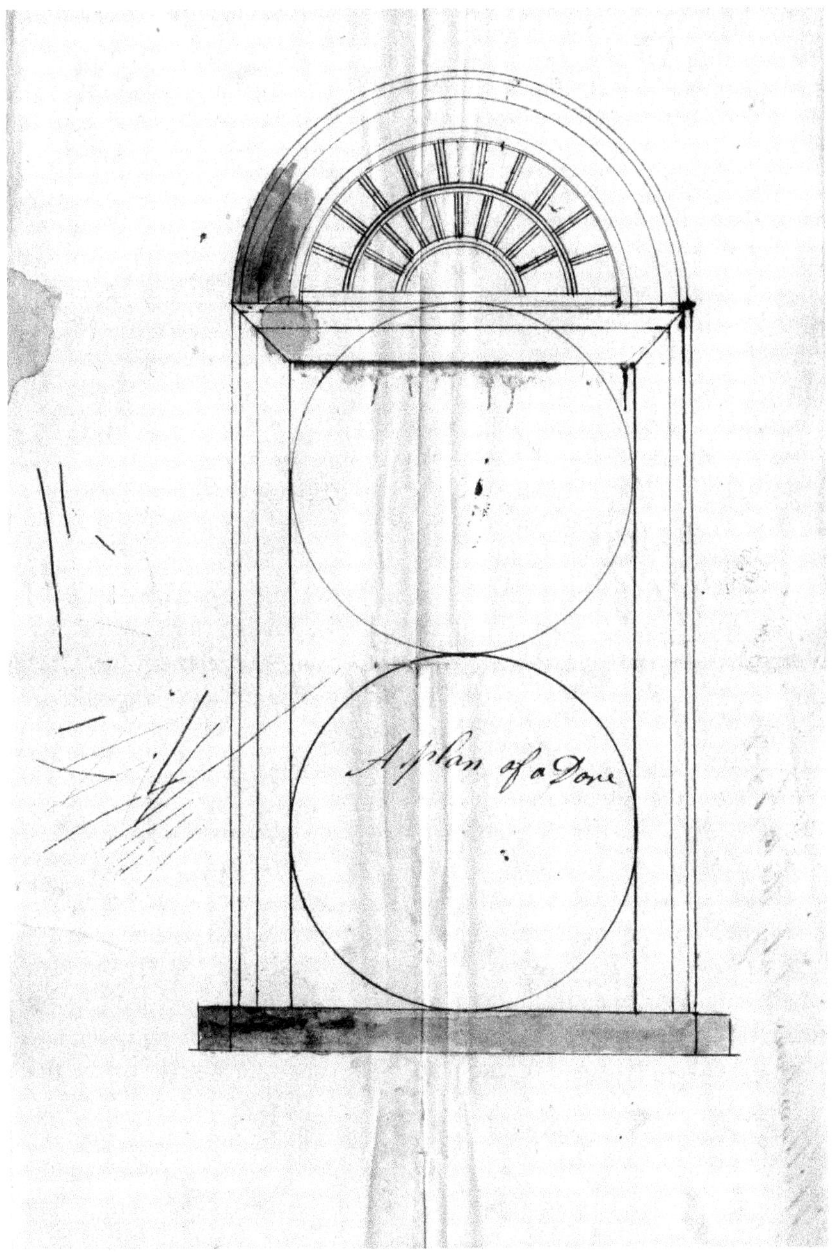

Figure 1.1. Williamstown, Vermont, meetinghouse door, 1804. The design of this meetinghouse door reflects the academic, neoclassical architectural style that emphasized order, symmetry, and geometric proportion. *Stevens Family Papers, University of Vermont Special Collections.*

like these signified deliberation and control: exactly the qualities many migrants feared lacking in the surrounding landscape.[29] Joseph Warren, a visiting minister in Pittston, Maine, predicted in 1793 that the meetinghouse under construction there would be "quite an elegant building."[30] Ephraim Abbot recalled that the meetinghouse in Charlestown, New Hampshire, had cost $7,500 to build and added that "few meetinghouses at that time in country towns were as large, as commodious, as handsome, or erected at so much expense."[31]

Investments in elegant church buildings did not reflect doctrinal change; the church remained a spiritual rather than architectural unit. But the newer architectural stylings did point to a perceived need to buttress that spiritual church with a physical landmark. From the 1790s on, towns across the region attempted to make grand statements with their meetinghouses. Hampstead, New Hampshire, which had built its meetinghouse in 1745, added a tower and spired belfry in 1792. The meetinghouses of Exeter, New Hampshire (1798), and Strafford, Vermont (1799), both featured octagonal, multi-level bell towers with ornamental detail.[32] The First Congregational Church in Bennington, Vermont (1806), featured an elaborate, three-level bell tower with Palladian windows—a highly academic, neoclassical design element that had recently become popular in British and New England churches (see fig. 1.2).[33] Similarly elegant belfries, which crowned decorative pediments, appeared on meetinghouses in Kennebunk, Maine (1804); Middlebury, Vermont (1809); and Troy and Fitzwilliam, New Hampshire (1812 and 1816).[34] By 1817, Montpelier, Vermont, had begun planning its own meetinghouse, complete with a "cupola or steeple" and 122 pews.[35]

Bell towers served both ornamental and practical purposes: they enhanced a church's appearance and linked dispersed town residents. Abigail Abbott of Peterborough, New Hampshire, announced in 1828 that her church had recently added a bell but noted that some outlying residents had already complained that the bell was "not quite heavy enough" for them to hear. She predicted that the town would soon replace it with a larger one.[36] Bells and bell towers served as conspicuous visual and auditory reminders of the town's spiritual (and often geographic) center. As such, they reinforced the church's centrality in the town's spiritual community, however fragmented that community might have actually been.

It was not just the embellished exteriors that distinguished meetinghouses as sacred space. Interior plans, particularly the arrangement of pews, reminded churchgoers of their roles in a stable, if not static, religious community. Towns normally sold pews to raise funds for church construction and upkeep, but pew sales also had spiritual significance. By buying pews, churchgoers made permanent and concrete investments in a town's church and (literally) situated themselves among others who did the same. The Waldoboro, Maine, meetinghouse committee designed its floor plan with one hundred pews: thirty-four in the gal-

Figure 1.2. First Congregational Church of Bennington, Vermont, 1806. The portico, bell tower, and Palladian windows typified embellishments to northern New England town churches in the early nineteenth century. *From a 1936 postcard; author's collection.*

lery level and the remainder on the main floor. Of these, the committee set aside only seven for open use, including one for the minister's family. In other words, just six out of one hundred pews—two on the main floor and four on the less-desirable gallery level—were left for public use (see fig. 1.3).[37] This emphasis on pew ownership had the dual effect of cementing each parishioner's place in the religious community and creating a barrier through which outsiders had only limited access. Just as pew ownership could confirm one's status in a stable town-church community, the lack of available pews could block outsiders from joining.

The meetinghouse interior was supposed to function as a microcosm of the larger community, or at least the idealized version of it. Church pews, purchased and occupied, suggested permanence. But towns were in constant transition; individuals and families came and went, and populations fluctuated over time. In many cases, families retained pews in the town church, even if they were no longer local residents or town-church members. The Dover, New Hampshire, meetinghouse committee fretted over the large number of empty—but spoken-for—pews. About one fourth of the pews were "owned by individuals not belonging to the parish, and who pay no part of the expense of religious instruction in said house." The committee proposed that if the parish could transfer ownership of those pews to "actual parishioners," the religious society would benefit from their increased participation, which would add not only to the "respectability of our society, but assist in the regular support of religious instruction."[38] As these records hinted, the overlap of town and church in one physical place (the meetinghouse) could create tensions among those who shared a civil community but did not fully share a religious one. Even though the meetinghouse was intended to weave together the secular and spiritual threads of a single town, it sometimes succeeded only in showing how those threads had frayed.

Just as ownership of pews in a church often revealed political tensions and fragmentation, so did the meetinghouse itself. For most towns, a meetinghouse not only provided a space for worship but also served as a powerful centerpiece for a town's political and spiritual affairs. But towns that could not build churches stood out as economically and socially fragile. Missionaries suspected that the absence of a meetinghouse signaled instability in a nascent religious community. Reporting from an 1827 missionary tour, Perez Chapin noted that the town of Raymond, Maine, did not "appear . . . to be in a state to render it suitable to form a society." The reason, he surmised, was that they lacked a meetinghouse. Only by building one could they truly unite as a religious body. "Till this is done," Chapin predicted, "such is the sectarian feeling among them, or rather *around* them that nothing can be of great avail."[39]

As it turned out, though, meetinghouses often came to symbolize conflict, not unity. A meetinghouse's location could become the basis for protracted bat-

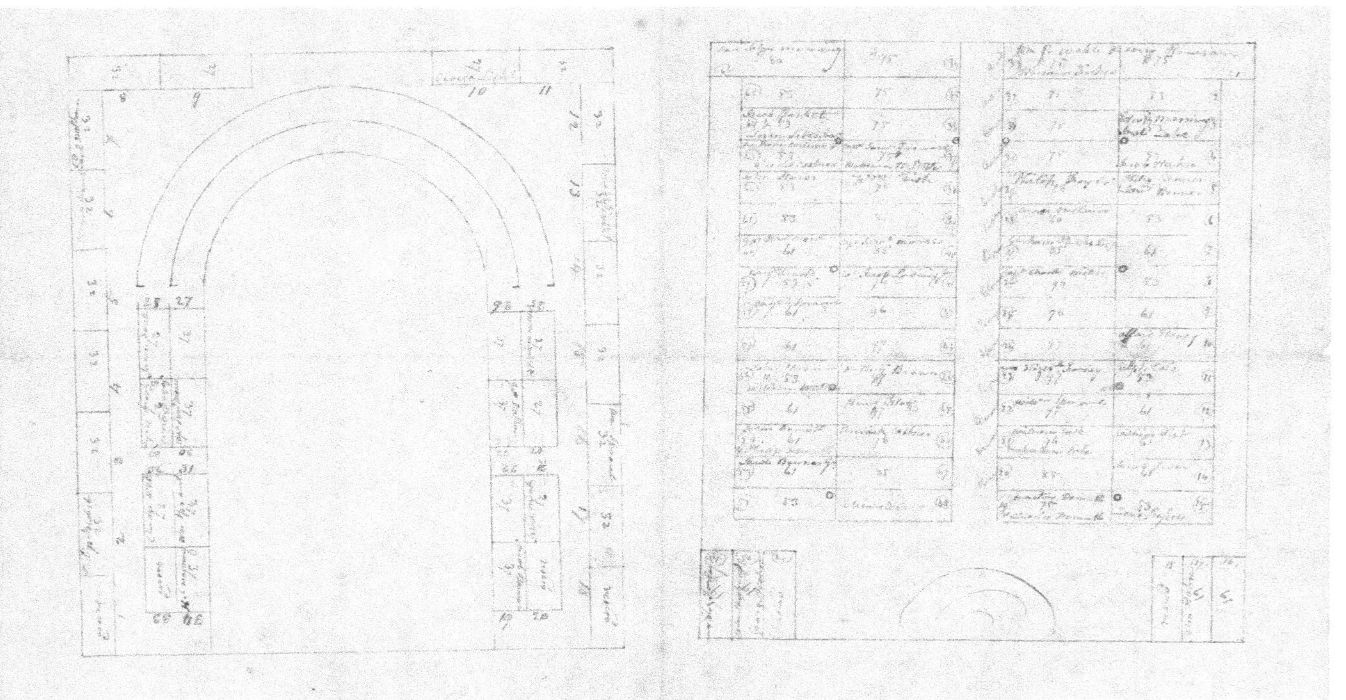

Figure 1.3. Waldoboro, Maine, meetinghouse plan, 1820. Above is the main floor plan; below is the gallery-level plan. The circled numbers are pew numbers; the uncircled numbers in the center of each pew refer to the price. Empty circles denote pillars, which explains the low asking price for those pews. Pew 48 (main floor, in front) was reserved for the minister and his family, and pews 1, 10, 18, 20, 33, and 49 were public pews. All other unlabeled pews were still for sale when this plan was drawn. *Congregational Conference–Maine Missionary Society Records, Collection 1704, Maine Historical Society.*

tles, especially when obstacles like ravines, forests, or mountains stood between outlying areas and town centers. The town of Belfast, Maine, endured years of wrangling between residents on either side of the Passagassawakeag River before they finally decided in 1792 to build one modest structure on each bank.[40] Residents of Pembroke, New Hampshire, similarly resolved to build a second meetinghouse to accommodate its outlying residents. Stephen Peabody, who visited the town in 1805, predicted that this decision would be "the foundation of their compleat ruin."[41] He thought the choice to build two meetinghouses marked not the resolution of a conflict but a surrender to unnecessary divisions. Rather than approve of a compromise that enabled more people to attend church, Peabody mourned the apparently permanent division of a religious community.

Belfast and Pembroke each settled on multi-church solutions, but these conflicts rarely resolved so neatly. Some residents of Wells, Vermont, remarked that they had no place to build a church due to the natural barriers that divided the town, including "vast and enormous mountains" and "a very well known and extensive Pond." These petitioners proposed one solution: to join with the town of Poultney, which already had a meetinghouse. But that plan left the remaining Wells residents to build their own meetinghouse with a smaller tax base—about which prospect they complained bitterly.[42] Even more controversial was a decision by a town with a meetinghouse to split into two parishes. In such an event, one of the resulting parishes would be deprived of this valuable asset. Those who stood to lose usually protested vehemently. Petitioners from Milton, New Hampshire, pointed out that a proposed division of their town would leave them with its least attractive areas and without the "large handsome Meeting-house which is completely finished, in the center of town."[43] For people like the Milton petitioners, splitting parishes amounted to more than an administrative division; such an action stood to fracture a unit both civil and religious. And the most valuable prize in this split—the meetinghouse itself—was also the most visible and central feature of that unit.

The town church, ultimately, defined membership by geographic location. Whatever else was essential to joining a church, the prerequisite to membership in a religious community was residence in a corresponding physical space. There, neighborly bonds superseded sectarian disputes, and the meetinghouse stood as a symbol of a shared investment in the greater spiritual good. By making that investment, northern New England's Congregationalists hoped to safeguard the ideal of town churches as religious centers of concrete places where believers could plant spiritual roots.

A church was more than just a neighborhood, of course. Ultimately, the town was a physical manifestation of the spiritual community that constituted a church. The spiritual geography of the town church took its shape from the relationships that formed in the town. Like the physical layout of the town church, the spiritual community also had its roots in the New England Way, the system in which the polity and the church collaborated to support and discipline the godly laity. The joint processes of church and town settlement spawned a patchwork of churchly communities in which parishioners surrounded their ministers in a shared religious enterprise. The clergy articulated a vision of their congregations as societies of believers and hopeful believers whose divine fates were inextricably linked through their common spiritual endeavor.[44] Even though each congregation was necessarily a collection of individuals—some saved and others not, some pious and others not—the church as a whole was greater than the sum of its churchgoers. Just as geographic proximity tied these parishioners together with neighborly bonds, a town church's sense of spiritual space tethered its members to the minister and each other in a web of mutual duty.

The Congregationalist tradition conceived of the town and church as a united and indivisible unit within which churchgoers might exhort together, commune together, and worship together. But whatever they did, the guiding principle remained that any person's spiritual condition was inseparable from his or her congregation's. And just as the corporate ideal implied mutual support in faith, it also required mutual watch in discipline. When a member failed in moral conduct, many churches not only disciplined the offender but also engaged in collective soul-searching. Often they concluded that no member could stray if the rest of the church had not allowed him to lapse. In an 1826 meeting of the Washington (Vermont) Church of Christ, a council found Ebenezer Bacon guilty of non-attendance. But the church also found itself guilty of lax enforcement of its own rules. Had they not "neglected [their] duty as a body and as individual members," the council concluded, Bacon would not have shirked his responsibility in the first place.[45] To maintain discipline, town churches turned inward to gather strength, renew their covenant obligations, and commit to the corporate ideal.

The town church's spiritual space encompassed more than just believers. It bound together a civil community that included church members, hopeful converts, and the unchurched. Among the town church's most important functions was to serve the whole community by advancing moral norms encouraging religious standards of virtue in secular relationships. The Church and Society of Bridgewater, New Hampshire, proclaimed that "the gospel in its genewine Operation has a Favorabele affect upon government regelating the morals of the People, and it has an incourageing influence to promote Education industry Agricultures and interprise." Town residents could rely on regular worship to "advance every Social blessing" and improve their earthly lives.[46] The Piscataqua (New Hampshire) Association similarly observed that public worship benefited a community because it tended to "promote the social virtues and is so influential in subduing the passions and prejudices among men, that it may well be considered one of the greatest bonds of society." It followed that "if public institutions of religion were laid aside, private virtue would not long remain behind."[47] Private piety might lead individual Christians to act properly, but a public and institutional religious presence enforced moral standards more broadly and nurtured a mutual vigilance among neighbors.

Northern New England's frontier conditions posed new challenges for the town churches' communal nature. In a region where people were always on the move, a town's borders could not always contain the town church. Both the physical and spiritual space that religious communities occupied extended beyond town limits when residents moved away, until they could show they were under a new church's watch. Ministers who tried to monitor the comings and goings of their parishioners relied on dismissions and recommendations to trace churchgoers' migrations and ensure their continued religious observance. Dismissions and recommendations were letters of introduction that allowed a departing churchgoer to prove good standing in a former church and gain membership in a new one. The minister of the new church would notify the original church that the migrant had arrived and transferred membership. Only then would the former church drop that parishioner from its register. Dismissions and recommendations were available only to converted members who had joined a church in full communion (usually by law, those who were not church members simply joined the parish where they settled, which required fewer formalities). Most Congregational churches received newcomers in the same manner as the church in Montpelier, which resolved that "Members removing into this vicinity from other Churches in fellowship with this Church" would, upon presenting a letter of recommendation, "be recognized as members of this Church."[48] Not only did these letters secure parishioners' access to religious worship and discipline, but they also extended town-church communities in intricate webs across the region.

It would seem at first glance that this system compromised town-church boundaries by extending churches' authority beyond town borders. But that geographic transgression was supposed to be fleeting. We might instead imagine a dismission and recommendation as an elastic band that a departing parishioner stretched from one church to the next. Once that migrant was safely situated in her new church, the band would snap back to its starting point, and the spiritual boundaries of each church would be restored.

Migration was a constant fact of life in virtually every northern New England town and church. Although few churches experienced rapid turnover, they tended to see steady trickles of churchgoers migrate elsewhere and greeted often larger streams of new arrivals. Most churches meticulously documented new and departing members' origins and destinations. Many migrants knew their destinations in advance, and letters of dismission and recommendation usually noted the name of the new church (and perhaps that church's minister). These records suggest largely regional migration patterns in which newcomers arrived from either southern New England or other towns in northern New England. Dismissed members generally headed elsewhere in northern New England (often in the same state), while a few went either to southern New England or west to New York or Ohio. Regardless, letters from their home churches would give them almost immediate entrée into new religious communities.

A sample of church records illustrates this point. Over the first two decades of the nineteenth century, the Congregationalist Church of Christ in Stratton, Vermont, accepted new members with recommendations from nearby towns such as Somerset and Wardsboro as well as more-distant places like Ware and Athol, Massachusetts; and it dismissed members to churches in Vermont towns like Townshend, Jamaica, Winhall, and Wardsboro, along with Rindge, New Hampshire. From its founding in 1807 through the 1830s, the First Congregational Church of Waldoboro received members with letters from Duxbury and Boston, Massachusetts; Concord, New Hampshire; Brooklyn, New York; and the Maine towns of North Yarmouth, York, Boothbay, Union, Hardwick, Blue Hill, and Hallowell. During the same period, the church recommended members to Boston as well as Belfast, Farmington, Thomaston, Hallowell, Portland, Calais, Bangor, Augusta, Wells, Robbinston, and Brunswick, all in Maine.[49] The sheer volume of letters reported in church records offers a sense of the constant movement across the region. It also shows how churches, clergy, and churchgoers stretched the spiritual boundaries of the town-church community.

Because a departing parishioner remained a member of his or her home church until a new pastor confirmed a transfer in membership, ministers and church councils monitored members who had moved beyond the town boundaries.[50] The Newbury (Vermont) Congregational Church learned in 1793 from the church in nearby Haverhill, New Hampshire, that two dismissed members had gone "astray from the path of duty." But instead of writing the two off as former members, the Newbury committee asked the Haverhill church for a list of offenses for which they might discipline the men. Not until four years later—after at least one church council meeting and much correspondence with Haverhill to address the problem—did the Newbury church finally excommunicate one of the offenders.[51] In some cases, church members discovered they needed their old churches' endorsements after they had already settled in new places. In 1829, a couple who had been excommunicated from the Bangor Congregational Church and had since moved to Philadelphia found themselves unable to join any church until they received proper dismissions from their former congregation. They wrote to Bangor to express "deep repentance and humiliation on account of their sins," and to ask the church to readmit them and grant dismissions and recommendations. With those documents in hand, the couple could properly withdraw from the Bangor church and unite with a new congregation.[52] For migrants like these, letters of dismission and recommendation extended the scope of the town church, but only temporarily. They allowed parishioners to migrate as if under their home church's canopy of protection until they could make a smooth transition to a new church, thereby minimizing the time that they were under no church's watch.

By design, dismissions and recommendations should have reduced the number of outsiders who lived among town-church members but did not fully participate in their religious lives. But church leaders still fretted over how many people lived in their midst but failed to transfer their membership. The reverse was also true: many town ministers worried about their own members who left and failed to join churches when they settled in new places. The Middlebury Congregational Church observed with alarm in 1826 how many of their members "have removed from this place without uniting with any Church in the vicinity of their present residence."[53] In response to such negligence, many congregations imposed residency rules that required eligible settlers to join churches no more than one year after moving to a new town. These ultimatums became more common as the pace of migration picked up. In 1824, the First Congregational Church in Freeport, Maine, decided that "members of Sister Churches who reside in town and occasionally commune with us" must obtain dismissions and recommendations from their home churches or forego the privileges of taking communion in Freeport.[54] One reason for these rules was financial: not until these uncommitted churchgoers united with a town church could congregations demand their full support. But it was also true that churches were wary of outsiders—even sympathetic ones. By using dismissions and recommendations, town churches positioned themselves (albeit often unsuccessfully) to keep watch over their members at all times. In doing so, they both shored up the geographic boundaries of local institutions and extended those boundaries to overlap with others across the region.

But these efforts to bolster spiritual communities could not mask the havoc that transience wreaked on town churches. Migration—and, along with it, economic instability and fragile social ties—meant that towns lacked both the financial resources and the longstanding residents who might invest in a church. More to the point, these residents might not invest enough in each other to submit to their neighbors' spiritual watch.[55] Settlers in Eden, Vermont, worried that their town could not support regular preaching for these very reasons. Writing to the Connecticut Missionary Society (CMS) in 1807, they explained that, although they appreciated a recent visit by a CMS missionary, they would be unable to establish a church at that time. Their population was too diverse, having settled "from Various States and Difrant towns," and they were not yet "Sufficiently acquainted with each Other to Proceed with Propriety" in gathering a church. They imagined themselves too unstable to settle a minister, as many were "young Men without familys and Nearly all . . . Strugling With the Wilderness under many Disadvantages." Until they could support the gospel in "its Proper Dignity," they asked for a steady supply of missionaries to visit so they might continue regular worship.[56] Many towns in similar circumstances failed for decades to support regular preaching. That is why the Cumberland County (Maine) Conference expressed so much concern in 1822 about the fate of the church in Raymond, which it described as "a feeble flock, few and widely scattered." The church's congregation had settled so thinly that "they can hardly be said to know each others state."[57] More than just a financial commitment, a town required deep personal commitments among churchgoers in order to maintain a church. Financial obstacles aside, many of northern New England's frontier settlements could barely manage that.

To nurture religious communities, town churches sought ministers who could weave disparate interests and religious orientations into a cohesive whole. Just as the meetinghouse lay at the center of a town church's physical landscape, the minister occupied the center of its spiritual landscape. Indeed, most towns placed a far higher priority on settling a minister than on building a meetinghouse. One church council likened the pastoral relationship to that between spouses: "very intimate, their obligations mutual and great, and their connection productive of eternal consequences."[58] And just like the spousal relationship, that between a pastor and his flock embodied a common commitment that, ideally, developed over decades. The church in Jericho, Vermont, declared that the connection between the church and his pastor should be "permanent, unless very Important reasons to the Contrary exist."[59] According to Ephraim Abbot, a permanent settlement fostered "that attachment which ought to subsist between a minister and his people." When he finally settled in Greenland, New Hampshire, the town initially guaranteed only a six-month tenure and allowed either party to terminate the relationship beyond that point. He complained that the proposal "savor[ed] of Methodism" in its impermanence.[60] Abbot, along with his colleagues, imagined the bond between the town and its minister as one that spanned the minister's career. Only by shepherding a community over a lifetime could the minister plant roots deep and wide enough to effect any spiritual consequence.

These roots spread beyond the meetinghouse doors, but (ideally) only as far as the town's borders. Within those limits, the minister oversaw, coordinated, and shepherded religious activity. Because a town minister's duties placed him in daily contact with parishioners—in their farms, workshops, private homes, and markets as well as in church—the lay-pastoral relationship interwove the minister's authority with a familial intimacy. It was crucial that this relationship remain exclusive. Interloping clergy not only interrupted worship, they actually dislodged the local minister from his central place in his town's religious life. One minister scorned the "traveling doctrines of the day" as unnecessarily distracting.[61] The Waldoboro Congregational Church similarly criticized clergy who preached uninvited in a settled minister's parish. The church feared that "this conduct directly tends to introduce confusion and disorder into Parishes; to alienate ministers from each other, to throw open our Societies to sectaries and to itinerant preachers of every description, and to impair the influence of the Regular means of Religious instruction."[62] Sectarian competition had no place in the town-church system; just as surely as physical boundaries marked the town's geographic scope, spiritual boundaries demarcated each minister's territory of religious work.

This work was all-encompassing, designed to reach believers and non-believers alike within the same community. The most obvious and public aspect of the minister's work was preaching. Although morning and afternoon Sabbath meetings were the most common venues for such labors, a minister's duties extended to other occasions, including monthly concerts of prayer, midweek prayer meetings, and communion seasons. These sermons and lectures reinforced both a church's corporate identity and the minister's doctrinal and ecclesiastical authority. Preaching was inseparable from every public observance in Congregationalist life: regular prayer and worship, conversion, communion, funerals, ordinations, fast days, election days, and any number of other public gatherings. Occasional sermons (so named because they marked occasions such as funerals or ordinations) were printed, circulated, and read widely, so that many ministers found audiences well beyond their own congregations. The omnipresence of the Congregationalist sermon in spoken and printed forms helped shape public discourse by weaving together threads of orthodox doctrine and the corporate ideal.[63] Town ministers integrated this discourse into their own sermons, which they generally intended to strengthen not only individual souls but also the covenanted communities to which those souls belonged.

Although official duties like preaching and administering communion were the most visible of the minister's duties, a typical minister spent most of his working hours outside the church and in direct contact with town residents. Ministers spent much of their time dropping in on private homes to talk about any topic that might arise—the weather, the soil, political affairs, and (most importantly) the states of parishioners' souls. Through these conversations, ministers could gauge who might be close to conversion, who was wavering in faith, and who seemed drawn away by encroaching preachers. Visiting allowed clergy to engage their neighbors in private spaces, thereby gaining close acquaintance with both the churched and unchurched in their towns. Whereas a minister might deliver sermons or lectures a few days per week, he visited families nearly every day. More than any other aspect of their jobs, visiting afforded the clergy a close peek into their parishioners' daily lives.

Both the clergy and churchgoers viewed visiting as key to a minister's leadership. A New Hampshire minister found that settled clergy were "necessary not only on Sabbath, but in the week; not only in the house of God, but in every house." Visiting, in other words, enabled ministers to carry out parts of their jobs that they might not accomplish in the more formal setting of church.[64] Churchgoers tended to agree, and they criticized ministers who did not attend sufficiently to visiting. When the parishioners of the Third Church in North Yarmouth, Maine, dismissed their minister, John Dutton, they complained that he neglected the "usual degree of visiting." They had other grievances—notably the poor quality of his preaching—but they thought that "friendly intercourse with his people" during visits could have done much to "heal divisions."[65] To be sure, some pastors thought visits too informal to be truly effective. New Hampshire minister Isaac Hurd wrote in 1828 that he had "reason to lament that my visits are not more strictly *pastoral* visits," and that he could not always "introduce religious subjects and endeavor to make conversation profitable."[66] Others grumbled that visiting only revealed their parishioners' impiety and lack of concern with matters of religious import. But the custom nonetheless remained vital to ministers' work and reinforced their place as the center of their religious communities.

Among the many advantages of visiting was that it allowed ministers to reach out to parishioners who were not converted church members or even churchgoers —or, commonly, who professed other faiths. So did another of a minister's usual roles: leading benevolent and educational endeavors that benefited the community beyond the church members. Ministers were instrumental in establishing libraries, founding academies, and hiring school instructors. Stephen Peabody, for instance, administered and raised funds for an academy in Atkinson, New Hampshire.[67] Ephraim Abbot hired teachers to keep schools in the towns where he ministered.[68] William Jenks, in addition to serving as a trustee of the Maine Missionary Society and founding a subscription library in Bath, also led the Bath Society for Discontinuing and Suppressing Public Vices, which sought to enforce Sabbath observance; "discourage and suppress" profanity, gambling, and drinking; and distribute religious tracts, thereby promoting piety and morality broadly throughout the town.[69] Just as the clergy exercised disciplinary authority over church members, they also oversaw the wider community's educational and moral progress.

A minister, in short, was the center of the town's religious gravity. Without someone to supply that office, the town church itself might disintegrate as residents fell away to other congregations, denominations, or worldly pursuits. Congregationalists feared for the spiritual state of towns that lacked ministers, however well-established their churches might be, and however well-served they were by missionaries and other visitors. When the Freeport (Maine) Congregational Church dismissed its minister in 1815 after a long salary dispute, an advisory council urged the town not to allow its pulpit to stand empty. As long as the church lacked a settled minister, the council warned, they left vulnerable "not only [their] own religious state, but the civil interests of this town, the moral habits of [their] children and families, and their unchangeable destiny in the world to come." Only with permanent clergy could the town secure its religious and civil well-being.[70] So believed Eli Moody, who fretted that his former church in Weybridge, Vermont, had allowed its pulpit to remain vacant for over a year. Moody advised church members to settle a minister soon, lest their church "scatter, as sheep upon the mountains, so that some, at least, will not find their way back into the fold."[71] As the hub of the town church, a minister extended his influence throughout his community as he preached, visited families, administered sacraments, implemented church discipline, and directed benevolent activities. By exercising these roles, he connected his parishioners more firmly to the church and to each other.

Ministers were also instrumental in leading the events that gave shape to a church's spiritual landscape. Among the most important of these were revivals. Although any given church experienced revivals only periodically, they were significant because they produced especially high rates of church attendance and conversion. Most Congregationalist revivals followed the pattern that Jonathan Edwards and others established in southern New England during the Great Awakening in the 1730s. In the tradition of the New England Way, these revivals were periods of heightened religious attention and conversion within one congregation, centered on the preaching efforts of one minister.[72] Even as settlement progressed northward after the American Revolution, village revivals continued to follow the Edwardsian pattern of a contained and communal affair.[73] Unlike other styles of revival at the time—such as the Methodist camp meeting, which welcomed participants from many towns and denominations who might have been strangers to each other—the Congregationalist revival revolved around the town church, its minister, and its members. Chester Wright, the Congregationalist minister in Montpelier, underscored the importance of community ties when he reported that sixty of the seventy members who had joined his church in an 1817 awakening lived "within a circle of about a mile in diameter."[74] Revivals depended much on town ministers' efforts—and, it followed, on the minister's relationship with his church. Because so many northern New England towns lacked ministers of their own, awakenings became especially anticipated and celebrated events.

A revival might begin with a particular turn of events—perhaps one person's dramatic conversion or a cluster of people suddenly on the verge—and it would continue with a period of frequent preaching intended to inspire further soul-searching, especially among those on the brink of conversion. Despite the excitement and commotion that might attend a revival, all of these steps proceeded in a somewhat orderly and decorous fashion, in stark contrast to the revivals led by some other denominations. Noting a spate of awakenings that had erupted in towns across New England, the *Adviser*, a Vermont Congregationalist magazine, observed approvingly that "in none of those places where revivals have lately prevailed . . . has there appeared, among those who have been awakened, any thing like wildness or enthusiasm." Rather, the new converts simply demonstrated "a deep and rational conviction of the importance of eternal things."[75] Similarly, a narrative of an 1824 revival in Vassalboro, Maine, described the event as "very rapid and powerful, yet still and solemn," and without "boisterous excitement of the passions."[76] And whereas more heated styles of revivalism threatened to distract religious communities, town-church revivals strengthened them. As the Rutland (Vermont) Association of Congregationalist churches noted in 1830, the "system of operations" that other groups favored "tends to interfere with the responsibilities of the established clergy and the sacred relations which they sustain to the church and to the world."[77] Only in an atmosphere of serious prayer and reflection, Congregationalists believed, could a true awakening take place. It was the minister's job to create this solemn mood so he might then focus his parishioners' attention on their own souls.

During the long stretches between revivals, ministers bemoaned their congregations' lukewarm piety and prayed for another revival to take root. Because their own preaching was so crucial to bringing about a revival, they often questioned the value of their endeavors if no awakening appeared on the horizon. "How can I bear," asked William Jenks, "to reflect on a state of spiritual deadness among Christians!" He ruefully observed that the situation in a colleague's congregation had been "favourable, exceedingly favourable" for some time, but he was somehow unable to inspire similar attention among his own people. "I shall be shown my worthlessness," Jenks predicted, "in some more striking manner than I have seen it yet."[78] Isaac Hurd similarly fretted in 1822 that he seemed "to be laboring almost in vain," with "but little fruit" for all his effort.[79] Even though revivals were rare in any given congregation, ministers still assumed the burden for initiating and sustaining them; failure to do so caused a town minister to question his own leadership.

But the ministers were not wholly in charge; indeed, a congregation had to come together to bring about an awakening and allow it to spread. To succeed, a town-church revival involved the entire web of relationships among church and clergy and was a truly communal event. This web formed the foundation not just for revival but also for the spiritual community that sustained the town church. The Congregationalist church took shape within both the town's physical space and the spiritual landscape that residents and their minister laid out. As an institution with a history in New England town settlement, the town church was an ideal (and idealized) fixture. It assumed specific communities in specific places were organic, stable, and whole. When this turned out not to be the case in northern New England, the town church faced new challenges to its very structure and orientation.

Although town churches were designed to be stable, northern New England's towns were rarely so. Despite the Congregationalist legacy and the careful layout of the town-church geography, the realities of backcountry conditions and religious competition frustrated attempts to implement the town-church ideal. The principal challenges were threefold. First, relationships between churches and religious societies—the spiritual and administrative entities that governed a parish—grew increasingly contentious as a rising majority of non-believers chafed against the Congregationalists' political power in their towns. Second, doctrinal divisions within Congregationalism itself split churches and parishes. Finally, dissenting denominations drew still more people away from town parishes, depriving them of financial support and driving wedges between churchgoers, who shared neighborhoods but not religious affiliations. All of these conflicts occurred against a backdrop of social and economic instability that depleted parish coffers, heightened competition for resources, and sent migrants across counties and states, thereby unraveling the ties of familiarity and mutual obligation that wove together covenanted communities. Should formerly united parishes disintegrate, leaders asked, what would remain to nurture piety and regulate morality—and to support the civil government in doing the same? If northern New England's town churches had ever managed to fulfill those roles, it became quite clear in the early nineteenth century that they would not continue to do so for long.

Because so much had depended on the perceived unity of town, church, and parish, divided parishes signaled troubling changes to Congregationalist communities. Perhaps the most significant gap was that between churches and societies. Religious societies represented the parishes as legal and administrative bodies. Run by lay members, they were responsible for raising money and financing ministerial salaries, building and repairing meetinghouses, administering charitable donations, and the like. Churches, on the other hand, were spiritual bodies, gathered according to the precepts and customs of the denomination in question. Church members were converted Christians who had joined their churches in full communion, whereas societies might include church members along with the unconverted. In towns where the churchgoing population was more religiously diverse, some society members might have affiliated with other denominations, even if they attended the town church by default. As a result, societies increasingly saw themselves in doctrinal opposition to the smaller church membership.

These tensions resulted from both greater religious diversity in the towns and many churches' exclusive standards for membership. Some congregations, hoping to enforce stricter doctrinal standards, abandoned the Half-Way Covenant, which had allowed children of any baptized churchgoer to be baptized themselves. This practice originated in the mid-seventeenth century, when New England churches sought to preserve their authority over an expanding population and diminishing membership. By baptizing children of baptized (but not necessarily converted) parishioners, churches could oversee a broader base.[80] But some worried that lower standards for baptism diluted their congregations' piety. And many churches, like the member congregations of Vermont's Windham Association in 1791, abandoned the practice. Over the next few decades, churches across the region followed suit, including the Union Church of Christ in Greenfield, New Hampshire (1800), the Congregational Church in Waldoboro, Maine (1808), the First Congregational Church of Freeport, Maine (1810), and the First Congregational Church of Bangor, Maine (1811).[81] By ending this privilege and baptizing only children of full members, churches created a two-tiered system in which unconverted (and unbaptized) churchgoers were expected to participate and contribute without hope of attaining the privileges of full membership unless they converted.

As church membership grew more selective and less representative of a town's population, the power dynamics between church and parish shifted. Although non-members did not sway church governance and discipline, they could gain control over religious societies. As a result, churches and societies often butted heads in matters of church funding, ministerial hiring decisions, and other disputes. In 1786, Jeremy Belknap resigned as the Dover (New Hampshire) Congregational Church's minister after a years-long struggle with the town regarding funding—a problem exacerbated, he thought, by repeated and divisive votes on the question. Although there were many in the parish "from whom I should not wish to be separated," there was also a large faction "with whom I cannot have any Connexion." In the end, Belknap resigned rather than allow the parish to split over his continued service.[82] When the church in Hopkinton, New Hampshire, settled Jacob Cram in 1789, a town-wide protest ensued, resulting in jailings, lawsuits, and a drive to create a new parish.[83] Although the church installed Cram nonetheless, his rocky tenure lasted only three years. Joseph Warren, a young Congregationalist minister preaching on a trial basis in Pittston, Maine, in 1793, was skeptical of his chances of settling there because the town was so divided. "There is two parties in the church," he wrote, "and I suppose one will oppose what the other does."[84] Similarly, political divisions led the religious society in Underhill, Vermont, to dismiss its minister, James Parker, despite the church's objections. Parker complained that some hostile society members had "profanely intruded" on Sabbath worship, and he despaired of forging spiritual unity in the town.[85] A council concurred and reluctantly recommended his dismission. In towns like these, a church's will could not match the parish's political power.

Along with parish divisions over ministers came contentious struggles over finances. One purpose of uniting towns as single parishes was to concentrate religious funding within one church, even if every taxpayer did not personally favor that church, minister, or doctrine. But Congregationalist ministers were expensive, compared with the clergy of other denominations. Not only did they tend to be more educated (possessing at least a college degree), but also, because of religious establishment, they were town officers as well as spiritual leaders. Moreover, unlike many dissenting groups that opposed a salaried ministry, Congregationalists funded ministerial salaries with compulsory payments. Consequently, in addition to benefits like the use of a ministerial plot and parsonage, and allowances of cut timber, grain, and other such enticements, settled town ministers generally netted salaries of over $350 per year. By contrast, ministers of other denominations could expect to earn less than $250.[86] To procure a Congregationalist minister, then, a town had to be willing to invest.

Even though Congregationalists agreed to fund their ministers' salaries, many clergy found that actually securing payments was a tricky matter. Stephen Peabody frequently had to call on his parishioners to collect his own salary, and he often struggled to do so. After visiting one family, he wryly noted that a woman "proposed to give me a puppy" instead of his ministerial rates.[87] Peabody tended to forgive his flock's tardy payments, but tugs of war over salaries could get far more heated. Often, a town simply could not afford a permanent minister, due both to its inhabitants' divergent sentiments and their poverty. Missionary Thomas Holt pointed out that places like Weld, Maine, might never establish churches without missionary support. Divided between Baptists and Congregationalists, Holt reported, "the town is new, the inhabitants poor." The church, he concluded, "must wither or be upholden by the Arm of omnipotence without the instrumentality of a preached gospel."[88] Whether due to inability or refusal to pay, a town's financial shortcomings often reflected or exacerbated deeper spiritual divisions.

Fractured parishes posed only one of many challenges to the town church's stability. Indeed, divisions within Congregationalism itself threatened the denomination's ability to unite its following and ensure its own survival. One of the hallmarks of Congregationalism was its system of local government. Without any centralized body to issue standard interpretations of doctrine or practice, each church developed (within limits) its own religious sensibility. And because each congregation was free to pursue its own brand of Congregationalism and ordain a compatible minister, proponents of competing doctrines tended to avoid each other, seeking associations of like-minded clergy and shunning others.

In northern New England, the theological range was vast. On the liberal side were a few Unitarians, along with latitudinarian Congregationalists like William Jenks and Paul Coffin of Buxton, Maine, who once proclaimed that he could not "reconcile Calvin's Institutes with the Scriptures."[89] On the other end of the spectrum lay conservative and New Divinity Calvinists who reacted against what they saw as a watering-down of true doctrine and called for a return to the uncompromising bent of Jonathan Edwards. Together with other strict Calvinists, New Divinity Congregationalists rejected the halfway covenant along with any notion that humans had the slightest influence over their own salvation.[90] Even though Congregationalists across the spectrum shared much—including their denominational history and the town-church system—their ministers and churchgoers often saw themselves in direct opposition to each other.

Ministers and churchgoers alike derided Congregationalists of different stripes and spoke of them with the same ire they usually reserved for Methodists or Universalists. Moderate Paul Coffin puzzled over the "Hopkinsian" view that God created sin and wondered how New Divinity Congregationalists could accept the "Divinity of the Devil" ("Hopkinsian" and its derivatives allude to Samuel Hopkins, a New Divinity leader).[91] Indeed, Coffin did not consider the New Divinity a branch of Congregationalism at all, categorizing it as a separate sect entirely. He complained that "people turn with every wind, are Hopkinsians, Baptists, Methodists, and Congregationalists," and refused to unite under one minister.[92] Stephen Peabody described the "Hopkintonians" he encountered as "rank," "zealous," and "rigid."[93] Strict Calvinists were equally hostile toward their more moderate counterparts. Maine minister Joseph Wingate described the Unitarians as "the most erroneous sect of Christians that I know of."[94] Increasingly, Congregationalist ministers severed ties to one another by refusing to join associations or exchange pulpits with any other than like-minded clergy. As one minister pointed out, "of all errors, those are the most dangerous, which come nearest the truth, and yet come essentially short of it."[95] Instead of creating communities of believers, they used the language of sectarianism to erect barriers.

Divisions within Congregationalism weakened the town church. Not only did congregations often fail to hire ministers because of doctrinal disagreements, but tensions also split churches and parishes. Raynham, Maine, had boasted a longstanding religious society of about one hundred members and a church of thirty-one members until doctrinal conflicts fractured the parish in the 1820s. Tensions erupted when Raynham's new pastor forbade his parishioners "the privilege of hearing any preachers except those of the orthodox stamp." Although he had publicly embraced a more liberal doctrine upon his ordination, he later gravitated to orthodox Calvinism. Believing that "duty obliged them to secede," the liberal churchgoers of Raynham did exactly that, even though they sacrificed a settled minister and access to their meetinghouse in the process.[96] Like others who peered across the wide gap between liberal and orthodox Congregationalism, the Raynham dissenters understood their conflict as one between religious traditions, not within one. As sectarian divisions strengthened, churches split, new parishes formed, and towns divided along doctrinal (rather than geographic) lines. Even without the challenges of other denominations, religious rivalries began to rearrange the region's town-church boundaries.

Divisions within Congregationalism did not pose the only threat to the town-church ideal. Other groups also drew parishioners away from town churches into neighboring—and competing—congregations. The longest-standing dissenters in northern New England were the Baptists. In some respects, they diverged little from conservative Congregationalists. They adhered to strict Calvinism, favored congregational autonomy, and emphasized the Bible as the sole religious authority. But significant doctrinal differences separated the two groups. Baptists rejected the Congregationalist practice of baptizing infants by sprinkling water on the head, arguing that it had no biblical basis. Instead, they insisted on baptizing adult believers and only by full immersion. The distinction was important. Whereas Congregationalists saw this ritual as a legacy of the Abrahamic covenant that brought infants under the church's watch, Baptists saw it as a symbol of spiritual death, burial, and rebirth. Because they believed that full immersion was the one way to bring about the new birth, Baptists considered anyone who had not undergone the ritual unconverted. Consequently, they also took issue with the Congregationalist tradition of open communion for all believers, insisting that they could commune only with those who had received what they judged an authentic baptism.[97] The ways in which Baptists and Congregationalists interpreted and used these rituals reflected their very different ideas about how to draw the boundaries of their religious communities. Moreover, Baptists' insistence on voluntarism meant that they opposed the church-state partnership and ministerial taxes. Their preference for voluntary churches contradicted the town-church ideal by making belief, rather than residence, the basis for church fellowship.

Baptist parishes—which either broke off from the town's first parish or combined residents of multiple towns—were usually the first dissenting societies to physically alter the boundaries of the town church. Although Baptists had founded churches in northern New England by the 1770s, their numbers did not grow dramatically until after independence. Their membership rose following the New Light Stir, a period of evangelical revival in the late 1770s and early 1780s that established them as the Congregationalists' principal competitors in northern New England.[98] In 1790, there were only twelve Baptist congregations in Maine, but that number doubled in the next decade and increased fivefold in the decade after that. By 1820, the Baptists had more churches in Maine (154) than any other denomination.[99] During the same period, they also became the fastest-growing denomination in Vermont. Although they did not expand as rapidly in New Hampshire, they grew from two churches in 1770 to seventy in 1826.[100] Because of their sudden rise and their preference for the congregational polity, Baptists positioned themselves to compete directly with town churches. Wherever a Baptist church organized and incorporated, it siphoned members from the local town parishes—and along with those members, their ministerial taxes and their fellowship with their neighbors.

Because Baptists organized on the congregational plan, a Baptist church might become the established church if it were the first to organize in its town. This turn of events was rare but not unheard of. The Middletown, Vermont, Baptists gained a majority in the town in 1805 and consequently assumed control of the town parish. Although proprietors could invite guest preachers of different faiths, they could settle only a Baptist minister.[101] The town of New London, New Hampshire, settled Baptist Elder Job Seamans as their first minister, thereby granting him the right to the ministerial lot and public support. Although he eventually accepted his salary through voluntary payments and survived many attempts to oust him, he retained the public land and remained the town's standing minister for decades.[102] Despite these footholds, the peculiarities of their doctrine (including adult baptism and closed communion) meant that the Baptists rarely dominated town parishes as Congregational churches tended to do. Whereas the Congregationalists increasingly failed to carry out the town-church vision, the Baptists did not even try.

Baptists usually separated from town parishes rather than try to overtake them. By doing so, they could devastate an established parish's finances and morale. Town churches increasingly found themselves contending with Baptists and other denominations, which divided parishes into ever-smaller units as parishioners left to join new churches. Congregationalist missionary Joseph Field noted in 1805 that the deep divisions between Congregationalists and Baptists in New Sharon, Maine, prevented its inhabitants from supporting a minister. "Nothing appears but union," he reported, "to be necessary for the settlement and maintenance of preachers."[103] The town of Blue Hill, Maine, experienced similar problems. Even though their pastor, Jonathan Fisher, had been settled for more than two decades, the town church lost so many parishioners to the Baptists by 1817 that they had trouble supporting him.[104] As one New Hampshire minister observed, divided parishes placed all churches in financial jeopardy. Jacob Abbot, who preached in Hampton Falls, New Hampshire, observed in 1809 that many nearby towns, all of which had recently supported ministers, now had empty pulpits—a trend he blamed on rising sectarianism. Writing again in 1825, he bemoaned the "breaking up of societies and churches by dividing them in to so small sections, that they will be unable to provide themselves the regular means of religion."[105] Just as the town church depended on the minister at its center, it also depended on the town's unanimous efforts to support him. Lacking one, the other was impossible to achieve.

Even if a Congregationalist parish remained intact, dissenting parishioners could overrule the church by dividing the use of the meetinghouse for various denominations, often without allotting time to the Congregationalists themselves. On a missionary tour in 1796, Paul Coffin noted that although the residents of Bath had a settled Congregationalist minister, his opponents had voted to reserve the meetinghouse for Methodist preaching half the time.[106] The town's dissenters lacked sufficient numbers to form parishes of their own, but they still managed to disrupt the town church by inviting strangers to its pulpit and pews. As in Bath, when churches and parishes diverged, new denominations, ministers, and churchgoers filled the gaps between them.

Congregationalists decried this sort of fragmentation as religious partisanship—a most undesirable path for communities that were supposed to unite in worship. Stephen Bemis, a student at Dartmouth, criticized the "silly, enthusiastic preachers" who set about "making divisions in towns and destroying the peace of civil society" at the expense of settled ministers.[107] Solomon Livermore, a divinity student from Wilton, New Hampshire, similarly declared that "a minister should be no party man."[108] William Jenks prayed for "less of a spirit of party in the different branches of Christ's visible church."[109] Likewise, Jacob Abbot decried the "sectarian and scismatical spirit," which he thought would prove "highly injurious to the interests of religion." There was danger, he argued, in the "party spirit and party religion" that resulted from "diversity of opinions and sects." Partisan religion could only excite "bad passions [and] bad dispositions," which, according to Abbot, made it "the worst kind of religion."[110] Of all the faults they found with these upstart religious groups, Congregationalists generally agreed that their worst evil was to factionalize town-church communities by encouraging individuals to break off from organic communities to pursue their own interests.

As an institution, the town church endured its share of challenges. By the close of the eighteenth century, new denominations had begun to expand in the region, new parishes had broken off, and older ones found themselves mired in conflict. But the town church had begun its decline well before dissenters posed serious challenges to the system of religious establishment that sought to preserve it. A new religious geography was taking shape in New England, one that altered and eventually erased the old town-church boundaries. What place the Congregationalists might find in this new geography would depend on how they negotiated the end of an ecclesiastical system that had defined them for two centuries.

Asa Lyon, a Vermont Congregationalist minister, appeared to have given up entirely on the principle of a town church by 1833. As he pondered whether those who embraced different doctrines should worship separately, he admitted that, in fact, they should. To commune with those who disagreed on the essentials of justification and salvation, he conceded, would deny believers the benefits of communion itself. It followed, then, that people who parted ways on matters of baptism, church discipline, the form of the Lord's Supper, or any other essentials of doctrine and practice should not pray together. In short, he argued, "we cannot commune with those who hold and teach principles, which if we experience all that they require, we cannot be saved." Far from William Jenks's earlier ecumenical vision, Lyon suggested that open communion could not serve the needs of any heterogeneous Christian town.[111]

Christians during the early republic generally agreed that religion necessarily bound society together, that only widespread belief and attentive worship could ensure that families, economies, and governments would function ethically and morally. As the locus of overlapping spiritual and secular communities, the town church served as a little polity that both bolstered piety and enforced morality. But the town church, which assumed its residents' full participation and cooperation in religious and civil undertakings, depended most of all on a homogeneous and undivided town. As Congregationalists confronted greater diversity both in their denomination and in their towns, they came to understand their own churches not in connection to particular places but rather to a particular set of doctrines.

Congregationalist communities in northern New England were always more ideal than real—more constructed than concrete. From their beginnings, the northern hinterland's towns were more diverse, less stable, and more permeable than their counterparts in Massachusetts and Connecticut. So, too, were their town churches. But the town-church ideal anchored an otherwise tenuous existence for the Congregationalist majority, who understood church and town as overlapping entities. The town church as an institution was certainly on the decline by the early decades of the nineteenth century. The dual questions of what would replace it—and how Congregationalism would adapt—only heightened its proponents' anxieties.

2 Zion Travels

The Itinerant Enterprise

THE AWAKENING IN York, Maine, began slowly, excruciatingly so. It started in 1801, when a number of the town's "principal people" traveled to nearby Berwick to witness a revival. York had no preacher, so its inhabitants remained anxious and aimless until they invited William Batchelder, a Baptist missionary, to visit four years later. Once he arrived, the revival progressed quickly, with several meetings in York and neighboring Wells, some attended by over a thousand people. They met in fields, orchards, and forests when churches would not hold the crowds. In one meeting, an audience of 1,400 collected in a grove "where the rocks formed like galleries, . . . [and] the trees formed an arbour to shelter us from the sun." Under that leafy canopy, observers listened for four hours as preachers addressed them from rock ledges and tree branches. The meeting culminated in a nighttime procession to the seashore. As some prayed, some exhorted, and others sang, the company gathered at a cove "where the water was as smooth as a sea of glass." The beach, "thronged with spectators," shone by the light of torches and lanterns as Batchelder led each convert to the waterside for a full immersion. "This was a time surpassing description," he reported, "but all was peace, order, joy, and heavenly music."[1]

Batchelder did not stay long to enjoy the fruits of his labor. He was due to preach in Quamphegan, on the Maine–New Hampshire border, the next day, and with twenty miles to travel, he left the seaside baptism for an overnight journey. Such was the life of a Baptist missionary: after his work in one place produced the desired conversions, he moved on to the next town, where he hoped to achieve the same results. Batchelder believed that these fleeting contacts produced lasting good. "There are thousands in these parts anxious to be acquainted with the truth," he estimated. A willing audience made for fruitful missionary work. Batchelder guessed that "nearly every preacher who has preached in [this] place since the work began, has been instrumental of awakenings."[2] Although many in their congregations had never heard preaching, missionaries like Batchelder expected they would not stay unchurched for long.

Baptists were used to sharing their ministers. The longest-standing dissenters in northern New England, they had, as of the early nineteenth century, never matched the Congregationalist parishes' power, wealth, or population. To compete, they found ways to organize within the existing parish system, dividing ministers' time among different churches, gathering members from many towns into single parishes, and challenging legal obstacles to church formation. By doing so, Baptists created opportunities to worship even when their ministers could not keep pace with demand.

By the close of the eighteenth century, other upstart denominations joined the Baptist dissenters in northern New England. These groups—especially the Methodists, Universalists, and Freewill Baptists—followed an itinerant model of church-building. They crossed parish (and state) lines, relied on itinerant clergy to minister to far-flung churches, gathered for large meetings and revivals, and developed centralized administrations—all of which suited a mobile, churchgoing population. Although they hired local clergy, their institutions transcended local parishes, and they conceived of their churches in expansive terms. Instead of focusing on building churches rooted in towns, these denominations found new ways to connect widely scattered followers.

The itinerant churches, just like town churches, took shape in physical and spiritual spaces that structured institutions' relationships to each other, their followers, and sectarian outsiders. But because they covered more physical ground, the itinerant movements created regional networks linked by ministers, correspondents, and conferences that rotated among distant towns. The itinerant system also created spiritual spaces where ministers connected the laity to central authorities who decided matters of practice and discipline. These denominations did not see itinerancy as a compromise to cope with ministerial shortages or the absence of local churches, but rather as an intentional strategy to extend shifting boundaries. Hoping to enforce uniformity across distance, the itinerant movements used their traveling corps to connect far-flung followers more tightly than did secular bonds between neighbors who did not share churches.

In the decades following the American Revolution, religious dissenters flooded northern New England and challenged both the orthodoxy and the boundaries of Congregationalist communities. Although they professed different doctrines and sometimes competed fiercely for followers, they had much in common—not least the unprecedented growth they all experienced during the early republic. They shared roots in the charismatic spirituality of the Great Awakening: a style popularized by George Whitefield that emphasized "heart religion" and attracted followers as much with dramatic flair as with doctrinal substance. Moreover, they objected to what they viewed as the liberal and moderate Congregationalists' emphasis on morality over piety.[3] And they all relied on itinerants and increasingly complex bureaucracies to administer their growing followings and extend their geographic reach while ensuring that consistent doctrine and discipline bound them together.

The Baptists, the longest-standing dissenters in northern New England, straddled the line between the town-church and itinerant styles. They saw each church as an independent body, and their preference for congregational autonomy meant that Baptist churches were tied to local communities and even served as town churches in a few places. But they never fully embraced the town-church ideal. Baptists opposed religious taxation and insisted on voluntary support, and so they rarely relied on towns as foundations for their religious communities. Instead, they drew their faithful out of town parishes, and they increasingly depended on itinerants to serve their growing following. As a result, Baptists, despite their congregational orientation, adopted newer strategies for organization and evangelism that reflected the itinerant model.

As itinerancy became a more important component of Baptism, the movement revolved less and less around its congregational polities. To coordinate the activities of missionaries, churches, and settled ministers, Baptists created associations.[4] Most associations in northern New England—including the Woodstock Association in Vermont, the New Hampshire Association in New Hampshire and Maine, and the Bowdoinham Association in Maine—were founded between the 1780s and the 1810s, a period of rapid Baptist growth. The New Hampshire Association (1785) saw its membership multiply almost tenfold in its first two decades. The Bowdoinham Association (1787) grew nearly ninefold in just thirteen years. Each association included about twenty churches and wove itself into a wider Baptist network by holding annual meetings, circulating pamphlets, and overseeing Baptist doctrine and practice.[5] Citing the "ecclesiastical licentiousness" of the era, which threatened to "enervate, if not Destroy, all Church Discipline," associations published covenants and articles of faith to which they expected member churches to subscribe.[6] They warned against partnerships with "those who propose a confederacy" founded on doctrines other than their own.[7] By doing so, they centralized authority, even within a denomination that prized congregational autonomy.

To maintain this authority, Baptists sent missionaries to serve the headless churches and societies that dotted northern New England. At first, associations set up exchanges in which settled ministers rotated to fill empty pulpits.[8] Exchanges still left many churches without clergy, though, so associations created missionary societies to fund preaching tours. The Woodstock Association had long sent preachers on informal assignments "to the northward" before it established a formal missionary society in 1806.[9] The Massachusetts Baptist Missionary Society and the Vermont Baptist Association also hired missionaries.[10] They distributed tracts, covenants, and periodicals to reinforce doctrine and discipline, spread news of revivals, and report on preaching tours. They evangelized, preached, and helped Baptists gather churches.[11] They reached tiny outposts like Gouldsboro, Maine, where missionary James Murphy found "neither church, meeting-house, nor minister of any denomination . . . that keep up the form of religion on the Lord's-day." Sensing that the inhabitants were eager for formal worship, Murphy advised "some, who were tender in their minds," to meet together on the Sabbath.[12] Churches like this one looked to associations for guidance in doctrinal and disciplinary matters as well as ministerial services. Linked together by missionaries, northern New England's Baptist churches joined a growing itinerant network.

As the denomination expanded, Baptists maintained an ever-shifting balance between congregational autonomy and authority that increasingly concentrated in associations. But other groups, particularly Methodists, Universalists, and Freewill Baptists, sought no such compromise. Instead of supporting local autonomy, they structured themselves largely on the itinerant model, with centralized and geographically far-reaching hierarchies that oversaw doctrine and discipline, and itinerant networks to tie local communities together.

Methodism emerged in eighteenth-century England, where it grew from a small prayer circle to a full-fledged religious movement under John Wesley's leadership. As it grew, Wesley developed the customs and rituals that would remain important in American Methodism. These included the love feast (in which members gave testimonials of religious experiences), public confessions of faith, and singing of hymns. Church members also gathered in class meetings: small groups within churches in which members gave personal testimony, studied the Bible, and enforced discipline. Class leaders reported to (primarily itinerant) preachers, whom Wesley supervised.[13] Wesley also developed a systematic theology, which borrowed from both the Calvinist conception of innate human depravity and the Arminian belief that humans could return to righteousness by choosing to accept Christ's general and unconditional offer of grace.[14] What began as a collection of voluntary societies became a formal hierarchy with its own discipline and liturgy.

Bishops Francis Asbury and Thomas Coke, along with a few followers, founded the Methodist Episcopal Church in the United States in 1784. They replicated and expanded the hierarchy that Wesley had created in England and revised the Methodist *Discipline*, which became the church's authoritative text in North America.[15] American Methodism took shape as a network of class meetings within churches and societies, which clustered in itinerant circuits, which fell within districts, which were run by conferences. Unlike most other American denominations (which used at least some lay governance), the Methodist Episcopal Church was run entirely by clergy, with bishops leading conferences, elders in charge of districts, itinerants overseeing circuits, local preachers manning church pulpits, and class leaders and deacons at the bottom of the hierarchy. The laity could occupy no higher office than class leader, and neither they nor local preachers voted on policy or discipline. The Methodist leadership gathered in quarterly and conference meetings, and conference administrators convened a general meeting once every four years.[16] With a line of authority that extended from classes up to Francis Asbury, the Methodist episcopacy maintained doctrinal and disciplinary consistency as the denomination expanded across a widening territory.

This episcopacy was largely in place by the time Asbury appointed Jesse Lee to form a new circuit in Maine in 1793. Lee, a Virginian, had been riding circuits in southern New England. Soon after he established the Readfield Circuit in Maine, he and his colleagues expanded the Methodist connection, creating the first New Hampshire circuit in 1795 and the first Vermont circuit in 1796.[17] Lee was a charismatic ambassador. Joel Winch, a Vermont Congregationalist who later became a Methodist circuit rider, recalled that Lee that "was not like other men, for he was much larger and his Clothes were made different than any that I had ever seen." Lee preached with a booming voice that commanded attention: "it was uncommon hevy, he preached with ease so that a child might understand him."[18] Under his leadership, the Methodists grew rapidly in northern New England. From a single circuit in 1793, the Methodists in Maine added nineteen circuits in two districts by 1810; by the time the Maine Conference formed from the New England Conference in 1825, it had added ten more circuits and another district. During its first thirty-five years, the New Hampshire District grew from one circuit to twenty-two. When the Vermont District was absorbed into the New England Conference in 1804, it included thirteen circuits, which were soon consolidated into six. By 1826, the Vermont District had expanded to include fourteen circuits, and the Danville District (containing eleven circuits) was added within the state of Vermont a year later. In 1830, the Vermont, Danville, and New Hampshire districts combined as the New Hampshire and Vermont Conference, which included three districts made up of fifty-five circuits.[19] By then, the northern New England Methodists had built an infrastructure that connected churches, circuits, and conferences within a shared discipline.

Universalism, like Methodism, began as a transatlantic movement, but it reached maturity as a doctrine and a denomination in the United States. Universalism emerged during the late eighteenth century, driven by a diverse set of preachers who criticized the Calvinist doctrine of particular election and favored the idea of universal salvation. They arrived at Universalism after circuitous spiritual odysseys. One early leader, John Murray, converted to Universalism in his native England at the end of a journey that led him from strict Calvinism to

Methodism to an ecumenical ministry in the tradition of George Whitefield. He eventually settled in Gloucester, Massachusetts, and the congregation he gathered there in 1779 became a Universalist center for followers in Boston, Portsmouth, and nearby towns in New Hampshire and Maine. Meanwhile, Isaac Davis (a doctor from Somers, Connecticut, who had been a New Light Separatist) and Adams Streeter (a Davis convert from Massachusetts who had been a Baptist) preached and circulated Universalist tracts in central Massachusetts. Caleb Rich, another former Baptist, preached in southern New Hampshire, where he attracted followers like William Balch, Thomas Barnes, and Hosea Ballou, who fanned out on their own preaching tours. These early evangelists attracted converts who had heard Universalist beliefs, local clergy who questioned Congregationalist doctrine, and networks of sympathetic kin who circulated ideas through migration and correspondence.[20]

Universalism imparted a rational theology of God's benevolence toward all people, but it also tapped into the tradition of charismatic preaching that evangelicals like Jonathan Edwards and George Whitefield had introduced during the Great Awakening.[21] It was this blend of intellectual substance and charismatic style that would attract so many converts in northern New England. But if its early leaders shared an evangelical sensibility, they differed in their interpretations of doctrine. Universalists agreed that Christ's death, atonement, and resurrection redeemed all of humanity. Yet some argued that only true believers would reach heaven, whereas others believed sinners would arrive in heaven after an intermediary period of punishment. Still others saw themselves as improving upon Calvinism, not breaking from it; they expanded the doctrine of election to include all of humanity among the elect.[22] Through the end of the eighteenth century, Universalists debated the particulars among themselves, uniting only on the broad principle of universal salvation.

In the early 1790s, Universalism was still a decentralized movement; early efforts to unite as a denomination had failed. The Philadelphia Convention of Universalists attempted to provide an organizational base beginning in 1790, and some churches proposed standard articles of faith.[23] But not until 1793, when the New England General Convention organized, did Universalism begin to coalesce under common institutions and doctrines. The convention included member churches from New England and New York, and it licensed preachers, sponsored educational efforts, and published circular letters and minutes. At the 1794 meeting, the convention chose about thirty ministers "to go forth in a circuitous manner and preach the everlasting Gospel" wherever Universalist churches or societies already existed. Gradually, the convention expanded its powers. Beginning in 1800, it consolidated its authority over local churches by approving ordination councils, mediating disputes between ministers and congregations, excommunicating errant clergy, and requesting that all congregations send representatives to annual meetings so as to ensure uniform practice in their churches. To underscore this point, the convention reminded followers that "God is a God of order" and admonished them to "pay peculiar solemnized attentions to regularity and discipline."[24] By concentrating authority in the convention rather than individual churches, Universalists hoped to establish a regular practice and uniform faith.

Those efforts culminated in the first decade of the nineteenth century, when the convention formalized its spiritual and bureaucratic authority. At the 1803 annual meeting in Winchester, New Hampshire, the convention approved the Winchester Profession, a common confession for all churches to adopt. The profession articulated a Universalist doctrine broad enough to accommodate the group's varied theological strains but narrow enough to promote doctrinal unity. It proclaimed the authority of the Bible, endorsed the doctrine of universal salvation and restoration, and asserted the equal importance of faith and works. Beyond those core principles, the profession included an additional "liberty clause" that allowed churches to devise their own articles of faith. The convention also established mid-level associations—beginning with the Eastern Association in Maine (1803) and the Northern Association in Vermont and New Hampshire (1804)—and assigned liaisons to connect the associations with member churches and the General Convention.[25] Later, the convention assumed more direct control over ordination and commissioned a hymnal for all Universalist congregations to use. With a centralized hierarchy to oversee doctrine, discipline, and practice, the Universalists expanded dramatically; between 1800 and 1820, the number of Universalist congregations increased from twenty-two to over two hundred, with most of that growth concentrated in northern New England.[26] Using the itinerant model, Universalists spread across a vast territory while maintaining control over its local churches.

Just like the Methodists and Universalists, the Freewill Baptists attracted followers and cemented their authority by creating a bureaucracy to oversee itinerants, churches, and societies. And just like Methodists and Universalists, Freewill Baptists traced their history to George Whitefield and his American evangelical network. The Freewill Baptist movement began in 1780, when Benjamin Randel underwent a conversion experience that led him to reject Calvinism for an Arminian doctrine of human perfectibility and free grace. Born in Newcastle, New Hampshire, in 1749, he was raised an Old Light Congregationalist who disapproved of the enthusiasm of the Great Awakening. He remained skeptical even after he attended what turned out to be one of George Whitefield's last revival sermons. Although the experience had no immediate effect, the news of Whitefield's death a week later set Randel on a spiritual journey away from Congregationalism. He landed first in a Calvinist Baptist church, which he served as an itinerant in southeastern New Hampshire and southern Maine. But his ties to that church frayed during the late 1770s, when he began to embrace a more radical theology. In 1779–1780, he experienced a series of visions that convinced him of the scriptural truth of atonement for all who accepted God's grace. He then set out to gather converts and mobilize Baptists who had begun to question Calvinism. He also wrote a confession of faith and covenant, which he presented to converts. Within a year, a core group of signers formed the earliest membership of the Freewill Baptist church.[27]

Having identified themselves as a separate group, Randel and his followers set out to formulate a clear doctrine and organize a governing body. Randel interwove many threads of his own religious background: the Congregationalist tradition of open communion, the Whitefieldian model of revival and conversion, the Baptist practice of believers' baptism by full immersion, and Arminian doctrines of free grace and free will. But because he had little formal education, Randel struggled to develop a systematic theology that could withstand mounting criticism. As he wrestled with this task, he encountered Henry Alline, a radical Congregationalist who itinerated through Nova Scotia and northern New England, preaching a doctrine that blended Calvinism, mysticism, and pacifism. Randel met Alline in 1783 and incorporated his theological treatises into Freewill doctrine, which remained a distinctive confluence of its Calvinist and Arminian forebears.[28]

This distinctive theology enhanced the Freewill Baptists' appeal, but the movement saw little growth at first beyond the Maine–New Hampshire border towns where it had taken root: Strafford, Loudon-Canterbury, and New Durham, New Hampshire, and Shapleigh and Hollis, Maine. Just like early Universalists, early Freewill Baptists attempted to expand by setting out on haphazard itinerant tours. Preachers targeted towns with Baptist congregations, where they hoped to spark revivals and convince converts to break from their churches. Elder John Buzzell defended this schismatic approach, claiming that "it was never [the clergy's] intention to . . . make any disturbance in any good societies." Rather, the Freewill Baptists simply drew people away from already-splintered churches. It was "not these traveling ministers," Buzzell insisted, "but the town ministers [who made] the divisions, by opposing the work of God." The itinerants often succeeded; together with Randel, preachers like Tozier Lord, Peletiah Tingley, Edward Lock, and Samuel Weeks formed new churches at New Gloucester, Gorham, Sanford, and Woolwich, Maine, and Gilmanton and Tamworth, New Hampshire.[29] But despite this success, the movement did not have the institutional framework that had helped other denominations manage far-flung congregations. Moreover, the new Freewill Baptist churches, which often lacked settled pastors, were left to their own devices between visits from itinerants. Without regular meetings to allow communication and enforce doctrine and discipline, the Freewill Baptist movement stood to lose as many followers as it had gained.

To prevent such losses, leaders established the first quarterly meeting in 1783, which rotated among New Durham, Woolwich, New Gloucester, and Hollis.[30] The quarterly meetings combined administrative and devotional activities; they offered a forum for churches to communicate and members to partake of the sacraments of the Lord's Supper, baptism, and washing of feet. But these gatherings alone did not unite churches. Quarterly meetings were poorly attended, they did not enforce discipline or doctrine, and the denomination still lacked enough itinerants to support new churches. Throughout the 1780s and 1790s, the quarterly meeting minutes listed a veritable catalog of complaints, ranging from disunion to lax discipline to assaults from other religious groups. New Gloucester complained of a "Verry Low and Dead time as to religion," Woolwich warned of the "Many Enemies that are watching for the halting of the Saints," and Little River, Maine, mourned the "Broaken Circumstances" that resulted in "Schisms and Divisions unhappily taken Place among them."[31] By 1791, many churches had lost members and clergy to the regular Baptists, Congregationalists, and Shakers. Some, like the flagship congregation in New Durham, dissolved entirely. The quarterly meeting had failed to provide cohesive authority and discipline, and the movement faltered.[32]

The 1791 dissolution of the New Durham church marked a turning point in the Freewill Baptists' governance. The church regrouped shortly thereafter, under a new covenant that extended the basic principles of Randel's 1780 covenant. The New Durham Covenant of 1792, which Randel devised with help from lay exhorter Mary Savage, required members to reject worldly fashions, amusements, and unethical commerce. Followers were to perform good works and conduct their lives within the Freewill Baptist spiritual family, using church authority and discipline to settle conflicts, regulate behavior, and nurture piety. The covenant also forbade signers to sue or bear arms against each other. Finally, it listed three essential rites: believers' baptism, the Lord's Supper, and the washing of feet. The covenant embodied the Freewill Baptist concept of "gospel union," a voluntary submission to church discipline that bound members as a community and distanced them from worldly affairs.[33]

This model of religious polity provided the framework for the Freewill Baptists' subsequent expansion. Quarterly meetings remained at the heart of its infrastructure, but Randel added or formalized bodies both below and above the New Durham Quarterly Meeting. With approval from the corresponding quarterly meeting, local churches could organize as monthly meetings to handle administrative and disciplinary matters and hear members' confessions.[34] Churches also met for Sabbath worship and sometimes divided into informal class meetings, which resembled Methodist class meetings in form and function. Some, like Elder William Babcock, proposed adopting the class meeting officially. He argued that classes nurtured "Social Conferences and Prayer," which he thought were the "life and Soul of Religion."[35] The Freewill Baptists did not go so far as Babcock suggested, but class meetings did become an important, if unofficial, component of many monthly meetings.

Quarterly meetings also expanded. Within a decade after they adopted the New Durham Covenant, Freewill Baptists added seven quarterly meetings in Vermont, New Hampshire, and Maine. This expansion helped them to administer and admit new churches, distribute itinerants, and maintain discipline over an expanding territory. In order to channel communication among quarterly meetings, Randel elevated the New Durham Quarterly Meeting to a new status as the sole yearly meeting—so named not because it met annually, but because it met once per year in each of four constituent towns. The yearly meeting drew representatives from all quarterly meetings, and it handled disciplinary matters on appeal as well as ordination, expulsion, and any questions referred by the quarterly meetings. Whereas the quarterly meetings handled financial and administrative matters, the yearly meetings increasingly served as spiritual gatherings. They attracted more and more participants—clergy, laity, and the curious—and hosted prayer sessions, mass baptisms, and large communion seasons. These meetings often produced fruitful revivals, but they sidetracked the ministers from their official work. Accordingly, Randel established the Elders' Conference in 1800, which met concurrently with the yearly meeting and allowed ministers to focus on policy and doctrine.[36] Designed to maintain gospel union, the Freewill Baptists' administration combined a centralized bureaucracy with a far-reaching itinerant corps.

By the 1810s, the Methodists, Universalists, and Freewill Baptists had joined the regular Baptists as northern New England's leading dissenters. Although they differed on theology and style, they all relied on centralized organizations to coordinate itinerancy, support new churches, carry out discipline, and clarify doctrine. By relying on traveling preachers, these movements changed the region's religious landscape in two major ways. First, their rapid expansion placed them in direct competition with the Congregationalist majority for members, resources, and facilities. Second, by placing so much authority in the hands of central bodies, these denominations crossed—and ultimately dismantled—town-parish boundaries and reoriented religious activity around new physical and spiritual centers. In doing so, they challenged both the independence and authority of the town churches.

Whereas the Congregational town church took shape within a town's borders, the itinerant church's physical boundaries were more permeable. The territory that the itinerant church occupied shifted constantly. Quarterly and annual meetings rotated from town to town, and churches gathered at various sites within their members' reach. The preaching corps, too, wandered great distances. Itinerants served as liaisons between distant congregations and centralized governing bodies, and the laity moved about to attend whatever meetings, conferences, and revivals they could. An itinerant church's physical geography, then, was not tied to a particular place but rather to a religious community more broadly construed: one that sought to establish ties under the umbrella of shared faith rather than shared location.

These groups arranged their physical space around the itinerant plan, which utilized traveling preachers instead of settled clergy to supply pulpits, lead revivals, administer sacraments, and enforce doctrine and discipline. The itinerant plan took shape somewhat differently in each denomination, but in all cases, a centralized authority directed the itinerancy. The Baptists used the least hierarchical version of the plan, with a hodgepodge of associations and missionary societies overseeing their own itinerants. Many Baptist missionaries started out as independent traveling preachers and only later sought sponsorship from societies. Isaac Case of Maine spent part of each year on independent missionary tours in Maine, Vermont, and Massachusetts during his tenure as a settled minister. Eventually, he resigned his pulpit to pursue full-time itinerancy for the Maine Baptist Missionary Society.[37] So did Phinehas Pillsbury, who received a license to preach in 1803 and toured Hancock and Kennebec counties until the following year, when he received formal assignments from the society.[38] Missionaries like Case and Pillsbury benefited from working for organizations because they received a steady income and tapped into an evangelical network. Missionary societies, for their parts, benefited from their itinerants' labor because it yielded funds (from churches that received missionaries) and news about revivals and church-gathering.

Both the Universalists and Freewill Baptists designed itinerant plans with more centralized control. The New England General Convention ordained Universalist ministers, issued preaching licenses, and commissioned missionaries for fixed terms (usually one year), encouraging them to "embrace every opportunity to travel among destitute and newly formed Societies."[39] The convention did not assign circuits or missionary fields, but it did suggest that itinerants visit towns where at least a few Universalists lived, to ensure a sympathetic reception. To help them, the convention recorded churchgoers' names and towns "as a guide to the pilgrim, who may journey to those towns . . . it being our hope that no brother will . . . close the door of Hospitality on the wayfaring man."[40] The convention also publicized itinerants' tours to attract large audiences on their routes. The *Christian Intelligencer,* for instance, notified readers in 1823 that Fayette Mace was about to embark on a tour of Maine, New Hampshire, and Vermont before heading to New York City and Boston.[41] Relying on a network of the faithful, the Universalists hoped itinerants could generate even more enthusiasm as they made their way farther afield.

Like Universalists, the Freewill Baptists ordained their elders at quarterly and yearly meetings. They also examined preaching candidates and issued certificates to itinerants at Elders' Conferences.[42] The yearly meeting exercised more oversight over teaching elders, who itinerated among churches within a quarterly meeting, than it did over unordained exhorters and ordained "public gifts," who were free to travel "from place to place and from meeting to meeting, preaching and baptizing, and assisting their churches in their necessary business."[43] The quarterly and yearly meetings examined all clergy to make sure they preached correct doctrine, just as the Elders' Conference did in 1802, when they threatened to rescind Silas Willey's preaching certificate because he associated with a preacher whom the church had excommunicated.[44] Without going so far as to decide itinerants' routes, both the Freewill Baptists and Universalists maintained close connections with their traveling preachers to ensure doctrinal consistency, however far those preachers roamed.

The Methodists subjected circuit riders to lengthy trial periods and exercised tight control over itinerant fields, including frequent and rigorous examinations of their clergy. When the New England Conference admitted John Jewett on a trial basis in 1810, it did so despite his youth (at seventeen years old) and his "poor delivery" of sermons. After two years, the conference judged him "solemn" and "devout" but still possessing "small abilities"; he remained on probation. One year later, though he had improved to only "middling abilities," the conference received Jewett into the "traveling Connection" and placed him on the Union Circuit in Maine.[45] Circuit riders like Jewett were subject to such stringent supervision because they bore heavy responsibilities: they rotated among assigned churches, preached, administered sacraments, raised funds, sold subscriptions to publications, and oversaw local preachers. Methodist missionaries escaped much of the supervision to which the conference subjected circuit riders, because they itinerated in regions where the Methodists had not yet created circuits. The conference required missionaries to keep journals of the miles they traveled, sermons they preached, towns they visited, societies they helped form, converts they encountered, and money they raised. They reported to presiding elders, who appointed them to one-year terms in areas "where the circuit preachers cannot attend."[46] Whereas circuit riders maintained existing Methodist territory, missionaries extended the front lines of the denomination's itinerant infrastructure.

All of these groups used the itinerant plan to meet demands for preaching, but their membership continued to outpace the supply of ministers. The Universalists complained in 1796 that though "the harvest is truly plenteous, . . . the laborers are few," and the General Convention urged its preachers to "listen to the voice of entreaty saying come ye hither and help us" and travel to any church that desired preaching.[47] Decades later, the convention still lamented that the movement was "destitute of a sufficient number to supply the regularly constituted societies in our connexion."[48] A Baptist missionary in 1804 told a typical story of a woman who had waited two years for a visit from a minister of her own denomination to baptize her.[49] The Methodists had similar trouble keeping up with demand. In 1810, they counted one preacher for every 135 members. Eleven years later, they employed only one preacher for every 220 members and bemoaned "our great deficiency in men" to fill the "many and pressing calls for ministerial labors throughout New England."[50] The leading clergy might have been frustrated in their efforts to fill pulpits, but they happily noted that the heightened demand signaled a growing following. "What is Incouraging," observed Benjamin Randel, was that "Zion travels with Strong Pangs."[51]

Itinerancy was not a last resort for denominations who hoped to supply preaching. Rather, they saw it as a positive good and the best way to plant roots in the hinterlands. "Itinerant preaching is calculated to advance the interests of the Redeemer's kingdom," wrote one Maine Baptist, "but in new settlements there is special call for it."[52] The newer religious groups lauded the clergy who heeded that call. Freewill Baptists boasted that their ministers were "not bound by any town or parish lines" but could "go forth from town to town and preach the gospel freely."[53] Whereas the town-church establishment hampered religious liberty, the Freewill Baptists equated itinerancy with spiritual freedom. Likewise, Universalists predicted that their missionaries' zeal and "renewed exertion" would "give a new impulse to the progress of the truth."[54] During what one Baptist minister called "the age of missions," the traveling clergy brought a new energy to their work, which they could impart to the churchgoers they encountered.[55]

Some denominations rewarded itinerants with higher salaries or greater prestige than settled ministers. Although Baptists encouraged settlements, many of their clergy gained prominence not as heads of churches but as missionaries. In Maine, both Isaac Case and David Nutter left their pulpits to pursue missionary labor; Nutter even confessed that he had "never been satisfied that it was his duty to take charge of any church in particular." Only after they became itinerants did both men rise to eminent positions among Maine's Baptists.[56] Freewill Baptist and Methodist itinerants held authority over local preachers.[57] The Methodists made no secret of their preference for circuit riders; the move from itinerant to located (or settled) preacher was a demotion expected only of elderly or feeble itinerants, and conferences hesitated to allow it for anyone else. When one itinerant petitioned for a settlement in 1803, he complained that his request was "treated with contempt."[58] Because missionary tours threatened an itinerant's financial and physical health, denominations continually added incentives to keep itinerants in the field, such as higher salaries, more advancement opportunities, and financial assistance for their families.[59] By endowing itinerants with greater authority and support, each group laid the groundwork to expand using the itinerant model.

With increased prestige and compensation came more responsibility and risk. The itinerant's life was fraught with uncertainty, even on a fixed circuit or in a missionary field close to home.[60] Preachers traveled long distances, encountered severe weather and other obstacles, and faced fierce opposition from established clergy. The strenuous travel was not for the faint of heart. On a tour of New Hampshire and Vermont in 1804, Baptist missionary Joshua Bradley rode 516 miles in 45 days.[61] Jonathan Wallace, a Universalist missionary in Vermont, divided his work "between four different places which are all from twenty to thirty miles distant, [which] is a perpetual source of much inconvenience and fatigue."[62] Another itinerant traveled "200 miles to git home when the traveling was extreamly bad, at the breaking up of winter, [with] a heavy load to carry on my back."[63] Methodist circuit riders frequently requested locations (their term for settled pulpits) after a few years due to "debility of body" or "slender health."[64] The Methodists even had a category for preachers who were "so worn out in the itinerant service, as to be incapable of preaching constantly." These "superannuated" preachers still attended conference meetings and preached occasionally but did not fulfill any steady commitments.[65] Across denominations, a traveling preacher's work was physically exhausting.

Along with the rigor of travel came seemingly unending duties. Traveling clergy sustained churches, raised funds, visited churchgoers, and attracted converts. Preaching was central to their work, and itinerants kept detailed notes on the sermons they delivered. Isaac Case, touring Maine in 1804, estimated that he preached forty-nine times in twelve towns over seven weeks.[66] Freewill Baptist Elder Ephraim Stinchfield preached 440 times and baptized 245 people during an 1808 tour.[67] But the measure of an itinerant's success was not the number of sermons preached; it was the effect on his hearers. The Methodist *Discipline* reminded circuit riders that "it is not your business only to preach so many times, and to take care of this or that society, but to save as many souls as you can."[68] On the leading edge of religious expansion, itinerants extended their denominations' boundaries.

Having identified the faithful, traveling clergy sustained these communities until they could hire permanent ministers. Joshua Young, a lay preacher, helped to found a Baptist society in Greene, Maine, in 1790. The society grew slowly, and with assistance from another itinerant, twenty-five members gathered a church in 1800.[69] The Windsor (Vermont) Universalist Society could pay for preaching only on every sixth Sunday when it was founded in 1798. Fifteen years later, they still depended on itinerants to lead Sabbath services.[70] Most churches and societies lacked clergy most of the time. The Eastern Association of Universalists admitted as much when it reassured its congregations that "if you are not favored with a preacher raised from among yourselves, one will be sent you."[71] Without visiting ministers to preach, administer ordinances, monitor doctrine

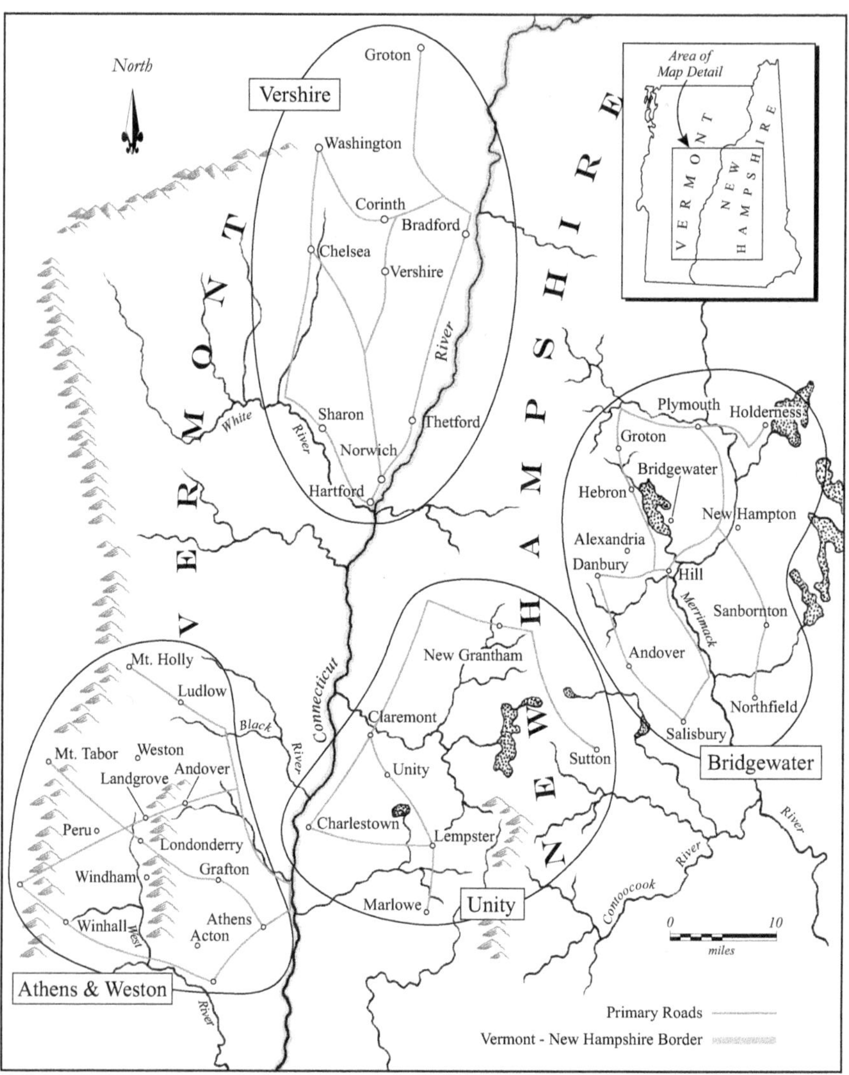

Map 2.1. Methodist circuits, ca. 1815–1825. These circuits, the Unity and Bridgewater circuits in New Hampshire and the Vershire and Athens & Weston circuits in Vermont, illustrate the typical size and scale of circuit riders' territories. It is difficult to pinpoint the exact locations of class meetings in a circuit at any given time, because conferences altered circuits frequently. This map shows what these circuits would have looked like through most of the 1810s and 1820s. *Map by Mark Cook.*

and worship, and establish liaisons to sectarian authorities, many of these headless churches might have dissolved. Because they lacked the relationship to their towns that Congregationalists enjoyed, local churches relied on other kinds of institutional support to survive.

Traveling preachers rotated between the churchly outposts they served and centralized meetings that drew the sectarian hierarchies together. The crowded calendar of meetings that most denominations expected the clergy to attend reinforced preachers' roles as the ties that bound the system together. John Buzzell remarked that ministers, "considering themselves under great obligation to attend . . . meetings, it kept them a great part of their time travelling from one meeting to another, and attending meetings of worship everywhere they went . . . so that they were almost continually preaching, either publicly, or from house to house."[72] An 1806 Freewill Baptist yearly meeting in New Durham drew believers "from Boston, from distant parts of the Maine, from Vermont near Canada line, and from the different towns around." After four days, during which participants crowded into homes, meetinghouses, and barns, and flooded out into orchards and groves, they dispersed again. At the meeting's close, "the people retired from the orchard and . . . went in different directions to their homes, carrying to their families, their brethren and friends, the pleasing account of the goodness of God."[73] The rotation of annual, quarterly, and monthly meetings kept ministers (along with many laypeople) on the move, which in turn opened new opportunities for preaching and worship.

Meetings not only offered chances for communal worship, they also made visible sprawling hierarchies with chains of command that connected governing bodies to their itinerant corps and distant churches. Associations, quarterly meetings, and conferences all monitored their preachers' teachings and moral comportment. Clergy accounted for all of their activities; those who could not attend meetings sent correspondence and journals. Elders examined traveling preachers and admonished them if they strayed too far from doctrine. In 1801, the Freewill Baptist Elders' Conference examined several preachers who had "become Entangled in that Dangerous Doctrine of the Imposability of falling away" (the Calvinist idea that salvation was irreversible). All but one renounced the error.[74] Methodists criticized their clergy for "preaching too much about the millennium," "entertaining doubts respecting the propriety of infant baptism," and spreading "doctrines contrary to Methodism." Doctrinal irregularity grew so rampant that the New England Conference resolved in 1817 to "ascertain whether any doctrines are embraced, or preached, contrary to our established articles of faith" and pledged to "prevent the existence and circulation of all such doctrines."[75] By using centralized authority, denominations tried to stamp out dissent and monitor their itinerants even as they traveled farther away from the centers of power.

So, too, did they police the clergy's personal behavior. In town parishes, itinerants provoked suspicion among local residents who saw them as interlopers.[76] Accordingly, it was paramount that preachers represent well. Itinerants were expected to carry proper licenses; presiding conferences disciplined preachers who bore false certificates or vacated their assigned circuits.[77] But even licensed clergy could cause problems. The Freewill Baptists disciplined Elder Simon Pottle in 1802 for intemperance, inattention to ministerial duties, "light and vain conduct," and "freedom with a sertain Betsey Kinney." After two years of complaints, the Yearly Meeting finally demanded that he return his preaching credentials.[78] The Universalist General Convention withdrew fellowship from Joab Young in 1810, because he "has given up habits to intemperance."[79] Among the most notorious Methodist offenders was Leonard Frost, who proposed marriage to six different women in his circuit. After charging Frost with un-Christian conduct, slander, uncharitable conversation, and falsehood, the New England Conference carried out a lengthy trial that culminated in Frost's expulsion in 1829.[80] Frost stood as an extreme example of what might happen if conferences let their itinerants escape oversight. To protect both their mission and their reputations, itinerant denominations tried to make sure traveling preachers never strayed from their superiors' watch.

Itinerant groups used meetings to open lines of communication among clergy, churches, and churchgoers. Churches sent in reports of spiritual states, forecast their revival prospects, and sometimes requested advice. The Freewill Baptist Church in New Gloucester, Maine, admitted to the New Durham Quarterly Meeting in 1785 that they were "In a low State as to Religion," but matters improved greatly over the next year, by which time they enjoyed "Sweet Breathings for Zion's Prosperity."[81] Others wrote with questions about doctrine or discipline. The Putney (Vermont) Baptist Church asked the Leyden Association in 1803 how to handle a church member who had "frequently gone contrary to the rule of the Gospel" but confessed his sins every time. The Association advised the church to "suspend travel with him" despite his confessions.[82] In dire cases, a meeting might appoint a committee to visit a troubled church, as the Vermont Baptist Association did when the church in Benson was "in a very tired state."[83] By arranging such visits, they could buoy a congregation's spirits and keep churches in the fold. Meetings also published news from member churches. The Universalists distributed circular letters for their own churches, as did Baptist associations, which also delivered corresponding letters to other associations. By providing forums for communication, public meetings structured churches' relationships around their associations and conferences.

The itinerant plan's physical landscape took shape not only within these organizing schemes but also in the places where worshipers gathered. Whereas a town's meetinghouse represented a community's joint political, financial, and spiritual investment, an itinerant church claimed no such backing. Because they lacked public funding, and their scattered followers took longer to gather churches, dissenters tended to build their meetinghouses far later than Congregationalists did. While Congregationalist church construction concentrated between the 1790s and 1810s, most dissenting groups built their churches in the 1810s or later. The Baptists of Blue Hill and Bath, Maine (which had organized in 1806 and 1810, respectively), built their meetinghouses in 1817.[84] The Freewill Baptists of Lewiston, Maine, built theirs shortly after their 1817 founding.[85] The Universalists of Portland commenced work on their meetinghouse in 1821, a little after they organized as a society.[86] Methodists in Rochester and Lamprey River Village, New Hampshire, incorporated meetinghouse societies in 1826 and 1827, respectively.[87] Compared to Congregationalists, dissenters needed more time to gather the parishioners and money they needed for church-building.

While they waited to draw up meetinghouse plans, they looked elsewhere for places to worship. The sites they found expanded the fluid sense of space that defined their religious geographies. When they could not gain access to churches, dissenters gathered instead on meetinghouse steps or in fields, groves, barns, private homes, courthouses, and schoolhouses. On a tour in Maine in 1803, Freewill Baptist William Babcock preached in a barn and led a "season of prayer in the fields."[88] At the 1804 meeting of the Methodist New England Conference, Francis Asbury preached in a grove.[89] Congregations often met in schoolhouses, as did the Baptist church in Bangor, whose six members could not claim a share of the meetinghouse.[90] Meeting in alternative spaces sometimes had unintended consequences. A New Hampshire Congregationalist observed that the sectarians had "some advantage over us in the winter." Shut out of the town church (which, like most town meetinghouses, was unheated), the Baptists met in the schoolhouse, which had a stove. "The place is warm," the minister noted wryly, "and many can attend there with comfort and safety, who would not venture themselves in a *cold house*."[91] Although most congregations would have preferred to build or share a meetinghouse than find other venues, their alternatives—including heated buildings or outdoor locations—may have attracted more churchgoers with their comfort and accessibility.

The spaces the upstart groups chose for worship stood in stark contrast to town churches. The Congregationalists' sense of sacred space was rooted in a particular place, contained within its borders, and arranged around its built landscape. But the sectarians laid out sacred space amid less tangible landmarks: the ties among churchgoers, clergy, and denominations.[92] Individual churches were building blocks in the itinerant plan, but unlike locally rooted Congregationalist churches, their importance lay in how they linked members to a broader community of believers. The itinerant enterprise joined outpost churches and their sectarian leadership in a web of mutual support and obligation. As a result, local church members looked past their neighbors to the traveling preachers, their distant supervisors, and the scattered faithful as they tried to sustain a larger spiritual body. These far-reaching interconnections, and the constant movement along strands of the itinerant web, gave shape to the ever-shifting physical layout of the itinerant church.

The regional network that linked distant churches framed their members' sense of spiritual space as well as their physical landscape. Unlike the spiritual orientation of Congregational town churches, which resembled self-contained series of concentric circles around each minister, the itinerant movements functioned more like spiders' webs. They sought to connect what one preacher guessed to be "many thousands of brethren . . . scattered about on nearly as many hills and dales."[93] Itinerants traveled the radial lines on these webs, tying far-flung believers on the perimeter to the sectarian hierarchy concentrated at the center by communicating doctrine and discipline to churches and relaying news back to leaders. These communities' fluid physical boundaries made them more permeable than they seemed at first glance. Whereas a churchgoer would have had to change residence to join a new town church, she needed only to change heart to join an itinerant church.

An itinerant church's spiritual geography, much like the town church, revolved around a communalistic vision that demanded a sense of mutual duty among like-minded believers. But whereas the town-church model of a covenanted community encompassed all who fell within its boundaries, the itinerant church applied the corporate ideal only to those who chose to join. Its members were bound to watch over each other and invest in each other's spiritual states. The General Convention of Universalists reminded its followers that a true church consisted of "every Member mutually caring for every other Member." With mutual watch came mutual obligation, so that "if one member suffer all the members suffer with it."[94] John Buzzell similarly wrote of the interdependence that bound Freewill Baptists. He considered "the members of the church as so many members of the body [who] were all necessary and useful in their several places," and who could function best in concert with each other.[95] To underscore this sense of mutual duty, churchgoers within denominations referred to each other as "brother" and "sister," as if they had joined an adoptive and extended family.[96] Itinerant churches broadened their understanding of religious community to emphasize common faith over common residence.

This corporate vision shaped all aspects of religious life, from church formation to discipline. Gathering a church gave hope and purpose to those who had heretofore lacked a faith community. Unlike most Congregationalists, whose parishes came into being along with their towns, sectarians created religious communities only through deliberate action. When believers founded a church, they separated from the world around them. Having done so, they saw themselves not as one church among several, but, in the words of Baptists in Shoreham, Vermont, as a spiritual island: "a feeble Band in this new settlement surrounded with enemies on every side."[97] Sectarians imagined their churches as outposts in a literal and figurative wilderness, which, without spiritual sustenance, would undermine a believer's resolve to live a godly life.[98] As churches gathered, they gave isolated believers institutional support as well as connections to a wider network. For that reason, the Rockingham Association reminded Universalists that each new church would become "the point of concentrated effort . . . around which rally the believers scattered abroad."[99]

Church-gathering was among the itinerant denominations' most important tasks, because a church could draw believers out of the hinterland and around a central gathering point. When the Freewill Baptist Strafford Quarterly Meeting organized in Vermont in 1802, its leaders discovered "about 330 brethren, scattered around the hills in that wilderness country" who might find a home in the quarterly meeting.[100] A Baptist who visited Salisbury, Maine, in 1810 felt "anxious to look up the scattered sheep and lambs of Christ and see how many could be found that ware fit members for a church." He reported that "after much labor," he gathered four men and five women into a church in that town.[101] Effective preachers left trails of new churches in their wakes. Freewill Baptist Elder Charles Bowles, after many tours in Vermont, helped form churches in Shelburne, Hinesburg, Huntington, Waterbury, and Stowe. He also brought fifty-six members into Washington's church and established a quarterly meeting in Huntington.[102] Itinerants were ever watchful for such opportunities; in 1819, a Universalist missionary in Maine reported that "several new societies of respectability" had formed, which "solicit the labors of more ministering bretheren."[103] New churches helped anchor the itinerant spiritual geography by creating communities where none had existed before.

To ensure doctrinal consistency in new congregations, ministers carried directives from governing bodies to the churches under their watch. At their 1826 annual meeting, the Maine Conference of the Methodist Church determined that all preachers should carry copies of the *Discipline*. To support their efforts, the conference appointed a committee to "examine into the state of Discipline within the bounds of our Conference, and to point out any departure, from Doctrine and discipline which may appear."[104] By extending a clear line of authority from the conference to the itinerant corps to infant churches, sectarian leaders strengthened the connections that ministers forged up and down the denominational hierarchy.

Having founded a church upon a specific doctrine, members separated themselves from their neighbors by enforcing strict discipline. Unlike Congregationalists, who only reluctantly dismissed members who embraced other doctrines, sectarian churches took swifter action. Methodists expected layfolk to attend Sabbath services, communion, love feasts, and weekly class meetings. Regular absence was grounds for dismissal. Some circuits also mandated attendance at quarterly meetings, as the Poland (Maine) Circuit voted to do in 1810.[105] The Freewill Baptists similarly expected attendance at all regular meetings and threatened to excommunicate any member who missed three biweekly conferences in a row without satisfactory cause.[106] Baptists also rejected members who flirted with other traditions. The Baptist Church of Christ in Mason, New Hampshire, excommunicated Willard and Anna Lawrence, who had adopted Universalism, "which this church cannot see to be Scriptural."[107] Similarly, the Baptist Church of Christ in Andover, Vermont, punished Benjamin Taylor in 1821 for "hearing Methodist preachers, to the neglect of the church meetings."[108] Lacking any geographic basis for churchly unity, doctrinal uniformity was paramount.

The itinerant denominations also enforced codes of morality and manners that separated members from worldly affairs. The Freewill Baptists imposed restrictions on amusements, fashion, and comportment, even requiring members to conform to a plain mode of speech and prose that departed from the era's more ornate styles. Benjamin Randel himself favored using the "Plain language . . . in wrighting," and the New Durham Quarterly Meeting chastised Ephraim Stinchfield in 1796 for "using Craft in a letter to Yearly Meeting" instead of writing "so plain as he should."[109] Other churches enforced codes of simplicity and modesty, prohibiting drinking, dancing, gambling, fornication, profanity, gossip, and quarreling. They also governed their members' financial affairs. Freewill Baptists and Methodists banned unethical commerce, usury, and indebtedness, and barred members from suing each other, requiring that "all Difficulties should be settled by the church."[110] Regular Baptists also prohibited unscrupulous practices. The Baptist church in Marlow, New Hampshire, threatened to excommunicate Zachariah Beebe after he "defraud[ed] people at his mill by Converting their grain to his own use." The Second Baptist Church of Clarendon, Vermont, disciplined John Bullard in 1811 for "Selling a Ram Lamb which was not his own Property." And in 1804, the Sanford (Maine) Baptist Church suspended Nathan Hill for stealing gunpowder during the town militia's muster day and for "Stabing his bayonet into a horse" (an offense, ironically, for which he did not need the gunpowder). By policing members' behavior, religious groups reinforced their communal ethic and created a buffer between their churches and the world.[111] And whereas town churches used moral restrictions to uplift the whole community, sectarian churches used them to separate their members from the wider community.[112]

By maintaining constant watch over each other, members broke from the prevailing religious culture, which they deemed impious. Before he discovered Methodism, Joel Winch had "concluded there was but a little in religion" because "Professors or non professors all lived alike as it appeared to me." But he later found that his problem with religion was that town churches did not demand piety. The Methodists offered a stark contrast. "There was not a People in the World," Winch concluded, "that had so much Scripture to prove there Doctrin and manners" as the Methodists did.[113] This interweaving of doctrine and discipline shielded sectarians within exclusive societies.

Because so many of their societies lacked settled clergy, ministers inhabited different places in the itinerant spiritual geography than they did in the town churches. Rather than occupying the center of each church, ministers in these denominations connected disparate bodies within their larger spiritual web. This was true even of settled clergy, who traveled more than their town-church counterparts did to attend meetings and assist other churches. As a result, religious life in these churches did not revolve around the minister's constant presence, and itinerant movements emphasized the importance of pastoral leadership less than Congregationalists did. Sylvanus Haynes, a Vermont Baptist, observed in 1811 that a recent revival had resulted more from lay efforts than the work of visiting preachers. He credited the "ingathering of souls to Christ" to the "conversation, relation of experiences, and the exhortations of young converts in conferences." Although preaching played a role, he suggested that "neither preaching, nor the exhortation of gifted brethren have been so instrumental of awakening sinners [as] *conferences*."[114] The Freewill Baptists, too, reported many revivals that took place without the clergy's assistance. A revival in Maine in 1810 "went on, generally, without the instrumentality of public preachers." Instead, churchgoers "met together and improved their gifts, and found that by waiting on the Lord, they renewed their strength."[115] The Methodists also depended on class meetings (often led by laypeople) to nurture their members' devotion. Joel Winch's first class meeting was a revelation: the class leader "exhorted till the Power of God came down in such a measure and I never knew it before . . . [and] my heart began to melt like wax."[116] Like many others, Winch arrived at this revelation not through a minister's constant guidance and preaching but through the efforts of lay exhorters.

For itinerant denominations, religious ritual dramatized the relationships among churches and hierarchies, ministers and layfolk, converted and unconverted. Their approaches to ritual ranged from the Universalists' minimal requirements to the Methodists' extensive catalog of meetings and rites. What they all shared, however, was the struggle to identify which rituals defined their churches and to determine how to use them to forge a spiritual identity.

Among the most hotly debated rites was baptism. It assumed different meanings with its different forms, whether it took place in infancy or adulthood, and whether it entailed sprinkling or full immersion. Universalists did not believe that baptism was necessary for salvation and tolerated either form at any stage of life. For Methodists, as for Congregationalists, baptism (preferably in infancy) allowed access to a religious community: a prerequisite to full membership. Regular and Freewill Baptists believed baptism symbolized the new birth. They baptized only professed believers over the age of consent and only by full immersion.[117] They invested baptism with enormous importance, not just because of its spiritual implications for individual converts, but also because it tangibly and dramatically demonstrated faith for all to witness. Believers' baptism was a spectacle by design, intended to impress upon observers both the precariousness of their spiritual states and the joyous transformation that could follow conversion. Ministers who led baptisms hoped for good weather (they attempted few immersions during the winter) and tried to set a dramatic scene. An 1808 Freewill Baptist revival in Saco, Maine, culminated with the baptism of 41 converts before 1,600 witnesses. The converts, who gave their testimonies in a grove, walked over a mile to the baptism site as observers thronged the roadsides. "The spectators were silent," one witness recounted, as they "situated themselves in a circular form, round the place designed for baptism." The clergy kneeled in the center of the circle, prayed, and led the candidates to the water, where they conducted one baptism at a time for forty minutes.[118] This ritual demarcated spiritual space by arranging observers on the perimeter and creating a (literal) inner circle of believers. The visual spectacle was carefully planned both to initiate new converts in the ways of piety and to stir witnesses to examine their own souls and strive for conversion.

Along with baptism, communion ranked among the most visible public rituals. Whereas the Congregationalists believed communion was rooted in the physical space of the town church, others believed it created the spiritual space where believers could mingle. But although all denominations prized the Lord's Supper, they fiercely debated who should gather at the communion table. Congregationalists and Baptists had long battled over whether to share communion services, and Baptists continued to insist that their own members should meet separately to partake of the Lord's Supper. Because they could commune only with those who had experienced a genuine conversion and spiritual rebirth, they argued, only those who had undergone a proper believers' baptism were candidates.

Others favored a more permeable border. Most itinerant groups other than regular Baptists held that communion joined the whole body of Christ. William Babcock, a Freewill Baptist, insisted that "the soul seriously engaged . . . thinks nothing of Sects or parties." He hoped Christians would break bread together—a stance he contrasted with the "wicked and uncharitable, illiberally narrow Doctrine of close communion."[119] The Universalists, who denied that any sacrament was necessary for salvation, also embraced open communion. The Langdon (New Hampshire) Universalist Church left the "different modes of participating of the ordinances of the gospel to every one's conscience" and gave each member "the free liberty of communicating with any other Christian community." Likewise, the church offered communion to "all professing christians present, of whatever church or denomination, that are in regular standing."[120] As with Freewill Baptists, Universalists understood communion as a ritual that created a common space for converted Christians and left the unconverted to watch from the margins.

Whereas these denominations invited observers to witness baptisms or communion, they retreated behind closed doors for rituals that demanded the uncompromised fellowship of a spiritual family. For Methodists, class meetings and love feasts prompted the inward search for piety along with heightened communal identity. In weekly class meetings, groups of about twelve church members prayed and studied the *Discipline* and the Bible, after which their class leader scrutinized their religious knowledge and the states of their souls. In quarterly love feasts, the members of all class meetings on a circuit broke bread together, prayed, and confessed their spiritual experiences and backslidings. The clergy sometimes opened these events to observers—especially prospective converts like Joel Winch, who attended three class meetings and two love feasts before joining.[121] But they were usually limited to converted Methodists, for whom these meetings offered a chance to refresh the spirit and establish bonds of faith under the canopy of a clear sectarian identity.[122]

But even though the clergy tried to use ritual to separate members from observers, non-conformity in the denominational ranks blurred those boundaries as religious movements tried to shield their tightly knit communities from the wider evangelical world. Freewill Baptists and Methodists, who both favored Arminian doctrine and public confessions of faith, struggled to reconcile their similar theologies with their separate religious identities. The Freewill Baptists maintained their own institutions, but they also tolerated some cross-pollination with like-minded Christians. William Babcock's parishioners tended to view Freewill Baptist and Methodist class meetings as all but interchangeable. In 1802, Babcock's monthly meeting even voted to dissolve one of its constituent class meetings because "our Methodist Brethren [have] established one out there." But the crossover among class meetings threatened to deplete the already-struggling Freewill Baptist churches in the region.[123] In response, the New Durham Quarterly Meeting demanded that its members commit to one group or the other. "It is inconsistent," the elders decided, "for a member of our Connection to Sign his or her name to a methodest Class Paper for the sake of Enjoying the Benefitt of a Method[ist] Class Meeting." Those who had already done so had three months to clarify their intentions.[124]

The Methodists, for their part, were even more suspicious of crossover meeting attendance. Joel Winch, after he became a Methodist circuit rider, despaired that one of the classes under his watch "had never had one Class meeting separate from the World." He feared that this problem signaled a broader decline in discipline, but the class members saw it differently. They explained that "the Preachers had always told them that Close[d] Class Meetings were only for Townes and Villages." To distinguish themselves from town churches, they defied their own organization and welcomed outsiders.[125]

The Methodist hierarchy continued to demand private meetings, even as many Freewill Baptists sought freer exchange between the two groups. Enoch Place, a Freewill Baptist itinerant, habitually attended Methodist quarterly meetings near his New Hampshire home.[126] William Babcock appealed to the Methodists in 1806 to open their meetings to the greater Christian community. On behalf of the Elders' Conference, he pledged that "our Meetings, our Conferences, our hearts are yours," and he asked them to welcome all "Brethren in the Lord." The Methodists declined, although interested guests like Place continued to frequent their public meetings.[127] These negotiations regarding meeting attendance reflected tensions within each denomination over where to draw boundaries around their private spiritual space. Whether and how to include the mass of believers depended on how each group balanced outward-looking evangelism against inward-looking communal sustenance.

The pinnacle of all discipline, ritual, and sacrament within the itinerant churches—and indeed within town churches as well—was revival. In fact, churchgoers and clergy alike so fervently desired revivals that they undertook most other religious activity, from baptism to communion to love feasts, to excite the spirit and bring about awakenings. Unlike the Edwardsian town-church tradition, the sectarian revival had its roots in the more fluid and dynamic style of George Whitefield. Whitefield and like-minded evangelicals like Gilbert Tennant had confronted ecclesiastical landscapes where dissenters were scattered across hinterlands and a concentrated elite feared that itinerancy threatened well-defined parishes. Whitefield adapted to these circumstances by preaching an ecumenical message that reflected his wide-ranging religious experiences, appealed to his diverse audience, and attacked what he considered the insipid Anglican style of worship.[128] Although he made a greater impact in the middle and southern colonies than he did in New England, his visits to the northern colonies deeply influenced those who witnessed them. He drew large crowds, especially in places like New Hampshire and Maine, where he visited several times and preached outdoors to audiences numbering on various occasions over a thousand.[129] Whitefield's legacy persisted in northern New England; not only did each itinerant group draw in some way on his doctrine or style, but thousands of New Englanders remembered his revivals. Enoch Place met a man in Loudon, New Hampshire, who "was almost 90 years old [and] Said he got religion when he was but 17 years old in the old whitfield reformation."[130] As sectarians organized and expanded after the American Revolution, the Whitefieldian model of revivalism—which interwove itinerancy, spectacle, and evangelicalism—provided a precedent for them to follow.

Itinerant denominations built on this tradition by blending an ecumenical style with rituals that clearly delineated spiritual space for believers. In particular, they used quarterly and annual meetings—which drew large crowds of clergy, laity, and other spectators—to shore up the faithful and welcome new converts. Conferences gathered to address sectarian business: the clergy handled financial and doctrinal matters, held prayer sessions, and admitted lay members for rites like foot-washing and communion. But these meetings also had an evangelistic purpose. By staging public worship and inviting observers to witness communion seasons, baptism, and the like, conferences were intentionally conspicuous.[131] Freewill Baptist quarterly and yearly meetings took on a revivalistic fervor that eclipsed the clergy's official business.[132] At a 1795 meeting, at least one thousand observers gathered in a pasture to hear Benjamin Randel and several exhorters. In an overnight prayer session, "Sinners . . . cried to God for Mercy, Backsliders came to themselves and came home confessing, and there appeared to be a great shout . . . and the noise was heard afar off." By the time the crowd dispersed in the early morning hours, they had witnessed "a Season long to be remembered."[133] Methodists, who divided their quarterly meetings into closed sessions for business and open sessions for prayer, hoped for similar results. In an 1804 quarterly meeting on the Durham Circuit in Maine, Elder Timothy Merritt preached from an oxcart in a grove before a large assembly. The next four days yielded over one hundred converts.[134] By combining private meetings with public revivals, groups attracted outsiders who might seek to become insiders.

This tradition of large prayer meetings gained momentum with the news of such a gathering at Cane Ridge, Kentucky, in 1801. The revival at Cane Ridge took place during a regularly scheduled Presbyterian communion season, but it was distinctive in two respects. First, the Presbyterian organizers invited Methodist participation, which lent the event an ecumenical flavor and an Arminian theological bent. Second, the sheer scale of the revival—an estimated twenty thousand people participated over six days—echoed a Whitefieldian past and raised expectations for similar events in the future. Presbyterians, Methodists, Baptists, and other sectarians all worked to replicate the stunning display at Cane Ridge. But Cane Ridge provided the template most of all for Methodist camp meetings. Camp meetings—Methodist institutions that welcomed a diverse lay participation—emphasized evangelical religiosity and fellowship through sacrament.[135]

News of Cane Ridge and the flurry of revivals that followed spread quickly. William Babcock in 1801 read about "the work of God in Tennessee and Kentucky, in which . . . the Baptists Methodists and Presbyterian ministers [were] breaking bread together." He thought the news was "so glorious" that he read an account to his own congregation.[136] Samuel Train, a New Hampshire churchgoer, also heard about the "grate Revival of Religion at Cantucky." He hoped that the spark would spread and that his church would "stand Strong Looking out for a shower of devine grace."[137] They did not have to wait long. Methodists staged the first camp meetings in northern New England within a few years of Cane Ridge, and the institution quickly gained popularity. William Babcock attended an 1805 camp meeting in Weathersfield, Vermont, where a Freewill Baptist elder numbered among those who preached to about four thousand participants. Babcock stayed through the next day to witness the "Preaching, Praying, Singing, and Exhortations," along with the "impudent opposition from the rabble."[138] The next year, Francis Asbury attended at least two camp meetings in the region: one in Canaan, New Hampshire, and one in Buxton, Maine, where twenty ministers preached to about five thousand hearers.[139] Although they appeared sporadically at first, camp meetings soon became a regular feature of northern New England's revival culture.

Methodists usually coordinated camp meetings with conference or quarterly meetings. Over the years, they encamped near Rumford, Farmington, and Gorham, Maine; Landaff, Chester, and Rochester, New Hampshire; and Brandon and Lyndon, Vermont, the last of which drew about three thousand participants in 1824. They chose sites with available water and space for wagons and tents, and they invited preachers from many denominations. In 1829, John Lord, the presiding elder on the Danville (Vermont) Circuit, developed an offshoot of the camp meeting that he called the four days' meeting. These protracted prayer meetings (which often lasted much longer than four days) gathered in churches instead of fields and always coincided with quarterly meetings.[140] Together with camp meetings, they united people from around the region in an intensely pious atmosphere where they heard preaching and exhortation and left, organizers hoped, with a change of heart that drew them to Methodism.

Skeptical observers shuddered at the apparent anarchy they associated with camp-meeting dramatics. Joseph Field, a Congregationalist missionary who came upon an 1805 camp meeting in Monmouth, Maine, criticized the event for being "to the highest degree enthusiastic and disorderly." He described a confusing scene in which hundreds of hearers stood "in every kind of posture and exercise, some preaching with a few to listen and hear, others stretched upon the ground, over whom a multitude of both sexes stood praying and clapping their hands . . . to bring them to conversion." In the midst of this chaos were clusters of onlookers discussing "matters of comparative indifference" while others kneeled, "praying with the utmost violence of voice and gesture."[141] John Flagg, a New Hampshire Congregationalist who witnessed a camp meeting in Mississippi, judged the event "too absurd and ridiculous to be allowed in a *civilized country*."[142] These observers, who were used to a more structured and clergy-centered revival, saw only anarchy and undisciplined enthusiasm.

But Methodists viewed these revivals differently: as orderly (if exuberant) displays of faith that tightened their communal bonds and opened doors to outsiders. Far from anarchy, supporters argued that camp meetings promoted "strict propriety" by requiring temperance and orderly conduct. More to the point, the temporary encampments extended the boundaries of Methodism by nurturing an intense piety that stuck with observers long after the meeting had disbanded. One Maine Methodist lauded camp meetings because they could draw hearers "from the east, west, north, and south, to the consecrated spot in the wilderness." When the meeting ended and its participants dispersed, converts and the hopeful would "carry to their homes a larger measure of the hallowed fire."[143] From the camp meeting's gathering point, the fervor coursed through the backcountry, creating spiritual inroads for Methodists to follow.

Not all revivals revolved around organized meetings. Most northern New England revivals started locally and expanded beyond parish limits. What we might call "cluster revivals"—which spread to surrounding churches and towns but did not accompany a planned event like a quarterly meeting—attracted observers of many faiths (and many unchurched) who crossed parish boundaries to take part. These revivals rarely erupted spontaneously; denominations relied on word of mouth and the religious press to report on any unusual activity, and they suggested specific strategies for preachers who hoped to spark revivals in their churches. The Freewill Baptist *Religious Magazine* instructed preachers to look for signs from their flocks, who might begin to "feel a constant and ardent desire for an outpouring of the spirit" or assume a "general seriousness and tenderness."[144] Periodicals also encouraged the faithful to submit accounts of revivals, so as to raise others' hopes and encourage their efforts.[145] Unlike a town-church revival, which reinforced the community's spiritual bonds, the cluster revival cast a wider net to gather new converts.

Such an event took place in Eaton, New Hampshire, in 1803, when Freewill Baptists announced that months of spiritual exertion had finally brought forth a full-blown revival: "For about a month, almost all the time, both Day and Night . . . were heard from the houses, Barns fields Roads and woods the Echoing of Praise and Prayer to God." The awakening consumed not just local churchgoers but also "many People from various towns" who came to "see for themselves," including hopeful converts and "Profain and Vicious Persons [who] Came to Laugh." Fifty-one converts were baptized—a relatively large yield that suggests an enormous audience.[146] An 1807 revival that began in the Stratton (Vermont) Baptist Church quickly spread to the neighboring towns of Wilmington, Winhall, Windham, Wardsboro, and Jamaica, leaving a few missionaries scrambling back and forth among them to gather churches, baptize new converts, and administer the Lord's Supper.[147] The following year, a Freewill Baptist revival that began in Saco, Maine, attracted witnesses "from every direction, to see and hear the young converts." One of these observers, a young girl from nearby Standish, experienced a dramatic conversion and inspired a revival in her hometown and neighboring Gorham and Raymond.[148] By crossing town borders, converts and observers reinforced the idea that a church's spiritual boundaries encompassed all believers, regardless of where they lived.

Revivals punctuated religious life, which consisted mainly of regular worship, attendance at conferences, and maintaining discipline. But because revivals interwove all of these elements, along with very public and dramatic conversions, baptisms, and communion, they achieved an importance that overshadowed their relative infrequency. Large revivals—whether they coincided with a meeting or followed awakenings in a cluster of towns—reoriented northern New England's spiritual landscape. By drawing participants from across the region, these revivals erased parish boundaries and established new communities based on shared religious devotion rather than shared geography. By pairing exclusive activities like foot-washing and baptism with open access to camp meetings or prayer sessions, revivals enabled the itinerant denominations to balance their twin goals of uplifting and expanding their membership. Even Universalists, who eschewed enthusiasm and emotionalism, hoped for large awakenings to expand their community. The Rockingham Association reported that its 1827 annual meeting drew "brethren of other denominations" and "naighbouring towns" who descended on the assembly in such numbers that the organizers had to improvise temporary seating for the congregation. "We regard this as evidence of an inquiring spirit," the association declared, "which is one of the most effectual agents in discovering truth."[149]

In defining the spiritual space of the itinerant groups, religious leaders and the laity negotiated between two competing impulses. First, they traced lines of authority that extended from governing bodies down to outlying churches and encouraged an insular communal ethic. With their backs to the world, sectarians focused on doctrine and discipline, looking to authorities to ensure that even far-flung communities moved in concert with each other. But as they turned toward the center, they still extended one arm outward, for only by doing so would they expand over new territory and attract new members. Public rituals identified the faithful, set them apart, and inspired others to imagine crossing the perimeter of the sectarian world. With traveling ministers to administer sacraments, monitor doctrine, and carry out discipline, the itinerant denominations managed to create clear but permeable and ever-shifting boundaries around their spiritual communities.

The delicate balance between looking inward toward the denominational center and outward toward the seemingly endless supply of potential converts became the defining paradox of the itinerant groups. On the one hand, the centralized governance and well-defined doctrinal and disciplinary standards made membership more exclusive than in a town-church community and fostered a sense of mutual obligation and support. Methodists—whether they lived in cities or outlying settlements, in mountain hamlets or port towns—all answered to the same authorities and built their spiritual lives according to the same *Discipline*. Indeed, the denominational guide to faith, conduct, and church authority structured their lives and oriented their faith far more than town churches ever attempted to do. In this light, church members identified more closely with the expansive Methodist network than they did with those "in the world" who lived just next door.

But even though centralized authority and uniform doctrine raised barriers between the itinerant churches and the world at their doorsteps, these denominations' expansive sense of physical space rendered barriers fluid and permeable. Popular and public religious practices like outdoor preaching, adult baptisms, large revivals, and rotating conference meetings served evangelistic purposes even as they nurtured the faithful core. The Freewill Baptists' habit of referring to churches as "branches" revealed much about how they understood their religious world: though every church extended out into its own space, it also enjoyed a strong connection to the Freewill Baptist network. Like the other itinerant denominations, this was a network defined by faith rather than neighborhood.

The paradox of the upstart religious movements—doctrinal rigidity paired with geographic fluidity—drove their evangelical efforts. Although they limited membership to converts, no physical boundary prevented them from seeking potential adherents. Unlike the typical town church, which situated itself within an ever-shrinking parish, the itinerant model enabled its leaders and followers to rearrange their religious space around growing networks of believers, clergy, and institutions. Itinerant groups, therefore, offered a new definition of religious community based on denominational affiliation rather than physical place. They challenged the town churches by reorienting their members' religious duties and corporate obligations. By shifting their focus away from their towns and toward a scattered, voluntary body of believers, these churchgoers traded one corporate ideal for another. As more believers followed, they left Congregationalists to fret over the moral future of towns adrift from churches.

3 Scrambling for the Right

Disestablishment and the Town Church

The first terrain that Congregationalists and itinerant denominations fought over was the established town church. For many—particularly Congregationalists—publicly funded worship in a town church had been the bedrock of a system that ensured a moral and pious society. With religious taxation came automatic membership in a spiritual community, even for those who had not joined a church in full communion, along with all of the privileges and obligations that membership entailed. Among the most important privileges were access to regular worship and the spiritual and moral edification that religious observance could foster; obligations included the submission to the community's religious and moral standards, which in turn ensured public peace and order. But to the upstart religious movements, the town church looked very different; hardly a basis for cohesive community, it was more like a restrictive spiritual mold, which they would need to break to achieve true religious liberty. As Congregationalists and the new evangelical groups competed for churchgoers and funds, the town church (especially its power to demand religious taxes) became the battleground where their rivalries played out.[1]

Vermont became in 1807 the first New England state to end its system of religious taxation. Aaron Cleveland, a Congregationalist missionary, spent that year in Vermont, and he noted with alarm the new law that ended public support for churches. Reporting back to the Connecticut Missionary Society in 1808, he fretted about the future of a godless Vermont. The legislators who passed the law, he wrote, were "infidels, Baptists, and nothingists" who desired nothing less than to "outlaw all religion." But they were also "the most popular and leading men" in the state, and Cleveland wondered if they would use their political power to take their secular aims to unprecedented lengths. To Cleveland, it seemed as if every law that protected religious worship and public morality now risked repeal. "Even the observance of the Christian Sabbath stands on slippery ground," he fretted, "as it respects the Legislature of Vermont."[2] Without public support for worship, observers like Cleveland wondered, what power would compel town residents to unite as church members? Would wandering preachers tear parishes apart? Would the state become indifferent to religion, or would it turn openly hostile? Having ended religious taxation, would it abandon its guardianship of religious authority? And if it did that, what would be the fate of public morality and order?

The answer, which Cleveland could not have predicted, was that Vermont—along with New Hampshire and Maine—would do nothing of the sort. Although all three states ended compulsory religious taxation, they did not sever ties with churches or religion more broadly. In fact, they kept old laws and even enacted new ones that both supported worship and protected religious institutions. Most importantly, though these states showed no *de jure* preference for Congregationalism, they continued *de facto* to privilege the town-church geography that was linked to the old Congregationalist establishment.

Even as lawmakers lauded religious liberty, they hesitated to break church-state ties. Further, they hesitated to abandon the town-church legacy on which states had long depended to uphold morality. Just as establishment in northern New England was never as all-encompassing as its opponents feared, disestablishment was an incomplete process: a legal fiction that masked ongoing state support for religion.[3] This is not to suggest that disestablishment never happened, but rather that legislative reform did not by itself cut church-state ties and alter the town-church landscape, as both supporters and detractors believed it did. Whereas the laws that ended religious taxation convinced citizens that they had attained religious liberty, other policies granted some churches public property and assigned churchgoers to parishes. Rather than sever church from state, the governments of Vermont, New Hampshire, and Maine merely shifted the relationships between the two as religious and civil institutions took new forms.

The Revolutionary War and its attendant rhetoric of liberty and equality stirred a national debate over the proper extent of religious toleration. Northern New Englanders, like other Americans, grappled with the implications of disestablishment when it seemed that churches alone retained the authority to compel moral behavior. At the Revolution's end, Vermont, New Hampshire, and the province of Maine (under Massachusetts's jurisdiction) all maintained religious establishments. Underlying these systems was the expectation that each town would support a church that represented most of its inhabitants' spiritual preferences by levying taxes to pay for ministers' salaries and meetinghouse construction and repair. Dissenters could gather in separate churches or seek exemption from paying ministerial taxes. But they relied on the good will of town leaders, who might enforce the law (or not) and respect exemptions (or not), depending on their own inclinations. Ultimately, however, each state's establishment collapsed under the weight of sectarian expansion. In the 1780s and 1790s, the Methodists, Freewill Baptists, and Universalists joined the regular Baptists' rallying cry to abolish the town-church system. They succeeded because of two confluent trends that rendered this system untenable. First, spiritually and geographically scattered populations could no longer support common churches. And second, the language of religious liberty framed the debate as a war against tyranny and lent revolutionary fervor to the struggle for freedom of conscience.

Vermont was the first New England state besides Rhode Island to join the United States without some constitutional basis for established religion—but the fact that the state constitution did not link church and state did not mean that such a relationship did not exist. In fact, Vermont's establishment, which lasted for thirty years after the territory organized a government in 1777, resembled systems in neighboring states, even though its political heritage was different. From the start, Vermont was more socially and religiously diverse than other New England states, and its diversity challenged the town-church ideal. White settlement in Vermont started in the mid-eighteenth century as migrants arrived from southern New England, New York, and elsewhere. Settlers included the prosperous holders of the Wentworth grants in the Connecticut Valley along with those of humbler origins, who migrated after the American Revolution to escape poverty and debt. Congregationalists were (and, through the early nineteenth century, remained) the most populous denomination. But they had a late start. Bennington organized the first town church in 1763, and the pace of church-building picked up only slowly thereafter. Congregationalists added four more churches in the 1760s, sixteen during the 1770s, and seventy-six over the next two decades, most clustered in southeastern Vermont.[4] The regular Baptists started just as slowly but eventually became Vermont's fastest-growing denomination. In 1796, Isaac Backus reported that the number of Baptist churches in Vermont had grown from two to fifty in sixteen years. Still, their numbers did not surpass the Congregationalists' through the early nineteenth century.[5]

Soon, Methodists, Universalists, and Freewill Baptists also found footholds in Vermont. Methodists, who first moved into the state in the 1790s, established thirteen circuits, containing 2,529 members, by 1804, when Vermont joined the New England Conference.[6] During that period, the Universalists expanded from a disconnected array of congregations to a more organized constellation of churches. In 1804, the New England General Convention created the Northern Association to oversee its growing following in New Hampshire and Vermont.[7] The Freewill Baptists, whose early growth concentrated in New Hampshire and Maine, organized their first Vermont church in 1800. Within a decade, they had added twenty-one more and two quarterly meetings.[8] By the second decade of the nineteenth century, these three denominations had joined the regular Baptists as Vermont's leading dissenters.

The resulting religious landscape resembled less a neat division of town parishes than a jumbled array of congregations, sects, and the unchurched. Nathan Perkins observed during a 1789 missionary tour that many of the settlements he encountered were full of "a miserable set of inhabitants—no religion, Rhode Island haters of religion—baptists, quakers, and some presbyterians." He estimated that "about 1/2 would be glad to support public worship and the gospel ministry," but that "the rest would choose to have no Sabbath—no ministers—no religion—no heaven—no hell—no morality."[9] As a Congregationalist missionary, Perkins might, out of prejudice, have lumped too many Baptists or other dissenters with the unchurched. But there was no mistaking the fact that Vermont lacked a prevailing churchgoing culture; by 1791, only about one-fourth of Vermont's towns had organized churches.[10] This deficiency probably resulted less from spiritual apathy than from the fact that religiously diverse towns lacked enough people in any single denomination to support a church. Nonetheless, the sparse distribution of churches around the state gave many Vermonters cause for concern.

Through its early constitutions and statutes, Vermont's legislators hoped to give religious institutions a secure foundation by creating an establishment similar to that used by other New England states. But unlike in New Hampshire or Maine, Vermont's church-state relationship developed without a longstanding tradition of one prevailing denomination. In their attempts to promote public piety and religious liberty, state lawmakers framed establishment in relatively flexible and ambiguous terms. Each of Vermont's early constitutions (successively passed in 1777, 1787, and 1793) included a provision in the Declaration of Rights to protect freedom of conscience. These articles identified the "natural and unalienable right" to worship according to one's faith and freed citizens from the compulsion to "attend any religious worship, or erect or support any place of worship, or maintain any minister" not of their own tradition. The constitutions further protected Protestant citizens—and after 1787, all citizens—from violations to their civil rights due to religious belief.[11]

Since the constitutions were silent on the overlapping questions of parish formation and religious taxation, lawmakers tried to clarify these matters through a series of parish and ministry acts. In 1783, declaring that Christian worship and education were "of the greatest Importance to the Community at large, as well as to Individuals," the General Assembly laid out how towns would form parishes, build meetinghouses, hire preachers, and collect religious taxes—and how dissenters could gain exemption from these taxes. The ministry act required that two-thirds of the eligible voters in each town agree on a place of worship and a minister (a 1787 act revised this language to include churchgoers in unincorporated areas). Dissenters could gain exemptions with certificates signed by officials who represented their congregations. This stipulation reflected the suspicion that some might "pretend to differ from the Majority with a Design only to escape Taxation." By default, each adult was assumed to be "of Opinion with the major part of the Inhabitants within such Town or Parish where he she or they shall dwell," until she produced a certificate.[12] Regardless of the certificate provision, however, many of Vermont's towns found it difficult to garner the two-thirds majority needed to form churches and settle ministers.

Vermont's parish and ministry laws comprised the most liberal religious establishment in New England at the time. Unlike every New England state but Rhode Island, Vermont's statutes did not specify which dissenting groups were legitimate and which were not.[13] And unlike Connecticut and Massachusetts, Vermont did not explicitly favor Congregationalism.[14] Vermont's establishment, then, emphasized consensus over orthodoxy. The state preserved not a specifically Congregationalist establishment but instead a general Protestant one in which the bounds of the community church took precedence over its members' particular beliefs.

But the very concept of the community church was rooted more in Congregationalist doctrines and practices than in those of other denominations, and Vermont's efforts to support worship through law proved incompatible with its complex religious landscape. At issue was not simply church-gathering (which any dissenters could do) but rather which churches could receive public funding. In the ministry acts of the 1780s, lawmakers underscored the importance of the town church in terms of its role in the "community," and they legislated with the tradition of the New England parish in mind. The town, according to law and custom, remained the default unit of civic and religious community.

By privileging the town church, Vermont's establishment helped Congregationalists and hindered dissenters. Dissenters complained bitterly about the certificate law, which required a signature by a verified leader of a dissenting church or society. In a state with few organized churches, such evidence was often difficult to obtain and easy to challenge. In Weathersfield, the Baptists did not file their certificates in time to gain exemption from taxes to build a meetinghouse. After the town tax collector seized their property in 1787 to make up for the delinquent payments, they petitioned the state assembly for relief to no avail.[15] The same year, sixty-five inhabitants of Chester petitioned the assembly for relief from a tax to fund a meetinghouse intended "for a Different denomination of Christians," but the Congregationalist majority challenged the petitioners' credibility. The Congregationalists argued that "there is but Six Baptists Male Persons in the town of Chester that have made So much Profession of the Baptist Religion as to be Baptised, and one of them is Their Preacher, Who is Ordained at Large and is not Obliged to Stay in Chester only During his Pleasure." As to the remaining Baptists, the Congregationalists guessed the petitioners "will be

Put to their Trumps to find them."[16] This time, the Baptists got their wish: the assembly exempted them from the meetinghouse tax. But it had become clear that the certificate exemptions did not function as smoothly as lawmakers had hoped.

Dissenters increasingly argued that the hallmarks of the Vermont establishment—majority rule in the towns and the certificate system—did not comport with the principle of religious liberty articulated in the state constitution. In an election sermon before the General Assembly in 1792, Baptist preacher Caleb Blood warned against "religious establishment by law, which never fail[s] of pernicious consequences to both church and state." To compel support for churches, he argued, "fills the mind with prejudice for both the doctrine and the preacher, and of course does hurt to the cause of religion."[17] Two years later, about two hundred Vermonters petitioned for the repeal of the 1787 ministry act.[18] They attacked the act on two grounds. First, they argued that it infringed on the right of conscience. Citing the third article of Vermont's Declaration of Rights, they pointed out that "civil Authority have no Right to intermeddle with ecclesiastical affairs" and maintained that the state violated the "sacred Rights of free citizens." Second, they claimed that the ministry act not only violated individual liberties, but it also harmed the cause of religion itself. They insisted that the act was "detrimental to the interests of true Religion" because it "has a tendency to increase the number of hypocrites and infidels," create "prejudices *among* different sects," and disturb "the peace of neighbors." Religion could prevail only when "the Church is in no sence dependent on the civil Power for its support." Calling the act the "bane of peace [and] the hinge of Contention," the petitioners urged its repeal.[19]

They did not immediately achieve their goal. But lawmakers responded by taking steps to bring the law into line with the state constitution. In 1797, the General Assembly broadened the guidelines for founding religious societies and parishes and building meetinghouses. Although it still required a two-thirds majority to found a town church, any group could now form a society, which could contract with ministers, build meetinghouses, and raise funds. The 1797 Act for the Support of the Gospel also liberalized the certificate laws by stipulating that any minister, deacon, or elder of the "sect or denomination" to which the dissenter belonged could sign a certificate, regardless of whether the dissenter was a church member. Further, anyone who moved into a town or parish now had a year to file a certificate.[20] The law still assumed that those who failed to do so favored the town majority and would be liable for town religious taxes, but now dissenters faced less of a burden than they had before.

Even so, critics thought the law did not go far enough to ensure religious liberty. The Council of Censors (an elective body charged with assessing the constitutionality of the government's actions and proposing constitutional amendments) proclaimed that the law was "repugnant to the Constitution" and ought to be repealed almost entirely.[21] They argued that, despite protections for dissenters, the 1797 act "expressly binds the citizens of this state, indiscriminately, to erect and support places of public worship, and to maintain ministers . . . provided they are so unfortunate as to be in the minority of any town . . . and who are not at the time of taking the vote, possessed of a certain prescribed certificate." That exemptions existed was irrelevant. Rather, the point was that "in no case have civil power any constitutional right to interfere in religious concerns."[22] In claiming such powers, the legislature overreached.

Over the next several years, the assembly gradually relaxed restrictions on dissenters. But the political momentum favored abandoning certificate laws, however liberal. In 1807, the General Assembly proclaimed that, "in the interest of "promot[ing] harmony and good order in Civil Society," the ministry act "ought to be repealed." With that, lawmakers removed the last provision for publicly funded religion in Vermont.[23] Congregationalist observers outside the state predicted that a wave of religious anarchy and moral depravity would follow. A writer in the *Dartmouth* (New Hampshire) *Observer* warned that disestablishment would lead to "the eradication of every moral, virtuous, and religious principle from the human heart." A Connecticut pastor worried that "we have almost ceased to be a Christian nation." But there was little outcry in Vermont, and the law seems to have had little practical consequence. Although missionary Aaron Cleveland feared that the repeal would "occasion the dismissal of many Ministers" in the short term, he also predicted that "those who are hereafter settled, will be settled on more permanent ground." A few years later, Baptist historian David Benedict wrote that none of Vermont's Congregationalist ministers had lost his pulpit due to disestablishment.[24] In Vermont, the severing of ties between church and state—somewhat weak to begin with—appeared to have been a smooth transition.

Like Vermont, New Hampshire's system of establishment was decentralized and ambiguous, leaving much room for interpretation. Unlike Vermont, however, New Hampshire's political and religious culture emerged directly from one source: Massachusetts and its Congregationalist establishment. During the colonial period, New Hampshire borrowed heavily from Massachusetts's ecclesiastical laws, which favored Congregationalism. But religious life in New Hampshire was quite different than in Massachusetts. New Hampshire's thin settlement and backcountry conditions required a more flexible establishment that could accommodate the diverse and unstable religious communities which gradually emerged there.[25] As a result, colonial laws left decisions about religious taxation largely up to the towns. Through the eighteenth century, these laws nonetheless protected town majorities (who were Congregationalist almost by default) and stifled dissenters. When the onset of the American Revolution necessitated a reappraisal of New Hampshire ecclesiastical law, calls for religious liberty abounded.[26]

The constitutional period in New Hampshire was long and contentious; voters debated several constitutions from 1775 to 1792.[27] Not all of these debates addressed liberty of conscience, but many did, and the constitutional definition of religious liberty remained contested. The first two proposed constitutions (drafted in 1776 and 1779) contained only vague references to liberty of conscience.[28] Voters rejected these, so a new convention gathered in 1781 to try again. This time, the drafters composed a much more elaborate statement of the extent and limitations of religious liberty. They devoted the fourth, fifth, and sixth articles of the Declaration of Rights to the subject. The first two of these articles declared the unalienable right of conscience and guaranteed each individual's right to worship according to his or her own beliefs. The sixth dealt not with individuals but with institutions: denominations and town churches. Claiming that "morality and piety, rightly grounded on evangelical principles, will give the best and greatest security to Government," Article 6 authorized towns, parishes, and religious societies to contract with and support Protestant clergy. Although a town's majority controlled its parish, Article 6 also protected individuals from having to support ministers of denominations other than their own, and it set every Christian denomination on equal footing before the law.[29] Taken together, these articles set forth a definition of religious freedom that was somewhat more liberal than that which had existed under colonial law. But the language on parish organization, taxation, and exemption was sufficiently ambiguous that the courts and legislature would battle over the dissenters' status for decades.[30]

The three articles respecting freedom of conscience survived two more revisions of the constitution, which was finally ratified in 1783 and amended again in 1791. But the relationship between church and state was hardly free of controversy. Many critics believed the constitution did not sufficiently promote religious worship. The Piscataqua Association of Congregationalist ministers complained of "the very inadequate Provision made by the N. H. Constitution for the support of the Ministers of the Gospel." Along with other Congregationalist associations, they urged the state to more aggressively support public worship and "improve the supply of the ministry."[31] Others opposed such a move. The delegate most responsible for stirring up the convention debate over religious liberty was William Plumer of Epping, the Speaker of the House in the General Court (not a judicial court, confusingly enough, but the name of the legislatures in both New Hampshire and Massachusetts). A rising political star, Plumer boasted a colorful spiritual past, having espoused at various times New Light Congregationalism, Baptism, and deism.[32] As an outspoken critic of establishment, he tried—unsuccessfully—to end mandatory religious taxation and religious tests for holding public office.[33] But his efforts reflected an intensifying statewide debate over the proper relationship between church and state.

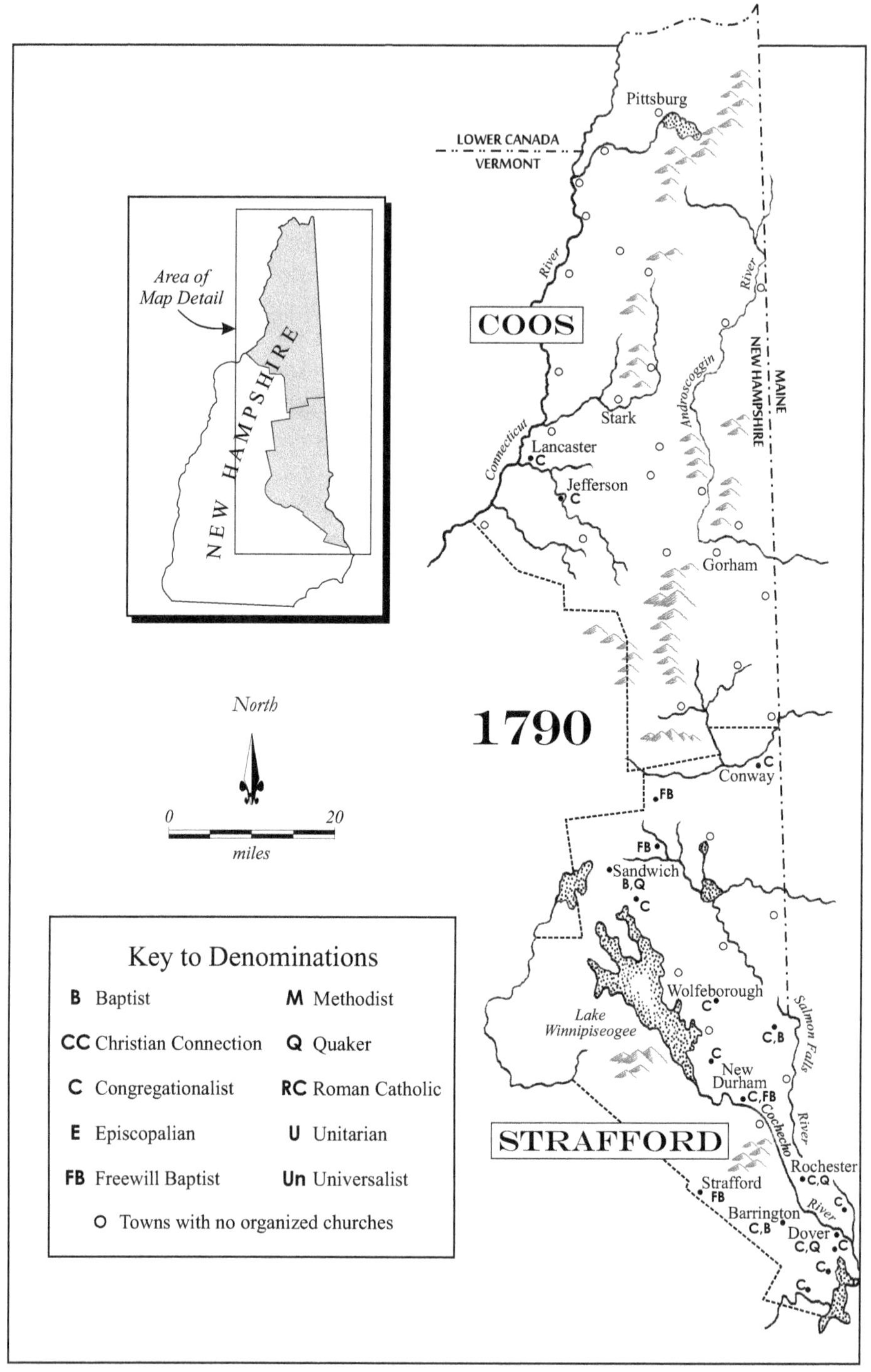

Map 3.1. The spread of churches in eastern New Hampshire, 1790–1830. These three maps show the pace of church-founding in Strafford and Coos counties, New Hampshire. The religious institutions on the map include incorporated and unincorporated churches,

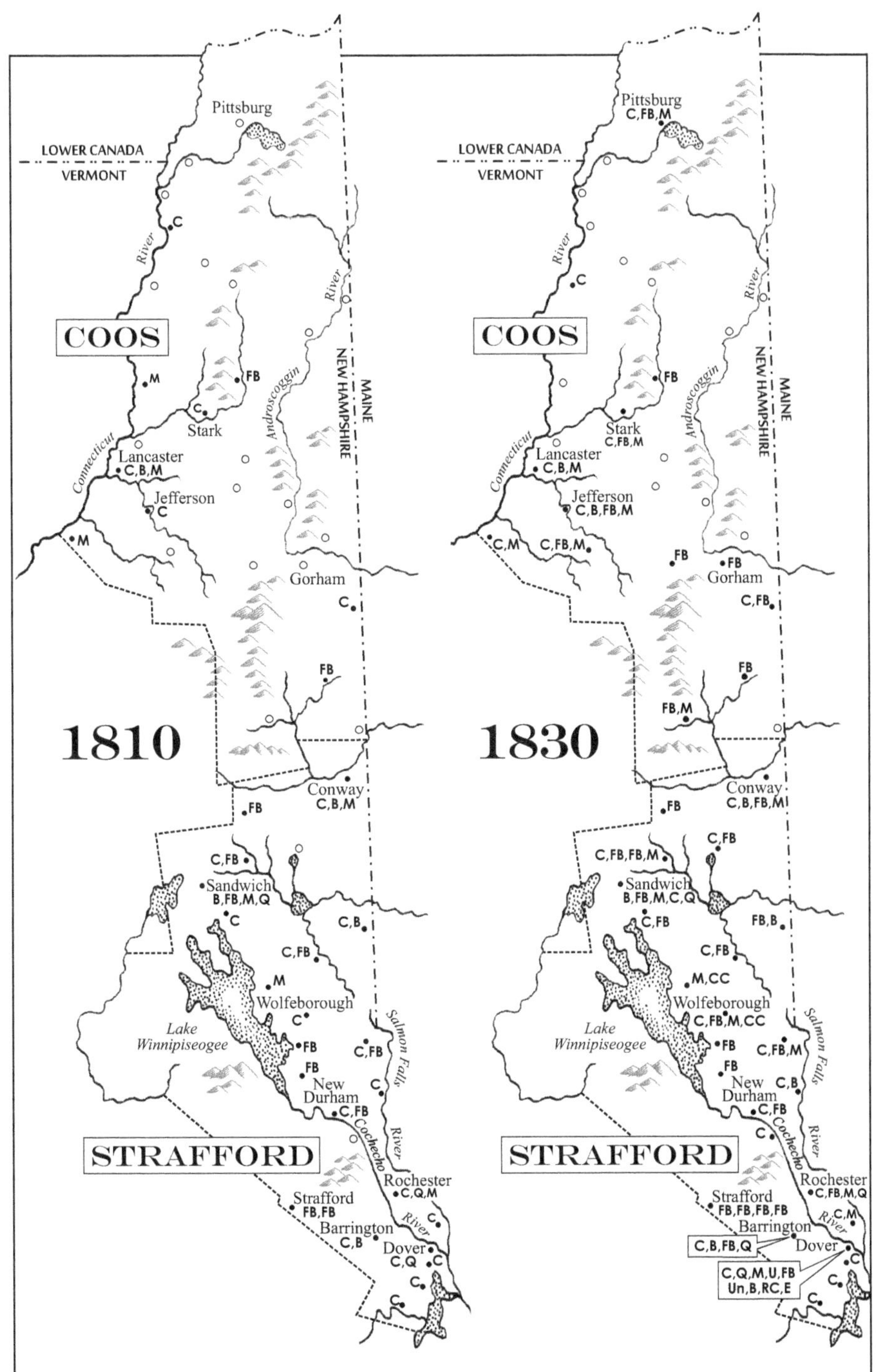

societies, and classes; they do not include legal parishes where residents had not organized churches or societies, or towns where concentrations of believers lived but worshiped elsewhere. *Maps by Mark Cook.*

The language of establishment in Article 6 left room for conflicting interpretations in the legislature, courts, towns, and churches. Article 6 failed to define dissenters' rights, much less identify the dissenters themselves; this ambiguity lay at the root of sectarian conflict in New Hampshire. Neither colonial precedent nor state law advised dissenters how to secure exemption from religious taxes. There was no certificate law such as those in Massachusetts and Vermont, and no law stated who was eligible for exemption. Did affiliation and regular churchgoing suffice or was a profession of faith necessary? What about those who had no regular church to attend, or those who attended a church in another town? Might the unchurched exempt themselves? The law failed to answer these questions precisely.

Adding to the confusion was the increasing proliferation of denominations, religious societies, and churches throughout the state. When the American Revolution broke out, New Hampshire boasted 84 Congregationalist churches, 15 Presbyterian, 11 Baptist, 3 Episcopalian, and 4 Quaker meetings.[34] Within twenty-five years, the number of Congregationalist churches had increased to nearly 145.[35] The Baptists had organized at least 41 churches by then.[36] The number of Episcopalians and Quakers remained stagnant, but new denominations overtook them. The Universalists, who formed their first society in the state in 1780, expanded to four societies by the beginning of the nineteenth century. The Freewill Baptists also gathered their first churches in New Hampshire during the 1780s, and within two decades, they had organized quarterly and yearly meetings that joined several branches in Maine with seventeen in New Hampshire. The Methodists founded their first New Hampshire society in 1795; within six years, they had gathered 675 members into four churches.[37] Although the Congregationalists held a majority and controlled most town churches, the new religious groups began to chafe against paying taxes to support the majority's worship. Without clear legal guidance, each town made its own arrangements to fund churches and societies.

In many towns, majorities forged peace with minorities simply by exempting them from ministerial taxes or allocating their payments to designated churches or societies. But elsewhere, religious minorities cried foul at what they perceived to be illegal taxation. Some dissenters devised artful schemes to avoid paying taxes. At a Conway town meeting in 1800, a Baptist faction waited until most voters had left before they proposed and approved a measure to absolve them of all past due taxes should they incorporate as a society. But that vote must not have solved the problem for all of Conway's Baptists. Seven years later, a small group petitioned the General Court for permission to be "annexed" to the Baptist society "in order to free them in a peaceable and regular way from paying a ministerial tax to any other denomination."[38] There were other ways to avoid paying taxes. In 1804, the Elders of the Freewill Baptist New Durham Quarterly Meeting permitted their clergy to provide shelters for dissenters by signing certificates to non-professors "who Desire to Come off from other Denominations" and attend their meetings "to Clear them from Paying Rates to others."[39] Whether the towns accepted these certificates is unclear; many exempted only professing church members. But the Freewill Baptists, through the liberal use of certificates, saw a way to circumvent local religious taxation and develop a greater following in their nascent denomination.

More commonly, dissenters tried to gain exemption using petitions and lawsuits. Edward Spalding petitioned the town of Hollis in 1785 to "exempt his estate from ministerial tax, for the reason that he belonged to the Baptist denomination." The town declined, ruling that his estate "shall not be freed from the minister's tax for the time past, present, or to come."[40] In Hampton Falls, the Baptists petitioned for years to gain exemption from ministerial taxes. After failing in these efforts, and after a home where they held their meetings was vandalized, they sued in 1809. The lawsuit, though it never came to trial, cost the parish about four hundred dollars.[41] In 1812, the Universalists of Marlow petitioned the legislature, claiming that they had been "oppressed by ministerial taxes raised by the Town" and requesting that they "be released from said burthen."[42] By this time, mandatory town-church taxes were no longer the rule—in fact, by the close of the decade, only about half the towns in New Hampshire levied religious taxes at all.[43] But for dissenters who had to battle these taxes, state law offered little recourse.

Bitter battles over taxation led dissenters to petition the General Court to allow them to be incorporated as separate parishes. These petitions often met with fierce objections from town majorities who feared losing the tax base they needed to support ministers and maintain meetinghouses. The residents of Surry protested that they had such a small community to begin with that they had "not one Inhabitant to spare" to a separate parish—and, furthermore, they doubted whether all of the Baptist petitioners were truly Baptist professors, arguing instead that not one of the petitioners "ever made any Profession of Religion of any Denomination that we know of."[44] Others cited their towns' spiritual, rather than economic, interests. Petitioners from Wentworth opposed an effort to establish a Universalist society in their town in 1807; they feared it would bring about the "corruption of . . . hearth and morals" by establishing "corrupt preaching among us" and turning the town into an "asylum" for outsiders who "wish to be freed from paying ministerial taxes in the towns where they reside."[45] Whether the towns saw themselves as protecting their economic, moral, or spiritual interests, the fight to maintain their original parishes could turn fierce indeed.

When Congregationalists or Baptists petitioned for incorporation, they usually succeeded. But some newer religious groups met with an unexpected obstacle: the state refused to recognize them as denominations, which undercut their legal arguments for tax exemption and incorporation. The first hint of this problem came in 1802, when Christopher Erskine failed to secure an exemption from paying religious taxes in Claremont. Erskine, who had attended a Universalist church there since the early 1790s, presented the town with a certificate in 1795. Although the town accepted the certificate at first, it refused to honor Erskine's exemption after 1799, at which point he sued the town and won. But on appeal, the court found for Claremont, deciding that the Universalists were "not such a sect, persuasion, or denomination as . . . are exempt from the payment of taxes for the support of a regularly settled minister of a Congregational Society."[46]

That the Universalists were not a denomination came as a surprise to Erskine.[47] The decision also astonished the Universalist Convention, which had lobbied the legislature and courts on Erskine's behalf. The convention argued that the judgment boded poorly for religious liberty in general and the Universalists in particular. They feared the decision "hath opened a wide and effectual door for the recovery of Congregational Ministerial taxes at the hands of all Universalists." And worse, the notion that they were not a denomination simply "blotted the whole body of professing members . . . from the volume of legal existence." To avoid this fate, the convention asked the court to reconsider its decision.[48]

The courts declined to do so. As a result, Universalists remained liable for ministerial taxes. And they were not alone. Methodists and Freewill Baptists, too, failed to gain recognition. Although the records of many early court cases have been lost, one pivotal decision by Chief Justice Jeremiah Smith epitomized the rationale for deciding which denominations were legitimate. *Muzzy* v. *Wilkins et al.* (1803) involved a Presbyterian plaintiff whose town had refused to exempt him from paying taxes.[49] In this case, the court found for the plaintiff. But Smith's broader arguments about the definition of "sect" and the nature of establishment shed some light on the Erskine case and similar disputes, and on the dissenters' status in early nineteenth-century New Hampshire.

By finding for the plaintiff, Smith affirmed that the New Hampshire constitution protected any member of any "sect" from having to pay taxes to support another denomination. But Smith employed a very limited definition of "sect." According to Smith, the distinguishing feature of a denomination was church polity, not doctrine. The Presbyterians, he pointed out, maintained a different organizational structure than the Congregationalists did. That distinction separated the two more than any variations in doctrine or confession. The same held true, he argued, with Episcopalians, Quakers, and Baptists, all of whom he recognized as sects. Conversely, doctrinal differences did not in and of themselves amount to sectarian differences, because any denomination's membership might include parishioners of varying doctrinal stripes. Groups like "Calvinists, Arminians, Hopkinsians, Universalists, &c.," he maintained, "are not distinct sects; they are found blended with all sects."[50] It followed, then, that they were not entitled to exemption from ministerial taxes in New Hampshire.

Smith's decision reflected an implausibly narrow understanding of the variations in church polity and doctrine. At the time, Universalists had adopted their own articles of faith and had begun to develop a cohesive hierarchy entirely separate from the Congregationalists (who, ironically, routinely shared ministers and resources with the Presbyterians under the Plan of Union).[51] By 1803, one could no more claim that the Universalists occupied a place on the Congregationalist spectrum than that the Methodists were still a radical group of Anglicans. But Smith argued exactly that. So, too, did he insist that under Article 6, only those who affiliated with recognized denominations were exempt from supporting other churches.[52] This provision was entirely fair, he pointed out, because it meant that everyone would support religious and moral instruction, whether to their own (recognized) denomination, or to the minister or church who served the town and, by extension, the general spiritual welfare. Public instruction in morality, funded by taxes, fulfilled a public purpose for which the community shared responsibility.[53]

Smith's decision in *Muzzy* v. *Wilkins* became the basis for the New Hampshire judiciary's treatment of religious minorities for over a decade. So, having learned they would make no progress in the courts, dissenters turned to the legislature. The first to do so were the Freewill Baptists, who sought state recognition in 1804.[54] The Universalists followed with a similar petition the next summer. Pointing out that they had been "denied a trial . . . on the ground that we were not a sect," they petitioned for recognition as such so they might enjoy the full benefits of Article 6. The legislature, clearly more inclined than the courts to accommodate religious pluralism, granted their requests with legislative resolves.[55] The Methodists followed suit in 1807.[56] Whether these resolutions carried the full weight of law was unclear.[57] But they served their purpose in that no one ever challenged them. The resolutions gave the legislature a legal basis to incorporate churches and societies, and they seem to have convinced most towns to exempt members of those institutions from religious taxation.

The tensions among dissenters, towns, and established churches reached a stalemate by the early 1810s. But a political realignment in the state revived the debate over religious liberty and establishment. As elsewhere in northern New England, the Federalists had long allied with the Congregational churches and supported the town-church system, whereas the growing Republican Party actively courted dissenters with their anti-establishment rhetoric of religious liberty.[58] The 1810s saw the Republicans—led by William Plumer, who was elected governor in 1816—challenge and eventually overtake the Federalist majority. The Republicans introduced moderate reforms at first, like an 1816 law that removed the tax exemption from ministers' personal and real property.[59] This measure fostered greater equality among the clergy of different denominations, though it changed little in terms of religious toleration and taxation.

But when the Republicans secured majorities in both legislative houses after 1816, they positioned themselves to tackle disestablishment. Among the earliest to attempt such a move was state senator Dan Young, a Methodist preacher from Lisbon who had spent the previous thirteen years traveling circuits in New Hampshire, Vermont, and Ohio. Only recently resettled in his home state, he claimed to have entered politics solely for the purpose of bringing about disestablishment.[60] The year he assumed office, Young introduced a bill intended to repeal the 1791 provision that authorized towns to levy religious taxes. Young's bill would have allowed any denomination, church, or religious society to tax its own members, provided those individuals had entered into a voluntary association with the body in question. Although the bill protected all pre-existing contracts between towns and ministers, it would have removed any future contracts from the towns' purview and placed them in the hands of churches and societies. The bill failed miserably in its first attempt at passage, garnering only four votes (including Young's) in the Senate. Young introduced it annually thereafter, and each year it gained more support. Finally, in 1819, the bill received strong enough backing in both houses to prompt serious discussion.[61]

The Toleration Bill passed easily in the Senate but became the center of fierce debate in the House.[62] Many opponents of the bill argued that under the 1792 constitution, New Hampshire already ensured perfect religious liberty and that no additional measures were needed. Edmund Parker insisted that everyone in the state was already "at liberty to worship God in the manner and season most agreeable, or not to worship at all." Thomas Whipple, who had introduced the bill in the House, countered that although all were free to worship as they chose, they might still be liable for taxes to support another denomination. This obligation violated the rights to conscience and property.[63] Supporters granted that the bill would shift the responsibility for supporting churches from towns to religious societies, but they maintained that doing so would not radically depart from the provision in Article 6 that provided for ministerial support.[64] Others disagreed. John Pitman pointed out that Article 6 clearly allowed the legislature to empower the towns to raise religious taxes, so any attempt to remove that power was unconstitutional. Moreover, opponents predicted that the bill would trigger a decline of public piety and morality that the Declaration of Rights was designed to prevent. If support for religion became a private and voluntary matter, what authority would ensure public piety? Without town churches, many feared, towns would splinter off into separate parishes. Henry Hubbard predicted that "every town in our State will contain as many Societies . . . as the passions, the prejudices, or the interests of individuals shall dictate."[65] If town churches could not unify communities, there would be nothing to stop them from dividing into narrow, self-interested factions.

The Toleration Act passed. It affirmed the towns' rights to levy taxes for civic purposes—for schools, roads and bridge repair, and aid to the poor—but nullified their authority to raise funds for meetinghouse construction or ministerial support, except where contracts were already in force. It affirmed the right of all Christian denominations to form churches and societies, raise funds, establish bylaws, build and repair meetinghouses, contract with and support ministers, and accept members under equal corporate powers. The law also ensured that all societies would be completely voluntary.[66] The act met with an enthusiastic reception. A commentary in the *Religious Informer,* a Freewill Baptist newspaper, celebrated the law as "a just cause of congratulation to the enemies of religious tyranny and intolerance." A Universalist society that formed in Alstead the following year pointedly called itself the First Christian Toleration Society. Despite the "senseless outcry" that erupted in some sectors, Republican newspaper editor Isaac Hill insisted that this act entailed no threat except to those who wished to "make use of extortion and oppression to support *their* system."[67] Rather, supporters hoped the act would allow Protestant Christianity to flourish in the state in all its forms.

The Toleration Act did not bring about a sudden break between church and state. To an extent, this process was already underway. About half the towns had already stopped levying religious taxes, and many others had long-term contracts with ministers, which the law could not break. All religious societies now had to seek incorporation from the General Court to gain legal standing, though this procedure had long been, and remained, a formality. The Toleration Act failed to address another form of state religious support—ministerial lands, which towns maintained for the use of the clergy of the longest-settled church. And because the Toleration Act was a law and not a constitutional amendment, it did not nullify the portion of Article 6 that allowed for public funding of religion. It left intact other facets of New Hampshire's church-state partnership: the state retained until 1868 the right to decide which denominations and ministers were legitimate, and the Protestant test for officeholders remained in effect until 1876. But proponents hoped that, at the very least, the Toleration Act ended the injustices that attended religious taxation. Whether their hopes would prove justified remained very much in question, just as the future of establishment in New Hampshire remained very much subject to debate.

In Maine, the separation from Massachusetts provided a chance to break with a long and contentious history of religious establishment. Although Massachusetts had by the late eighteenth century long abandoned its active persecution of minority religious groups, it maintained an establishment that balanced explicit privileges for Congregationalists with a grudging toleration of dissenters. Colonial law allowed dissenters to file for certificates of exemption rather than fund the Congregationalist ministers, who (in Massachusetts) were virtually always the choice of town majorities. These laws contained loopholes, however, and local parishes often abused them.[68] And Massachusetts's ecclesiastical law was a poor fit for Maine, where the Congregationalists clung to a much more tenuous majority in fragile parishes as they watched new religious groups sweep in toward the close of the eighteenth century. Rather than settle the issue of establishment, ongoing disputes over dissenters' status only stoked debates over the church-state relationship.

As Massachusetts lawmakers wrote their state's constitution, dissenters urged them to codify a more expansive religious toleration. The final result, the Constitution of 1780, included two articles in its Declaration of Rights that dealt with the extent and limits of religious liberty. Article 2 protected individual liberty of conscience. It declared the "right as well as the duty of all men in society, publicly, and at stated seasons, to worship the SUPREME BEING" and ensured every person's right to do so "in the manner and season most agreeable to the dictates of his own conscience."[69] Religious liberty was conditional; not only the right to worship, but the *duty* to do so became enshrined in the constitution. Liberty of conscience, then, did not extend to unbelievers, or even to the unchurched faithful. By tying liberty to duty, the framers supported a vision of a Protestant republic in which the state fostered piety. Even dissenters embraced this vision—for all the uproar over the Constitution of 1780 and its implications for religious liberty, Article 2 and its reference to duty provoked little, if any, protest.

But Article 3 was another matter. Whereas Article 2 applied to individuals, Article 3 addressed the legal status of denominations, parishes, and religious societies. It proclaimed the equality of "every denomination of Christians" under the law, banned "subordination of any one sect or denomination to another," and guaranteed that all religious bodies could elect, contract with, and support the clergy of their choice.[70] But Article 3 also established a mutually dependent relationship between church and state, and it framed that relationship so as to call the rhetoric of equality into question. Because churches benefited civil society by fostering "piety, religion, and morality," the legislature had the right to require towns and parishes to levy religious taxes.[71] This provision represented a step back for Baptist and Quaker dissenters, who had been categorically exempt from ministerial taxes for decades under colonial law. And even though Article 3 ensured that each individual's share of these funds would support the "public teacher or teachers of his own religious sect or denomination," it made no exception for those who did not or could not attend a church of their choosing. Instead, those dissenters' ministerial taxes would support the clergy "of the parish or precinct in which said monies are raised." The Constitution of 1780 assumed that the town was the default religious community for all of its residents. Only when a churchgoer could provide evidence to the contrary would his ministerial taxes support a separate church or parish.

Opponents of Article 3 decried the inherent contradictions to the principle of religious liberty. They suggested that under the Constitution of 1780, "church and state are not barely to be brought together, but are to be really *united*."[72] Some critics noted that the provision for majority rule over religious matters would make sectarian equality impossible to achieve. They argued that minorities might never enjoy religious liberty so long as "the majority in each town and parish [had] the exclusive right of covenanting . . . with religious teachers and so of excluding the minority from the Liberty of choosing for themselves."[73] This provision would leave dissenters in a state of perpetual subordination. Article 3 not only betrayed the promise of religious liberty, but it also cemented a system in which dissenters could never attain it.

Amid an enduring dispute over the proper relationship between church and state, the Massachusetts government reinforced its ties to religion, which facilitated the spread of Congregationalism in Maine. Massachusetts towns had long been expected to support churches and supply their own preaching; this expectation was part of the legacy of Puritan settlement. But the newer, sparsely populated settlements in Maine rarely met that requirement. Although white settlement in Maine dated back to the seventeenth century, most migrants were recent arrivals, transient and poor. They hailed from the economically stagnant port towns and farming communities of Massachusetts, where hardships brought on by war and a shaky recovery had forced them to seek opportunities elsewhere. Those who arrived in the latter decades of the eighteenth century endured a series of environmental misfortunes, ranging from grasshopper infestations to droughts to unseasonable frosts.[74] As a result, migration was frequent—not just to Maine but also within the province, as settlers wandered in search of viable opportunities.

The population explosion was dramatic. Congregationalist minister Paul Coffin observed in the late 1790s that Davistown had increased from 6 to 40 families in just a few years, and that Livermore had grown by two-thirds in the same period, to about 130 families.[75] Such rapid growth, along with economic insecurity, made for fragile communities unable to support preaching. Missionary Daniel Little noted in 1792 that only four towns in Lincoln County—one of the most populous in Maine—had settled preachers, which left about 25,000 people without regular clergy.[76] As elsewhere in the region, some towns were limited by their own geography. Levi Frisbie, reporting from a missionary tour northwest of Augusta, doubted that the settlements he encountered would ever be able to support preaching; the "Scatter'd situation of the people" prevented them from even learning about his visit. Other settlements, "being nearly surrounded by Mountains can never be large," he predicted, and "can never support a Minister."[77] Poverty, transience, and geography conspired to impede the spread of religion.

Legislators read reports like Frisbie's and committed to ensuring that Congregationalism would prosper in Maine as it had in Massachusetts proper. At first, they tried to compel Maine residents to support ministers. In 1786, citing a "parental regard" for Maine's backcountry outposts, the Massachusetts General Court hired a preacher who could serve Lincoln County's unincorporated areas. A tax on the county's inhabitants would defray the expenses.[78] But stopgap measures like this one proved insufficient. So Governor John Hancock asked the General Court in January 1791 to support a newly formed missionary society, the Society for Propagating the Gospel among the Indians and Others in North America (SPG). Hancock observed that frontier settlers endured a "peculiar disadvantage" in funding churches and would remain, if left to their own devices, "almost intirely destitute of that knowledge, and information, which render other parts of their Country so respectable." The General Court agreed to contribute annually, citing their concern that Maine residents, "from their particular situation & circumstance," could not support religious worship "without the aid of Government." The state was obliged to assist where its citizens could not.[79] And by supporting the SPG, the state implicitly endorsed a Congregationalist establishment. With state support, the SPG extended its influence in Maine, helping Congregationalist churches remain viable as they faced competition from Baptists, Methodists, and Universalists. And unlike other disputes over liberty of conscience and religious taxation, this form of establishment met with little controversy.

State support of the SPG allowed the Massachusetts legislature to hold Maine towns just as accountable for religious maintenance as they did the towns of Massachusetts proper. Accordingly, citizens in Maine joined other Massachusetts residents as they debated the state's religious establishment. In the 1780s, both the courts and the legislature sifted through the ambiguities surrounding the legal definition of "religious society" in Article 3. This definition increasingly became a matter of controversy because some Congregational parishes argued that unincorporated societies (which at the time included nearly every dissenting church or society) did not meet the legal standard of a body politic, and were therefore ineligible to receive and control the tax funds raised from their own members. In 1785, the Supreme Judicial Court upheld the dissenters' right to direct tax payments to their own ministers, but it also found that only incorporated societies were legally entitled to those funds. Town parishes were incorporated by default, since they had been created in the same acts of incorporation that recognized the towns themselves. But dissenting congregations had never sought recognition in Massachusetts as public entities and thus were not recognized as such.[80]

The General Court weighed in on incorporation in 1786, when it declared each parish (of any denomination) a corporate body and empowered the qualified voters of any parish to allocate funds for ministerial support, meetinghouse construction, and the like.[81] The original town parishes, however, retained some privileges that subsequently formed parishes did not enjoy. When a dissenting parish set itself off from the town, the original parish retained its rights to the meetinghouse, ministerial lands, and tax revenue from every estate not explicitly attached to the new parish, including past-due tax payments from individuals who joined the new parish. The law now recognized sectarian parishes, but it still privileged town churches.

These actions by the court and the legislature muddied the waters of religious toleration—waters already made murky by the town parishes' inconsistent treatment of dissenting churches. Whereas some towns diverted funds to these churches as taxpayers directed, others required certificates, and still others ignored the law entirely, forcing lawsuits before they allocated funds. To safeguard their privileges, more minority churches sought incorporation. The first dissenting parish in Maine to do so was the Baptist Religious Society in New Gloucester and Gray, which formally separated from the Congregationalist parishes in those towns in 1790.[82] A trickle of Baptist parishes followed.[83] So, too, did several Congregationalist parishes, whose members sought incorporation either as newly formed town churches or as second parishes breaking off from growing congregations.

Although the 1786 parish act promised that all religious societies would stand equally before the law, differences in Baptist and Congregationalist incorporation acts belied that claim. In both cases, the law required individuals to present written proof of church or society membership. But Congregationalist church members merely needed to present evidence "in writing under their hands" to the town clerk so that he could record their status. Baptists had to present an additional certificate, signed by the Baptist minister or clerk whose parish they joined, to the clerk of the parish they left.[84] Although either transaction was simple enough, the difference between them assumed different relationships between town and church. The law treated Congregationalist parishes as connected to the town. But Baptists who left the Congregational parishes joined communities with no organic boundaries. The law distinguished between the very foundations of these communities—one defined by place, the other by denomination.

The law also privileged incorporated parishes but remained vague about the path to incorporation. The court, however, held that a congregation required a legislative act of incorporation to claim any rights.[85] The Supreme Judicial Court of Massachusetts confirmed this principle in *Barnes* v. *First Parish in Falmouth* (1810), in which the court held that only "a public Protestant teacher . . . of some legally incorporated society" could recover religious taxes.[86] This case concerned a dispute between Thomas Barnes, a Universalist minister in Falmouth, Maine, and the town's Congregationalist parish. Barnes had requested that the parish earmark Universalists' taxes to pay his salary and argued that by failing to do so, the town violated his parishioners' freedom of conscience. But the court distinguished between religious freedom and religious taxation. In a decision that echoed Jeremiah Smith's in *Muzzy* v. *Wilkins,* Chief Justice Theophilus Parsons agreed that the Massachusetts Constitution protected liberty of conscience, but he found that this right was not at issue. Instead, the question was whether the state could appropriate money for the common good. Parsons wrote that funding public worship served society by supporting "the practice of a system of correct morals among the people," even if an individual taxpayer did not attend the town church. Parsons also distinguished between public and private societies in terms of their claims to town funds. An incorporated society, he argued, was "formed by the public authority of the state," and therefore eligible for public funding. A private or "voluntary association" derived its powers "from the individual consent of each member," not from the law. Private societies had no legal claim to public funds.[87]

The General Court weighed in on the matter once more with the 1811 Religious Freedom Act. Citing the constitutional promise of equal protection for all Christian denominations, the act ensured that any Protestant minister was entitled to his share of ministerial taxes, whether or not his society was incorporated. It also provided the text of the certificates dissenters would file to have their taxes allocated to their own ministers or societies. Finally, it empowered unincorporated societies to manage their financial assets.[88] By standardizing the means by which churchgoers joined and separated from religious societies, and by granting unincorporated societies basic financial powers, the act eliminated the ambiguity that had clouded these matters and compelled towns to treat dissenting groups equally. Even more importantly, the Religious Freedom Act effectively nullified the *Barnes* decision by tying liberty of conscience to religious taxation. The framers of the act rejected the argument that religious taxation promoted the broader public good more than it did individual churches. Rather, religious liberty meant that taxpayers should direct their payments as they saw fit.

Congregationalist ministers accepted the law reluctantly. William Jenks of Bath lamented the "late act of the [General Court] respecting 'religious liberty'" and predicted that it would bode poorly for Congregationalists. Having already seen many of his own parishioners gravitate toward Bath's Baptist church, Jenks hoped that the act might "be overruled for good."[89] He need not have worried. Although some Congregationalist parishes made do with less public funding, the Religious Freedom Act of 1811 did not seem to affect church membership, nor did it seem to fuel the growth of new dissenting societies. In fact, its consequences were fairly limited—the act simply ensured public funding for unincorporated congregations. Massachusetts still required taxation to support religion, and taxpayers who did not identify with a particular religious group (or who did not have access to a church of their preference) still paid taxes to support the local parish. Because Congregationalists usually controlled the original parish in each town, the law still privileged that denomination. But by linking religious liberty and religious taxation, the act at least ensured that each religious society would receive equal treatment under the law.

The Religious Freedom Act of 1811 forged a truce in the debate over religious taxation. But for Maine residents, that debate reopened when the vote for statehood brought the issue of religious liberty to the fore. To apply for statehood, Maine had to draft a constitution. Two hundred seventy-four delegates gathered at the First Parish Meeting House in Portland in October 1819 to create that document. Of these, only a handful (about thirteen) were ministers. Of those, all but one were dissenters.[90] Among them was Ward Locke, a Freewill Baptist preacher who represented Chesterville. As an itinerant, he faced repeated obstacles in towns where "the freewillers and the congregationals had no dealings together." He often found himself locked out of meetinghouses and prevented from preaching. Although he had entertained doubts about whether a preacher could appropriately act in a political role, he ultimately decided to serve so he might represent dissenters' interests. "If the foundation of religious Liberty was not Laid in the constitution," he wrote later, then "it would be hard to precur it after ward."[91] As it had for Dan Young in New Hampshire, the issue of religious liberty convinced this dissenting preacher to participate. It is impossible to say whether the other dissenter-delegates saw their roles primarily as safeguarding toleration, but they almost certainly brought to bear similar histories of their dealings with the Congregationalist establishment.

It was not the Protestant dissenters but rather the Catholics who initiated the discussion of toleration on the convention floor. On Tuesday, October 19, a group of Catholics from Damariscotta presented a memorial to the delegates asking that the state constitution ensure equal status for all denominations, thereby granting them rights and privileges they had not enjoyed under the Massachusetts government.[92] The memorial was uncontroversial. The delegates were amenable to protecting religious freedom to an extent that far surpassed Massachusetts precedent; the new constitution would guarantee equal religious liberty to all citizens, without placing special restrictions on non-Protestants or even non-Christians. Section 3 of the Bill of Rights borrowed much of its language from Articles 2 and 3 of the Massachusetts Declaration of Rights but with entirely different consequences. It provided for all citizens the right to worship undisturbed according to the dictates of conscience, forbade legal preference for one denomination over another, and granted all religious societies equal rights to choose and support their own clergy, regardless of corporate status.[93] But the debates over the meaning of religious liberty and the relationship between church and state revealed deep divisions over the proper place of religion in civil society.[94]

Although no one disputed the principle of equality, there was much debate about whether the equal *right* to worship entailed an equal *duty* to do so. Almost as soon as Section 3 was introduced, many delegates proposed to insert the phrase "to exercise the duty" so that the first sentence might read, "All men have a natural and unalienable right to exercise the duty to worship the Almighty God according to the dictates of their own conscience."[95] Supporters of this motion resisted using the word "right" alone because they thought it suggested the right *not* to worship, or the right to worship only at one's own convenience. But others argued that the state had no business deciding whether religious worship was a duty—and, furthermore, that such a requirement would indeed violate the principle of equal religious liberty. Ward Locke echoed many dissenters' sentiments when he supported strict separation between church and state. "The Legislature is departing from its proper sphere," he claimed, "when it undertakes to regulate the intercourse between man and his Maker."[96] Religious duties lay within the purview of the church and conscience, not the law.

Whether to include the term "duty" in Section 3 was more than a question of semantics. Delegates on both sides articulated opposing ideals of the relationships among church, state, and community. Those who hoped to amend Section 3 predicted that if the constitution did not require worship, public morality would surely deteriorate. "If . . . morals depend on religion and the support of civil government on morals," asked Ezekiel Whitman, then "is it not the duty of every government . . . to *uphold* and *encourage* the institutions for public instruction in the principles of religion?" He suggested that the state *should* "encourage and support the institutions of public worship."[97] Most delegates agreed that widespread piety would strengthen society. But they also thought the state should not dictate religiosity. If the state attempted to do so, Locke predicted, "we may make hypocrites, but not Christians."[98] Any ties between government and religion could destroy the very religious liberty the constitution sought to protect. Better to sever that relationship entirely than risk dire consequences.

In the end, the delegates sent the constitution to Maine voters with the original version of Section 3 intact, containing no references to pious "duty." All of the proposed amendments failed, as did suggestions to include religious tests for public offices.[99] At least one implied limit to religious liberty did survive, however. Henry Hobbs of Waterboro proposed an amendment to protect any individual from obligations to pay taxes to support the construction and repair of meetinghouses, "contrary to his own voluntary engagement." It, too, was voted down. According to delegate John Holmes, that provision would "destroy all corporate powers" of religious societies and leave them powerless to raise funds from their own members.[100] The convention thereby transferred the power to levy religious taxes from town to parish. Whereas the decision to join a church was voluntary, a churchgoer's financial obligations were not.

When the delegation distributed the constitution for voters' consideration, it eagerly proclaimed the principles of religious liberty, toleration, and equality that it hoped Section 3 would promote. The framers declared that the "the worship of Jehovah, to be acceptable, must be a free will offering," and that piety "cannot be regulated by human legislation." Accordingly, the constitution guaranteed the rights of conscience, "placing all denominations on the footing of the most perfect equality."[101] The delegates certainly anticipated some protest of this departure from Massachusetts precedent. And to be sure, many citizens expressed apprehension about the extent of religious liberty that the constitution endorsed. Elijah Kellogg, an SPG missionary, predicted that the new constitution would "induce many to move into the District, who have been told that religion would be proscribed." Jonathan Fisher, one of Kellogg's colleagues, similarly feared that irreligion would ultimately prevail. "It is astonishing," Fisher remarked, "how many professors of Christianity in this new state have voted for a Constitution which makes no provision for the sanctification of the Lord's Day, nor the support of public worship."[102] Such reservations aside, the constitution passed overwhelmingly with more than 90 percent of the vote.[103] For the new state of Maine, the legacy of Massachusetts's establishment lay in the past.

By 1820, all three northern New England states had ended the legal financial ties between town and church that had inextricably joined the two and left minority congregations at a distinct disadvantage. In each state, debates raged over whether religious taxation violated freedom of conscience. Proponents of local establishment argued that the close ties between town and church enabled the state to ensure public piety and morality, and—by extension—public order. These outcomes benefited the state and all of its citizens, and therefore merited all citizens' support, even those whose churches did not receive public funds. Ending this system, they argued, would create a religious landscape that was so fragmented and factionalized that churchgoers might barely be able to support religion at all. But those who argued against the town-church system countered that religious taxes violated religious liberty if these funds supported a mode of worship that the taxpayer opposed. And though they celebrated the anticipated liberties that would follow the end of religious taxation, many who had pushed for this change watched anxiously, along with their opponents, to see what might happen should the government sever all ties with religion. But the break between church and state was not so clear-cut as they imagined, and the results were not so dramatic as they predicted.

After they ended compulsory religious taxation, the northern New England states witnessed neither the dawn of religious liberty nor a slide into godlessness. In fact, little changed. States continued to encourage worship and buttress religious institutions, often through similar means as before. Like other states, Vermont, New Hampshire, and Maine endorsed the churches' roles as guardians of morality by empowering them to enforce Sabbath worship and moral norms such as temperance. But the northern New England states went further than that, using law and jurisprudence to promote a particular kind of religious community: a stable congregation built around the long-term partnership between a town and its settled minister. They bolstered that partnership by preserving physical spaces in the town for Congregationalists and by defining the town's spiritual space to include as many people as possible within its scope. Dissenting churches that broke from their towns were left with their own committed followers and perhaps some church property but no space that the law called their own. Even as they removed the legal backing for religious taxation, northern New England's states continued to use the law to support the town-church religious geography.

The basis for this support, before and after disestablishment, lay in longstanding legal definitions of two kinds of religious entities: territorial parishes (the original town churches) and poll parishes (which separated from the town). Territorial parishes existed as geographic and spatial units, whereas poll parishes existed only in a legal sense, without any inherent claims to physical space. State laws and constitutions alike granted territorial parishes legal privileges that poll parishes did not enjoy, including the rights to ministerial land and meetinghouses. In other words, these laws denied the dissenting communities' geographical existence in a system that defined churches by the ground they occupied. By tying some religious communities (and not others) to physical townscapes, post-establishment law placed these parishes on unequal footing.

As territorial parishes, town churches continued to control the physical space that their religious communities occupied. The New England states (and, prior to the Revolution, colonies) had long privileged these parishes by granting them plots of public land, which, according to town charters, were reserved for each town's first settled minister. These provisions assumed that only one minister would serve each town at a time, that he would be a Congregationalist, and that the established church would settle a minister before any of the town's dissenters did. But the ministerial lots did not always work as planned. Moreover, the laws that protected them grew increasingly out of step with the realities of religious life, which featured not united churches but fragmented populations, empty pulpits, and increasingly worthless and vacant public land.

As these incongruities became more apparent, the northern New England states grappled with how to handle ministerial lots that appeared to have outlasted their purpose. Whereas New Hampshire generally let the town charters stand, Vermont and Maine modified them with laws to suggest how towns should lease, administer, and distribute ministerial lots. In 1798, Vermont allowed towns that had not yet settled ministers to divide the lease income from such plots to benefit all of the churches in each town. But as soon as one of those churches settled a minister, the plot would revert to him.[104] Maine standardized the means by which towns either assigned plots to the first settled minister or divided the proceeds from leasing the plots, so long as the ministers who reaped the benefits could verify that "their places of public worship fixed within said town or parish."[105] But even though state laws tended to support dividing ministerial lands to accommodate multiple ministers, the wording to direct such action was often so vague and contradictory that the towns found little guidance in deciding how to allocate land. As a result, local conflicts over land rights erupted.

A public lot of as many as three hundred acres could be a great boon to a church that would otherwise have to provide a parsonage through its own means, so many congregations raced to settle clergy before their neighbors did. Such "scrambling for the Right" to the ministerial land, complained some Vermonters, tended to produce a decidedly un-Christian climate.[106] In some cases, towns refused to grant the land to the first settled minister if he was a dissenter. The Methodists in Bucksport, Maine, settled their minister before any other church in town, but the Congregationalist minority seized the ministerial lot for their own minister, who occupied it for twenty-five years.[107] In New Hampshire, the Superior Court of Judicature decided in 1822 that a poll parish could claim neither the ministerial plot nor the income derived from its sale. The court distinguished the town of Wilton (and its Congregational church) from the Baptist Society in Wilton and found that the ministerial lands remained "the absolute property of the towns"—meant not for the first minister who took residence but for the first minister who served the town church. Maine's Supreme Judicial Court echoed that principle in 1826, when it decided that only a minister recognized by a town could occupy that town's ministerial plot. It was that minister who served most of the town's churchgoers, the courts insisted, and it was he who served the town's public interest, which in turn entitled him to the land.[108]

Even when towns wrangled over the rights to public land, the question of who claimed those rights was often moot. Plots stood empty as churches and societies in splintered towns failed to settle clergy. Many towns often had to liquidate the ministerial land so they could divide the funds among their churches, but ambiguous laws impeded their efforts. The Baptist and Congregationalist churches of New Boston, New Hampshire, butted heads in 1821 over what constituted a fair division of proceeds from the sale of ministerial lands.[109] Petitioners from Shapleigh, Maine, reported in 1824 that the "several denominations of Christians" in their town, "each doubting the right of the others" to use the lot, had allowed the land to remain vacant, as they did not know how to divide it.[110] The selectmen of Ripton, Vermont, complained in 1831 that the rules governing the use and distribution of ministerial plots were obsolete. Not only did the old town charters fail to account for the "great increase of religious sects" and the "liberal views" about religion that had become the norm, they also contradicted the 1807 law to abolish public religious funding. "How a Minister can be settled in any town under the present existing laws," the selectmen wondered, "your petitioners are unable to perceive."[111] Even when a town's citizenry tried to abandon the older strictures of establishment, the law got in their way.

Meanwhile, vacant public lots diminished in value with each passing year that their fields stood fallow and trespassers stripped them of timber, fences, and other assets.[112] Town residents viewed these lands as wasted opportunities for income. The plots remained uncultivated and unattractive to potential occupants because anyone who signed a lease would face eviction as soon as the first minister was settled. Many town residents argued that they could put the plots to better use by leasing or selling them to augment public school funds instead of religion.[113] But despite some exceptions that allowed towns to modify how they used or distributed ministerial lands, the institution of the ministerial plot remained intact.

So, too, did the meetinghouse, another physical space reserved for the town church. Whereas town parishes continued to control meetinghouses, sectarian churches that broke off as poll parishes entered a legal limbo that could vary according to arbitrary enforcement of property laws. In some cases, a new poll parish sacrificed use of the meetinghouse entirely. In others, poll parishes struck deals with neighboring territorial parishes to divide meetinghouse access according to their respective shares of their towns' population. Bedford, New Hampshire, was typical in deciding to distribute assets like time in the meetinghouse among poll parishes in shares that corresponded to their proportion of the town's population, with the territorial parish claiming the remainder. But these equations did not account for the unchurched or for unconverted churchgoers who affiliated with dissenting denominations (but were not considered full members), both of which groups were counted by default as members of the territorial parish. As a result, territorial parishes claimed disproportionately large shares of their towns' populations and assets. As late as 1865, the General Court endorsed those claims and passed an act enabling towns to distribute property and funds originally designated for religious purposes.[114] Regardless of how states, parishes, and towns handled these decisions, competition to use the meetinghouse had many dissenting congregations jockeying to protect property rights.

A town's changing denominational makeup might ignite new conflicts over long-decided agreements regarding how to divide religious assets. In Craftsbury, Vermont, where the religious society had once been multi-denominational, Congregationalists eventually gained a majority and took control of the meetinghouse. But then the Baptists enjoyed a resurgence and made up about half the town's churchgoers by 1810. That year, they petitioned to use the meetinghouse half the time for Sabbath worship (proportionate to the taxes they paid to build and maintain the house).[115] In a contentious town meeting, the Congregationalists prevailed by two votes and so retained control. One Baptist partisan immortalized this "late unjust event" in a satirical poem that portrayed the Congregationalists as conspiratorial villains who gathered in a "secret conclave" to "rule and reign o'er rights divine." The poet saw their victory as a startling coalescence of political and religious power—made more shocking because the vote took place three years *after* Vermont had disestablished religion. In this light, the Congregationalists' actions smacked of tyranny. Writing from what he imagined to be the Standing Order's perspective, the poet predicted a grim future for dissenters:

> All, that against *our Church* rebel,
> By Inquisition, we'll compell
> To own, by force, our potent sway,
> And all our covenants obey. . . .
> All sects obey our will, divine,
> And Church and State, in one combine,
> To make us *great,* our power enhance
> And us to rank supreme advance. . . .
> Now, Democratic rights must fall,
> And Church and State be all in all.[116]

Using the rhetoric of religious and civil liberty, this Baptist suggested that disestablishment had done little to sever the church-state relationship.

To resolve conflicts over meetinghouse time and similar disputes, the Vermont legislature in 1814 guaranteed incorporated status—including the right to acquire and manage property—for any legally organized religious society.[117] But even this measure did not resolve all property disputes. Several sectarian churches (or their members) petitioned the legislature for special resolves to help them acquire or protect church property that the officers felt was vulnerable due to town or inheritance disputes. Usually the General Assembly granted such requests. But when the Baptist Church in Brandon asked for a special law to protect the property of *unincorporated* churches, the legislature declined.[118] Baptists resisted incorporation because the resulting regulations violated their beliefs. Incorporated societies, for example, were expected to command financial support from their members, but doing so contradicted the Baptist insistence on voluntary contributions. So when unincorporated Baptist societies sought limited legal protection, they failed to secure it. Only parishes that organized according to state law could expect to protect their property. Those that did not, even for doctrinal reasons, were denied equal legal status.

Just as northern New Englanders struggled to demarcate the physical space of the meetinghouse, they also negotiated over spiritual space delineated by church and parish membership. Membership—how churchgoers identified themselves and how churches identified their followers—had lain at the heart of the town-church establishment, and now it became a core problem that post-establishment law sought to solve. Would parishioners remain members of their town parishes until they indicated otherwise? Many towns and churches assumed they would. As poll parishes broke from territorial parishes, towns tried to sort out who belonged where. But the task of separating towns from parishes raised more questions than it answered about how churches, societies, and parishioners could navigate the spiritual space among the religious communities in their midst.

Prior to disestablishment, all three states assumed that the town was the default religious community for all of its residents—only those who furnished evidence to the contrary could direct their taxes to another parish. Vermont's parish laws charged towns with hiring ministers and building meetinghouses, even if parishioners represented different faiths.[119] New Hampshire allowed each town's majority to decide how to support religion and maintain ministers.[120] Massachusetts went even further by requiring towns to support churches. Maine dissenters who did not specifically direct their religious taxes to their own ministers saw their money support the town parish.[121] In each state, ill-defined procedures for incorporation set poll parishes at a further disadvantage, which ignited firestorms over arbitrary rules that determined how to allocate dissenters' taxes and define poll parishes' rights and responsibilities.

Territorial parishes held an advantage in claiming members and their money, even after disestablishment. Vermont, New Hampshire, and Maine all allowed establishment-era ministerial contracts to remain in effect. As a result, many people found themselves still liable to support churches they did not attend. This issue especially affected those who had not formally withdrawn from territorial parishes, because members of poll parishes almost always joined by choice rather than default. The General Convention of Universalists decried this problem in 1828, urging its followers to gather churches so they could avoid supporting other clergy. The convention observed that many Universalists remained "members of other societies . . . taxed for the support of doctrines they believe to be false and injurious," and urged them to "form themselves into societies according to law" to avoid those liabilities.[122] Universalists still fell under the purview of town parishes until they formally identified themselves as members of another church. Even though the states no longer levied ministerial taxes, they still supported a system of religious funding that supported the town-church tradition.

State law continued to treat territorial and poll parishes differently. Although Vermont had abandoned religious taxation more abruptly and completely than New Hampshire and Maine, remnants of the old system persisted. Along with the ministerial contracts that remained in place, the first section of the 1797 Act for the Support of the Gospel, which authorized towns, parishes, and religious societies to enter contracts and raise taxes to support churches, continued as well.[123] Anyone who paid religious taxes prior to 1807 would, barring a formal separation from a town, parish, or religious society, continue to do so. And because Vermont law considered all taxpayers to be part of their town parishes unless they filed certificates to indicate otherwise, some people continued to fund churches whose doctrines conflicted with their own.

Town churches expected their parishioners' support. The Middlebury Congregational Church repeatedly confronted members who were delinquent in paying taxes. In 1815, the church charged Levi Hooker with failing to pay his ministerial tax. A few years later, the church challenged Bela Sawyer's certificate (filed with the town clerk), which claimed he no longer owed taxes because he no longer believed in Congregationalist doctrine. A similar conflict arose in 1829 when the church complained that Jonathan Sawyer filed a certificate with the town "which prevents his supporting the gospel in common with his brethren."[124] In all of these cases, the church challenged current and former members even when they had filed certificates to withdraw. More to the point, by the time these members filed those certificates, they had spent months or years after disestablishment paying taxes to support a church they did not attend or with which they did not agree. Even after 1807, such arrangements were still the norm, and the town clerk, more than one's own conscience, remained the arbiter of church funding.

Tussles over membership and parish funding were even more contentious in New Hampshire, where the 1819 Toleration Act did little to calm the uproar that preceded its passage. Although most people seemed to support disestablishment, the Toleration Act left many questions unresolved. How should towns dispose of the trusts and property they held for religious purposes (and that had previously benefited town churches)? How should churches and societies ensure reasonable financial support? How were parishes that split off from each other supposed to divide their assets—or were they obligated to do so at all? Questions like these lay at the heart of the continuing debate.

Protests against the Toleration Act persisted well into the 1820s. The Methodist *New England Missionary Intelligencer,* which defended the act, warned that its critics "resolved on one mighty effort to get the law repealed."[125] The true extent of this repeal movement is unclear, but the Toleration Act certainly had its detractors. Shortly after it passed, the New Hampshire General Association claimed that many churches, "once flourishing," found themselves "reduced to a very few members . . . pining away in a famine of the word."[126] By 1823, sympathetic legislators proposed a bill that would have allowed towns to set up public trusts to fund religious worship and instruction. This bill, supporters argued, would correct what they saw as a "radical defect" in the 1819 law: by ending religious taxation, it seemed to imperil every church that had ever depended on state support. If citizens were given the "*unbounded freedom to the purse,*" they would abandon churches in droves. Untethered churchgoers, instead of maintaining "common and sacred places of union," would attend "*all* [churches] *in their turns,* and contribute to the support of neither." Such fickle habits would tear at the fabric that bound churches together. Whether these fears had merit, they nonetheless fueled predictions of spiritual demise. "How could a clergyman be settled for even a term of years, or a house of worship be built," many asked, so long as anyone could "certify himself off by his own written declaration and leave the remaining members saddled with the burthen?"[127]

Fearing that New Hampshire might have moved too quickly to sever church-state ties, legislators spent years modifying the Toleration Act to restore income for churches. In 1823, the General Court enabled any religious society to tax its members and keep permanent funds to finance ministerial salaries and meetinghouse construction.[128] In 1827, the legislature confirmed that contracts between towns and settled ministers which predated the Toleration Act would remain in effect, and that towns could levy taxes to maintain town-owned meetinghouses. The law reiterated that no person should pay taxes to support a minister of another denomination, but it kept in place pre-1819 certificate laws that required dissenters to file their certificates with towns, not churches.[129] In other words, towns continued in their former roles as the collectors and distributors of religious funds. In effect, the General Court reestablished the partnership between town and church and restored many of the town parish's functions.

Although the General Court hoped to calm fears of an abrupt break between church and state, their revisions to the Toleration Act made matters even more confusing. Frequent conflicts between towns and poll parishes erupted throughout the 1820s and for decades thereafter. When the Congregationalist Church of Christ in Lyndeborough received requests for dismission from church members who moved elsewhere and hoped to join Congregationalist churches in other towns, it complied. But when Uriah Cram requested a dismission in 1821 to join a new religious society in the same town, the church refused, judging his request to be "out of order."[130] Whereas the Lyndeborough Congregationalists followed the standard protocol for departing churchgoers, Cram violated those same expectations by asking to break from his territorial parish. Even after disestablishment, the ideal of the town church held sway.

The courts failed to settle these disputes conclusively. In 1822, New Hampshire's Supreme Court of Judicature ruled that poll parishes were not entitled to a share of the town ministerial fund because they had separated from the town parish. The town rightfully retained control of the fund and could continue to use it for religious purposes.[131] The court upheld this precedent through the 1850s, adding that towns with contracts that preceded the 1819 Toleration Act could continue religious taxation. In 1860, the court maintained that even though towns lacked the power to assess religious taxes (by that time, virtually no town had a contract dating from before 1819), they still claimed responsibility to "hold funds in trust, to aid in supporting religion within their limits." The court's rationale was that towns, as branches of the civil government, were entrusted to "advance the general good of the people," and that the maintenance of religious institutions fell within that responsibility. Therefore, the argument concluded, towns had "at least an indirect interest in promoting religion" and could act in ways that served that interest, the constitution, and the act of 1827.[132] The courts did not suggest that towns had a right to endorse any single denomination nor did they come down unconditionally in favor of religious taxation. But they consistently granted that towns had a responsibility to support religion, and they suggested that the proper way to fulfill this duty was through the workings of the territorial parish. Although New Hampshire had abandoned compulsory taxation decades earlier, it continued to maintain a general Protestant establishment that both endorsed the towns' responsibility to support religion and privileged the town-church model.[133]

Just as in New Hampshire, Maine legislators tried to preserve the town parish while removing the legal apparatus of religious taxation. Although the constitution abolished religious taxation by the towns, the 1821 Act Concerning Parishes (and its 1825 addendum) preserved parishes' rights to assess and collect taxes from members. The 1821 act outlined how parishes and religious societies could become incorporated and detailed how they could elect officers, call meetings, and acquire and hold property. It also spelled out how individuals could join or withdraw from incorporated parishes or societies, and it confirmed every parish member's obligation to pay religious taxes and resolve any outstanding debts to a parish before leaving it. Finally, the law confirmed the clergy's right to hold public or private lands intended for the use of the ministry. The 1825 addendum further detailed the parishes' powers of tax collection.[134] These laws in and of themselves did not violate the principle of equality among individuals and denominations; anyone was free to join or leave any parish, and only those who had joined a parish were subject to religious taxes. But the courts' decisions regarding the rights of territorial and poll parishes, the relationship of each to the town, and the extent to which membership (and thus financial obligation) was fully voluntary showed that the laws did not truly embody the basic promise of religious liberty.

Maine, like Vermont and New Hampshire, continued to privilege territorial parishes over poll parishes in questions of religious funding. In doing so, Maine courts drew upon Massachusetts precedent. In other words, after dismantling the Massachusetts establishment, Maine turned to that very same church-state system to balance religious and civil authority. Courts continued to define territorial parishes as geographic entities that shared boundaries with their towns and poll parishes as administrative units that lacked physical boundaries.[135] Accordingly, they continued to conflate towns and town churches, which in turn implied unequal privileges for the parishes and their members. In *The Inhabitants of Alna* v. *Plummer* (1824), the Supreme Judicial Court found that towns without organized churches could assume parochial duties, such as meetinghouse construction and ministerial funding. Inhabitants who had not withdrawn to another parish, the court concluded, "constitute but one corporation" that served religious and civil functions. In the absence of a town parish, those functions were joined under the town's corporate body. When the first parish organized in such a town, it would become a territorial parish and stood to inherit all of the town's religious assets.[136] Subsequent parishes—poll parishes—could claim none of these benefits. The Supreme Judicial Court confirmed as much in *Osgood* v. *Bradley* (1831), which held that the relative status of territorial and poll parishes did not differ substantially from that under Massachusetts law. Rather than "derange, disperse, and destroy all parish funds," Maine sought merely to liberalize Massachusetts law while preserving continuity in its essential functions.[137] As a result, territorial parishes retained automatic privileges and claims to public assets that poll parishes did not.

The status of territorial and poll parishes also hinged on how the courts identified their members. Under Massachusetts law, everyone was automatically a member of the territorial parish in which she lived, unless she produced a certificate to show she had joined a poll parish.[138] No one could abstain from parish membership. Maine liberalized that law, making it legal to decline to join a parish. But the courts still held that, given no evidence to the contrary, each person belonged to some parish. And they determined that membership was based on residence and family ties—not attendance, participation, or even sectarian preference.

Maine's Supreme Judicial Court confirmed this principle in two cases that resulted from similar disputes in the same town, Turner. In each case, the plaintiffs had attended meetings of Turner's first parish (a Congregationalist society), claimed membership, and tried to vote. When the presiding officer refused their votes, they sued. Both plaintiffs had participated more often in the town's Universalist society (a poll parish created in 1805) than in the Congregationalist parish. They attended Universalist meetings, professed Universalist doctrine, and helped fund Universalist preaching. But they also affiliated with the Congregationalist parish. One plaintiff, identified as Mr. Bradford, had purchased a pew in the Congregationalist meetinghouse, sometimes attended meetings there, and had paid taxes to the first parish in the early 1810s. Based on his participation in the town's Congregational church, he claimed parish membership and the right to vote in parish meetings. The other plaintiff, identified as Mr. Jones, had also paid taxes to the first parish before he adopted Universalism, and he continued to worship with the Congregationalists occasionally. The Supreme Judicial Court found against Bradford (deciding he was in fact a member of the Universalist society and could not vote in the Turner parish meetings) and for Jones (deciding that he was a member of the Congregationalist parish and could vote).[139] On the surface, these decisions seem contradictory—but the reasoning behind each revealed the extent to which the courts tried to preserve the town-church model.

In each case, the court found that personal history—not doctrinal preference—was the key factor in determining parish membership. And someone could change parishes only by filing certificates, not by attending a new church or professing a new faith. In Bradford's case, the court decided that a minor continued as a member of his father's parish after reaching adulthood unless he filed a certificate to indicate otherwise. Because Bradford's father had been a member of the Universalist Society of Turner, and the plaintiff had never formally left that society, he was not a member of the first parish. Doctrine, pew ownership, and financial contributions were irrelevant. So, too, was the case with Jones. Having been born into a family that belonged to Turner's first parish, Jones never filed a certificate to withdraw, even though he embraced Universalist doctrine and attended the Universalist church. The law considered him to be a member of the Congregationalist parish.[140]

Taken together, the two decisions showed explicit favor neither for Congregationalism as a denomination nor for the first parish of Turner. But they still revealed a state preference for a town-church model that emphasized continuity of membership and each citizen's default status as a member of some religious society, whatever the denomination. The majority decision in *Bradford* pointed out that church membership must be inherited—otherwise, what would happen if, upon reaching adulthood, each person were left "without any connection with the religious society of their parents, in which they were brought up"? Surely the law intended no such gap in membership. The court likened parishes to towns and counties as bodies that served both "civil and ecclesiastical" purposes and organized and governed individuals, sometimes "without their choice or election, and sometime against their will."[141] According to this view of the parish's public role, the legal status of membership remained more significant than personal belief. Even with constitutional guarantees of freedom of conscience and proud declarations of religious liberty, Maine saw parish membership as a matter to be governed by law.

Other court decisions reinforced these principles. The Supreme Judicial Court found that anyone who moved into a territorial parish automatically became a member unless he filed a certificate to withdraw. Further, a parishioner's tax obligations did not change even if the parish church adopted new articles of faith that contradicted his religious beliefs.[142] In these cases, the court limited the freedom *not* to join a church by compelling anyone who wished to withdraw to follow legal procedures. Until he did so, the legal standards for parish association—family history and town residence, instead of doctrine or participation—supported the town-church notion of a stable and organic community rooted in a particular place. By emphasizing these standards, the state helped churches and societies monitor membership and secure financial contributions. Just as importantly, the state asserted its right to govern matters of church membership, even as it insisted that membership and taxation were entirely voluntary.[143]

Despite the widespread acceptance of disestablishment across northern New England, publicly supported religion survived in new ways. The states determined how parishes should raise funds, and they asserted the right to define parish membership. In doing so, the states involved themselves in the private matters of religious association and identity. Even though parishes, rather than towns, now raised their own funds, they determined each member's financial obligation in much the same way as before (through property assessment), and these obligations continued to be mandatory by law. Most religious societies even continued to call these assessments "taxes," despite the fact that religious—not civil—institutions now collected them. Regardless of each state's guarantee that no one would pay taxes to support a minister of a different religious tradition, the law still determined how individuals should withdraw from parishes. Sometimes, the criteria for membership might place individuals in parishes without their consent. Because states and towns continued to set these criteria, people did not always enjoy the right to define church membership for themselves on their own terms. In this sense, the old system of compulsory support persisted with only slight modifications. Parish laws supported a partnership between churches and towns that privileged territorial parishes and their ministers. By granting those ministers public funding and property, the states favored the Congregationalist assumption that a minister served all the people in his town, converted and unconverted alike. More importantly, they continued to envision religious life playing out over a town-church topography.

If we define disestablishment as the cessation of ministerial taxes, it is easy to pinpoint when it happened in each state: 1807, 1819, 1820. But if we define disestablishment more broadly by looking at how states attached churches and ministers to parishioners and property, the process becomes more complex and difficult to untangle.[144] The northern New England states, though they unquestionably embraced religious liberty and refused to endorse any particular denomination, did not fully break the ties between church and state. The end of ministerial taxation left a wake of ambiguous laws and court decisions, which raised knotty questions about the relationships among citizens, churches, and governments. New laws transferred responsibility for religious fundraising from town to parish, but the states continued to define parishes and delineate their corporate powers to manage membership and property. By classifying different kinds of parishes—and assigning them different privileges to claim public lands and town funds—the states created a hierarchy of wealth, privilege, and authority among territorial and poll parishes. As they did so, legislatures and courts proved hesitant to sever completely the longstanding alliance between church and state.

This relationship reflected a continued preference for the town parish over the poll parish. Lawmakers adamantly denied that they favored one denomination over others, and their proclamations of religious equality were most likely sincere. But as long as towns and states allocated church funds and property, the town church would retain its legal privilege. And this legal privilege meant that some version of establishment persisted—one that came to embody a much more complicated dynamic between religious and civil authorities. So indelible was the town church's imprint on northern New England's religious landscape by the early nineteenth century that the states could not easily reshape its contours.

The remnants of establishment would eventually fail to preserve the town church as the prevailing model of religious community. Changes in church membership and styles of religious organization, along with continued migration and instability among northern New England's population, ultimately remapped the region's religious culture. So, too, did the laity's insistence on creating religious communities of their own designs. But these shifts would take place in spite of—not because of—legislative change. Ultimately, a transformation in religious life and culture in northern New England set in motion an extra-legal disestablishment that rendered lawful restrictions weak or moot.

4 'Tis All on Fire

Landscapes of Religious Community

To SUGGEST THAT "religious community" was a contested ideal in northern New England would be an understatement. The states had long been in the dubious business of attaching people to parishes. And as new religious groups planted roots in the region, they, too, tried to steer inhabitants into spiritual communities bounded by denominational lines. But however the states or the clergy organized parishes and tried to impose expectations for religious life, the laity did not always defer to those demands. Their wide-ranging spiritual inclinations operated just as powerfully on northern New England's religious geography.[1] Rather than follow the maps that churchly and political authorities drew for them, the laity plotted their own religious geography in the hinterland.

Such was the case with Joanna French, a New Hampshire Congregationalist who found herself too ill to attend church one June morning in 1817. Having missed Sabbath worship the day before and still feeling "very unwell," she skipped the monthly concert of prayer in her town of Epping. Recuperating at home, she felt isolated, "unworthy," and "stupid," but she consoled herself with thoughts of the concert of prayer: a day designated each month for New England's Protestants to pray for revival. The tradition was relatively recent—introduced in her town only a year before—but churchgoers welcomed the addition to the schedule of Sabbath meetings, midweek lectures, and communion seasons that already filled their calendars. French had learned that concerts of prayer had prompted revivals in nearby Raymond and Exeter. Knowing that believers around the state and beyond had convened at the same time and for the same purpose buoyed her spirits. "O will it not be animating to reflect," she asked, "that thousands are assembling (though but few in a town) to pray for the outpouring of the spirit?" Even as a homebound invalid, she, too, felt part of the assembly.[2]

For French, the concert of prayer represented not just another opportunity for worship but also a chance to forge spiritual union with other believers. It spoke to her own understanding of religious community: whether participants prayed in the same church, the same town, or distant corners of New England, the common enterprise of worship connected them. Although the clergy supported concerts of prayer wholeheartedly, they probably did not intend these meetings to supplant local churches. But French, whose daily spiritual life had turned dull and whose church had descended into listless inertia, sought communion both among her neighbors and among the untold thousands whose piety inspired her. She was not rejecting her town church. Rather, she was augmenting it, exploring spiritual outlets as she situated herself within a religious community partly of her own making.

Northern New England's inhabitants tackled religious community-building with no small degree of creativity. A dynamic of mobility coursed through the region's towns, churches, and families. Geographic movement was certainly not unique to northern New England; as elsewhere, migrants came for many reasons, but economic factors played the largest role. Maine drew poor migrants from Massachusetts port towns who hoped to escape postwar economic stagnation. Many farming families who faced debt, high taxes, and foreclosure in Connecticut and western Massachusetts followed the Connecticut River Valley north to New Hampshire and Vermont, hoping to find cheaper land and markets for their labor.[3] Other influences also came into play, like the extended networks of relatives and friends who preceded each other in migration and guided each other's choices about where to settle. And missionaries, preachers, and religious seekers looked to the northern frontier as a vast spiritual vacuum waiting to be filled. Whatever their reasons, migrants to northern New England headed to remote settlements, only to find themselves surrounded by others who had done the same.

How, then, to forge spiritual ties and create religious communities? Sectarian hierarchies, town churches, and itinerant routes all played their parts, but we cannot understand northern New England's religious geography without examining the laity's role in creating it. Seekers found religious experiences in meetinghouses but also in homes, forests, and fields. Their secular and religious lives intermingled. So did institutional and lived religion, which took shape both in conflict and in concert with each other. Lived religion—all the ways in which people derived spiritual meaning from their surroundings—meshed seamlessly with the stuff of everyday life.[4] The clergy and laity were neither inherently at odds nor mutually reinforcing: they could be either or both. What is important is that they engaged each other in a complex conversation about the nature of religiosity. As they negotiated the meanings of practice and prayer, northern New Englanders navigated a religious culture that encompassed their diverse spiritualities.[5]

The laity did not speak with one voice. They affiliated with many denominations and embraced doctrines and rituals that varied among and within religious groups. They mapped out spiritual worlds that coincided with and transcended sectarian geographies. The private domain of personal piety bled into local communities, which forged bonds of shared faith. But many believers who felt surrounded by strangers looked beyond their town lines when they joined virtual spiritual networks. Atop the town-church and itinerant systems, the laity superimposed its own religious geography, which coalesced in concentric circles around individuals, families, towns, and the region. The overlap between lay and sectarian geographies profoundly shaped northern New England's emerging religious culture.

Personal piety—individual collections of spiritual beliefs and habits—moored religious experience and stood at the hub of believers' spiritual maps. Layfolk nurtured piety through private reading, prayer, and devotion; they expressed it by attending church, debating doctrine, and exploring belief in speech and writing. Churchgoers and the unchurched alike gleaned doctrines and rituals from what they read and heard. They encountered diverse sectarian offerings, a wide-ranging print culture, and a social world that offered all manner of secular distractions. They negotiated with each other and the clergy over the meaning of practices, the necessity of public worship, and the content of devotional texts. From these influences, they constructed religious identities from complex and often contradictory sets of beliefs and behaviors, which defined their relationships to ministers, churches, and a wider network of believers and abstainers.

At the core of personal piety lay individual knowledge of—or attempts to know—God. Christians and hopeful converts tried to achieve godly experiences in many ways: through reading the Bible, attending worship, taking communion, and consulting with ministers, to name a few. As they did so, they came to embrace particular doctrines and rituals that best fit their sensibilities, but they also forged new spiritual paths when personal belief demanded it.

Among the most important private expressions of belief was secret prayer. Believers who obeyed the scriptural injunction to "enter into thy closet" to pray engaged in silent meditation to restore their spirits and commune with a divine audience.[6] Secret prayer, along with family and communal prayer, formed a triad of worship that structured people's spiritual lives, each piece complementing the others in method and purpose.[7] In private devotions, the language of prayer was less important than its authenticity; whereas well-chosen words could mask impiety in public, secret prayer laid one bare before God. As one minister pointed out, words "are of no consequence, when we appear in *secret* before the prayer-hearing God, who attends not to the language of the *lips*, but to the voice of the heart."[8] Because of its solitary nature, secret prayer was at once the hardest form of worship to undertake and the easiest to forgo. But that was the point; secret prayer was meant to impress no one, to bolster no one's pious reputation, but rather to allow "an intercourse and communication between the invisible God and the soul."[9]

Those who were spiritually troubled or yearning relied on secret prayer to shore up their piety. Joanna French, having sunk into a low spiritual state, longed for "former experiences in which I got near to God in secret prayer," when "the meditation . . . was sweet and . . . removed all slavish fear."[10] Abigail Bailey also sought solace in private devotions. A New Hampshire settler caught in an abusive marriage, Bailey lived too far from her church to attend meetings. So she retreated to her "retired room" for secret prayer at least twice each day. When her unconverted husband asked why, she explained that she "esteemed it a great privilege to seek to God by prayer at any time, and at all times [and that] we were commanded to pray always—to pray without ceasing."[11] By doing so, she could find peace that her daily life did not afford.

For many seekers, their natural surroundings intensified secret prayer. The woods could be a place of revelation, as they were for Betsey Carroll, who settled in "the wilderness" of northwestern Vermont. There, "in the deep silence of the primeval forest," she enjoyed "the most delightful seasons in reading the Bible and in prayer."[12] New Hampshire churchgoer Sarah Livermore suggested to a friend in Massachusetts that her state's remote location and rustic landscape inspired more devotion than the "hustle and bustle of less retired situations." In New Hampshire, she thought, "a solemn silence pervades the whole scenery of nature," and "we wish to be in union with everything around."[13] With physical isolation in a wilderness setting, she thought, came the private space to commune with divine creation. For seekers and converts, whose spiritual lives played out in northern New England's woods, gorges, and river valleys, the landscape meshed seamlessly with their religious sensibilities.

The ethereal calm of secret prayer might even spark conversion. Churched or unchurched, one's religious identity hinged on whether one had undergone conversion: the pinnacle of individual religious experience. Although each denomination understood original sin, election, and salvation differently, they mostly agreed that an unbeliever could attain salvation only by surrendering to God and undergoing a cataclysmic conversion experience. Conversion could happen quickly or after years of yearning and backsliding, and it followed a consistent pattern across sectarian lines. During a period of preparation—which included intense prayer, religious reading, and spiritual conversation—the hopeful convert gained a sense of his or her own sin. This awareness deepened as desperate shame, feelings of contempt toward God, and utter hopelessness at the prospect of salvation overcame the prospective convert. Despair gave way to hope as she came to realize that the only way to be saved was to submit completely to Christ. With surrender came justification (the removal of original sin), regeneration (entry into the state of grace), and the abandonment of the saint's former self.[14]

The conversion process was largely a private ordeal, known only to the convert and perhaps a few confidants.[15] The journey could seem endless. Nathaniel Cheever of Hallowell, Maine, waited four years from when he first gained "a sense of my situation" to when he perceived "a work of heavenly grace operating on my heart."[16] Elijah Fisk of Levant, New Hampshire, remarked in 1830 that he had "bin in a strange way ever since 1805." At times, he found that his "passions often are raised so high of grief and joy mingled together that it is almost impossible . . . to contain myself in the meeting house." But he still had doubts. "I should need a greater evidence than common," he imagined, "before I can believe that I have met with a saveing change."[17] James Wentworth of New Hampshire spent most of his youth struggling with a conversion that began before he turned ten years old and proceeded in fits and starts, punctuated by moments of crisis: a violent storm, the death of one sister, the conversion of another. After he witnessed a religious revival at the age of twenty-one, he renewed his efforts. More backsliding followed until the next year, when another revival refocused his attention. In a moment of panic, he "looked up and saw . . . a God who seemed to be angry with me and If I looked down I saw a gaping hell . . . ready to devour me." The next day, he went "to the wilderness" to pray for evidence of his conversion and finally received it in the form of an inner peace.[18] Converts found that seething doubt eventually gave way to confidence—but for many, this transformation occurred at the end of a grueling journey.

Many found that the trials of doubt and faith outlasted the initial conversion process, especially Methodists and Freewill Baptists, who maintained that believers could backslide out of the state of grace. Some endured so much emotional trauma that they contemplated suicide. Joel Winch, who began to "experience religion" at the age of eleven, spent over a decade backsliding and returning to faith as he drifted between churches. Unsatisfied with his conversion to Congregationalism and overcome with spiritual isolation, he "was temted to Kill myself" with a razor blade, but he believed God stopped him from doing so. When he finally communed with the Methodists two years later, he "felt Heaven flowing into my soul."[19] James Wentworth, who eventually joined the Freewill Baptists, experienced a similar crisis. During an 1827 journey to Vermont, he sank into a depression as he grappled with a nagging call to preach. He pondered suicide twice: once during a sojourn into the woods and again as he crossed a bridge over a steep chasm. Only then did he feel "a stream of light" that convinced him of God's presence, and the suicidal yearnings ceased.[20] Most converts likely did not ponder such drastic steps, but they did confront despair and self-doubt. Furthermore, these spiritual transformations served as the pinnacle of private piety for those who experienced them. More than providing fuel for revivals and foundations for church-gathering, conversions also opened doors to private spiritual worlds.

Converted or not, most of northern New England's seekers expressed private belief by choosing a faith: adhering to a particular denomination and whatever version of Protestant doctrine they believed correct. Laypeople asserted their prerogative to decide such matters for themselves. Sarah Livermore maintained that Christians could arrive at their beliefs through rational inquiry. "We have a preached and written word," she explained, and sufficient "understanding to practice according to its divine precepts." By listening to sermons and reading the Bible, Livermore suggested, each churchgoer could select the doctrines he or she favored. "If we do not," she added, "the fault is ours."[21] In fact, anecdotal evidence suggests that most who chose a faith cited substance more than style as the reason. Doctrine, then, figured among the core elements of religious belief and identity.

Layfolk did not shy away from doctrinal debates, particularly when they clashed with their own churches. In 1799, a group of Mount Desert, Maine, Congregationalists asked to be re-baptized "by plunging." One of their number, David Wasgatt, explained that he "never was satisfied with his infant baptism." The church pointed out that Congregationalists did not sanction baptism by immersion and asked Wasgatt why he did not join the nearby Baptist church—to which he replied that he "could not put up with the close communion."[22] Others tried to blend new practices with old. Job Seamans, the Baptist minister of New London, New Hampshire, was surprised to find that "the washing of feet was under consideration amongst some of the members of the church." Foot-washing, a practice favored by Methodists and Freewill Baptists, was not part of regular Baptist worship—and yet Seamans's parishioners had already "had 1 or 2 conferences upon the subject," without his knowledge, by the time he found out.[23] Believers who assembled doctrine piecemeal posed a particular challenge to ministers, because they threatened to upend the rational underpinnings of religious practice.

But such creativity was exceptional. Rather than mix and match doctrines to their liking, most believers found spiritual homes in religious movements that meshed with their leanings, and they openly contested other denominations. Laity tended to be quite specific about their preferences. Solomon Bunnel of South Hero, Vermont, announced to his Congregationalist church in 1806 that he had rejected the Calvinist doctrine of election. "It does not feel to me," Bunnel explained, "that [God] Dooms any Infants (not capable of knowing good and evil) to eternal condemnation."[24] Dissenters also railed against infant baptism. Nashti Bingham sought to leave the Cornish (New Hampshire) Congregational Church in 1803 and join the Baptists because she had experienced a "change in sentiment" that convinced her that infant baptism was unscriptural. When her church demanded that she discuss the matter, she declined, insisting "the best way for me was to read the word seriously and ask the wisdom of god to direct me in the matter."[25] Elizabeth and Kenelm Winslow, Freewill Baptists of Lewiston, Maine, similarly requested a dismission from the New Durham Quarterly Meeting in 1790 on doctrinal grounds. "We cant stand in Fellowship with you," they explained, because "you Deny Election and the Perseverance of the Saints . . . [and] we believe the Lord knows his own." Freewill Baptists held that no salvation was secure, but the Winslows favored the Calvinist view that salvation, once conferred, was permanent.[26] Seeking answers in scripture, believers articulated defenses for newfound faith.

Religious identity could change over time, as became clear in church records that noted the comings and goings of members who chose new denominations. The First Congregational Church of Bangor, Maine, accepted former Baptists and Methodists, and the New London (New Hampshire) Baptist Church lost members to the Universalists and Freewill Baptists.[27] In one year, the Voluntary Congregational Society of Chelsea, Vermont, lost five members to the Universalists and four to the Baptists.[28] In its first three years, the Freewill Baptist Monthly Meeting of Springfield, Vermont, lost at least seventeen members to the Methodists.[29] And for decades, Congregationalists and Baptists in Woolwich, Maine, forged a two-way path between their respective churches as they traded sentiments and memberships.[30] One Baptist missionary wearied of the flux. "They say they want to go to heaven," he reported, "but they are determined to go their own way, or not at all."[31] But despite his impressions of fickle churchgoers, few truly decided to go "their own way." Believers rarely embraced a freethinking impulse to reject dogma; rather, they traded one spiritual authority for another as they sought doctrines that best fit their personal religious sensibilities.

Just as belief tapped into different faiths and doctrines, so too did behavior, which included participation in rituals and other visible religious expressions. The most obvious religious behavior was church attendance, but attendance did not necessarily correlate with belief. Regular worshipers tried to attend churches that reflected their religious views, or at least offered palatable substitutes. But most northern New Englanders were not regular churchgoers. Some abstained entirely, others attended sporadically, and still others alternated among other churches' meetings and their own.[32] Sometimes a churchgoer's choice to join or reject a congregation reflected social and political divisions in his town. Daniel Prouty requested a dismission from the Universalist Church in Langdon, New Hampshire, in 1811 because he could not "feel free to Set Down in Communion with John Sartwell," another member. The church granted Prouty's dismission and issued an open invitation to him to return "when he Can feel free to . . . walk in fellowship with the Church."[33] Similar conflicts drove believers to competing faiths. In 1820, the Sedgwick (Maine) Congregational Church admitted William Gray, a Baptist who had lost a property dispute with a fellow Baptist. When he accused his adversary of "swearing to what was false," the Baptist church excommunicated him.[34] Gray's desire to take part in any religious community outweighed his attachment to Baptist doctrine. When complicating factors intervened, even a pious church member might make unexpected choices.

Layfolk frequently visited other churches out of curiosity or necessity, even if they also attended regular preaching in their own faith. Freewill Baptist minister William Babcock reported in 1803 that he had just preached a Sabbath sermon "to Deists, Calvinists, and Quakers—Backsliders, Freewillers, unconverted, and Nothingists—O my soul what a medley."[35] Such diverse audiences were common, and exposure to new movements could lead a believer to question his own faith. Congregationalist minister Stephen Peabody visited a parishioner who was "almost beside himself on acct. of his having attended . . . meetings of the Baptists Methodists, etc. etc." Peabody advised him to be "not too hasty in determining upon any thing," but he worried that fickle churchgoing might weaken the man's resolve.[36] More commonly, though, visiting other churches simply allowed more chances to worship. The Methodists often drew outsiders like sisters Betsey and Mary Barrell, Congregationalists in York, Maine, who attended a camp meeting in 1829. According to their aunt Charlotte Cheever, the sisters had reported that "a great solemnity pervaded the whole scene," and guessed that many conversions resulted from the gathering.[37] Believers like the Barrell sisters freely attended other churches, supplementing their usual meetings with additional activities because all of these outlets were available. Fluid behavior did not shake firm religious identities.

While some attended church erratically or sampled from different denominations, others abstained almost entirely. After Sarah Livermore observed many empty pews on a typical Sunday in Wilton, New Hampshire, she suggested that "if [the abstainers'] hearts were not harder than flint, such excellent preaching might bring them to see the evil of their ways."[38] Samuel Goddard became quite discouraged about the state of religion in Maidstone, Vermont, after he struggled to gather just a few worshipers there. He had announced his four o'clock meeting and waited over an hour for hearers, but only "the two families which lived in the house where I preached" showed up. He was especially irked at the "number of men collected at a blacksmith's shop a few rod distance, and idle."[39] The *Religious Intelligencer* made light of poor church attendance by printing a humorous catalog of reasons why respectable Christians might skip worship, including such excuses as "Stump'd my great toe," "Can't leave the house for fear of fire," and "Letters to write to my friends." And, for the especially sheepish: "Snored aloud last time I was there—shan't risk it again."[40] As this light-hearted ribbing implied, and countless ministers' complaints corroborated, non-attendance was rampant.

Attendance and belief—and failure at both—often went hand-in-hand. Hiram Harwood of Bennington, Vermont, rarely attended church, much to his devout family's chagrin. And when he did, he often brought books or newspapers to pass the time, and sometimes "easily and unconsciously dropped into a pleasant sleep." He shrugged off his family's criticisms, remarking that "no one can make himself a christian."[41] Lois Gould of Greenfield, New Hampshire, admitted in 1831 that she had skipped worship "for eight or nine years" because she had been "too cold in religion [and had] not shown all that interest and made those efforts to attend, as I ought."[42] The Congregational Church, with apparently little debate, restored her to full standing. But it is even more noteworthy that they had not sought Gould for disciplinary proceedings in the previous eight or nine years. As egregious as her violation was, it seems to have caused little alarm and attracted little attention. By backsliding for years and returning to the fold, Gould typified frontier inhabitants who commonly drifted in and out of religious communities.

Some of the unchurched were simply undecided. Religious pluralism confounded many who wanted a spiritual home but could not find the right fit. William Babcock met a man who explained that "he wished to have Religion, if he knew which way was right, but there were so many."[43] A woman near Blue Hill, Maine, told Jonathan Fisher that she "was entertaining a hope" but was "not satisfied with either of the three denominations" that held worship in her town.[44] She joined many other pious unchurched people who could not find a group to match their spiritual needs but remained confident in the state of their souls. One woman wrote to her sister that "I am perfectly easy in my mind with regard to the salvation of my *soul,*" even though she had not "wept and spoke in public, been wash'd by a priest and joined a church." Such rituals, she thought, were unnecessary to salvation, and she found nothing in "christ's testament to induce a belief of their importance."[45] Without a minister or church to guide her (whether by her own choosing or accident of residence), she had relied on biblical reading and private reflection to order her spiritual world. Unchurched did not necessarily mean impious.

Habits of worship only weakly reflected one's religious leanings because church attendance stemmed from many variables that had little to do with affiliation. To discern how laypeople constructed religious identities, we must look beyond institutions to other contexts. The laity engaged in many activities that both intersected with and transcended institutions. They read and wrote, interacted socially with the clergy, and even engaged in lay exhortation and mysticism. Typically "unchurched" behavior like dancing, playing cards, and reading novels can also shed light on religious identity, because believers had to reconcile their worldly pursuits with their spiritual aspirations. Taken together, the laity's extra-institutional behavior interwove popular culture and individual spirituality with belief to create religious experience.[46]

Religious reading revealed much about how northern New England's laity vested the written word with spiritual meaning. Literacy endowed readers with agency in their spiritual lives. Not only did it confer the ability to read the Bible and other devotional texts directly; it also bestowed the power to negotiate the meanings of these texts.[47] Literate habits, however, are notoriously tricky to pin down. It is one thing to catalog the books, pamphlets, and periodicals that scattered about New England's hinterlands or the reams of letters and countless diaries that layfolk tucked away or shared with confidants. It is another matter entirely to figure out who produced or consumed these materials, how they understood them, and where reading and writing fit into the wider scope of their spiritual lives.[48] We do know that literacy shaped most New Englanders' lives—more so than it did those of other Americans. Given the Puritans' emphasis on reading the Bible, New England had long required nearly universal primary education; thus, the region's literacy rates had, since early in the colonial period, surpassed those elsewhere in British North America and the United States.[49] Northern New England was slower to provide public schooling than southern New England, but even there, literacy rates generally exceeded 90 percent for men and 80 percent for women.[50] It is likely, therefore, that reading figured into most people's religious experiences.

Northern New Englanders shared a religious print culture that, to borrow from historian Candy Gunther Brown, was made up of "a distinctive set of writing, publishing, and reading practices" premised on the potential of the Bible, doctrine, and religious news to draw far-flung Christians together.[51] They benefited from a printing industry that grew rapidly during the early republic, thanks in part to new commercial markets and transportation networks that extended into the backcountry.[52] Increasingly, traveling ministers peddled tracts, periodicals, and Bibles along with spiritual counsel. They hoped religious media would foster habits of active reading and spiritual reflection—and that sales and subscriptions would keep their denominations afloat.[53] But what we know about how and why ministers distributed printed materials tells us little about how the laity actually used them. Laypeople read privately, beyond the watch of the clergy or anyone else who might hope to influence how they digested and responded to what they read. Largely conducted outside the bounds of formal worship, private reading figured in a mosaic of extra-institutional activities that framed piety and religious experience.

Layfolk often approached reading as private seekers, absorbing bits of news and doctrine and filtering them through their own experiences and inclinations. By all accounts, they snapped up religious literature whenever they could. Joseph Field observed as much when, on an 1805 tour of Maine, he stocked libraries and filled requests from "a number of men desirous of books."[54] The Baptist Church of Greene, Maine, informed the Maine Bible Society in 1811 "of the deficiency of bibles in the town."[55] Elijah and Hannah Batchelder and David Hammond, all of Georgetown, Maine, also sought Bibles. "If you have aney Bibles to dispose of to the poor," they wrote in 1812 to the Massachusetts Bible Society, "we think our selves as much a deed of Cherity as a most aney you can bestow uppon."[56] Readers also sought newspaper subscriptions; the Freewill Baptist *Religious Informer* reported that its subscriptions jumped from 140 to 800 in the latter half of 1819, its inaugural year.[57] Through such requests, readers made clear their demands.

Many readers sought out Bibles and religious literature to edify the spirit and engage the soul. One New Hampshire churchgoer studied the Bible to jar herself into serious introspection. Fearing her own "wicked heart," she examined the fourth chapter of Hebrews and prayed "to be earnestly engaged for the salvation of my soul." She remained spiritually listless, so she turned to books by well-known theologians for inspiration: "O for the zeal of a Davis or a Doddridge," she wished, "to warm my frozen soul."[58] This woman may have feared her efforts were for naught, but others found that reading paid spiritual dividends. After years of living as a "great sinner," Congregationalist Nathaniel Cheever of Hallowell, Maine, believed his conversion sprung from reading "with attention and . . . a desire of improvement much of God's Holy Scripture." His concerted study "served to confirm my faith" and produced "this happy effect on my own immortal soul."[59] As Cheever found, reading could inspire hope for one's own salvation and perhaps bring it about.

Many layfolk read not to bolster their faith but to challenge it. One Maine churchgoer, a lukewarm Congregationalist, began to read "sermons written by Arminians" when his neighbors (lacking a minister) decided to conduct their own Sabbath meetings. He continued with wide-ranging selections: Universalist tracts by Elhanan Winchester, histories of religion and doctrine by Hannah Adams, and discourses on "the Quaker sistem of religion." Dissatisfied, he turned to the Bible, which "now appeared to be my best companion and the study of it my greatest delight." Reading the Bible led him to convert to Baptism.[60] Joel Winch, whose father subscribed to the town-church library in Hartland, Vermont, read many devotional texts as a youth, including several volumes of sermons and some of Philip Doddridge's writings. Then, he came upon a copy of the Methodist *Discipline*. Reading that book sped along his eventual conversion to Methodism.[61] Both of these men eventually became ministers—but not in the faith in which they were raised. For each, religious reading guided an odyssey to an unexpected destination.

Just as religious reading allowed churchgoers to construct private spiritual worlds, religious writing gave shape to those worlds by allowing writers to record, scrutinize, and even create religious experiences. Diarists wrote of daily routines punctuated by worship, struggles with spiritual coldness, hopes for awakening, and musings over doctrine and chapters of scripture they had heard or read. By addressing these topics along with day-to-day minutiae, diarists integrated the godly and the mundane as they worked out their spiritual identities.[62]

In settings where church attendance was sporadic and religious institutions weak, diarists often wrote of feeling isolated in a godless world. The realities of settlement—transience, poverty, and a dearth of churches—amplified the effects of apparent moral decline. John Clark, a recent migrant to Vermont, joined a small and struggling lay society in the 1780s but observed that most of his neighbors were unchurched. "In my daily intercourse among men," he recalled later, "I found evidence of the desparate deceitfulness and wickedness of the Human Heart."[63] Stephen Bemis, a Dartmouth student and part-time schoolteacher, tired of the "immoral, irreligious, [and] disspirited people" he encountered. "Such Sundays I never saw before," he bemoaned.[64] Others complained that their towns were "cold," "stupid," and "lamentable," populated by "impenitent sinners" who said "nothing . . . upon the subject of religion."[65] Far from finding solace in a covenanted community, these writers portrayed themselves as islands of faith in a godless sea. They defined themselves not by the bonds that tied them to other churchgoers but by the barriers between them and their unchurched neighbors.

In this spiritual solitude, diarists examined their souls for every stirring of piety. The Loudon, New Hampshire, churchgoer who scorned herself as a "backsliding daughter" with a "wicked deceitful heart" asked herself, "what progress do I make in religion?"[66] Phinehas Bailey of Waitsfield, Vermont, also wrestled with profane thoughts. "Can any person be a Christian," he asked, "who is so easily drawn from heavenly to worldly things" and whose thoughts "turn from religion to vanity?"[67] Joanna French agreed that even the most pious needed to guard against spiritual laxity. True piety demanded self-scrutiny. "O may all of us who have professed to be subjects of the new birth," she implored, "carefully examine ourselves and see whether we live new lives."[68] In their diaries, professors and hopeful converts did exactly that.

Diaries provided private space for introspection, but many people also expressed themselves publicly by preaching and exhorting. These two kinds of discourse differed in content and style. Sermons were formal addresses that expounded on Biblical texts, and exhortation was extemporaneous, aimed at converting the damned. Depending on the denomination, either the laity or the clergy could preach and exhort. But the unrehearsed style of exhortation especially suited the untrained laity, who spoke spontaneously in church or conference settings, camp meetings, field revivals, and prayer meetings.[69] The groups that supported lay preaching and exhortation—Freewill Baptists, Methodists, and regular Baptists—differed on proper training and licensing, the ideal settings for these activities, and whether women could speak.[70] But regardless of those distinctions, they held that lay speakers exercised a divinely inspired gift that others should heed.

Lay preachers and exhorters stirred religious fervor and challenged the unconverted to examine their hearts for signs of piety. The Methodists licensed lay exhorters, but unlicensed exhorters also appeared at love feasts, prayer meetings, and camp meetings, where they prodded backsliders to repent. Freewill Baptists endorsed lay preachers and exhorters "to certify that they have the fellowship of the Connection to which they belong" so they might "Improve [their] gift[s] any where and in any way which God may from time to time call" them.[71] But most exhorters were not certified; they spoke when inspiration struck. The New Durham Yearly Meeting set aside time during its gatherings for lay exhortation, when any church member had "the privilege of relating what they have seen of the displays of divine power where they have travelled, and every brother or sister enjoy the same privilege."[72] Baptists allowed unlicensed lay exhorters to speak as they saw fit. The Sanford (Maine) Baptist Church, for instance, urged "any Brother to speak in public if he thinks he is moved by the Spirit of God."[73] After Baptist itinerant Henry Hale preached at an 1807 meeting in Falmouth, Maine, "a number exhorted and prayed, [and] this was a wonderful season of divine power indeed."[74] Lay preaching and exhortation imbued meetings with a fervor that a minister preaching alone could rarely impart.

For women in particular, exhortation afforded a public outlet to voice spiritual passions. Despite Biblical injunctions to "let your women keep silence in the churches" and "suffer not a woman to teach," many denominations skirted these prohibitions by distinguishing between preaching and exhortation. Preaching was public teaching (a man's domain), but exhortation allowed any Christian to exercise her "public gift." In keeping with the scriptural imperative that "your sons and your daughters shall prophesy," many argued that any Christian had license to testify to the workings of her soul.[75] The Baptist Church in Londonderry, New Hampshire, maintained that "women are not to be received as public Teachers, yet they may improve the Gift of Exhortation and prayer in subjection to the Chh."[76] William Babcock drew a similar distinction when a churchgoer confessed that she had wished to speak during worship but did not know if she should. He explained that "Praying and Exhorting Publickly; and preaching and Church government were different gifts, the first two being equally bestowed on all Believers as God saw fit, and the two last Women had no right to meddle with." Babcock urged her to speak "if the Lord should give her the Spirit again," to which she agreed.[77] A fine line separated preaching from exhortation. By distinguishing between them, religious movements allowed for spiritual equality while still reserving doctrinal authority for the male clergy.

Many women enjoyed acceptance, and even renown, as exhorters. The Pittsfield (New Hampshire) Freewill Baptist Church noted that Molly Savage "gave us some Comferting discourse" during a 1794 monthly meeting, which she followed with a "very weighty word of Exhortation" at the New Durham Yearly Meeting later that year.[78] Enoch Place encountered several women at prayer meetings who "exhorted with understanding and edification." One confessed that she "had known religion for many years but never felt as she did now in opening her mind to others."[79] Methodists like Nancy Caldwell, Fanny Newell, and Anna Nickerson also gained fame as exhorters; a minister described the latter as having "a peculiar gift to speak of her religious views and experience."[80] And some women established preaching careers despite the controversy over that calling. Sally Parsons, a Freewill Baptist, itinerated throughout New Hampshire and Maine, often traveling with Elder Benjamin Randel, delivering sermons at prayer meetings and conferences.[81] Clarissa Danforth, one of the best-known female preachers of the early nineteenth century, embarked on several preaching tours during the 1810s and 1820s. In June 1821, she preached at the yearly meeting in Weare, New Hampshire, and then traveled to Candia, where she preached alongside Elders Mark Fernald and John Buzzell. During a preaching tour in Maine, one of her hearers informed Elder Ephraim Stinchfield that she "Had good Lebearty in preaching."[82] Despite official injunctions against women preachers, these women often found receptive audiences.

Preaching and exhortation allowed women to act in a quasi-institutional role, supporting churchly authority even as they defied its strictures. So, too, did charismatic episodes, which included trances, dreams, and fits during which subjects saw angels, heard divine messages, and uttered prophecy.[83] Congregationalists categorically disapproved of visionary behavior. One missionary watched with unease as two sisters collapsed in "Convulsion fits" during a Sabbath meeting in Trenton, Maine. He had recently scolded one of the sisters for an unnamed offense, which raised suspicion that the fits were a deliberate attempt to disrupt worship.[84] Most visionary behavior occurred among the radical denominations, though it was not always welcome. Enoch Place, on a preaching tour in Maine and New Hampshire, saw a young woman fall "out of her Chair, as one dieing" during a meeting. Witnesses brought the woman to a bed, where she "lay for Some time apparently in great distress," until she "came to and praised the lord." Not long afterward, Place met Sister Mack, a Freewill Baptist from Old York, Maine, who had begun to see "Strange apparition[s]." Although Place respected the intense religiosity that fueled these visions, he hoped they would pass. "It appears she has got into a great extreem of earnestness and a firy Zeal," he thought, "which I hope she will change for a holy Zeal for the Lord of Hosts."[85]

Among the more notorious visionary incidents was the "Angel Delusion," which took place in Springfield, Vermont, between 1805 and 1811.[86] At the eye of the storm were William Babcock and his wife, Betsy Merrill Babcock, who reported having "manifestations" in which an angel shared divine messages. Betsy's dreams brought the couple together. As a single minister ripe for marriage, William heard "Sister Betsy Merrill tell her Dream of the Camp Meeting" in 1805. For months, William took notes as Betsy entered trancelike states in which she spoke "very sensibly" before "labouring some time, heaving her breast, as if much oppressed, breathing very short, . . . sighing and groaning," and falling into a deep sleep. Riveted, and not a little jealous of Betsy's gift, William proposed marriage.[87]

Their household became the center of a charismatic movement that transfixed the church and nearby towns. The angel visited not only Betsy but also a small circle of women who related his (often contradictory) revelations in sensational episodes.[88] Before long, Babcock's followers sought the angel's advice on matters ranging from finance and travel to doctrine, discipline, and church polity. The angel told William (through Betsy) when to preach, whether to buy land, and how to phrase his church's declaration of faith. He also saw Betsy through three difficult pregnancies that bore even more difficult results: a miscarriage and two sons who died in infancy. Finally, the angel stoked local tensions, first by advising William against befriending Clarissa Danforth and then by accusing several parishioners of immoral conduct.[89] After the Babcocks' son Joshua was born in 1810, the visions slowed to a halt. In their wake, the troubled Springfield-Fishersfield Monthly Meeting broke up. The Babcocks sold their farm and moved to Barrington, New Hampshire, where William, his reputation in tatters, retired from preaching.[90]

These visionary episodes were private spiritual moments when the subject saw and heard only heavenly beings and godly decrees. But they took place in a public context and had broader implications for religious communities. A visionary —especially a woman who was otherwise excluded from churchly roles—could upend a church by detracting attention from ministers and formal worship.[91] Sometimes, a church might tire of a visionary and wish to restore proper order. But in cases like Betsy Babcock's, a visionary might supplant the local church as the center of spiritual authority. Whereas critics derided these incidents as products of emotional frailty or overactive imaginations, those who trusted the visions insisted that they were physical manifestations of true faith and a divine presence.

From public worship to readership to mystical fits, churchgoers drew on a long menu of religious behaviors that informed and expressed their spiritual identities. But even the most observant church member did not live in a vacuum. Although the pious tried to shut out secular distractions, their communities included taverns alongside churches, novels alongside Bibles, and dances alongside prayer meetings. Whatever their views of worldly amusements, northern New Englanders negotiated permeable boundaries between their secular and spiritual lives.

Drinking, dancing, card-playing, and the like quickly became marks of impiety during the early nineteenth century, but they had not always been so. Through the late eighteenth century, many ministers thought little of (moderately) enjoying worldly pleasures. Congregationalist Stephen Peabody drank and socialized often with his parishioners in Atkinson, New Hampshire. After a 1785 Thanksgiving service, he shared "a drink of flip" and then "drank and had an excellent entertainment" while "the young people met and had a fiddle and a dance."[92] But many factors conspired to end these gatherings. Newer denominations shunned secular diversions, and as the temperance movement gained force, even moderate Congregationalist ministers urged churchgoers to refrain from activities they had condoned only a few years before.[93] Increasingly, ministers and layfolk fiercely debated the proper limits of such behavior.

Despite warnings to abstain, many churchgoers sampled worldly amusements.[94] Betsey Carroll of Vermont, her religious conversion well underway, nonetheless attended dances with her husband and "opened our doors for balls."[95] Eliza Bryant, a young parishioner in southern Maine, habitually skipped Sabbath worship and "stayed home a reading" fiction: romances and comedies such as Charlotte Smith's *The Old Manor House,* Elizabeth Inchbald's *Lovers' Vows,* and Eliza Parsons's *Women as They Are.*[96] Unlike sermons and serious literature, which critics argued could broaden the mind and elevate the spirit, novels promised fantasy and escape, and typically portrayed illicit romance that ended in moral collapse.[97] Carroll and Bryant appear to have escaped serious consequences for their transgressions, but others courted more severe punishments. Polly Phillips, a member of the Greene (Maine) Baptist Church, risked excommunication when she "joined in the world with their own amusements and recreation."[98] Churchgoers enrolled their children in dance classes, prompting at least one church to remind parents that "it was inconsistent with the duty of professors of religion to send their children to a dancing school."[99] Although many ministers dismissed such diversions as vain and godless, the laity took a more complex approach. That they joined in worship on the one hand and dances on the other suggests that the boundary between the two was never as fixed as churches and clergy might have wished.

Whereas some people either rejected or embraced religion definitively, most lived their lives in a hazy zone between perfect devotion and complete depravity. Many believers were ambivalent about drinking. Betsey and Timothy Carroll, having learned (like others raised before the nineteenth century) that alcohol preserved health, "supposed liquor was as essential as any other article for housekeeping." For over a decade after they joined a Methodist church, which demanded abstinence, the couple "continued to use spirituous liquors" daily. Only when Betsey feared Timothy's excessive drinking did she abstain and implore him to do the same (he complied).[100] Similarly, Nathan Fisk had been a Baptist believer for many years before he thought himself "fully prepared to go all lengths in entire absence." By that time, he had abstained for "nearly three years . . . unless I thought I really needed it."[101] Although clergy expected abstinence, believers balanced churchly edicts against the habits of everyday life.

Drinking was one of many practices that believers clung to, even if it seemed to preclude a godly life. Sarah Livermore insisted that most amusements posed no threat to piety. Although she agreed that card-playing could drag participants into "a licentious and dissipated course of life," the same did not hold true for other pastimes. Dancing and attending the theater, she thought, allowed respite from "the more intense application of the mind and body to mental pursuits and laborious exercise." She did not propose that entertainment should "encroach on the more important duties of religious, literary, or worldly pursuits." But surely a little levity had a place alongside piety. "Must a person to be religious," she asked, "cease to be joyful?"[102]

Livermore's rhetorical question points to the complex nature of religious identity. Members of religious communities were also members of secular communities. These identities continually overlapped and diverged. A churchgoer could adopt seemingly contradictory beliefs and behaviors—by reading novels along with tracts, or attending a dance one day and worship the next—with no injurious effect to his or her piety. Engaging in these practices, layfolk constructed religious worlds on their own terms. Spiritual identity comprised not just belief but also countless private decisions: to attend church or not; to sample different denominations or not; to seek spiritual fulfillment in meetinghouses, camp meetings, or forests; to read the Bible or novels; to drink, dance, or abstain. In the spaces where institutional and popular religion intersected, laypeople wove together the unruly strands of spiritual life into meaningful religious identities.

Personal piety formed the bedrock of religious experience, but a believer's religious life was never a wholly private affair. Churchgoers and the unchurched shaped each other's spiritual worlds by mingling in households and villages. Early republican society idealized well-ordered families as building blocks for well-ordered churches and towns. Settlers created religious communities that fanned out beyond church walls and the clergy's reach. Extra-institutional settings like family worship, reading circles, and prayer societies dominated churchgoers' religious experiences. These overlapping patches of family and neighborhood reoriented local communities so that they included, but did not revolve around, local churches.

Like the larger community, a typical family included believers, abstainers, and hopeful converts. According to an ideal of family governance, the father exercised authority over all who shared his home: his wife and children, hired hands, boarders, servants, and other relatives. As a spiritual unit, the family stood as a metaphor for the church, with a head leading the body and the whole united in prayer. But frontier life—marked by frequent migration and economic instability—offered few supports for pious families. As a religious community writ small, the family offered its own spiritual opportunities and challenges.

Where a precarious existence frayed neighborly ties, the family formed the foundation of religious life. As the *Christian Almanac* explained, "a family is a little community . . . and no community can prosper without religion."[103] Indeed, the household had long lain at the core of religious worship. In early New England, families acted in concert with churches and the state to enforce Puritan culture, which combined Calvinism with an ethical code of conduct and assumed a community's collective responsibility for its members' moral well-being. Each family (and especially each householder) was to create a home environment that nurtured and enforced the communal values of piety, obedience, and industry.[104] By doing so, they ensured that the intertwined moral and religious legacies of Puritanism would persist through the generations.

The challenges of religious pluralism, political upheaval, and economic insecurity underscored the family's importance in New England's religious culture. To make sure families remained godly instruments, the established and dissenting clergy alike promoted "family prayer" or "family worship," in which members of a household met at appointed times each day for prayer and other formal religious exercises. Family worship fulfilled different purposes than both public services and private prayer; it promoted individual piety, strengthened family governance, and tightened the connection between church and household.

Family worship took on particular significance in the northern frontier. Lacking ministers or congregations in many settlements, the home offered the best venue for regular prayer. Clergy of all denominations urged parents to attend to this duty. The West Shaftsbury (Vermont) Baptist Church proclaimed that all parents should "make their daily practice to call upon God's name by prayer with their families."[105] The New Durham Quarterly Meeting advised that "good Family Government may be universally set up and maintained in scriptural Love, faithfulness, and Strictness."[106] The General Convention of Universalists called on its members to "teach your children and domestics to reverence prayer."[107] Itinerants, too, urged families to pray, so they might set the best example for their children. Congregationalist Thomas Holt spent part of a mission teaching a "young married couple . . . the importance of personal family religion."[108] With instruction from missionaries, well-meaning couples could implement family prayer in their households and thereby lay the groundwork for healthy and vibrant religious communities.

Even in communities with organized churches family worship played a central role, because it reinforced the church's mission to safeguard public morality and piety. Accordingly, local churches reminded members to remain diligent in practicing family prayer. The Congregational Church in Jaffrey, New Hampshire, pledged that "in our families, we will Diligently Read or cause the word of God to be red and attend the same with sincerity of heart that it may dwell richly in us." The Union Church of Christ in Greenfield, New Hampshire, alerted its members to the "duty of family worship." Similarly, the Middlebury, Vermont, town church reminded churchgoers "who are heads of families" of their "indespensible duty . . . to maintain regularly family worship."[109] Families that gathered in prayer furthered their churches' interests by nurturing piety and maintaining moral governance.

But many clergy feared their efforts to encourage family worship fell short. Elder Ephraim Stinchfield lambasted Freewill Baptists in 1793 for "omit[ting] the worship of God in their families." He especially criticized those who claimed that they were "so full of the worries of the World, . . . they can't spend time all week" in family prayer. Nonsense, he proclaimed: "I cannot see how you are a going to manifest to your Families that you are a Christian, except in this way."[110] Nathan Douglas, a Congregationalist missionary, also complained about parents who raised children "to whom even the first principles of religion had never been taught."[111] Such negligence was inexcusable. Others feared that the failure of family worship boded poorly not just for religion but for communities. Stephen Bemis decried what he saw as the decline of the well-ordered family. "O Parents," he wailed, "you are destroying your own peace, ruining your children, and ruining society."[112] The Windham Ministerial Association, in more measured tones, pointed out that "family government is the basis of all government, and family religion of all religion." Where churches were often weak, ministers looked to the family to enforce moral standards. In the effort to maintain civil and godly order, they concluded, "we view FAMILY PRAYER to be of essential importance."[113]

An array of manuals and articles appeared to help families conduct worship. These guides spoke to well-meaning heads of households who did not know how, when, or why to gather the family in prayer. One manual, which urged parents to "no longer neglect a duty so plain and important," included special word for those who had "lately entered a family state" and did not know how to hold family prayer.[114] Another spoke to those who had "a rational conviction in the truth of religion" but "at the same time wish to have some assistance in this duty."[115] To help, guides provided prayers, sermons, hymns, and devotions for morning and evening services on Sabbath and weekdays, and suggestions for how to lead worship.[116] One manual directed families to worship twice daily at regular times, "that the family may be trained to punctuality and system." Worship should include servants and other household employees, "because they are immortal beings, who must be saved or lost forever." And prayer should be "fervent" and should "specify circumstances in which they are interested as a family" so as to make "their *common interests*" known to God.[117] Worshiping this way, writers hoped, would unite parents and children, strengthen family governance, and preserve a stabilizing force in a changing society.

Advice like this, however, was merely prescriptive; it is impossible to know how many families followed suit. Many did, especially when pious parents took the lead. Diadama Harwood, a recent Congregationalist convert in Bennington, evangelized to her unconverted children. She sang hymns "until a late hour in the evening," according to her son, and read tracts and religious books "on which she very amply dealt out comments."[118] But many others let this duty slide, and their violations appear in church records. In 1805, the Chelsea (Vermont) Congregational Church excommunicated Daniel Lad for "disbelieving in the Bible, [and] habitual neglect of public and family worship."[119] Preston Jones faced the same sanction in Bangor when his church found that he "neglected the duty of family prayer and . . . did not consider himself a Christian."[120] By shirking their responsibilities, these (former) church members failed to govern their families and maintain order in their homes. Their laxity, the clergy feared, left families open to vice and unsound doctrine.

Entreaties to family prayer and instructions to praying families idealized households as places where parents, children, and servants gathered happily for worship. But families often divided over faith. Women in New England (as elsewhere) joined churches in higher numbers than men.[121] It followed that many households included unconverted husbands and believing wives.[122] In these marriages, religion engendered conflict. Such was the case with a Methodist woman on Joel Winch's New Hampshire circuit, whose husband was a "hard drinking wirthliss man" who "shut her out a number of times . . . because she staid at Class meetings." She decided to leave her husband and return to her father's house—a decision Winch tacitly condoned.[123] When Betsey Carroll, a Methodist, asked her unconverted husband to lead family prayer in 1813, he refused. When she offered to officiate herself, he "said that I could if I wished, but . . . that he should not hear me." True to his word, he left the house when she began to pray.[124] A Congregationalist in Bangor admitted in 1817 that her husband had forbidden her to attend meetings and threatened to bar her from visiting her family if she disobeyed.[125] Even without such threats, believers and unbelievers endured strained unions. George Freeman, on a missionary tour in 1825, met a woman near Montpelier, Vermont, who had been active in her church and "instrumental in getting up a Tract Society." But this "truly good woman" was "obliged to mourn over an unbelieving and opposing husband."[126] A circle of New Hampshire women in similar straits met regularly to "pray for the salvation of their unconverted husbands."[127] Others warned against entering into such marriages in the first place. A churchgoer whose husband had never converted advised a friend to remain single unless she could "get a favourable opinion of [a suitor's] disposition and a satisfactory evidence of his new birth."[128] Lacking these assurances, she warned, a Christian wife faced a grim future.

Marriages in which partners professed different faiths were equally fraught, especially when couples had to decide whether to baptize their children. Because different denominations imbued baptism with different meanings but still considered it essential, spouses often locked horns over how to proceed.[129] Missionary Samuel Goddard visited a "poor pious woman" in western Maine whose Methodist husband had left her when she refused to abandon Congregationalism and adopt his faith. She asked Goddard to hear her profession of faith and baptize her children—something her husband had forbidden her to do outside a Methodist church.[130] Goddard helped her, but not all ministers would have. When the (Congregationalist) Cumberland Association in Maine considered whether to baptize the children of a believing mother after her husband had prohibited the practice, they deferred to the children's father. "If suitable efforts to conciliate the husband were unsuccessful," a committee found, "the duty must be omitted."[131] The association abdicated its watch over the children to preserve family governance. By favoring a wife's preference over her husband's (even if her beliefs comported with their own), they might undermine the very authority that was supposed to keep the couple's spiritual house in order.

Families, whatever their religious inclinations, gave crucial support to the diverse contingent of itinerants and other clergy who traced paths through backcountry towns. Households became hubs of religious activity when their members hosted ministers and opened their homes, barns, and fields for the clergy's use. When Methodist preacher Epaphras Kibby filled in on a Maine circuit, the circuit's usual preacher, Timothy Merritt, directed him to sympathetic households where he could lodge or preach. "You may put up at Mrs. Standishes, the place where I board," he advised, or "if you do not arrive till Satterday you may put up at Equr. Webbs." As for preaching, "on Sab. evening I preach at Mr. Brown's at Mill Cove, on Mon. at Mr. Cliffords, on another day in the week at Mr. Welch's . . . [and] you will perhaps be able to meet the Class at Mr. Murry's."[132] During an 1811 mission to Maine, two households in Calais and one in St. Croix allowed Ephraim Abbot to preach in their barns and homes, one of which accommodated 150 hearers.[133] Similarly, a Universalist churchgoer identified as Mrs. Bartlett regularly allowed the Rockingham Association of Universalist ministers to meet in her home.[134] Whether these hosts saw their actions as expressions of piety, acts of duty, or simple gestures of courtesy is usually unclear. But their behavior at least reflected sympathy toward their own denominations and a desire to interweave their homes with their religious communities.

When the laity hosted ministers of other faiths and in rare instances opened their homes to other churches' meetings, their motives were even less clear. Surely, some courted alternatives to their own denominations. But most voiced satisfaction in their beliefs and tolerated harmless conversation with ministers who hoped to change their minds. Warren Gardiner, a Baptist in Pennamaquan (since renamed Pembroke), Maine, not only allowed Ephraim Abbot to lodge at his house, he also hosted a meeting during which Abbot preached two sermons—yet he never hinted that he might adopt Congregationalism.[135] Jonathan Fisher spent many hours in friendly discussions with Baptists and Methodists he met (he found the Universalists less hospitable). In Sedgwick, he "conversed several hours with Mrs. S[now] in a friendly way" about her Methodist faith and her "great opposition to her daughter's joining the Congregational Church."[136] Although these encounters did not always achieve the clergy's aims, their hosts allowed themselves to be evangelized by ministers of other religious traditions. These layfolk illustrate the frequent incongruities between belief and behavior. By reaching out to ministers who hoped to convert them, they straddled hazy lines between sectarian communities, even if they had no intention of crossing over.

The clergy clung to their hopes that households would act as little churches. But in unchurched communities, families lacked guidance to carry out family prayer and teach Christian precepts. Where the pious lived among the irreligious, attention to faith could isolate praying families amid their indifferent neighbors. To be sure, many pious families lived up to the clergy's hopes for well-ordered religious households. But those who were lax in worship and divided in belief were probably more the norm. These flawed and fragmented households functioned as microcosms of frontier settlements—but not in the ways that the clergy had hoped.

Families, as it turned out, were imperfect building blocks for imperfect religious communities. But these communities formed nevertheless, born of the intimacy of kinship and neighborhood. One reason that laypeople were so active in forming religious communities was that they rarely had clergy to do it for them. It is impossible to know just how many of northern New England's churches lacked ministers at any particular time, but church and conference records document the undersupply of clergy in all denominations. The headless church, then, became a common feature of the new religious landscape.

Many churches started out with no clergy. The Goffstown (New Hampshire) Baptist Church resolved in 1795 to "joyn together to hold meeting on Lords day when we have not a pubblic gift as well as when we have one."[137] The Baptists in Bangor also gathered a church when they had no hope for permanent preaching. "Though few in number," one member explained, "we do feal it a duty which is binding on us . . . to be embodied together in order that we may more carefully watch over each other . . . [and] enjoy Church ordinances and privileges."[138] Other churches became headless when they could not replace ministers who had left or died. For example, the Manchester (Vermont) Baptist Church dismissed Joseph Cornell in 1793 when it could not pay his salary; the Sedgwick (Maine) Congregational Church lost Daniel Merrill when he converted to Baptism in 1805; and the Jericho (Vermont) Congregational Church's minister, John Denison, died around 1812.[139] However a church found itself without a minister, its members had to navigate doctrine, discipline, and ritual themselves.

Whether (and how often) headless churches relied on outside ministers depended on their access to nearby clergy or an itinerant network. Some congregations—especially those too remote to merge with other churches—simply gathered when they could and improvised services. In 1792, missionary Levi Frisbie encountered a Maine settlement so isolated that "no minister ever before visited them, and they have . . . heard but very few sermons of any kind." However, he reported, "they hold meetings on Sabbath days."[140] The Baptist Church in Livermore, Maine, founded in 1793 without a minister, kept Sabbath worship and biweekly conferences. Churchgoers volunteered to lead meetings where worshipers prayed, sang hymns, read the Bible, and "offer[ed] some thoughts on what was read."[141] Without guidance from clergy, these headless churches settled into patterns of worship of their own design.

Other churches sought help from nearby ministers. When the Baptists in Shoreham, Vermont, decided to form a church, they called on local clergy to help them compose a covenant and articles of faith. They also asked a Baptist elder to administer communion four times per year "till we should become so established as not to have need of further troubling [him] in this way."[142] When a few Freewill Baptists gathered in Montpelier in 1808, they drew up a covenant and held monthly meetings on their own until Elder Ziba Woodsworth arrived to offer periodic assistance. To integrate the Montpelier church fully into the Freewill Baptist hierarchy, Woodsworth ordained one of its founding members.[143] Most headless churches hoped for a similar outcome. But because they might wait months or years to settle a minister, they relied on outside clergy to carry out official functions.

Since a headless church could not perform baptisms or communions, most of its activities consisted of Sabbath meetings, midweek conferences, and prayer sessions. To assist churchgoers, ministers published guides to holding services. The 1794 edition of William Enfield's *Prayers for the Use of Families* contained a new section for "congregations when destitute of a minister," including morning and evening services and funeral prayers. Headless churches relied heavily on such advice.[144] Ephraim Abbot met two elderly men in Robbinston, Maine, who "from the first settlement of the town have assembled every LORD'S day as many of the inhabitants would meet them." Because they rarely saw clergy, they used tracts to guide worship. "The custom," Abbot reported, "is to read some select discourse and to perform the other parts of worship as is usual in congregational societies."[145] With a plan for worship and religious texts, these churchgoers managed to hold meetings even without a settled minister.

Ministers urged headless societies to maintain worship. The Universalist General Convention suggested that "all Societies who are not favored with constant preaching . . . assemble on the first day of the week [and] attend to the reading of the scriptures."[146] The Rockingham Association similarly advised its members to hold regular Sabbath meetings "for mutual exhortation and prayer." Churchgoers might read a "printed discourse or a moral and religious article" to "keep a society constantly in profitable action."[147] Congregationalist missionary Robert Cochran advised a society in Putnam, Maine, to meet on the Sabbath, even if they had no preaching. At the very least, "they could read some good sermon which would be usefull."[148] By reading sermons, churchgoers could glean elements of correct doctrine and take advantage of Christian fellowship in whatever form they could.

When churchgoers concentrated their efforts in communal reading and prayer, they sometimes sparked revivals. Visiting ministers often discovered budding awakenings in churches that had not heard preaching for some time. In Winhall, Vermont, a revival erupted in 1806 among Baptists who had not yet organized a church but met regularly for worship. Within a few months, the awakening had spread to the nearby (and also largely unchurched) towns of Jamaica and Windham.[149] Lay preaching was a mainstay of headless revivals, especially in denominations that condoned exhortation. The Freewill Baptists in Limerick, Maine, sparked an awakening shortly after they gathered a church. Although they lacked a minister, one of their six members preached and proved "a great instrument of the late revival there."[150] Even among Congregationalists, who placed the highest premium on a minister's preaching, headless churches might stir up their own awakenings. The members of the Second Church in North Yarmouth, Maine, having recently lost their minister, continued to meet for worship, conference meetings, and monthly concerts of prayer—all, evidently, to good effect. In 1822, the Cumberland County Conference reported an "unusual spirit of prayer" that signaled an emerging revival.[151] However effective in starting revivals, headless churches still needed clergy to finish them with the usual culmination of confession, baptism, and communion. But by igniting awakenings themselves, the laity sustained and extended religious communities and so reinforced bonds of piety.

In addition to headless churches, expanding denominations also encouraged lay prayer societies, class meetings, and conferences to anchor fragile religious communities. Once peripheral to formal church functions, these semi-institutional bodies wove themselves into the fabric of religious life. Prayer meetings met weekly or monthly.[152] Although most members were churchgoers, these societies organized separately from the churches with which they affiliated. Prayer societies often segregated by sex; women's groups far outnumbered men's, perhaps because they offered venues for religious discourse and leadership that women rarely enjoyed in church. The Freewill Baptist "Sisters meeting" in Springfield, Vermont, organized in 1803 and met weekly for prayer and exhortation, after which members shared their "particular trials and experiences."[153] The Shelburne (Vermont) Female Religious Society, which accepted any female "Regular member of any particular church," gathered around 1816 and met biweekly "for social prayer and praise and religious instruction and edification."[154]

The Female Religious Society in Jericho, Vermont, held biweekly meetings that opened by "singing a Psalm or a hymn" and continued "by reading a portion of the Scripture and by prayer and reading such other religious Books as may be deemed proper."[155] Many churches appreciated the prayer meetings' potential to intensify piety. The Methodist Vershire (Vermont) Circuit urged members to "establish select prayer meetings for the purpose of encouraging and praying for holiness of heart."[156] Others were more skeptical. Ephraim Abbot, having attended a Congregationalist prayer meeting with "15 of the Ladies of Greenland," New Hampshire, thought that "some of the young ladies appear in some measure thoughtful" but wondered if "any lasting impressions are made on their minds." He kept his misgivings to himself, however, admitting that his "friends are in favor of the conference."[157]

Many people credited women's prayer societies for exciting revivals. An 1817 revival in Gilmanton, New Hampshire, began in a women's "reading circle" when religious fervor overcame one member as she read a tract.[158] Diann Smith's prayer meeting in Jericho helped start a revival after "one of the sisters of this church" challenged a backslider to ponder the state of his soul. His change of heart had a wider effect in the town, which joined in fasting and prayer. Smith credited her prayer meeting, which met on the morning of the fast, for furthering the effort. "All knelt," she recounted, "and I trust some felt the spirit of prayer."[159] Charlotte Cheever hoped her Hallowell, Maine, prayer meeting would similarly feed a wider awakening. After one "delightful" meeting, she reported, "I had almost faith to believe the work would be revived among us, and I yet trust it will be."[160] Prayer meetings shifted the gravity of religious fervor outside the church.[161] Looking to lay institutions to spark awakenings, churchgoers rerouted the usual pathway from preaching to revival.

No lay society succeeded more at concentrating spiritual efforts than the class meeting, the most frequent and intensive gathering on the Methodist calendar. Classes fit neatly into the Methodist hierarchy. Lay leaders maintained discipline, recorded attendance, and levied rates for ministerial support. They reported to circuit preachers and presiding elders, and could lose their positions if they became lax enforcers.[162] Not for the faint of heart (or soul), classes followed a more or less strict template in which leaders questioned churchgoers, demanding raw honesty about sins committed, temptations weathered, and the soul's relation to Christ.[163] Nathan Fisk lauded the class meetings in Bangor, during which "every member of their Church is requested to tell the exercises of their minds." He thought the meetings "edifying" to the soul. "By proceeding this way when they have no preaching," he observed, "their number increases while their Class meetings serve as a means to stir up their minds."[164] Although Fisk was a Baptist, he admired the classes' dedication. His own church, he thought, might do well to follow their lead.

As one of the most constant and central features of a Methodist's spiritual life, classes signaled something new in northern New England's religious life: the institutionalization of the headless church. Classes themselves had long been a fixture of Methodism. But in New England, where the clergy had traditionally occupied a town church's spiritual center, a deliberately headless religious body offered a new model. Classes gathered more regularly, and under steadier leadership, than Methodist churches led by clergy. They also demanded more of their participants. A lay institution by design rather than default, the class meeting demonstrated how churchgoers could maintain a religious community that honored both doctrine and discipline.

Lay societies also grew popular in other denominations. Freewill Baptists created their own class meetings, which were so like the Methodists' in form and doctrine that some members of each group saw them as interchangeable. William Babcock's Springfield Monthly Meeting divided into classes led by church members who answered to ruling elders. Methodists and Freewill Baptists sometimes mingled in the classes until the Freewill Baptists ended the practice in 1805.[165] Churches of all traditions held conferences: weekly lay meetings featuring singing, prayer, and religious conversation. Conferences could be ecumenical. Baptists and Congregationalists in Dennysville, Maine, for instance, met monthly to "converse on the importance and nature of religion and on the state of their own minds."[166] The meetings encouraged worship and reflection; more than that, by uniting two groups who were separated by faith but joined by geography, the meetings could reorient a town's spiritual map around the bridge that connected them.

Just as religious identity emerged from a complex set of beliefs and behaviors, religious communities coalesced around overlapping social circles and local institutions. Families, churches and societies, empty and occupied pulpits, reading societies, prayer meetings, classes and conferences—each marked a focal point in a constellation of spiritual centers. As kin and neighbors combined and recombined in different religious settings, they created spiritual communities beyond the church, and—because anyone's home, barn, or field could become the locus of spiritual activity—they blurred boundaries between sacred and secular places. Churches and ministers remained important. But shared reading, singing, prayer, and conversation outweighed the preached sermon, both in terms of the numbers who took part and the time and energy churchgoers spent in the effort. Although layfolk might have thought themselves isolated from metropolitan New England and the tradition of the settled church, their communal religious enterprises linked them to a wider religious culture.

Just as individuals, families, and congregations blended into local communities so, too, did local communities merge with the wider hinterland. Kindred spirits could be hard to find in fledgling towns where neighborly ties proved elusive. Thus, as laypeople crisscrossed northern New England, they forged complex social networks of families, friends, and former church-mates. Travel and correspondence sustained these relationships, creating borderless communities of like-minded believers who relied on each other for news, advice, and encouragement. Making do despite the miles that separated them, far-flung migrants situated themselves not just in local churches but also in extended networks.

Newcomers to states and towns fueled dramatic growth in the region through the first quarter of the nineteenth century (see map 4.1). Vermont's population nearly tripled between 1791 and 1810, and New Hampshire's nearly doubled between 1790 and 1820. Maine's population increased even more sharply: more than fivefold in four decades.[167] But even when this growth leveled off, migration continued, especially to remote and recently settled areas. In other words, people moved within the region, back and forth between states and locally among towns.[168] These are the patterns missionary John Sawyer detected when he helped organize a church of ten members in Sangerville, Maine, in 1828. "This is the third time I have assisted to organize 5 or 6 of the members into churches," he noted, "first in Garland, then in Foxcroft, and now in Sangerville."[169] These towns are close but not quite contiguous; they lie in a jagged north-to-south chain, about thirty miles long, that roughly traces the border between Somerset and Penobscot counties. That Sawyer organized churches with the same handful of founding members in all three towns suggests the extent of local migration in the region, which did not change statewide population counts but nonetheless affected the makeup of towns, churches, and neighborhoods.

Church dismissions and recommendations also illustrate these patterns. During the 1790s and early 1800s, the First Baptist Church in Livermore, Maine, accepted new members from Newton and Charlton, Massachusetts, and Buckfield, Maine, and dismissed members to such Maine towns as Sanford, Jay, Farmington, and Lebanon. Between 1803 and 1823, the Free Baptist Church in Barnstead, New Hampshire, dismissed members to churches in Centre Harbor, Strafford, Portsmouth, and Durham, all in New Hampshire, along with unspecified towns in Vermont and Maine. Between 1822 and 1830, 118 members of the Weathersfield Circuit in Vermont requested dismissions—nearly one quarter of the circuit's membership during that period. Of the departing members, few moved farther than New York or New Hampshire. Destination towns included Holland Purchase, New York; Waitsfield, Richmond, and Ludlow, Vermont; and New London and Haverhill, New Hampshire. Moreover, many members moved among class meetings within the circuit, signifying changes in neighborhoods.[170] This was a society on the move, but most of this movement was local.

Migrants traversed the region in cross-currents to seek better land and economic opportunity. John Clark had migrated from Connecticut to Clarendon,

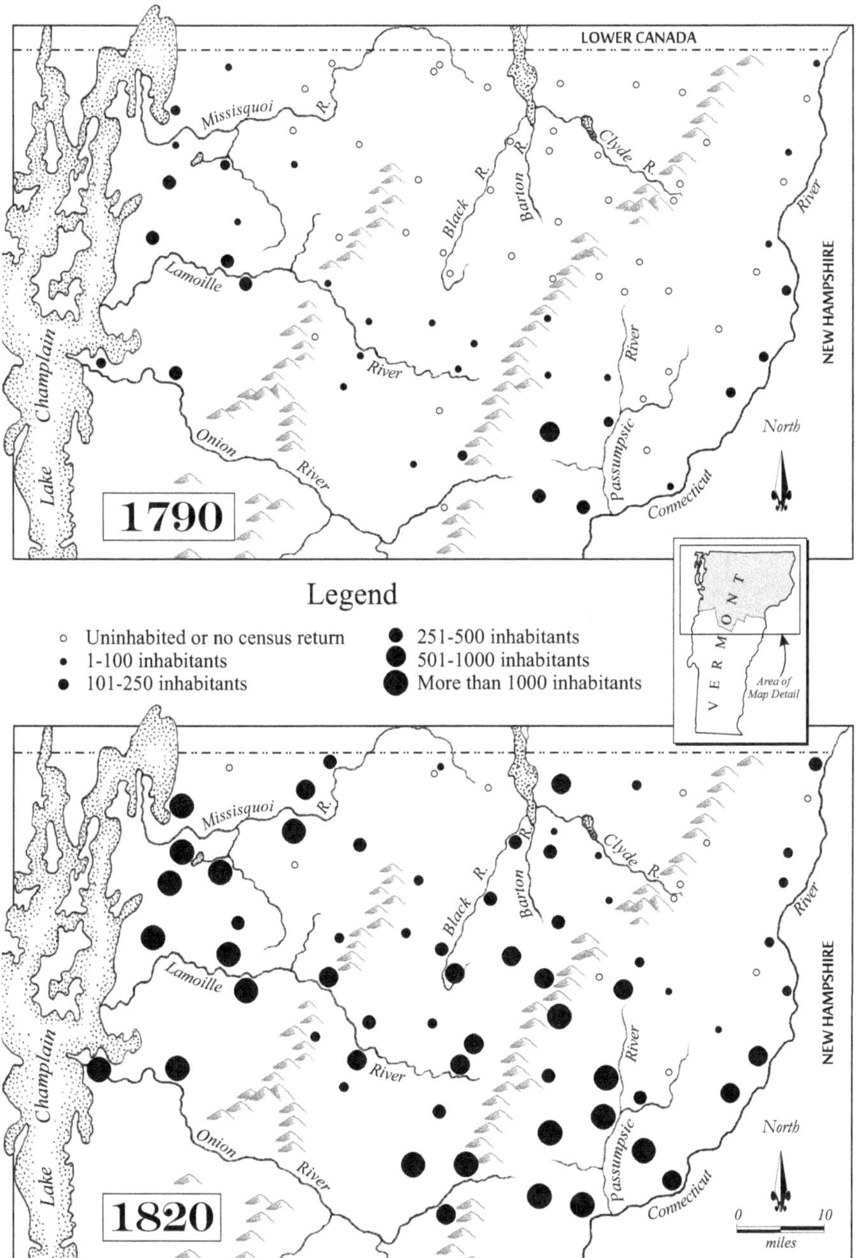

Map 4.1. Population growth in northern Vermont, 1790–1820. Northern Vermont, which was sparsely populated in the late eighteenth century, attracted many new migrants over the ensuing decades. All of Vermont's towns were chartered by the late eighteenth century (and thus existed legally and geographically), even if they were not populated. Several fledgling towns in 1790 appear to have been abandoned by 1820, while many towns uninhabited in 1790 gained stable populations by 1820. These patterns of growth suggest widespread regional mobility. *Maps by Mark Cook.*

Vermont, in 1784 after falling on hard times. There he "connected with a heterogeneous mass of people from all parts, lately relieved of the incurtions of open Enemies [and entertaining] hopes of better times." He worked in Clarendon until 1785, when he earned and borrowed enough to buy a small farm and bring his wife and six children from Connecticut to join him. The Clark family's journey was not over. In 1786, a fire destroyed their property, leaving them in abject poverty. Unable to rebuild, they moved to the town of Hartford in eastern Vermont, where he settled into a "peaceful Neighborhood with Christian friends," and his family finally enjoyed the economic security they had sought.[171] Joel Winch, the future Methodist circuit rider, spent much of the 1790s moving about with his family after they left their Massachusetts home to seek a stable livelihood. First, they moved to Fitzwilliam, in southwestern New Hampshire, where their father failed to secure an income as a tanner. Then, he decided to "try farming," and the family moved to Hartland, Vermont, on the Connecticut River. There they bought a small farm on a credit arrangement that required Winch's father to "work out by Dayes" and "work the chief of the Night on his own farm."[172] Also typical was Nathan Fisk, a cobbler who left his home in Washington, New Hampshire, for Bangor, Maine, sometime in the mid-1810s. He spent the next two decades moving among neighboring towns along the Penobscot River.[173] Clark, Winch, Fisk, and countless others sought relief from poverty by migrating, often repeatedly. The endless flux was a conspicuous feature of the region's social (and spiritual) geography. Stephen Chapin, a Society for Propagating the Gospel (SPG) missionary, described Maine as a place with "no fixed character, except it be constant variation."[174] Beneath the New England landscape lay an undercurrent of continuous movement.

Many of these migrants mourned the loss of community. Settlers, especially churchgoers, eyed their new neighbors with suspicion. John Clark was shocked to find "irreligion almost epidemical" in Clarendon. Although he met "some good Christians here and there," he witnessed more "profanity, debauchery, drunkenness, [and] quarreling," and doubted "whether this could be a peaceful or profitable religious retreat for me and my family."[175] Solomon Stevens, a teacher in northwestern Vermont, complained that he lived in "a state of nature." He thought his neighbors and students "poor, ignorant, and inbred." Only one family, he judged, had "any claim to respectability, and they, in [southern] New England, would be called brutes."[176] Nathan Fisk found Brewer, Maine, just as hostile. With shortages of cash, supplies, and goodwill, settlers seemed rough and opportunistic. They were "as Civil here as could be expected in such a place," he wrote, but "most of the people are one for self, forgetting their Neighbors."[177]

Settlers longed for any semblance of home. Rebecca Brown French, a settler in Cavendish, Vermont, begged her parents for news in 1795. She had not heard from them in so long, she wrote, that she feared "my Parents and friends have forsaken us and forgot that we are in a wilderness . . . Surrounded with many temptations." Some word might ease her loneliness.[178] A couple from Weybridge, Vermont, sorely missed the "sweet bonds of fraternal affection" they had left behind when they moved. "One day we are surrounded by a circle of friends, near and dear as life," they wrote, "and the *next* we find ourselves among strangers, surrounded by a new set of beings, of whose existence till *now* we had no knowledge."[179] Migration, though it could bring new opportunities, came with costs.

But just as itinerants connected distant villages in prayer networks, the meandering laity wove webs of friendship and kinship through communication and travel.[180] Correspondence cemented relationships and channeled religious news and discussions over distance. Letters were rarely one-way communications. Writers invited postscripts by other friends and relatives, and recipients circulated letters among interested readers. The semi-public nature of correspondence amplified its impact. Loved ones exchanged word of revivals, judged preachers' performances, compared notes on tracts they had read, examined their own spiritual struggles and conversions, carried on doctrinal debates, and monitored each other's piety and morality. In doing so, they sustained religious communities that transcended town borders.

Since local communities often lacked clergy, many layfolk preserved ties with favorite (but distant) ministers through letters. Rebecca Miller of Middlebury carried on a lengthy correspondence with John Clancy of Castleton, Vermont, who trained for and then joined the Congregationalist ministry during the course of their friendship. They were especially close; she helped finance his education at Andover and was bitterly disappointed when he accepted his first pulpit in Virginia rather than returning to Vermont.[181] Miller sent Clancy news of revivals, conversions, and deaths. As a revival erupted in 1821, she reported that "sisters [were] collecting for special meetings from different parts of the town . . . with a view to stimulate each other to *feel* and *act out* more of the spirit of the times." She hoped they would "exert an influence favorable to the promotion of a revival of religion and even strengthen the hands and encourage the heart of their Pastor." She also sought counsel from Clancy and confessed her doubts and spiritual longings in her letters. At times, she wrote, "there is . . . a want of sufficient *love* . . . as well as trust" in God—and as a result, she found herself "shrink[ing] back from the Redeemer instead of fleeing to him as the only refuge."[182] By confiding in Clancy, Miller forged the kind of relationship that churchgoers sought with local pastors. Perhaps she never found the same affinity with her minister in Middlebury, or perhaps her friendship with Clancy provided a necessary spiritual outlet. Whatever the reason, Miller and Clancy sustained a traditional pastoral relationship in untraditional ways.[183]

Whether they wrote to pastors or (more commonly) relatives and friends, correspondents made a point of spreading religious news, and they asked the recipients of their letters to do the same. Reports of local preaching—both its quality and content—appeared frequently in letters. New or visiting ministers especially merited mention. Clarissa Clark seemed optimistic about a "young man from Andover who will probably spend several months with us" in Craftsbury, Vermont. With steady preaching, she hoped, "our prospects [for] the enjoyment of the Word of Life are rather more favorable."[184] Sarah Watts described her minister, recently settled in Kennebunk, as "nearer perfection than any one I ever knew"; his weekly lectures were "exceedingly interesting and instructive."[185] Elizabeth Cheever, on the other hand, criticized a decidedly less talented minister, whom she described as "theatrical," "affected," and "self-conceited," adding that her mother was "much disgusted with him." Although she tried to illustrate his many faults in a letter to her brother, George, she claimed she could not "succeed in writing as well as acting him out, which I can do quite well."[186] Although George Cheever presumably did without his sister's impersonation, her account still provided a vivid depiction of weekly worship. In doing so, she helped him stay connected to his home church.

Preachers and their performances provided fodder for discussion, but no religious news was more eagerly anticipated than that of revival. Just as religious periodicals published revival narratives to inspire their audience's hopes, correspondents' recountings of awakenings cheered readers who longed for similar inspiration. Letter-writers depicted days or weeks of preaching, conversion, and fervor, as Daniel Skinner did in 1816 when he described a "powerful and extensive" revival in Middlebury to his friend Harvey Leavitt. With at least eighty converts, the awakening had been "the most glorious season Middlebury has ever saw."[187] Nathan Fisk of Bangor informed his father in 1817 that "the Lord has been Pleased to call up the attention of many in this Place." He added that Congregationalist and Methodist "meetings are held often and much crowded and solemnity appears in almost every Countenance."[188] Betsey Walker, a Maine Baptist, reported breathlessly on a revival in Arundel, where she had spent four weeks so she could attend twice-daily prayer meetings. She guessed that few remained unconverted. "Tis all on fire," she wrote to minister Timothy Remick, "such times I never expected to see."[189]

Correspondents eagerly awaited news of awakenings, especially if their own towns were undergoing lackluster times. Churchgoers often despaired of their neighbors' spiritual apathy, as did George Cheever, a student at Bowdoin. "If ever a revival of religion is anywhere needed," he informed his mother, "it is here in college." Everyone he knew was "so utterly insensible of his situation, . . . and so entirely indifferent to every thing of a serious kind, that nothing less than the immediate power of God . . . can arouse and reclaim them."[190] Writers hoped for good tidings. Mary Ingalls, a recent migrant from New Hampshire to Vermont, complained to her friend Susan Craige about the "lamentable state" of her new town and asked Craige to "pray earnestly that these Mountain towns may be mountains of holiness."[191] Diann Smith of Jericho asked her friend Charity Bryant for news about a Middlebury revival. "We wish to hear more of the particulars," she added, because "*we* are stupid!"[192] Churchgoers like Smith relied on letters to nurture piety. Correspondents created virtual communities that provided what their real communities often could not: encouragement, spiritual sustenance, and the sense of a shared endeavor.

Letter-writers often concentrated on a much smaller task: giving strength to loved ones who hoped for conversion or feared backsliding. Mary Mann sought that kind of support when she wrote to John Fisk in New Hampshire of the spiritual isolation she felt in Dexter, Maine. "I am one alone in the wilderness," she mourned, "I am surrounded by Universalists." By connecting with other Congregationalists, she hoped she could "be kept from embraceing that Doctrine . . . [and] press forward in the strait and narrow path."[193] Correspondents urged each other to do just that. When Elijah Fisk's son moved from New Hampshire to Maine, Fisk warned the young man not to "fall in with the freewill Baptists," among whom "there [were] many Dangerous Principles Preach't up."[194] Anna Weeks urged her brother, a student at Middlebury College, to confess his faith so he might resist the "many temptations to lead you from your duty." The stakes were high, she insisted; a profession would determine "which side you will be, whether for Christ or against him."[195] Phebe Abbot scolded her friend Sarah Livermore for spiritual laxity, but she also asked Livermore to reciprocate, so the friends might watch each other's conduct. "I have many faults," she admitted, "which I am prone to overlook and indulge." What she needed was "some friend" who might "reprove me when I go astray." "Will not Sarah be that friend," Abbot implored, who would "use her influence to accelerate my progress in the christian course!"[196] Like members of the same church who confronted each other to maintain discipline, correspondents used letters to exhort like-minded believers to action.

Their efforts sometimes paid off. Whether prodded by parents, encouraged by friends, or counseled by ministers, churchgoers who finally experienced conversion often set pen to paper to share the news and wonder at the transformation. Melville Cox informed his friend Henry Hilton in 1821 that, "by prayer and supplication," he finally became convinced of his own conversion. He now enjoyed "uninterrupted peace" and felt "as though I could . . . sleep in the arms of Jesus." He could barely contain his exuberance, exclaiming "God is mine and I am *his,* shall I say it!"[197] Charlotte Cheever's husband, Nathaniel, was more guarded. He was traveling in Augusta, Georgia, when he sensed that his own conversion lay within his grasp. More than ever, he relied on "the converse of religious and pious friends" back in Maine. "They could assist me by their own experience," he thought, "and more especially by their prayers to seek and to find that strict and narrow road, which leadeth unto life eternal." He was sure that like-minded souls existed in Georgia, "but they are strangers to me." Instead, he wished to keep familiar company, even if only from a distance.[198] Private confessions in correspondence to friends and relatives were intimate, impassioned, and spontaneous. A letter might not supplant one's home church as a space for a conversion narrative, but it did provide a virtual space for public profession.

Correspondence, however, was not merely a confessional exercise. Letter-writers were also readers. Writing naturally intersected with religious readership, both by circulating written material and by giving friends and relatives a forum within which to discuss their latest reading. Nathan Fisk commended *Zion's Advocate* to his son and daughter-in-law, who had expressed interest in subscribing to a religious newspaper. "It is an interesting paper," he thought, "and conducted with prudence, avoiding disputations and controversies."[199] Correspondents sent clippings, books, or even their own autobiographical writings along with letters. Rebecca Miller sent John Clancy an article from the *Christian Messenger* about a mutual acquaintance's death and a funeral sermon, the latter of which she asked him to return "if opportunity allows."[200] Charlotte Cheever sent sermons and tracts to her son George. After she sent the text of a sermon by their minister in Hallowell, George wrote to thank her, praising the sermon as "really excellent" and "truly beautiful" in parts.[201] As the Cheevers' example suggests, correspondents could share published material to which they might not otherwise have had access. By sending sermons, pamphlets, and clippings with their letters, they extended the boundaries of both private religious discourse and the public culture of reading.

Private correspondence provided a shared space for devotion. Through their letters, believers engaged in worship, relatives simulated family prayer, churchgoers spread news, and kindred spirits encouraged each other's piety. In short, they used correspondence to welcome faraway loved ones into their spiritual midst. As Sarah Livermore explained to a distant friend, "A long space of country stretches itself between us, but still this does not intercept the interchange of thoughts."[202] Religious correspondence allowed like-minded believers to forge religious communities that transcended physical boundaries.

Sometimes they created these communities in a public fashion, by sending reports to religious publications. Publishers depended on layfolk to fill their pages with accounts of revivals and conversions. The Freewill Baptist *Religious Informer* requested "the lovers of the cause of Christ, whither a brother or sister, in a public or private station, who knew of . . . revivals of religion where they reside" to submit articles. According to the editors, "it will be equally desirable to the brethren in Vermont," to take one example, "to hear of the outpouring of God's spirit in New-Hampshire, New-York, Rhode-Island, Massachusetts, Maine, or elsewhere, as it is to hear from Vermont."[203] The faithful had an inherent interest in others' spiritual welfare, even people they would never meet. The laity participated in a regional culture of readership—not just as consumers of print material but also as producers.

And they participated eagerly, most often by submitting revival narratives. After an 1811 revival in Pittsford, Vermont, Holland Weeks excitedly informed his brother that his narrative of the event would soon appear in the *Adviser*, a Congregationalist magazine. "I sat up all night," he reported, and "wrote it, imperfectly, and sent it on without looking it all over so much as once." The magazine published the piece in three monthly installments.[204] A Baptist in Bristol, Vermont, wrote that, after years of spiritual lethargy, an 1810 revival tripled the church's membership.[205] And a "Gentleman from Fairlee," Vermont, reported an awakening that swept Lyman and Thetford in 1821, drawing hundreds of participants to meetings, and sparking two hundred possible conversions. The writer noted that the revival started among the Baptists and quickly spread to the other churches, and diverse crowds convened "without any jarrings." He believed that "such a time has not been known since Whitefield's day."[206] Such news not only called attention to the awakening's results, it encouraged churches in the midst of their own "low times." Just as importantly, these reports sustained a public conversation among churchgoers who desired to know how religion progressed in distant parts.

Revival news made up much of this conversation, but churchgoers published other pieces as well. Lay preachers, for instance, sent details of their preaching tours. In 1819, Clarissa Danforth informed the *Religious Informer* that she had completed a tour from Weathersfield, Vermont, to Providence, Rhode Island. At each meeting, she encountered "a loving company of brethren," witnessed many baptisms, and heard several exhortations.[207] Churchgoers submitted conversion accounts and other personal narratives. The *Massachusetts Baptist Missionary Magazine* published a letter in 1806 from a "pious woman" to her brother, which the editors judged would "promote the interest of religion." The writer, who had migrated from Massachusetts to Vermont, detailed her conversion during a revival. She also underscored the importance of spiritual correspondence. "Ever since Providence has placed me at so great a distance from my friends and former acquaintances," she explained, "I have felt a great solicitude to learn more of their spiritual concerns and to communicate to them the great things which God hath done for me."[208] By publishing her account, she could connect to her extended social circle—and she could also join the swirl of correspondence that joined scattered believers.

These extended networks—created through migration, correspondence, and print—helped define northern New England as a religious region. The region's ties extended beyond its borders, too, especially to southern New England and New York. But the tightest bonds concentrated in the northern frontier, where local migration patterns, itinerancy, and sectarian hierarchies reinforced spiritual connections among churchgoers who traveled near and far to pray together. The expansive and shifting geographic scope of religion gave rise to a flexible conception of spiritual community. As much as personal belief and membership, geographic fluidity shaped religious experience.

Annual, quarterly, and monthly meetings attracted motley collections of churchgoers from all over northern New England's map to central locations, and then flung them back again across the region. The Freewill Baptists' New Durham Yearly Meeting typically drew thousands. One participant in the 1806 yearly meeting noted that worshipers came from "Boston, from distant parts of Maine, from Vermont near Canada line, and from different towns arround."[209] Annual meetings of Methodists and Universalists also involved thousands of lay participants. The 1802 meeting of the Methodist New England Conference drew about three thousand people to Monmouth, Maine. A mere fraction were actually converted Methodists; during the public portion of the meeting, only 230 took communion.[210] More local gatherings, such as quarterly and association meetings and Methodist love feasts, attracted smaller crowds from nearby towns. At an 1828 Universalist quarterly meeting at Craftsbury, local churchgoers and "many from adjacent towns" requested that the planned one-day gathering continue for an extra day to allow for more preaching and worship.[211] In public sessions, conferences offered gathering spaces for mixed crowds to pray together.

Whereas yearly or quarterly meetings attracted geographically distant worshipers to central locations, regional revivals united large swaths of territory in a common undertaking. Revivals typically spread beyond town limits, affecting neighboring towns or counties. In 1818, Nathan Fisk informed his father that "the work of God prospers" all along the Penobscot Valley. Almost every day, Fisk heard of "some one who is brought into the liberty of the Gospel or of some new revivals of Religion." The awakenings extended far and wide: "not confined to one order only, but amongst Baptists, Congregationalists, and Methodists in almost all parts of Maine and it even appears in . . . abandoned places."[212] But that revival paled in comparison to the fervor that swept Maine's Oxford, Franklin, and Kennebec counties several years later. In 1824, the towns of Augusta, Bowdoin, Chesterville, Farmington, Hallowell, Jay, Lisbon, Livermore, Readfield, Sidney, Vassalboro, and Winthrop all witnessed waves of revival. The work spread through Congregationalist, regular Baptist, Methodist, and Freewill Baptist churches, where hundreds of people converted, received baptism, or joined churches.[213] Such widespread revivals assumed almost mythic proportions. Dramatic, potent, and seemingly boundless, regional revivals stood at the pinnacle of spiritual devotion.

When an awakening spread, churchgoers rushed among meetinghouses, fields, and groves to catch the fervor. In 1808, a revival spread from Pittsford,

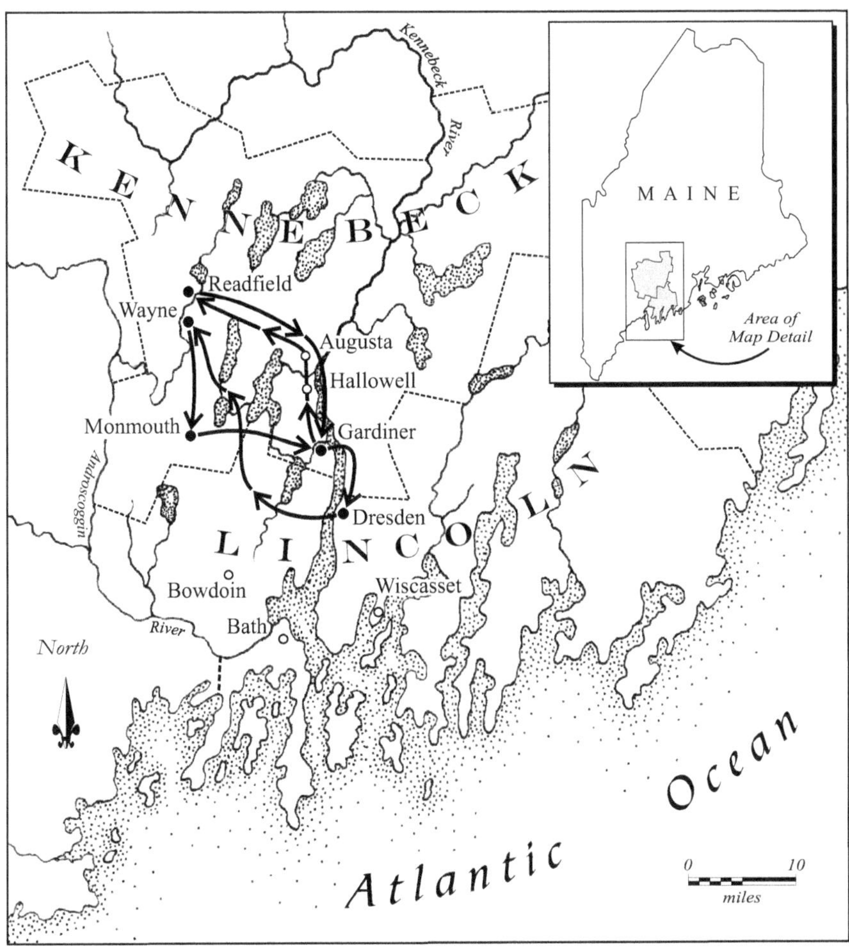

Map 4.2. Asahel Moore's revival tour, 1829. This map traces the approximate route that Moore, a young Methodist, would have followed as he visited several revivals and camp meetings during the fall of 1829. He crossed parish, town, and county lines to make his journey. His travels suggest the extent to which northern New England's religious culture depended on a geographically mobile laity. *Map by Mark Cook.*

Vermont, to Rutland, Ira, and Clarendon, mainly through the laity's efforts. From Pittsford, church members went to Rutland to pray with that town's residents. Their efforts paid off, and Rutland soon found itself caught up. Not much later, a churchgoer in Ira invited the Rutland converts to lead conferences in her home, and then the revival spread to Clarendon by similar means. Conferences, exhortation, and prayer spawned more of the same until the meetings were so "frequent, and often so crowded, that scarce any house would make the people comfortable."[214] Believers, hopeful converts, and the curious traveled from town to town to follow an awakening. When a revival spread among the Methodists of Kennebec and Lincoln counties in 1829, Asahel Moore, an eighteen-year-old churchgoer, traced a path among local religious gatherings. He traveled from his home in Gardiner to a camp meeting in Readfield, which yielded a dozen converts. He then rode back to Gardiner "and from thence to Dresden to attend another meeting in the woods of the same description [where] God blessed us with his converting grace." Soon afterward, he traveled to Wayne and Monmouth before returning to Gardiner. All told, his odyssey took him to two camp meetings, three four-days' meetings, one prayer meeting, one class meeting, and two "preaching meetings."[215] When people like Moore traveled to follow revivals, they blurred the boundaries between local churches and outlying congregations by crossing parish lines, mingling with other churchgoers, and forging connections with distant religious communities.

The very roadblocks that stymied local church-building—instability, transience, and diversity—cut paths for religious networks. Migration separated families and friends, and it left towns without means to support churches. But it also extended social ties and broadcast spiritual news and conversation across great distances. Correspondence strengthened personal relationships and sustained religious communities, even as their participants dispersed, and religious periodicals supported those correspondence networks writ large. Lay writers made distant events in unknown places immediate and concrete. In doing so, they connected remote readers and fostered a shared sense of religious experience. So, too, did the increasingly regional nature of religious organization. As sectarian infrastructure centralized, and revivals spread widely, churchgoers grew accustomed to worshiping in unfamiliar settings with unfamiliar people. The geographic and spiritual fluidity that increasingly characterized public worship only added to the sense of an all-encompassing religious community.

Layfolk dissolved the geographic and spiritual barriers that separated them. Individuals forged their own spiritual paths, sometimes tethered (and sometimes not) to larger spiritual communities. Families served as the building blocks of Protestant churches by enforcing religious and moral strictures and training dependents in the ways of piety. Headless churches and societies emerged within the parish system, assumed administrative duties, and offered outlets for prayer and religious conversation that regular public worship could not. And by partaking in northern New England's print culture, either as readers or writers, laypeople furthered their denominations' goals of spreading news of conversions and awakenings. By exercising the initiative to keep up religion in their homes and towns, and by joining sectarian communications networks, the laity furthered the denominations' goals to expand and plant roots.

But lay communities did not serve merely as auxiliaries or function solely within churchly frameworks. Families that divided over faith or neglected worship did not reinforce communal ties—they weakened them. Tensions between lay societies and clergy obscured sectarian authority and worked at cross-purposes with the hierarchies that tried to administer them. And when revivals took root in lay communities, ministers (perhaps contrary to their own expectations) often served ceremonial roles by offering sacraments after the revivals were well underway. By the time they did so, the laity themselves had already done the work of stirring souls, holding conferences, and urging their neighbors to spiritual attention. As with other lay institutions, lay-led revivals did not necessarily contradict the clergy's aims. But they did progress independently of the clergy's supervision.

Northern New England's layfolk could not rely on stable institutions to guide their religious lives, nor could they wait idly for such institutions to take root. Without ministers to provide consistent religious leadership, individuals wove personal piety from the threads of the doctrines, theology, and practices they encountered. In settlements marked by constant movement, they relied on families and friends to join them in praying communities of their own making. Local communities branched out into social networks, where the laity's spiritual world encompassed a tangle of beliefs, behaviors, and experiences. These lay communities—whether they gathered in local settlements or spread across the hinterland—formed the social basis for northern New England's religious culture. They were neither anti-clerical nor antinomian; their overriding goal was to flourish in spite of the clergy's absence, not because of it. Overlapping with sectarian maps but not bound by them, lay communities transcended both geographic and doctrinal boundaries to mitigate the spiritual instability that attended frontier settlement.

5 Fairly Missionary Ground

The Congregationalist Turn to Itinerancy

MEANDERING ITINERANTS, COLLAPSING parishes, and rootless layfolk: to a Congregationalist missionary, spiritual life in northern New England was tantamount to religious anarchy. The settlements that these ministers encountered little resembled those they had come to know in southern New England. They found the northern hinterland both familiar and foreign. Northern New England extended geographically, politically, and demographically from southern New England. It also extended spiritually, having inherited southern New England's dominant religious institution, the town church. But that institution had not survived unchanged. The town church weathered both economic instability and demographic mobility, forces that strained it even as the law attempted to preserve it. Congregationalists feared their efforts to transplant their denomination in the northern frontier had resulted only in a hodgepodge of unchurched towns, headless churches, and revolving pulpits—all of which created a spiritual vacuum that the few settled ministers in the region could not possibly fill.

In that vacuum, however, an ambitious missionary would find opportunity. So promised Asa Carpenter, who reported to the Connecticut Missionary Society (CMS) on Vermont's religious prospects in 1806. Carpenter told of migrants' crowding new settlements—lacking churches and religious leadership but desiring both. In Hopkinsville, he preached to recent settlers who told him "this was the first time that ever a sermon was delivered within the limits of the town." He met others who "were very ready to attend on public worship" but had "never been visited by Missionaries." Carpenter urged the CMS to send more missionaries soon. Sectarian itinerants had already made inroads, dividing towns and blocking Congregationalist church-building. "There is a great need of able and pious missionaries," he insisted, "to counteract the pernicious effects arising from corrupt and ignorant preachers who are exerting themselves in this part of the land." Should the Congregationalist clergy miss this chance, they might well abandon the "pious few" who scattered about the frontier to the evils of sectarianism and irreligion.[1]

Congregationalists eyed the region's unorganized parishes and unsettled churches, and they resolved to protect what they saw as vulnerable territory that rightfully belonged to them. But they realized they would not succeed using the same church-planting strategies that had worked so well in relatively uncontested southern New England. Toward that end, they organized missionary societies and sent ministers to preach, administer sacraments, admit church members, and provide spiritual guidance to frontier settlers. Missions were not a permanent solution; according to the Congregationalist ideal of the covenanted community, a permanent church needed a permanent pastor at its head. But as a stopgap measure to assist congregations until they could manage their own affairs, missionary work seemed the best approach.

The missionary enterprise, as it turned out, both solved and complicated the Congregationalists' dilemma. On the one hand, missions kept Congregationalism afloat in northern New England. More than that, they helped it thrive by allowing the faithful to gather new churches, hear regular preaching, and receive the sacraments. But even as Congregationalist missionaries cataloged their victories, they unwittingly rearranged the geography of the town church. Although they still aimed to build town churches with fixed boundaries, Congregationalists gradually adopted the sectarians' expansive and fluid spatial understanding of religious community. Ultimately, using missions to protect and spread Congregationalism both undercut the town church and reformed Congregationalism to fit the itinerant landscape.

Congregationalists began to talk of northern New England as a missionary field as early as the 1770s, when waves of New England's migrants started to fill frontier settlements. The Connecticut General Association sent missionaries to Vermont in 1774, but poor organization and wartime upheaval stymied their efforts. Consequently, the missionary enterprise did not begin in earnest until the 1780s. As the war ended, the pace of migration picked up, but the pace of church-building did not. Newly settled towns could rarely afford to hire ministers—and even when they could, the local clergy could not possibly meet the demand. Congregationalists looked to the backcountry with apprehension. Without churches to curb immorality and nurture piety, what would prevent the northern settlements from succumbing to irreligion and vice? Never mind that sectarians had already planted roots there; Congregationalists saw the region as a place to extend their own religious culture, not create a new one. They designed the missionary enterprise, which emerged from these fears and misgivings, to help northern New Englanders replicate the Congregationalist town-church geography.

When missionary societies expanded into northern New England, they encountered a town-church landscape already modified by a makeshift itinerancy. The Congregationalist clergy had long coped with widespread ministerial vacancies by rotating through each other's churches and supplying empty pulpits. Ministerial exchange, which could take pastors away from their churches for weeks at a time, was not unusual; the practice was common in southern New England as well.[2] But northern New England's exchange networks were more extensive, often choreographed far in advance by local ministerial associations. Stephen Peabody regularly exchanged with colleagues in his association, joining a "triangular exchange" in 1793.[3] Joseph Warren, a newly settled minister in Maine, predicted exchanging "almost every fortnight."[4] Associations used exchanges not just to trade pulpits but also to supply empty ones. The Cumberland Association in Maine urged members to visit the "destitute Parishes and Plantations . . . in the back parts of the County" as often as possible, and the Associated Ministers of Windham County, Vermont, required each member to preach at least one Sabbath per month in a vacant pulpit.[5] Some ministers also set out on their own itinerant routes. Paul Coffin of Buxton, Maine, traveled regularly to assist nearby churches, and Alfred Johnson of Freeport, Maine, traveled "sometimes 30, 40, 60, and 90 miles from home" to help congregations gather a church, administer sacraments, or ordain a pastor.[6] Exchange revitalized small churches that might have waited months or years to settle ministers. The practice also introduced a limited itinerancy that missionary societies would soon integrate more fully into Congregationalism.

Ministerial exchange remained common, but Congregationalist itinerants like Coffin and Johnson increasingly worked under the auspices of missionary societies. Several factors prompted them to make this decision—first among which was the promise of a salary. Although churches helped defray missionaries' expenses, not every church would (or could) contribute. A missionary society promised a base salary, struck agreements with beneficiary churches to contribute, and authorized missionaries to collect funds. Accordingly, many traveling ministers looked to missionary societies for steady employment. Job Chadwick requested a mission from the Society for Propagating the Gospel because his tours between the Kennebec and Penobscot rivers in Maine failed to support his "destitute family."[7] Others flocked to missionary societies so they could obtain valid credentials. Frontier inhabitants had no way to judge visiting ministers' qualifications, and in an era of proliferating itinerancy, many infant Congregationalist societies eyed outsiders with suspicion. Missionary Alden Bradford warned that settlers, weary of "persons in the character of clergymen" who carried no endorsements, "are now very cautious of strangers unless they come very well recommended."[8] A minister with a valid license would likely find a receptive audience. As missionary societies absorbed independent itinerants through the early 1800s and increasingly coordinated their activities, they began to play a central role in shaping the Congregationalist itinerancy.

Congregationalists started forming missionary societies during the decades following the Revolutionary War, just as migrants from southern New England headed to points north and west. Individual societies differed in their doctrinal preferences or selection of missionary fields, but they shared some characteristics in common. First, although many organizations hoped to send missions among American Indians (and did so in other regions), they eventually concentrated their efforts in northern New England among unchurched white settlements. Indian villages in the region were few, and most had longstanding ties to French Catholic missionaries that Congregationalists generally chose not to contest. Because white settlers who hoped to gather churches or hear preaching placed overwhelming demands on missionaries, visiting ministers decided to address those needs instead. Second, most missionary societies rejected the aggressive evangelism they associated with the itinerant churches. Rather than seek out new converts, Congregationalists hoped to keep the faithful under their watch.[9] They tended to designate missionary fields that had absorbed their own states' migrants: the CMS sent its ministers to Vermont (which attracted a large contingent of Connecticut migrants), and the Society for Propagating the Gospel among Indians and Others in North America (a Massachusetts organization) and the Massachusetts Missionary Society sent their missionaries to Maine. Early missionaries remained faithful to the town-church ideal by viewing frontier outposts as geographic extensions of their own Congregationalist communities.

Connecticut's Committee on Missions, the antecedent to the Connecticut Missionary Society, was the first such group. The Connecticut General Association (the colony's Congregationalist governing body) created the committee in 1774, when its members expressed alarm that so many Congregationalists were migrating beyond their churches' oversight. Concerned for the "State of the Settlements now forming to the Westward and North-westward of us, . . . many of which are . . . Emigrants of this Colony," the committee set out to serve these new communities.[10] Northern New England—especially Vermont and the eastern bank of the Connecticut River in New Hampshire—was one of the committee's missionary fields, along with New York and (after the Revolution) the Western Reserve, which also attracted many Connecticut migrants.

Missionary labor, with its low salaries and harsh conditions, proved a hard sell at first. Many ministers declined to serve, pointing out that their congregations did not wish to sacrifice the services of settled (and salaried) ministers. Theodore Hinsdale thought the "proposed Compensation inadequate," and he doubted that he could "obtain the consent of my People and a supply for them." Noah Meruen protested that his congregation "appeared opposed to my going upon a mission."[11] So, as postwar migration increased, and with it the need for missionaries, the committee found itself unable to meet demand.[12] Accordingly, in 1798, the association created the CMS, which assumed sole authority over missionary operations in the areas the Committee on Missions had managed.[13]

As the CMS began its work in Vermont, other organizations tended regions east of the Connecticut River. The Society for Propagating the Gospel among the Indians and Others in North America (SPG) figured among the most important of these, both because the scope of its work was so broad and because it was unique among other missionary groups for receiving state support.[14] The SPG, as its full name suggests, intended to Christianize Native American communities. But its missionaries found their efforts stymied both by Indians' lack of interest and the longstanding presence of French Catholic priests in Indian towns. The SPG's first missionary, Daniel Little of Wells, Maine, encountered a Penobscot settlement where a French priest "prevented my access to them on religious subjects, as a publick teacher." After Little persisted for two weeks, the priest "collected the Indians together near the uppermost branches of the river." Even those who stayed behind resisted Little's offers of instruction, as they "were apprehensive that their religion should be in danger." Failing in his initial assignment, Little turned his attention toward the white settlements along the Penobscot River, where "my services were acceptable and I hope useful."[15] It was among those communities where he covered the most ground. Little's early failure among the Penobscots and eventual success among white settlers foreshadowed the SPG's role in Maine. Although its missionaries continued to serve Massachusetts Indian communities in Stockbridge, Martha's Vineyard, and elsewhere, they focused their work in Maine among white inhabitants who lacked the will, knowledge, and resources to organize churches. The society's progress in the region (along with its public funding) gave Massachusetts grounds to expect Maine residents, like their counterparts in Massachusetts proper, to supply their own ministers. By offering clergy and subsidizing the cost, the Massachusetts Congregationalists made clear their expectation that migrants would carry the state's town-church culture with them to their destinations.

Before long, SPG missionaries found their field crowded with colleagues from other organizations. The Massachusetts Missionary Society, founded in 1799, hoped to "diffuse the knowledge of the Gospel among the Heathens, as well as other people in the remote parts of our country, where Christ is seldom or never preached." Like the SPG, the Massachusetts Missionary Society intended to focus much of its efforts on American Indian settlements in Maine, but its missionaries soon found that the need for clergy in the white settlements outpaced the supply. Citing the "vast line of new settlements" in frontier regions, "peculiarly embarrassed with respect to their religious interests," the society pledged to "put forth every exertion" to counteract the "wickedness, infidelity and atheism" that interfered with efforts to gather godly communities.[16] The Massachusetts Society for Promoting Christian Knowledge (MSPCK) was founded in 1803 as a tract society with a small missionary operation. Organizers hoped to forestall the "decay of evangelical piety" by distributing Bibles and religious books among the poor—particularly those who lived "where the means of religious knowledge and instruction are but sparingly enjoyed."[17] Smaller societies also formed, including the Hampshire Missionary Society (1802) and the Berkshire and Columbia Missionary Society (1804).[18] When the Evangelical Missionary Society (EMS) jumped into the fray in 1807, its founders acknowledged that "many Missionary Societies we know already exist" but pledged nonetheless to "lend our aid, and to emulate the pious zeal of those who have gone before us in the benevolent work." In their search for proper missionaries—those who had demonstrated sound faith and exemplary ability—this group directed that "the preference be given to settled ministers." All the better, its organizers reasoned, to extend Christian knowledge and institutions to "the infant settlements of our own country."[19] Like others of its ilk, the EMS hoped to use its most trusted clergy to implement New England's town-church model in the region's northern reaches.

As more southern New England missionaries forged itinerant routes to the north, northern New Englanders founded their own missionary societies to serve nearby towns. Their goal was not to shield frontier émigrés under an uninterrupted spiritual canopy but to acculturate new settlements (and settlers) in their midst by creating town-church communities to absorb them. Missionary fields were local: the New Hampshire Missionary Society (1801) served northern New England and northeastern New York, the Vermont Missionary Society (1808) served Vermont and eastern New York, and the Maine Missionary Society (1807) served Maine.[20] Local ministerial associations, many of which had long been sending clergy to preach in empty pulpits, also formed missionary societies. After years of hand-wringing over the ministerial supply and perceived "indifference to the settling of the Gospel" in New Hampshire, the Piscataqua Association founded its own society in 1803 to serve New Hampshire and Maine.[21] Missionaries directed their work to the "northern and thinly inhabited parts" of the region, where "the means of evangelical instruction are very sparingly enjoyed" and "ill-informed" preachers "sow the seeds of religious discord, and disaffect the minds of people to a regular ministry." To promote the town-church ideal, the Piscataqua Missionary Society sought itinerants who had been settled ministers themselves and could exert more influence as they gathered churches.[22]

Missionary societies quickly gained support from settlers, whose eager requests for missionary aid outpaced the supply of traveling ministers. Churches and societies that applied for assistance explained that poverty, isolation, and sectarian division conspired against towns that hoped to support Congregationalist ministers. The church in Georgia, Vermont, insisted that "able and faithful preachers in the gospel are greatly needed in these parts," despite reports that some churchgoers had treated a recent missionary "very disrespectfully." Other Vermonters asked that missionaries tend the "vacant Churches and Congregations Scattered up and down in the Northern Wilds," where towns contained "so many Various Denominations" that inhabitants could not settle clergy.[23] Parishioners in Washington, Maine, claimed that a missionary would elevate their town by "ameliorating the manners of the inhabitants and preventing the visits of Itinerant sectarians."[24] Churches also reminded missionary societies of their promises to watch over migrants' spiritual well-being. When the Congregationalists in Burke, Vermont, requested a minister to serve "this benighted part of the American Israel," they accused the CMS of neglecting northeastern Vermont, even though many of its inhabitants "originated from Connecticut and assisted to establish your worthy Society."[25] That sense of reciprocity drove both the missionary impulse and the ever-stronger calls by frontier churches for assistance.

By the early nineteenth century, the missionary enterprise in northern New England was well underway. The Connecticut Missionary Society rotated as many as seven full-time missionaries per year through Vermont's northern counties. The New Hampshire Missionary Society expanded from three missionaries in 1803 to sixteen who fanned out across New Hampshire and Vermont by 1820. The SPG sent as many as eighteen missionaries to Maine in a single year.[26] And the Maine Missionary Society saturated its field with as many as forty-eight missionaries per year during its first two decades. Other local societies managed more modest efforts that, taken together, added up to a large missionary presence rivaling competing denominations' itinerant corps.[27] As missionary societies expanded into new fields, they integrated itinerancy into Congregationalist communities.

Missionaries were hopeful but not a little apprehensive about their prospects for success. Many ministers understood the physical and spiritual landscapes of northern New England as unruly and untamed, and their grueling treks through the backcountry only reinforced their fears. The missionary enterprise took shape in part around the clergy's suspicion that vaguely defined evils—instability, sectarian opportunism, and irreligion—were already too ingrained ever to be eradicated. But it also carried the conviction that the town-church system could and should migrate northward as an extension of New England civilization. These competing perceptions of the northern frontier as part of New England's sphere and also foreign to it framed the missionaries' perspective. As they gained more intimate knowledge of the region's landscapes and communities, they expressed greater ambivalence about their undertaking.

The New England clergy by the late eighteenth century had long fixated on the landscapes that surrounded them. They took many of their ideas from their

Puritan forebears, who defined their natural environment as a wilderness that was both sanctifying and corrupting. For them, the wilderness symbolized believers' relationships to ministers, congregations' relationships to God, and the covenant of grace itself. Successive generations imagined New England as a paradise, the Mosaic desert, and even the Devil's territory, where temptations and evil threatened to lure godly people from a righteous path.[28] Nature was full of promise and temptation, and whether colonists could thrive there depended on whether they could untangle divine messages from the obstacles the devil had placed in the wilderness.

By the late eighteenth century, notions of a demonic landscape had faded, but ambiguous understandings of natural places had not. The wilderness continued to pose dark threats but also offer godly redemption.[29] Missionary Nathan Perkins, who toured Vermont in 1789, articulated this paradoxical view of wilderness. On the one hand, the Vermont woods struck him as threatening, desolate, and dangerous. He fretted that he "got lost twice in the woods already," where he heard "the horrible howling of the wolves." As he tried to find his way, he found himself increasingly "far absent in the wilderness—among all strangers—all alone." But he also perceived an innocence in frontier communities where people had "nothing to eat, to drink—or wear," but still treated each other with kindness. Rather than harbor evil, he concluded, "woods make people love one another."[30] This alien landscape seemed to pose countless physical and spiritual dangers—but it also promised that missionary work would prove worthwhile. Like Perkins, missionaries understood the northern hinterland within an intellectual framework that posited the entire region as a geographic and spiritual wilderness: not a howling desert but rather a place where crude towns, churches, and souls all awaited cultivation and refinement.

Missionary societies sent clergy into the field armed with lengthy instructions, contact information for local supporters, and stacks of books to distribute. But they offered little preparation for the physical trials and harsh conditions missionaries faced. Like other itinerants, Congregationalist missionaries confronted severe weather and forbidding geography. They covered long distances, often on unfamiliar routes, to reach missionary ground. Samuel Mills traveled 900 miles on a 1793 tour in Vermont, and William Miller rode 1,088 miles in 1802 through "the most mountainous part of creation I ever saw."[31] Even part-time missionaries who stayed close to home endured strenuous travel. One minister, who toured Hancock and Washington counties in Maine, rarely spent more than two consecutive days in one town. In one typical week, he started in Goldsboro and moved through the harbor and island towns along Frenchman's Bay: Taunton Bay, Mount Desert, Union River, Trenton, and Eden.[32] Jonathan Fisher, who divided his missions into short trips so he could remain close to his Blue Hill church, usually traveled between thirty and fifty miles per week on foot and horse.[33] On top of their other duties, the considerable distance and constant movement defined a missionary's work.

Missionaries gained a more than passing familiarity with northern New England's wilderness environment. They complained of all manner of hazards, from crude roads to steep gorges to impenetrable forests. Not surprisingly, northern New England's weather preoccupied most missionaries who visited the region, and they painted grim pictures of the perils they faced. In cold weather, missionaries encountered heavy snows, which sometimes made for easy travel by horse-drawn sleigh—but only to a point.[34] More often, they endured storms "raging with violence" that left roads "filled in many places above the fences." Spring thaws swelled rivers and flooded roads to make them virtually impassable, often miring horses "up to [their] knees in mud." Summer, in turn, brought extreme heat that could "make the travailing so uncomfortable as to make but little speed."[35] The rigors of travel left missionaries exhausted and often ill. Ephraim Abbot described one particularly rough day that started on horseback, continued downstream in a canoe, then on foot (carrying the canoe), and ended by poling the canoe upstream. Likewise, Perez Chapin complained of a long spring tour that left him "wet and cold and hungry" and eventually quite sick.[36] Regardless of the season, northern New England's inhospitable climate made the typical missionary's long itinerary seem even longer.

Missionaries worried not just how the climate inconvenienced them but also how it affected the settlers. Samuel Mills warned against winter travel, pointing out that newer settlements barely had the means to shelter their own inhabitants, much less a visiting minister and his horse. He reported that settlers viewed a winter missionary as "a calamity [rather] than a favor." In new towns, where "you would scarce find a barn or a board, [and] the houses are principally of Logs covered with Bark," hosting a winter traveler "would be inconvenient."[37] Others complained that the season was "unfavorable for public worship" because the cold and snow kept parishioners at home.[38] All seasons presented obstacles. Ephraim Abbot complained that summer storms made the roads so muddy that "it is difficult getting from town to town, and difficult for people to come together."[39] To their dismay, missionaries learned to expect lower church attendance on rainy days. After preaching to a scant audience during a summer storm, Amos Cooke wryly noted that "no more could *conveniently* attend." Surely Cooke knew that many churchgoers would have had to trek for miles in the rain to hear him. But he still derided them for giving up so easily. "It is lamentable that so few can have a disposition to serve the Lord," he commented, "unless it can be made a matter of convenience."[40]

The missionaries' understanding of the wilderness environment prejudiced them against its inhabitants, whom they considered products of untamed surroundings. Traveling ministers reported that their audiences were rough, uncultured, and given to sinful lapses. Nathan Perkins complained that Vermont churchgoers were "nasty—poor—low-lived—indelicate—and miserable cooks."[41] Settlers struck the clergy as "deeply affected with licentiousness," "loose in their manners," and "deficient in civil and religious knowledge."[42] But just as the wilderness corrupted its inhabitants, it also offered chances to reach unchurched but receptive hearers. Some ministers insisted that remote settlers bore little responsibility for their destitute circumstances; one explained that they were "driven by poverty . . . to seek asylum in the gloom of the forest."[43] Such people, he thought, could hardly be expected to organize churches, but they might accept whatever help missionaries offered. Jedidiah Bushnell agreed, observing that the "mountain towns" of Vermont contained many "valuable people" who had been "too much neglected by Missionaries."[44] And Job Chadwick remarked in 1804 that the settlers he met were "in low and destroying circumstances," but he still thought the Maine frontier could be fruitful missionary ground. "No people need teaching and preaching more than these," he remarked, but "I think none could be more thankful for the privilege."[45] Although the settlers suffered for lack of religion and education, they came to hear the clergy who passed through. Unchurched by default rather than design, they confirmed many missionaries' images of godless but benign settlers who lived, as one missionary suggested, "literally and spiritually in a wilderness."[46]

Because local environments and natural resources were so closely tied to local economies, missionaries depicted these factors as intertwined influences on the settlers' piety and character. They tended to distinguish between settlers in the more prosperous farming regions and those in the more volatile lumbering or shipping towns, who often squatted on land and moved about to pursue their trades.[47] Most missionaries believed the northern frontier's agricultural hamlets promised the most fruitful return on their efforts, because they already boasted the makings of ordered communities.[48] John Brewer of the Evangelical Missionary Society praised Maine's farmers for having "carried their habits of industry, sobriety, love of order, or literary and religious institutions along with them." But others—including "seafaring people and traders, [and] those who turn their *chief* attention to the lumber trades"—were less cultivated. They set up "camps in the woods, . . . leaping from river to river, and from bay to bay, . . . leaving the rivers and bays streaked with settlements but society and morals very little improved." Unlike farming towns, which settlers had "improved" both physically and spiritually, Brewer feared these ephemeral settlements would only foster irreligion and vice.[49]

Other missionaries observed the same, and they wished the backcountry settlers would adopt the virtuous and rooted ways of farming, however unlikely their success might have been in northern New England's unforgiving climate. Edmund Easton suggested that the failure to establish permanent farming communities impeded the progress of learning and religion. "The unsettled state of the soil is a subject of great . . . and continual contention," he wrote of Maine's Kennebec and Lincoln counties. Conflict over land use and ownership "greatly damps the spirit for agricultural improvement and greatly lessens their exertions for the promotion of religious order."[50] Stephen Chapin similarly lamented what he perceived as an "adversion to agriculture," which would have instilled the values of hard work and sobriety. "They have no patience," he complained, "to wait for the slow, but sure grains of the farmer." It followed that these settlers had just as little patience for their own moral and spiritual improvement. "It is obvious," Chapin insisted, "that the steady pursuits of the farmer are much more favorable to morality and religion than [other] employments."[51] In keeping with a long New England tradition that paired improvement of the land with improvement of the soul, these missionaries suspected that transient settlers in fragile outposts were failing to do God's work either in the fields or in their own hearts. The insecure hinterland economy (and the poor farming conditions) made northern New England a challenging but vital missionary ground.

Those challenges would persist, missionaries predicted, so long as settlers remained entangled in the unending cycles of poverty, landlessness, and transience. Amos Cooke observed of New Hampshire that although "the soil in these new towns and back settlements is . . . very good and well adapted to tillage, the face of the new country is mountainous." The settlers, he thought, fit their surroundings; their "habits, tastes, [and] minds . . . will be rough and require much cultivation."[52] Silas Bingham found in Vermont that "the Towns in general on the Mountain are peculiarly needy." Although populous, "they are generally poor [and] have very little munny circulating among them." Poverty was so rampant that frontier inhabitants succumbed to what Bingham's colleague Chauncy Lee described as "an amoral spirit of speculation and smuggling," which left "little temper or disposition to attend to their spiritual and eternal interests."[53] Just as they associated agricultural landscapes with moral order, each of these missionaries suggested that mountainous terrain bred instability and vice. Until settlers could plant roots in places that promised a secure living and nurtured steady habits, well-ordered communities that might support town churches lay far in the future.

Missionaries thought they could overcome many of these obstacles, like the settlers' crude manners and lack of education, with time and effort. But other challenges, especially the northern frontier's changing sectarian landscape, posed more difficulty. The upstart denominations' rapid growth dismayed Congregationalist missionaries, who worried that dissenters—one missionary called them "disorganizers"—would draw away churchgoers and alter town-church boundaries.[54] The missionaries complained about "Sectarian preachers . . . rush-

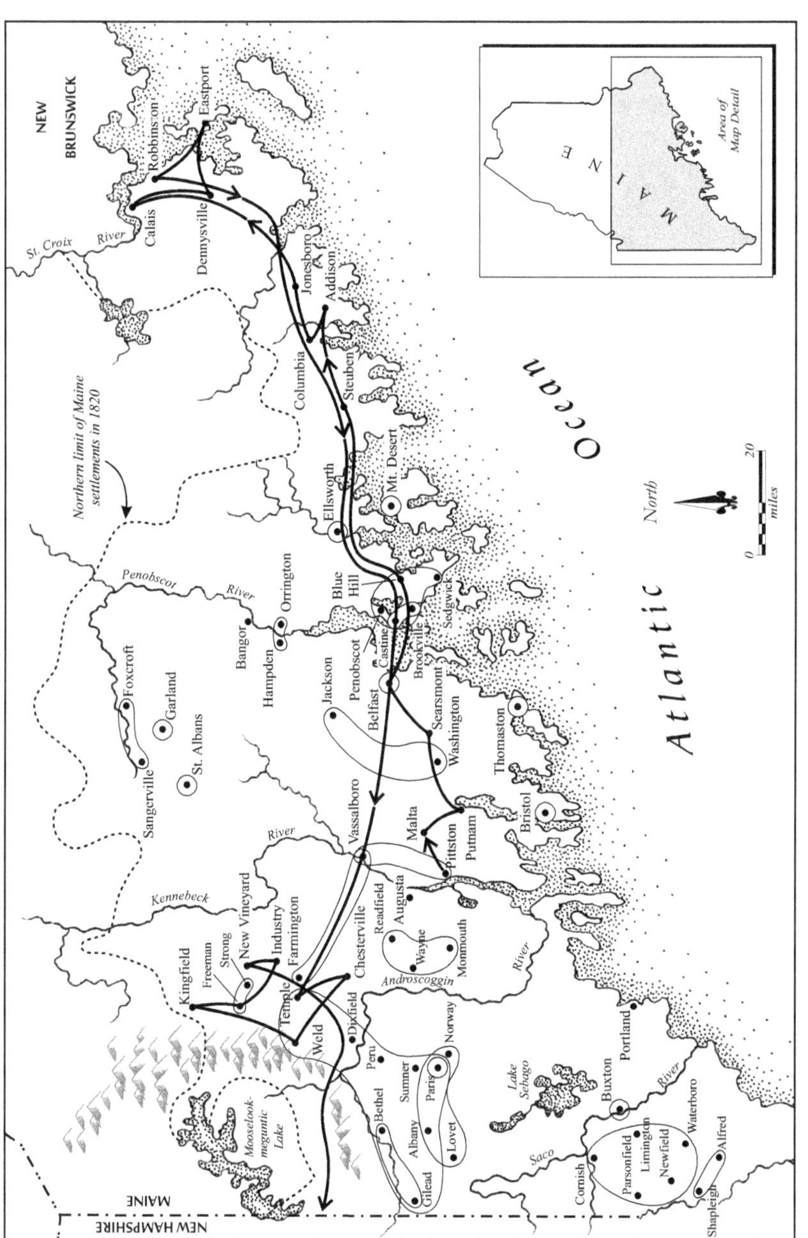

Map 5.1. Missionary fields in Maine, 1817–1818. It is impossible to know exactly how many Congregationalist missionaries were on the ground in Maine at any given time, but it is likely that more than sixty served the province in 1817–1818. They were not in the field all at once; a typical mission lasted one to three months. This map depicts twenty-three known tours during these years. Some assignments focused on just one town (circled) and its vicinity; other circuits saw missionaries cover two to six towns. A few ministers undertook much longer tours, such as Jotham Sewall, whose 1817–1818 tour of Maine is shown in bold. *Map by Mark Cook.*

ing in from every quarter" who taught "various species of delusive wildfire" and interfered with Congregationalist efforts to gather churches.[55] Paul Coffin shared these fears. "The religious State of *Maine* is not as one could wish," he reported to the SPG in 1797. "The People are visited by 2 sorts of *Baptists,* by *Quakers,* and by *Methodists*" who, he suspected, "are zealous to make followers."[56] Missionaries derided itinerants who spread unorthodox doctrine, and they portrayed the frontier inhabitants as innocent victims of sectarian designs. "I consider them as sheep left in the midst of wolves," wrote John Lawton of the parishioners in Eden, Vermont. "This country swarms with sectarian preachers," he added, "who are greedy to devour the little flocks that are gathered in these destitute towns."[57] These preachers would succeed, missionaries feared, in a frontier that isolated towns and robbed communities of the stability they needed to nurture town churches.

Despite the annoyances of travel, the settlers' peculiar habits, and the challenges posed by sectarians, ministers still sought missionary assignments. Missionary fields varied by location and scope. Some were quite specific; the EMS, for instance, assigned each minister a town or pair of towns, and the Maine Missionary Society designated "stands," or circuits of three or four towns per minister. Other societies issued more general instructions, like the SPG, which designated one or two counties, and the CMS, which instructed ministers to preach in northern or western Vermont (sometimes both), and perhaps suggested several towns to visit.[58] All societies allowed missionaries to preach elsewhere in the vicinity as the need or opportunity arose. Societies charged missionaries with wide-ranging duties, including visiting homes, preaching on the Sabbath, holding midweek lectures, distributing Bibles and tracts, selling subscriptions to religious periodicals, soliciting donations, administering sacraments, gathering churches, admitting new church members, catechizing children, and establishing (or even running) libraries and schools. In addition to these duties, missionaries kept journals, which they submitted after each mission. These journals not only documented their own labors; they also shed light on the religious and social climates the missionary encountered and identified potential new fields for work.

Societies expected ministers to be charitable in their personal dealings with settlers but uncompromising in their command of doctrine. Correct preaching ranked high among a missionary's duties. Ministers averaged about one sermon per day. Joseph Field preached 85 times during a summer tour in Maine, for example, and Samuel Goddard preached 157 times during a six-month tour of Vermont.[59] Asa Carpenter stressed the importance of preaching by noting that the towns he visited had "but little preaching of the right kind . . . except what is afforded by missionaries."[60] Because sectarian itinerants abounded, preaching of the "right kind" was crucial. John Brewer found, to his dismay, that layfolk favored a more animated style of preaching, and they rejected ministers whose sermons were "too plain, pointed, or severe." He blamed popular tastes on "those itinerant sectaries who sometimes preach in the corners of our towns," pointing out that "the most acceptable preaching is *not always* the most profitable."[61]

But missionaries did not shy away from the sectarian challenge. One guide defied conventional wisdom and suggested that missionaries "should [learn] to preach *without notes*" to attract hearers who were used to the evangelical style.[62] Samuel Brimblecom suspected that Congregationalists would fail if they tried to gather town churches without confronting the spiritual attractions that lured people away. Warning of the "very particular evil" of sectarianism, he suggested that "as long as the questions between different denominations remain unsettled, many who have never attached themselves to any religion will still continue neutral, and the Gospel in any form will fail of support."[63] To draw people away from sectarian enticements, missionaries would have to jump into the fray and combat error. Otherwise, he warned, Congregationalists would lose members to preachers who captivated them with style and emotional impact.

Ministers knew that Congregationalist churches could not afford such losses, and that they would remain vulnerable without a steady influx of new churchgoers. Accordingly, they placed a high priority on administering the sacraments: rites of membership that only ministers could perform and that therefore transpired rarely in backcountry settlements. William Miller, who preached to a packed house in Charlotte, Vermont, in 1802, administered the first communion the town had enjoyed in nearly four years.[64] Despite a growing missionary presence, many Vermont towns continued to do without sacraments. When Joseph Larabee toured the state in 1817, he visited many places where no one had administered communion "for two years past"—and, indeed, where Congregationalists had not preached "more than 1 or 2 Sabbaths."[65] Because baptism placed prospective members under the church's watch, and communion conferred membership, these rituals helped sustain churches by reaffirming members' covenant bonds. Missionaries seized every opportunity to build up churches through the sacraments, knowing that years could pass before an outlying settlement would have another chance to partake.

Preaching and the sacraments, however, occupied only a fraction of a missionary's time. Just like their counterparts in the settled ministry, Congregationalist missionaries devoted much of their work to visiting individuals and families. Whereas they averaged about one sermon daily, they paid between two and five visits per day to private homes. Jonathan Calif performed 156 visits, compared with offering 46 sermons, during a two-month tour. Jonathan Fisher paid 257 visits and preached 62 sermons on a tour of the same length, and Thomas Holt paid 435 visits on a tour twice as long, during which he preached 66 times.[66] Missionaries generally thought the hours they spent visiting numbered among their most productive. Abiel Abbot and Daniel Little reported in 1791 that "free conversation with families and individuals" proved "popular and useful." Not only did visiting allow the missionaries to use "every fragment of time," but it also gave them the chance to share "serious truth" with settlers, which "thus communicated [was] transmitted neighbor to neighbor," uniting the town in religious conversation.[67] Visiting not only afforded a missionary the chance to talk privately about spiritual matters, it also could turn a town's attention to religion even in the minister's absence. It is no wonder, then, that many missionaries thought their most important work took place in the home rather than the pulpit.

Instead of limiting their visits to fellow Congregationalists, traveling ministers tried to meet as many potential churchgoers (of any denomination) as possible. Some of these visits could be awkward; a missionary who met with a Methodist family reported that "tho treated with much respect I did not enjoy myself there being a disagreement in our sentiments and professions."[68] But these meetings could also be fruitful and cordial, as Jonathan Fisher discovered when he enjoyed a "friendly interview" with a Baptist minister.[69] Missionaries and settlers alike concurred on the value of visits. Robert Cochran decided to preach less and visit more, having become "convinced more good may be done by family visits than can be by preaching lectures." Churchgoers in one town urged Jonathan Calif to "spend most of my time in visiting from house to house." That way, he could understand "the state of religion among them, and how to administer instruction to them"—all the better to guide an infant church.[70]

Just as visiting gave missionaries entrée into hinterland communities, so too did teaching. Congregationalist missionaries sought to improve instruction because they thought an educated population would ensure their denomination's survival. The CMS credited much of the frontier's rapid population growth to young families "full of children."[71] This young generation inspired hope among those who believed Congregationalism would take root in growing communities. Stephen Chapin thought missionaries could expect to accomplish little among older migrants whose "opinions, habits, and prejudices [were] too deeply rooted to be eradicated." Rather, "it is among the rising generation that we must look to for a reformation."[72] Peter Nurse of the EMS also prized education as a complement to worship. Nurse arrived in Ellsworth, Maine, in 1811 and later settled in that town's pulpit. Noting the settlers' "strong desire that I should take charge of their schools as well as preach to them," he worked as hard to build up education as he did to establish religion. Like many town ministers who also oversaw schools, Nurse introduced students to the "interesting facts and momentous doctrines of the Bible," trusting that a generation exposed to religious education would someday form a more godly community.[73] Missionary societies hoped education, along with worship, would cultivate their charges' manners, morals, and spirituality so they might create ordered and pious societies.

Learning was not solely for the young. Missionaries also distributed Bibles, hymnals, and tracts to children and adults alike to encourage pious reading and reflection where books (and clergy) were scarce.[74] Most, like Ephraim Abbot, reported that they "visited many poor families, many destitute of the Bible." In one pair of townships, for example, Abbot discovered "not more than four or five bibles" along with "a few [New] testaments and mutilated bibles."[75] Samuel Goddard similarly found "great need of Bibles" during his tours of Vermont and New Hampshire.[76] To address these deficiencies, missionaries worked with a growing number of Bible and tract societies to find out how many frontier families lacked Bibles so they could supply as many as possible.[77] Missionaries and tract-society agents coordinated with each other to distribute shipments more efficiently. After Mighill Blood received several shipments in 1807, he distributed to three missionaries a Bible, 4 New Testaments, 2 hymnals, 5 spelling books, 17 copies of Philip Doddridge's *The Rise and Progress of the Soul* (a staple devotional text), and 187 sermons and tracts. The remainder of the shipment, which he reserved for other missionaries, included 2 spelling books, 3 New Testaments, 6 psalm books, 22 copies of *Rise and Progress of the Soul,* and 224 sermons and tracts, along with an extra box of Bibles and New Testaments.[78] Missionary and tract societies channeled a constant supply of reading material to distant settlements. By doing so, they hoped to encourage religious attention even when missionaries or settled clergy could not personally guide churches.

Because of the constant shortage of Bibles and other religious texts—and the limits to what they could carry—missionaries tried to be judicious when they handed out this material. In Norridgewock, Maine, Joseph Field left one Bible for Betsy Longley, whom her neighbors had described as "destitute and a proper object of charity." Samuel Goddard similarly delivered Bibles to "a poor family [who] lived a great distance from public worship and had no horse," and one "poor man with a considerable family."[79] Others used more choreographed strategies. One Vermont missionary entrusted a supply of books to a settler in Cabot, who ran a lending library for the members of his religious society. He loaned one book at a time to each borrower, who could make exchanges only on Sundays. The policy not only allowed him to distribute the books fairly, it also drew "the people to meeting for the sake of having a New Book."[80] Amos Cooke used a similar plan. Faced with the task of distributing a limited supply over five towns, he divided the Bibles as evenly as possible "among the most deserving." He also left one copy of *The Rise and Progress of the Soul* with a "poor but . . . trusted" churchgoer "on condition that it should be read by every family in the towns." As a reward for carrying out the plan, the original recipient of each volume could keep the book "as their own property."[81] Sharing the responsibility of distributing books with local residents, missionaries hoped that widespread reading would strengthen nascent churches by sparking religious conversations among neighbors and encouraging them to invest more care in each other's spiritual state.

Missionaries generally assumed that any assistance they provided—from preaching to visiting to instruction—could not match a settled minister's services. They had little patience for towns that relied on visiting preachers long after they might have filled their pulpits. Silas Bingham supposed that Leicester, Vermont, was "proper missionary ground, if a people's neglecting to procure the means of grace" was the only measure. But, he pointed out, the town had been settled for twenty-five years by the time he visited in 1809, and "as a people they have never taken any regular measures to have the gospel preached among them."[82] The people of Leicester had worn out their welcome in the missionary field. Other missionaries also wearied of towns that failed to settle clergy, and they refused to accept the common protest that poverty kept parishes from raising ministers' salaries. "If you are too poor to support the gospel," one suggested, "you are demonstrably too poor to do without it."[83]

Almost as soon as their work commenced, missionaries confidently reported that their efforts had begun to pay off. Archibald Bassett, who toured Vermont and New Hampshire in 1798, saw abundant proof of "the good effects of the labours of former missionaries," including "the frames of meetinghouses" that had begun to dot the land. But it quickly became clear that most settlements were ill-prepared to covenant as churches. David Huntington observed that "the towns are fast filling up with inhabitants, and as they come from different places they bring with them different customs, a considerable time must elapse before they can assimilate and unite in any important object." This instability underscored the "urgent necessity" of sending "judicious and pious missionaries" who could guide settlements as they coalesced into communities.[84] The period of assimilation proved long indeed. By the late 1820s, a town-church culture still seemed far in the future. Samuel Brimblecom observed of Maine that "the country is still new [and] many of the inhabitants not thoroughly settled on their farms." This precarious situation made for difficult church-gathering. "The settlers," he reported, "do not feel able nor interested to aid the establishment or support of a religious society."[85] It appeared that the Congregationalist missionary effort had evolved from a stopgap measure to a fixed institution.

Most missionaries conceived of their roles primarily as advancing Congregationalism by seeking out, gathering, and guiding infant churches. They hoped to replicate southern New England's religious geography by extending the town-church system, even though they, as itinerants, worked outside of that system. But town churches proved difficult to assemble where the realities of a spiritually diverse and economically insecure society conspired against religious unity. The missionary enterprise, its proponents argued, was a necessary bridge between an unstable wilderness and an ordered society that could support worship. During that transition, they relied on itinerancy to stem the tides of sectarianism and irreligion while they worked to nurture covenanted communities.

Unlike denominations that depended on permanent traveling ministries, Congregationalists accepted itinerancy only as a means to a greater goal: organizing town churches and settling ministers. By reaching unchurched settlements, sending ministerial candidates into the field, and offering assistance to new churches, missionaries hoped to extend the town-church system into the northern frontier, where they hoped it would take root and render missionary work obsolete. But the very nature of itinerancy detracted from those goals. Missionaries could gather churches but not shepherd them. They could baptize infants but not catechize those same children years later. They could hold communion but not promise to repeat the ritual during the next sacramental season. In other words, itinerancy was incompatible with the very core of the town-church community: the long-term moral and spiritual commitment between churchgoers and their settled minister. As Congregationalist itinerancy became more entrenched, its traveling ministers found themselves working at cross-purposes. They could extend Congregationalism or preserve the town-church system but not both. This inherent conflict not only shaped the missionary effort but also reshaped its religious communities in the northern frontier.

Missionaries noticed immediately the conspicuous absence of permanent clergy in northern New England. In 1793, Samuel Mills found that no towns had settled ministers on either bank of the Connecticut River along its northernmost eighty miles.[86] The situation improved little over time. Ephraim Abbot discovered in 1811 that no minister served the townships east of Machias, Maine.[87] In 1817, another missionary reported only eight settled Congregationalist ministers in Vermont's four northernmost counties. "Darkness covers the land," concluded the Vermont General Convention about this state of affairs, "and gross darkness the people."[88] Curtis Coe discovered the same situation in the border region between New Hampshire and Maine. New Hampshire's pulpits were empty between Exeter and the boundary with Lower Canada (present-day Quebec), a distance, he judged, of about 190 miles. In Maine, he reported similar circumstances north of Lebanon.[89] Like most Congregationalist missionaries, Coe sought ways to fill pulpits as fast—and permanently—as possible. Because a town church depended on a minister at its spiritual center, Congregationalist missionaries found northern New England's ministerial shortfall particularly alarming.

Congregationalist settlers who appealed to missionary societies only confirmed the general impression of northern New England as a vast unchurched territory. One hopeful churchgoer in Vermont claimed in 1801 that some of the state's "new towns" had not heard a Congregationalist minister for over three years.[90] The Union Consociation, which included towns on both sides of the Vermont–New Hampshire border, reported in 1812 that its member churches were "almost all destitute of the gospel ministry" and requested missionary assistance so they might combat the "pernicious errors" of other preachers.[91] Congregationalists in Ellsworth, Maine, similarly complained of "low bred Preachers . . . lurking about," who attracted dissenters' support and stymied the town's plans to build a meetinghouse and settle a minister.[92] Other churches requested missionary aid for similar reasons: they were too small, poor, or divided to support worship, and no suitable ministers preached nearby.[93] The Congregationalist laity and missionaries were equally anxious about the ministerial shortfall in northern New England. And both groups seemed convinced that, should the problem persist, rival denominations and creeping apathy would soon crowd out town churches.

Missionary societies tried to address the shortages within the Congregational model by encouraging churches to settle clergy whenever possible. Accordingly, they often assigned missionaries to churches that sought to ordain clergy, and sent financial aid to those that risked losing the ministers they already employed. The Evangelical Missionary Society eschewed the usual tactic of assigning broad missionary fields and instead located each missionary within one or two towns to foster a relationship between pastor and parishioners—one that would ideally lead to a settlement. Although the EMS expected each minister to preach in nearby settlements as well, it intended missionaries to serve primarily in their assigned locations. Such was the case with Silas Warren, a missionary who "objected to traveling" and served the Maine plantations of Jackson and Washington. The church in Jackson ordained him in 1812, and he remained there at least through the 1820s, though he continued to preach in nearby towns.[94] Peter Nurse, who also settled in his assigned church, insisted that "it is the duty of the people of every town . . . to have [a minister] ordained and established over them." Likewise, his church favored the Evangelical Missionary Society's policy of "conferring the labors of one Missionary to one Society or neighbourhood." The EMS surely concurred with Ellsworth's churchgoers, who suggested that "the labours of cultivation too widely diffused are like seeds sown on stony ground." Better, they thought, to concentrate a missionary's work in one town and build a lasting relationship. Peter Nurse, they claimed, had "done more good" by staying in Ellsworth "than ten such Missionaries could have done traveling in the usual manner."[95]

Like the EMS, other societies funded churches that could not raise adequate ministers' salaries by themselves. The church in Fryeburg, Maine, appealed to the SPG for direct aid when its congregation decided to settle Carleton Hurd, an SPG missionary, in 1823. The church offered Hurd two hundred dollars for the first five years of his pastorate, and five hundred dollars for every year thereafter, and they asked the SPG whether the "deficiency in the salary for five years may be made up in foreign aid." The society agreed, and to good effect. When Hurd thanked the SPG for their assistance, he added that the extra funds made possible the pastoral relationship that Congregationalists prized. "They are now my church and my people," he explained, "and upon them I look with more than the eyes of a Missionary, who is to spend but a few weeks in their service."[96] Clinging to the town-church ideal in a place where few churches achieved it, Hurd believed his greatest potential to serve lay in the settled pulpit, not the missionary field.

Still more common were part-time settlements that churches and missionary societies funded jointly. In these arrangements, a settled minister performed missionary work for part of the year because his church could not pay his full salary but did not want to dismiss him. The Maine Missionary Society agreed to pay over half of Daniel Kendrick's four-hundred-dollar salary as Pittston's ordained minister "in order to encourage his settlement." In exchange, Kendrick spent six months of each year on missions. The society invested more money than usual in Kendrick, but such agreements were typical, with most annual contributions ranging from fifty to one hundred dollars.[97] The Vermont Missionary Society similarly agreed to help Luther Leland keep his pulpit in Derby. Leland, who had preached in Derby as a missionary before settling there, earned one third of his salary from the society and continued to perform missionary work. Later, he sought a similar arrangement with the CMS. He proposed a six-month mission during which he would preach half the time in Derby and the rest "in this County or in the northern part of the state of Vermont." The church supported Leland's appeal for help, citing his "great service to this place, [and] also to the neighboring towns who are destitute." Leland remained committed to his church and explained that "there are but two settled Ministers in this County and should I be dismissed there would be but one." But he acknowledged that "I must not in [the] future preach where I am not paid."[98] Like many other ministers who had to choose between a salary and a settlement, cooperative efforts between churches and missionary societies allowed them to have both.

Despite efforts to settle ministers, even part time, the number of available clergy could not match the number of empty pulpits. Regardless, missionaries gathered as many churches as they could, trusting that an organized church (even a headless church) could better regulate and guide its members than no church at all. In their effort to gather churches, missionaries contributed to a major Congregationalist expansion in the decades following the Revolutionary War. Throughout northern New England, the number of new Congregationalist churches nearly tripled between 1780 and 1830 (see table 5.1). Even in New Hampshire, which boasted the longest-standing Congregationalist establishment by 1780, the number of new churches roughly doubled during this period. Not all of these churches were founded with missionary aid. But the largest overall gains in church-gathering coincided with the peak of Congregationalist missionary ac-

Table 5.1. New Congregationalist Churches in Northern New England through 1829

YEARS	VERMONT	NEW HAMPSHIRE	MAINE	TOTAL
through 1779	24	90	32	146
1780–1789	30	22	6	58
1790–1799	38	14	20	72
1800–1809	52	17	36	105
1810–1819	29	18	28	75
1820–1829	29	27	28*	84*
Total(post-1779)	178	98	118*	394*

* Statistics for church-gathering in Maine are available only through 1826.
Note: This table indicates the number of new churches in each decade—not the number in existence at any given time. When a church disbanded and regathered years later, it factors in these statistics twice as a new church. These reconstituted churches, however, make up an insignificant proportion of the whole.

tivity, with new missionaries societies organized, new fields opened, and more itinerants assigned to the frontier. Whether they drove the trend or benefited from it, these ministers enjoyed tremendous success in their efforts to organize new churches.

The best candidates for new churches were towns with stable communities, where sectarians had not already made inroads, divided settlers, and claimed shares of ministerial funds—in other words, towns with a unified social, religious, and economic base. Cotton Mather Smith thought he had found such a place in West Haven, Vermont, where he visited in 1793. His audience appeared "well united in sentiments, and but few Sectarians," and they seemed prepared to "exert themselves to procure the Settlement of a Gospel minister."[99] Missionaries sought towns like West Haven, which were either ready to form a church or might be soon with help from visiting clergy. Mighill Blood thought Lincolnville, Maine, was an "excellent township" when he visited in 1810, though its residents could not yet support a minister. He predicted, "there will, in a few years, be a

Map 5.2. *Facing page*: Town churches and settled ministers in central Vermont, 1800–1820. Orange and Addison counties comprised a mix of long-settled towns and remote mountain outposts. This map shows how the distribution of town churches and settled ministers changed during the 1800s and 1810s, at the height of missionary activity in the state. Three towns in southern Addison County (Brandon, Orwell, and Sudbury) had joined Rutland County by 1820, and two towns in the northwestern corner of Orange County (Berlin and Northfield) had joined Washington County by 1820, but they are shown on the latter map for the sake of consistency. *Maps by Mark Cook.*

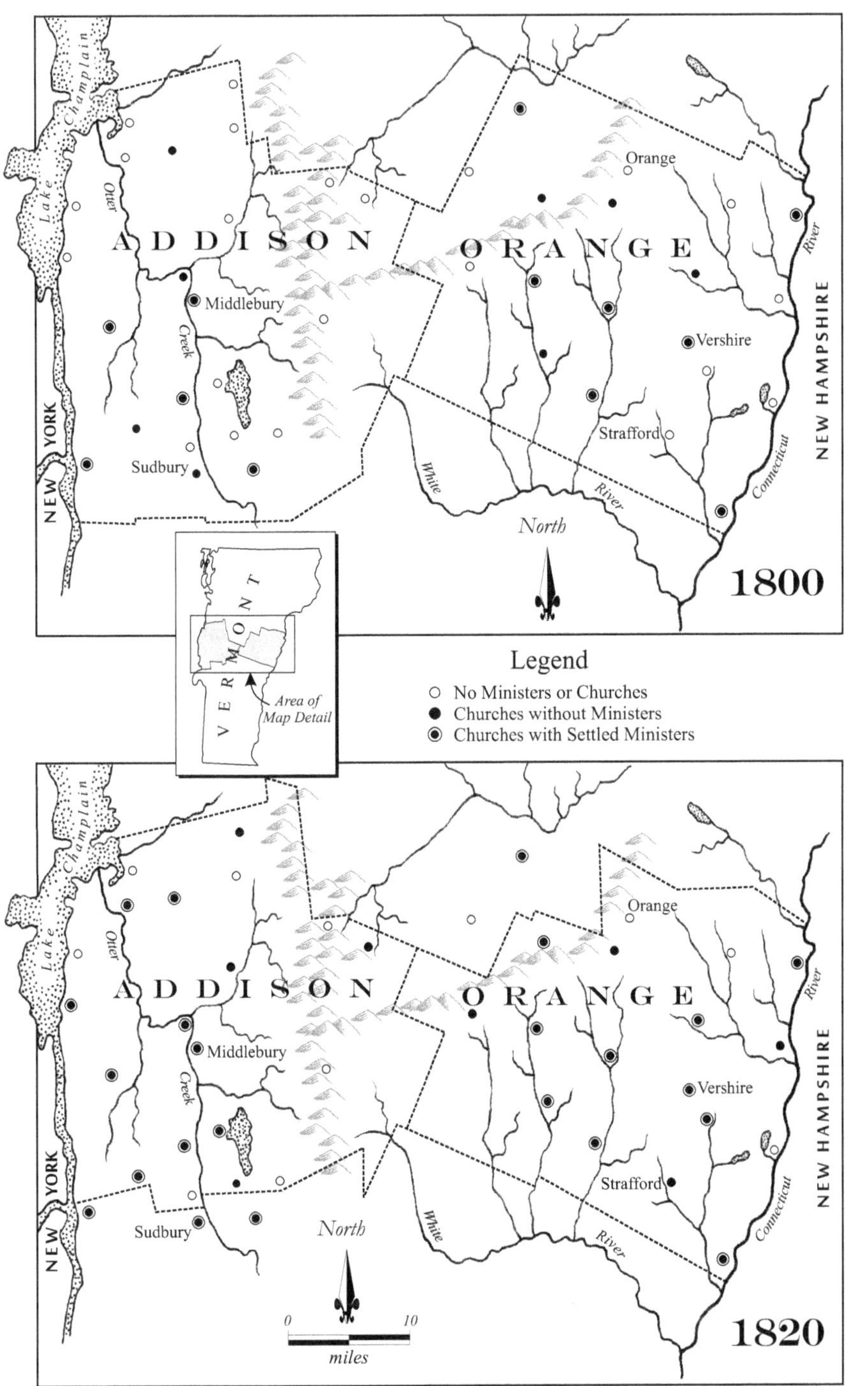
Lake Champlain
Otter
Creek
ADDISON
ORANGE
Middlebury
Sudbury
Orange
Vershire
Strafford
White
River
Connecticut
River
NEW YORK
NEW HAMPSHIRE
North
1800
VERMONT
Area of Map Detail
Legend
No Ministers or Churches
Churches without Ministers
Churches with Settled Ministers
0
10
miles
1820

very respectable, harmonious . . . Church and Society there," which could protect its members from "those who throw themselves into the ministry, and scatter errour, delusion, and sedition among christians."[100] A promising new church could set an example for neighboring towns. So thought Elijah Kellogg, who considered Lubec, Maine, the "only favoured spot" for a new church in a "destitute and disordered region," thanks to the town's recent prosperity and the relatively shallow inroads sectarians had made there. He began to gather a church there in 1818, hoping that it "would be a light shining in a dark place."[101]

Missionaries agreed that one successful church could anchor Congregationalism in an unchurched territory. Faced with a choice between ministering to scattered people and focusing on receptive towns, many chose the latter. A missionary in New Hampshire thought diluted efforts would produce weak results—in which case, "we lose our object, in assisting them at all." Better, he thought, to nurture one infant church. "If one Society in this desolate region can be established," he predicted, "it will do more to encourage and eventually establish others, than the *occasional* efforts of *many* ministers in *many* years."[102] Over time missionaries hoped they would make themselves obsolete by planting town churches that had no need for itinerants.

However missionaries tried to extend and strengthen the town-church legacy, the fact that they used itinerants to do so both furthered and hampered their efforts. Most missionaries served many churches, towns, and counties. Even settled ministers who relied on outside support accepted part-time itinerancy as one of the costs of leading poor congregations. Although many lauded the societies' efforts and celebrated new churches and expanded memberships, they still regretted the itinerant compromise. Sometimes, the cost of itinerancy was too high; when missionaries set out on tours, they left their home churches and families without clergy. One minister reluctantly sought assignments even though his absence would leave his family "with no meeting to attend better than the Methodist, which perhaps are worse than none."[103] Others observed that missionaries could only offer limited assistance to the churches they visited. Stephen Chapin wrote that "moral instruction has not much influence when it is not enforced by good example." Without a constant and trusted ministerial presence, he thought, churches would remain susceptible to sectarian influences. Therein lay the itinerant ministry's fatal flaw. "Your traveling missionaries have done much good," Chapin advised the SPG, "but perhaps not as much as they would have done, had they been stationary."[104]

Missionaries undoubtedly furthered the Congregationalist cause and did much to preserve the town-church system in the New England frontier. But the missionary effort both weakened and restructured the town-church boundaries—and, by extension, Congregationalism itself. The missionary enterprise dissolved the town church's physical boundaries, compromised its autonomy, and imbued its sacred space with a fluidity that was new to covenanted communities. In doing so, itinerancy fundamentally altered the relationships among town, church, and minister that had defined the Congregationalist geography.

Missionary work rearranged the town church's physical geography most of all by introducing the itinerant plan to Congregationalism. Traveling ministers crossed parish boundaries and connected individual communities within sprawling networks, thereby reordering the town church's spatial plan. Most importantly, itinerancy dissolved the borders between religious communities. Because missionaries made rare appearances in any particular place, they drew churchgoers from nearby towns who wanted to attend whatever meeting they could. When Ephraim Abbot preached in Denny's River, Maine, in 1811, his audience of two hundred included residents of several towns and unincorporated plantations, all at least ten miles away.[105] As missionaries welcomed churchgoers from the wider vicinity, they learned to expect movement back and forth across town lines and began to see their congregations not as locally rooted entities but instead as gathering points for far-flung believers. Jedidiah Bushnell reported in 1801 that "my congregation" in New Haven, Vermont, "is now sixty miles long and thirty broad." He still conceived of his church as having geographic bounds—but these clearly did not coincide with any town lines.[106] With itinerancy came a new understanding of geographic community, one that allowed movement beyond traditional town limits.

The changing physical geography of Congregationalism also applied to its religious infrastructure. Towns that benefited most from missionary labor were poor, divided, and only recently settled—in other words, the places least likely to have built churches. As a result, missionaries grew accustomed to preaching in barns, schoolhouses, homes, and the like. During a mission in 1812, Ephraim Abbot preached in a few schoolhouses, many private homes, and one Baptist church.[107] On a two-week tour in 1818, Jonathan Fisher preached in one schoolhouse and two private homes.[108] Without meetinghouses to mark their geographic, political, and spiritual centers, towns also lacked church seating plans and proprietary pews: the concrete markings of a closed religious community. And as congregations increasingly worshiped in alternative structures, they came to accept the open access those buildings allowed.

Chauncy Lee, who preached in many untraditional spaces during an 1808 tour of northeastern Vermont, officiated over one meeting in Hinesburg that epitomized a new Congregationalist community's permeable borders. Lee reported that "the people poured out in multitudes to the place of worship, which was a large Brick School house." So many attended that the congregation exceeded the building's capacity. To accommodate everyone, some churchgoers "remov[ed] the lower half of a window [and] formed another congregation without doors." Once his large audience was properly situated, Lee carried on with Sabbath worship, preaching two sermons, administering communion, and baptizing a child.[109] As he discovered, meeting in a schoolhouse (or any other secular structure) blurred the lines between sacred and profane space and literally dissolved the barriers between a community's insiders and outsiders. As the religious gravity of Congregationalism shifted to the expanding missionary field, worship in improvised settings became less the exception and more the norm. So, too, did the fluid boundaries between religious communities.

Itinerancy also rearranged the physical layout of Congregationalism on a broader scale. Although the town-church system in northern New England never quite worked as ministers had hoped, the northern frontier's Congregationalist churches had claimed local autonomy and local roots. But as itinerancy increasingly interwove with Congregationalism, the town churches' ties to organic communities faded. This shift resulted partly from disestablishment and sectarian expansion, both of which weakened parishes and fragmented previously united towns. But the changing Congregationalist geography also resulted from the missionary effort, which linked churches within an expansive network. Unlike the sectarian bureaucracies, no unifying hierarchy emerged in this relatively decentralized system. Instead, missionary societies occupied the centers of overlapping webs of religious activity and communication. Within this hodgepodge, each society both concentrated its authority over churches and broadened its geographic reach, thereby reorienting Congregationalism around a regional framework.

Missionary societies extended their influence first of all by directing the path of Congregationalism through northern towns. The town-church model held that congregations alone should choose their clergy. But communities that sought missionaries shared decision-making authority with the societies that supplied those ministers. These societies hired clergy, selected their missionary fields (sometimes choosing which churches they visited), and monitored their activities through their journals and correspondence. Moreover, each society favored a particular doctrinal bent. The Society for Propagating the Gospel embraced a centrist orthodoxy and dismissed ministers whom they considered too liberal. The Evangelical Missionary Society, which hired both liberal Congregationalists and Unitarians, shunned "Calvinistic zealots."[110] On the opposite end of the spectrum, the Connecticut Missionary Society embraced New Divinity theology and hired ministers who subscribed to strict Calvinism. Their missionaries' doctrinal influence may partly explain why the New Divinity took root in Vermont (where the CMS concentrated) whereas more moderate doctrine prevailed in Maine (where groups like the SPG and Maine Missionary Society held sway). By exercising authority over the doctrines their clergy taught and the places where they ministered, missionary societies helped determine Congregationalist orientation within their itinerant fields.

Because they decided which ministers would fill empty pulpits, societies also influenced churches' decisions about whom to settle. The societies' control over churches was not absolute; missionary appointments tended to be flexible, and any congregation could reject any minister. The decision to ordain a minister remained the church's alone. But missionary societies paired traveling ministers with needy churches, and when these churches decided to settle a minister, they often chose a familiar missionary. Such was the case with Benjamin Wooster, whose visit to Cornwall, Vermont, resulted in a settlement there; Ephraim Abbot, who visited Greenland, New Hampshire, as a missionary before the town offered him the pulpit; and Freeman Parker, whose preaching in Dresden, Maine, won him that town's loyalty and support.[111] To be sure, missionary societies strove to gather independent churches that could ordain whomever they wished. But by offering only approved candidates, societies narrowed churches' options. As they filled more and more pulpits, these few organizations held sway over decisions that individual churches had handled independently in the past. In doing so, the missionary societies reoriented each town church's focus away from its private, local affairs and toward a regional network of like-minded churches connected within a web of missionary activity.

Missionary societies strengthened regional ties not only by centralizing authority but also by creating a print network of religious magazines and newspapers that itinerants delivered to frontier settlements. Because they were so easy to produce and transport, the number of periodicals rose sharply in the early nineteenth century, paralleling the expansion of print culture more broadly.[112] Congregationalists used their publishing enterprise to share news of revivals and missionary activity, expound on doctrinal or moral lessons, and reinforce ecclesiastical or disciplinary standards. Their periodicals—such as the *Christian Monitor,* the *Connecticut Evangelical Magazine,* the *New Hampshire Chronicle,* the *Piscataqua Evangelical Magazine,* the *Religious Intelligencer,* and the *Vermont Evangelical Magazine*—documented and supported the missionary enterprise by sharing news and doctrine. As one newspaper claimed, religious periodicals "are made instrumental in bringing nigh those who were afar off."[113] Distant towns and churches that might have held little stake in each other now connected through reading, which reinforced their common faith. For two or three dollars per year, subscribers could keep abreast of "the most important accounts of the operations of Bible, Missionary, Tract, and various other societies." This news was especially important in light of the rapid expansion into the frontier. As the *Religious Intelligencer* reminded its readers, "scattered as Christians are in this part of our country, . . . without this means of information, it is impossible for us to know the conditions of other churches, or to act in concert with them."[114] The Congregationalist print culture broke down physical barriers by establishing a regional network among missionary societies, itinerants, and congregations.

Just as missionary activity altered the town church's physical dimensions, so did it rearrange the institution's sense of spiritual space. In its ideal form, the town church existed as a self-contained spiritual unit with a settled minister at its center. But when towns shared missionaries, the pastoral relationship fundamentally changed. No longer could a settled pastor pay constant attention to his church. Although expanding missionary activity allowed towns that had done without clergy to enjoy a ministerial presence, they could do so only for a fraction of the time. Moreover, they had to grow accustomed to not just one missionary passing through periodically but perhaps several in rotation, with little advance warning as to which one might show up or when. As a result, the town's spiritual gravity no longer concentrated in one pastor, but instead dispersed between the local laity and transient ministers.

Many missionaries regretted their fleeting presence in their churchgoers' lives. Paul Coffin, having preached near Caratunk Falls, Maine, in 1797, found the people there "serious . . . and very teachable." He was "sorry, very sorry," that he had to leave the next day to honor another appointment. With more time, he thought, "I might have fixed them in the knowledge of essential truths and the duties of the gospel." Therein lay the cost of itinerancy: Coffin served as many congregations as he could reach, but he also felt "much grieved to lose such a prospect of usefulness."[115] Many Congregationalist itinerants shared Coffin's misgivings. Ephraim Abbot, having completed an 1811 mission in Washington County, Maine, worried for the spiritual fate of the region's inhabitants—both the "children of G[od]" and the "many souls who are sleeping on the brink of destruction." With no other Congregationalist ministers in the county, Abbot asked, "how can I leave them alone?"[116] Justin Parsons was equally dismayed that he had to leave Kingston, New Hampshire, in 1818 just as an awakening began to stir the congregation. "I wish I could stay," he informed the Vermont Missionary Society, "but I cannot [as] I am engaged elsewhere." He requested that the society send someone else for the next Sabbath to help the revival along.[117] Missionaries who straddled the breach between a town-church ideal and an itinerant reality questioned their responsibilities and usefulness as ministers.

The relationships between itinerant and settled clergy also proved difficult to navigate. Alden Bradford complained in 1811 that many SPG missionaries had preached in towns that had settled ministers—a practice that "is not in conformity with their instructions" and "has a tendency to create divisions and disorders in our churches."[118] Never mind that the missionaries about whom Bradford complained (including luminaries like Jotham Sewall and his brother Samuel) were of his own denomination and had already spent considerable time in these places. According to the town-church ideal, the bond between a settled minister and his flock reigned supreme; a missionary's role was to offer a substitute for that relationship without supplanting it.

Not all missionaries agreed. Some claimed that visits by new ministers could breathe life into struggling congregations by offering fresh preaching and changes of pace. Jonathan Harvey praised the efforts of "Eight Labourers in the course of Eight or Ten months" who effected a "powerful display of divine grace" in the congregations he visited in Vermont.[119] Timothy Hilliard, on an 1817 tour of New Hampshire, also observed that ministers "from abroad" seemed "to raise the interest" in an otherwise quiet congregation. Before long, he questioned "the necessity of confining my labors to [one] people."[120] Hilliard's musings departed sharply from the Congregationalist assumption that the bond between a settled pastor and his flock lay at the core of the town church. Not only did the missionary enterprise alter that relationship, it also altered how at least some Congregationalists idealized religious community.

Itinerancy strained but did not completely break the bonds between congregations and ministers. Many missionaries found it possible—and even beneficial—to build long-term relationships with many churches. Repeated visits proved fruitful; as each minister became a more familiar presence, he attracted more followers. For that reason, Paul Coffin asked to repeat a previous missionary assignment "as nearly as may be" on a new tour, "hoping thus to be more useful."[121] Amos Cooke noticed the effects of repeated appearances when his second visit to a church drew "a greater audience than on the former occasion," including many from nearby towns. His third appearance attracted still more hearers, giving Cooke "reason to rejoice on my success as a Missionary" and, indeed, gave him "greater confidence."[122] George Freeman, too, found that he drew larger audiences with repeat visits. In Worcester, Vermont, he preached in the same private home twice within several weeks. For his second appearance, "though the traveling was worse a larger number attended," including some who had trekked for miles on a "verry muddy road" through the woods. His efforts in Worcester continued to pay off. A month later, he preached to "the largest number ever assembled to divine worship in this town." A few months after that, he gathered a church there, to which he admitted over a dozen members.[123] The place these missionaries occupied in their congregations paralleled that of a Methodist circuit preacher more than a Congregationalist town minister: they enjoyed a familiarity bred through repeated, but not constant, contact. In these towns, persistent and frequent interaction nudged along a pastoral bond and nurtured spiritual communities that otherwise had little chance to take root.

Some ministers developed still longer-term relationships with the congregations they served, even if they never settled in those towns. Few achieved greater status among the people they visited than Jotham Sewall. Sewall preached in New Hampshire and Maine for the Maine Missionary Society, the Massachusetts Society for Promoting Christian Knowledge, and the Massachusetts Missionary Society between 1801 and 1850. Throughout his career, he preached in

234 towns in Maine and 41 in New Hampshire. In many places, he appeared well over 200 times: 210 in Industry, 222 in Augusta, 233 in Machias, 497 in Farmington, and 1,369 in his home church of Chesterville.[124] He was, to say the least, a constant and well-known presence in the missionary field. Joseph Field, who encountered Sewall in Norway, Maine, credited Sewall with founding and directing many nearby churches and observed that nearby Congregationalists "look up with great veneration to Mr. Jotham Sewall as their Spiritual father and founder." Ephraim Abbot concurred, calling him "the father of almost all religion in this country."[125] Even though he never settled in these churches, Sewall used missionary tours to offer the leadership, discipline, and guidance that a town minister would have provided. His experience shows that an ongoing ministerial relationship remained central to Congregationalist communities. But missionary work compromised a minister's ability to shepherd any single congregation. Whatever bonds he forged with his congregations, therefore, signified an adaptation to itinerancy and a departure from the town-church ideal.

So, too, did new models of revival that emerged in this itinerant context. In the town-church context, the village revival epitomized the network of personal ties and mutual obligations in the covenanted community. This pattern contrasted with other styles of revival, such as the Methodist camp meeting, which welcomed participants from many towns and denominations who might have been strangers to each other. But village revivals could take weeks or months to build before they peaked in a spate of new conversions and memberships, so missionaries could not see them through. Without a typical town church's spiritual layout, the basic forms of revival changed, and so did a missionary's role in leading them.

Under a missionary's guidance, "town-church" revivals often involved multiple towns, churches, and ministers. Much like in the "cluster revivals" over which other itinerant ministers officiated, these awakenings drew large audiences, and spectators carried the momentum back to their own towns. Stable pastoral relationships rarely nurtured these revivals. Rather than hinging on one minister's labor, a new Congregationalist awakening depended on whatever clergy happened through. A small headless church in Washington, New Hampshire, had hosted several visiting ministers over the winter and spring of 1817 by the time a revival erupted in May. When a pair of missionaries arrived in August, the awakening was well underway. A final minister saw the event through its peak in the fall and winter. By the time the revival subsided the next spring—one year and several itinerants later—the church boasted forty-seven new members, and the town of eight hundred included about sixty-five new converts.[126] The collaboration between itinerants and churchgoers proved essential and profitable.

The notion that visiting ministers might coax along a village revival had never been consistent with the town-church ideal, but it became popular in northern New England. One minister even proposed that Congregationalist clergy work in itinerant revivalist teams: pairs of ministers "always . . . in company," collaborating "to stir [the faithful] to prayer and to duty."[127] This idea never caught on among Congregationalists, but ministers did join forces to bring about awakenings. The *Vermont Missionary Register* recommended in 1823 (based on anecdotal evidence of the method's success) that a succession of ministers rotate through each other's churches to create a "circle" of exhortation and prayer. With luck, they might ignite a revival, which would then spread throughout the several communities.[128] This proposal clearly conflicted with the town-church model of revival. Indeed, the suggestion that many visiting clergy could—and should—contribute to an awakening signified new thinking about the pastoral relationship that had been so central to the town church's spiritual landscape.

The itinerant form of Congregationalist revival signified a broader shift in the town church's geographic orientation. Thanks to the missionary enterprise, Congregationalist churches across northern New England enjoyed periodic (and sometimes frequent) preaching, partook in the sacraments, and received financial aid to help gather churches or settle ministers. It is impossible to know whether Congregationalism would have survived in the frontier without missions, but given the region's dispersed settlement and the meager supply of ministerial candidates, the clergy's early fears of losing out to sectarians seem well-grounded. By adopting some of their rivals' itinerant methods, missionaries extended their denomination's geographic reach and secured their foothold in northern New England. Their means of expanding Congregationalism, however, also weakened its core institution. The town church epitomized the covenanted community's independence and interdependence as a spiritual and geographic unit. As its once-shared boundaries dissolved into a new religious landscape, the clergy and laity alike grappled with how to reconcile the older town-church ideal with the realities of an itinerant system.

By all accounts, missionaries succeeded in their efforts to shore up Congregationalism in the northern frontier. They attracted new members and kept longstanding churchgoers in the fold. They gathered (and re-gathered) congregations, oversaw church construction, settled new ministers, and helped struggling towns keep their existing clergy. At least partly due to missionary labor, Congregationalist church membership expanded through the early decades of the nineteenth century.[129] Given the new challenges to the faith—disestablishment, denominational competition, and social instability—the missionaries seem to have carried out their principal directive to preserve and expand Congregationalism.

But in doing so, they remapped their denomination's religious geography. To preserve the denomination, missionaries had to sacrifice aspects of the town-church culture that had not only typified Congregationalism but defined it. They disregarded town borders to allow nearby churchgoers to attend worship and join communion. They led meetings in barns, schoolhouses, and the like: places that failed to distinguish insiders from outsiders as neatly as village meeting-houses did. They gathered headless churches with vague hopes that missionaries would pass through often enough to keep the congregations intact—or, alternatively, they left their own churches for months on end, hoping that their part-time missionary income would save them from losing their pulpits. Rather than leave each town church to its own devices, Congregationalists looked to missionary societies to decide which ministers to hire, where to send them, and which doctrine to preach (or shun). Rather than plant roots in particular places, missionaries linked towns through their travels and reoriented churches so they looked outward toward sympathetic believers around the region.

Without abandoning any tenet of Congregationalist doctrine, missionaries transformed the denomination by dismantling the most essential features of the town-church model. Although many Congregationalists held fast to the ideal, they refashioned the denomination around an emerging frontier religious culture. The missionary enterprise succeeded, in other words, by turning Congregationalism into an itinerant movement.

6 A City Set on a Hill

Northern New England's New Religious Geography

MISSIONARIES AND ITINERANTS, churchgoers and unchurched, settled clergy of all stripes—they all helped dismantle the framework of the old town-church system and build new structures in its place. But even those who brought about this transformation had trouble navigating the religious landscapes they created. This was certainly true in the neighboring towns of Barnet, Vermont, and Lyman, New Hampshire, during the fall of 1816, when local Methodists and Congregationalists waged a turf war. Congregationalist missionary Samuel Goddard, who was working to gather a church in Barnet, noticed that the Methodists had begun to struggle in Lyman, which lay on the opposite bank of the Connecticut River. He reported that "the Methodist have occupied this ground allmost intirely since the first settlement of the Town," but their grip was slipping. Of their two local preachers, one had renounced Methodism for Congregationalism. But the Methodists refused to give him a proper dismission, thereby compelling him to remain in a church he no longer supported. Meanwhile, the other local Methodist minister and a third preacher, a circuit rider, tried to add to their membership. But they faced such indifference that they "proposed to give up trying to preach" to nearby settlers.[1]

When their former colleague began leading Congregationalist conferences, however, the Methodists redoubled their efforts. They appeared in the midst of Barnet's Congregationalist revival and offered to help. But Goddard suspected that they secretly planned to siphon off new converts. The Methodists "are very much engaged to occupy the ground," he noted, "and seem to claim it aright and the young converts as their property." He believed the Methodists' efforts were in vain; the converts (by his tally) were all "Calvinist in sentiment, so far as they understand doctrine."[2] Armed with new members and a new church (that later comprised both towns), the Congregationalists emerged from this episode victorious.

This skirmish across the Connecticut River revealed much about the state of religion in early republican northern New England. A Congregationalist missionary sought to plant a town church, but with spiritual boundaries that extended into the next state. The Methodists, much feared by the Congregationalists for their purported knack for seducing churchgoers, scrambled to retain members and even their own clergy. The opposing churches worked together in a multi-denominational revival that masked furtive attempts to lure converts to one church or another. Among the revival's leaders was a former Methodist preacher with Calvinist sympathies, who awakened sinners in Congregationalist conferences. Goddard should have given the settlers more credit for their ability to "understand doctrine"—given the commotion that reigned in their neighborhoods, they seem to have sorted out the confusion rather well.

By the 1820s, northern New England's principal denominations were neither remote strangers nor intimate friends. Familiarity had bred both contempt and collegiality, suspicion and admiration. Denominations competed for funding, meetinghouses, and followers. Their constant struggles over these assets brought them into close, if awkward, contact with each other. But they also cooperated in the interest of nurturing piety in backcountry communities. Ministers preached together and provided mutual assistance in the itinerant field, members of the laity pooled their resources to build churches and hire preaching, and denominations sought ways to bridge the gaps that separated them. These denominations were in constant dialogue with each other, and their extended conversations and negotiation over sectarian territory, lay followings, and religious truth bound them in a common enterprise.

The town-church and itinerant cultures intersected and diverged as their adherents mingled in overlapping spaces. As northern New England's religious geography took shape, layfolk and clergy tried to reconcile shared religious interests with fierce rivalries over spiritual ground. Their efforts gave rise to a religious culture that borrowed from both the town-church and itinerant traditions. Churches and lay communities confined themselves within walls of doctrine, ritual, and social habit in their efforts to preserve faith. But they also extended hands of fellowship to Christians whom they increasingly recognized as earnest, if errant. By doing so, they permeated boundaries of their own making. Even more, they settled among themselves—albeit uneasily—on the features and fixtures of northern New England's new religious landscape.

The visceral enmity that often soured encounters among post-Revolutionary denominations did not quite fade over the early decades of the nineteenth century. But it did take on a different hue as persistent rivalries became entangled with tentative alliances. Churchgoers who seized meetinghouses from each other one day worshiped together the next. Ministers who attacked each other's teachings might also hear each other's sermons and even offer closing prayers. Believers lobbied the unconverted and plotted to draw the faithful from one church to the next—but they also acknowledged their rivals' piety and lauded their awakenings. The clergy praised any Christian advances into the hinterland, but they still competed for new ground on behalf of their own denominations. Sectarian conflicts set partisans at odds over both theological and geographic territory. These conflicts reflected honest doctrinal differences, but the persistent town-church system also underlay the heated discourse. That system, which continued to privilege town churches with access to assets, framed denominations' relationships by forcing them to compete or negotiate over scarce resources and followers.

The legacy of establishment, even after states ended compulsory religious taxation, compelled denominations to compete over ministerial funds, meetinghouses, and the churchgoers who filled them. Such was the case in Poultney, Vermont, where a settled Baptist church and a headless Congregationalist church repeatedly bickered over the town meetinghouse. According to a visiting missionary, the Congregationalists had largely financed the house's construction, but "there being no record found of the original contract" that divided use of the meetinghouse, the Baptist majority voted it to themselves in 1802.[3] In Alfred, Maine, dissenters overtook the town parish by joining it. Once they outnumbered the Congregationalists, they elected their own officers and assumed control of the meetinghouse and ministerial fund—both of which had been endowed by a bequest "for the use of the first Congregational parish."[4] In each town, the dissenters asserted their majority power over the local establishment by working within the town-church system.

Most such rivalries entailed more incremental struggles, not sudden, wholesale takeovers. Ephraim Abbot encountered several New Hampshire towns where Congregationalists and Methodists struggled to control meetinghouses. In Newcastle, he noted that "there is no room for Congregationalist preaching" because "the Methodists preach in the [meetinghouse] about 3/4 and the Freewillers have a constant meeting." In Newington, control of the meetinghouse came down to a town vote, which the Congregationalists won, but the Methodists continued to insist on a share. In Greenland, where Abbot eventually settled, negotiations turned particularly bitter. He reported that the Methodists were "doing all in their power to prevent" his settlement, including "meeting every Sabbath for a month past" so they might secure the meetinghouse for themselves. At the same time, the Congregationalists raced to incorporate their society so they, too, might stake a claim. The town approved Abbot (by a two-thirds margin) shortly thereafter, which allowed the Congregationalists to claim the meetinghouse. But bitterness prevailed on all sides. The Methodists "were very angry when the meetinghouse was voted from them, and they said very hard things, such as tyranny, injustice, no more religion than the d[evi]l, etc."[5] As Abbot discovered, verbal sparring turned especially heated when competitors tussled over a financial boon like a share in a meetinghouse.

Battles over buildings went hand-in-hand with competition for churchgoers. With parishioners came the town-church spoils, so clergy went after potential converts for reasons both practical and spiritual. Ministers who vied for adherents sometimes confronted each other face to face during church meetings. When Joel Winch was flirting with Methodism, he went to hear the famed itinerants Jesse Lee and Lorenzo Dow preach. After Dow completed a sermon on "the possibility of falling from grace," Winch's own Congregationalist minister rose to speak. He addressed Dow directly, "testifying that there was no such thing as falling from grace."[6] Rather than a deliver a sermon, the Congregationalist minister engaged in a personal attack. Samuel Goddard experienced a similar episode. He had just finished preaching to a mixed assembly in western New Hampshire when a Methodist preacher "rose and spoke in great confusion and extreamly loud for near an hour."[7] Clashes like these signaled more than simple sectarian disagreements. Indeed, they reflected some ministers' urgent desire to correct publicly—before their own churchgoers—what they viewed as errant doctrine. All the better, they hoped, to stifle the visiting ministers' influence and appeal.

Public skirmishes made for good theater, but more often, ministers competed secretly behind each other's backs. Visiting clergy regularly tried to edge one another out of prime meeting times and audiences. Joel Winch, after he joined the Methodist ministry, noticed that the Freewill Baptists on his circuit heavily advertised their monthly meetings, hoping to recruit new members from the Methodist churches. "That is how the Methodist ware all a going to become Freewillers," he surmised.[8] Others employed similar tactics. Missionary Thomas Holt reported after one Sabbath meeting that his audience in Lovell, Maine, had been uncharacteristically small. The reason, he suspected, was that the visiting Methodist preacher had told residents "that I was to be absent."[9] Stealth campaigns only added to the friction between itinerants and set denominations at odds with each other in the race to pack their respective meetinghouses.

If ministers could gather audiences, then they could appeal directly to outsiders and perhaps win them over and prompt conversions. They worked furiously to pluck prospective members from rival churches—and complained vehemently about competitors who did the same. Congregationalist missionary Stephen Chapin bemoaned the Baptist preachers who were "laboring to prejudice the minds of the people against our order." In particular, he reported that Daniel Merrill of Sedgwick, Maine, charged the Congregationalists with "denying and crucifying Christ, and persecuting the true church."[10] Whether or not these reports were true (and whether or not Chapin had any firsthand knowledge of Merrill's remarks) seemed beside the point; inflammatory rumors of this sort circulated widely and heightened suspicions between denominations. In August 1802, two visiting ministers—Congregationalist William Miller and a Baptist whom Miller identified as Mr. Beal—decided to preach a Sabbath together in Castleton, Vermont. As Miller recounted the story, Beal "passed the house where he knew me to be preaching and went directly to the house of a gentlemen who had a daughter propounded for admission into the church the next day." Beal spent the night with that family and used "all the arguments in his power" to dissuade the girl, unsuccessfully, from joining the Congregationalists.[11] It so happened that both Merrill and Beal had been Congregationalist ministers before they converted and preached for the Baptists—a fact not lost on Chapin and Miller, and one that no doubt heightened each missionary's concerns about the Baptists' motives. But as they surely knew, the Baptists did not have a monopoly on proselytizing. In a competitive zeal to attract (or keep) fickle audiences, many ministers resorted to aggressive tactics.

Although Congregationalist ministers portrayed themselves as victims of sectarian designs, they were not above scheming to get the upper hand. William Miller offered the Connecticut Missionary Society this advice on how to combat the Methodists, whom he thought had "the most dogmatical brass of any people I ever saw." The only way to "effectually . . . destroy [their] influence," he advised, was "to take a wild goose chase with them, and follow them in all their absurd spoutings." Direct confrontation, armed with "a memorized knowledge of the scriptures," was the only way to beat them; otherwise, they might imagine silent rivals to "be acknowledging their superiority."[12] Other Congregationalists also kept watch for sectarian encroachments. When Nathan Douglas left his pulpit in Alfred, Maine, for a mission, he learned that local Baptists had hired a Methodist itinerant to preach. "It was their design," he explained, "to draw off my people to their house in my absence." But Douglas countered with his own tactics. He rushed back to Alfred and invited the Methodist to preach in his own church—all the better to mitigate his evangelical efforts. The strategy worked. In the end, Douglas had "no reason to believe that [the Methodist] will try any further to make proselytes among us."[13] The Congregationalists learned to assert their influence to keep their own adherents in the fold.

Denominational rivalries did not simply pit Congregationalists against everyone else; the upstart groups also competed among themselves. The Freewill Baptists worried that too much intermingling among their followers and the Methodists would draw members away to Methodism. Perhaps that is why, when Joel Winch made a regular stop on his circuit, a "Freewill professer swore that he would lick me if I ever came that way again."[14] Universalists likewise fretted over the apparent attractions of Methodism. Minister David Pickering worried especially about young men's seeming proclivities to "preach Methodism, &c. in prefference to Universalism." He suggested that some ministerial candidates craved the spotlight in settings like camp meetings and revivals, which encouraged theatrical preaching. "Men are proud animals," he reasoned, and "they love to be revered, whether they deserve it or not." Although Pickering worried mostly about men's decisions to join the clergy, his comments also applied to the wider lay audience. He explained that Universalism did not offer a simple, dogmatic message that would appeal to those seeking an easy faith to grasp. "Universalists have never concentrated their forces" to reach a consensus on doctrine; they had only to offer "that diversity of sentiment which perplexes and intimidates young minds."[15] By flattering his faith's liberality, Pickering explained away other denominations' apparent ability to edge them out in the religious marketplace.

Competition over churches and churchgoers sometimes plunged entire communities into hostilities. James Turner, a Congregationalist minister, encountered fierce opposition in Kingston, New Hampshire. The Congregationalists supported him, but they were, according to Turner, in the minority. "The opposition to gospel ministry," he reported, was "great—very great." He encountered "a perfect union" of Baptists and Methodists that pervaded town politics as factions attempted to allot shares in the meetinghouse and ministerial fund, and even decide the fate of Turner's own preaching candidacy. Led by local politician and Baptist Levi Bartlett, this coalition voted the majority share of the meetinghouse away from the Congregationalists and invited a succession of visiting preachers to replace Turner—a decision, Turner claimed, that violated the wishes of "every pew owner with the exception of five," who would have to "vacate their seats to make room for strangers, who were never in the habit of worshipping God in this place." In other words, a coalition of religious minorities and outsiders from other towns had completely upended the church's place in the Congregationalist landscape. Despite Turner's objections, a new minister appeared every Sabbath. And each week, the Baptists and Methodists guarded the church doors to prevent Turner's entrance until their itinerant occupied the pulpit.[16]

Tensions peaked several weeks later, when the Congregationalists prepared for their communion season. "Notwithstanding the [communion] table was spread," Turner reported, guards blocked the meetinghouse doors until the visiting Baptist preacher was ready to begin. Weary of this routine but lacking recourse, the Congregationalists waited their turn. When they began their service later that day, the Baptist minister and many of his followers stormed the meetinghouse. "He went into the pulpit," Turner recounted, "and they gathered upon the pulpit stairs, in the pulpit, and in the parsonage pew." He then faced the awkward challenge of administering the Lord's Supper with unruly dissenters milling about the communion table. Such behavior, he added, "could hardly be expected this side of the bottomless pit."[17]

The Congregationalists and their rivals settled into a stalemate after that, but tensions threatened to erupt at any time. Turner later described a Methodist army that had staged a scorched-earth campaign through Congregationalist strongholds. They had abandoned towns where "they have prevailed and destroyed the regular order of the Gospel," leaving those places without preaching and turning instead to towns that "have yet the order of the Gospel among them, are struggling for life, [and] are inundated with [Methodist] preachers."[18] Turner thought the Methodists cared little about religious life in the towns they visited; rather, they sought only to topple the Congregationalist establishment and move on.

Turner's account reflected his bias toward Congregationalist doctrine and polity—and ardently against all things Methodist. Even though the Baptists staged the takeover of the meetinghouse, Turner blamed the tensions on itinerant Methodist preachers and their supporters. Levi Bartlett, for his part, located the problem elsewhere. He blamed Turner: "a vicious, hollow hearted unprincipled Priest who a few people have palmed on this Town in the shape of a Minister of the Gospel." As Bartlett told the story, the conflict in Kingston resulted from a lopsided meeting in which a small faction pushed Turner's candidacy through as a ploy to seize control of the meetinghouse. The Baptists and Methodists acted in self-defense by protecting their shares of the house and recruiting "steady rational Christians" to preach.[19] Whatever the truth, the conflict between the town-church and itinerant systems was partly to blame for underlying tensions. Speaking for the town-church tradition, Turner maintained that Kingston had settled him, and therefore the town church should control the meetinghouse. The pew holders, whom Turner included within the church's purview, had an inherent interest in public worship and should not have to move aside for strangers. But Bartlett bristled under what he saw as an undemocratic settlement and sought visiting ministers who could serve what he thought to be the popular interest. He also objected to the legal establishment that privileged town churches in the first place. "We here are in a ferment," he informed his brother, "and I suspect shall boil in the law, about religious controversy."[20] With that, at least, Turner could agree.

Many tired of the intense competition that set believers at odds. William Miller despaired of ever uniting the "flourishing" but divided town of Poultney, where "warm disputes upon sentiments" precluded efforts to support religion. "As well may oil and water be permanently mixed," Miller predicted, "as congregationalists and baptists form a lasting union."[21] Freewill Baptist William Babcock, too, lamented that the "enmity" between denominations was "as rancourous as ever." He wondered at those who "in every other concern of Society and good Neighbourhood are obliging Friends" but who assume the "ferocity of Savages, and . . . the bitterness of Enemies" when the topic turned to religion. Such behavior, he thought, was "the very marrow and essence of Persecution."[22] Although neither Miller nor Babcock wished to sacrifice his own denomination's success to aid his competitors, both men regretted the incessant rivalries that impeded Christian fellowship.

But even in the midst of such heated competition, northern New England did not succumb altogether to sectarian warfare. Although they often clashed over doctrine and financial resources, competitors also collaborated to promote general piety. And like mutually suspicious churchgoers who nonetheless mingled in each other's congregations, rival clergy came to see each other as colleagues in a joint Christian endeavor. This spirit of cooperation emerged in the context of an ecumenical culture that had its roots in at least three precedents. First, the tradition of multi-denominational revival that had first emerged during the Great Awakening provided a context for shared worship among Protestant evangelicals. Second, many early-nineteenth-century benevolence movements emphasized common Christian bonds more than exclusive sectarian ties. Benevolence societies that offered poor relief, promoted temperance, and distributed Bibles and tracts tended to define themselves by a mission to serve common Christian interests, and they united Protestant ministers and layfolk.[23] Members of a Portland Bible society, for example, set aside sectarian differences to focus solely on distributing the Bible, "a single object, in which christians of every denomination can unite."[24] And, finally, as parish lines gradually wore down in some places, ministers saw their relationships with each other less in the context of a battle for scarce resources and more as a collaboration in a wider Christian enterprise. As more ministers of different stripes converged in revivals and joined forces in benevolence, it followed that they might find some common ground in their day-to-day religious work as well.

If they had nothing else in common, ministers of competing denominations at least shared the experience of itinerancy, which broadened their perspective beyond the narrow confines of towns, churches, and circuits. Even ministers who had never traveled circuits or missionary tours had contact with those who did, and thereby connected with a larger itinerant network. As a matter of professional courtesy—and despite sectarian rivalries—the clergy often smoothed each other's paths by hosting traveling ministers in their homes and opening their meetinghouses to accommodate itinerants. On an 1806 mission through the "back settlements" in Maine, Baptist Phinehas Pillsbury preached in a Methodist minister's home near Brewer.[25] Congregationalist Asaph Morgan, on an 1813 mission in Fishersfield, New Hampshire, visited families with a local Baptist deacon "upon whom Congregational as well as Baptist ministers call" and whom churchgoers of both denominations trusted.[26] Samuel Goddard, on an 1814 tour of New Hampshire, lodged with a Methodist preacher in Lyman, whom he judged "an intelligent man." Goddard "had much conversation with him on important doctrines," and he found his host "embracing the Calvinistic system generally," though he alluded to "some difficulties on some points." In general, however, the two men found they had enough in common to pass a pleasant evening.[27] As they discovered, their shared experiences of itinerancy superseded religious differences that, in another context, might have set them at odds.

In the same collegial spirit, ministers also allowed each other to hold meetings in their churches, even if the hosts and guests embraced opposing doctrines. The Universalist Society in Norway, Maine, allowed Congregationalist Joseph Field to preach in its meetinghouse in 1805.[28] When Congregationalist Thomas Holt arrived in Paris, Maine, on an 1818 mission, the town's Baptist minister offered his church instead of directing Holt's audience to the much smaller schoolhouse. Largely because of this surprising (and welcome) gesture, Holt judged his Baptist counterpart a "benevolent, candid, [and] humble man."[29] Rival ministers did not always cooperate. When the Rockingham Universalist Association asked to use the Congregationalist meetinghouse in Epping, New Hampshire, for their 1829 annual meeting, the minister refused—despite his congregation's willingness to consent. But the Universalists found favor elsewhere; the Methodists offered their church, which easily accommodated the two hundred members in attendance.[30] The Universalists and Methodists usually considered each other rivals. But when ministers gave their meetinghouses over to visiting clergy, they extended a hand of religious hospitality that counterbalanced the harsh words their respective groups exchanged in other contexts.

Loaning sacred space was one matter; sharing it was another. Increasingly, ministers of competing denominations joined forces to lead services before mixed audiences. These efforts mainly united clergy who could agree on some points of doctrine: Congregationalists and Baptists preached together, as did Freewill Baptists and Methodists. Benjamin Chadwick, an SPG missionary, reported in 1804 that he had preached with Baptists on many occasions. "The Calvinistic Baptists and I have agreed well," he wrote, explaining that he had "preached before four Calvinistic Baptist preachers and there was no disagreement." But, he added, "I am too explicit in my sentiments . . . to please those who are either in the freewill or Universal scheme."[31] Despite the misgivings that Baptists and Congregationalists harbored toward each other, individual clergy forged collegial bonds. Congregationalist Timothy Hilliard and a Baptist missionary visited schools together and alternated delivering sermons before their young audiences.[32] Jotham Sewall, on an 1818 tour of New Hampshire, "got a young Baptist preacher . . . to assist me by making some of the prayers" at one meeting.[33] These partnerships benefited colleagues by allowing them to collect larger audiences in small settlements. They also built a collegial network that might open doors to other preaching opportunities.

Some ministers worked together despite more pronounced differences. Baptist Job Seamans regularly preached with a nearby Methodist minister, whom he complimented for using "a great deal of workmanship" in his sermons, concluding that "his sentiments [were], mostly, good."[34] Freewill Baptist preacher Adam Grant of Jordan Brook, Maine, invited Phinehas Pillsbury to preach before his congregation.[35] Ephraim Abbot joined a Methodist minister, whom he lauded as a "prudent exemplary and pious man," to lead a service in Calais, Maine.[36] And Congregationalist Edmund Easton preached in Bethel, Maine, before an "assembly composed of three denominations and three of their Preachers." The ministers, he thought, "appeared harmoniously to unite and rejoic[ed] most of all to behold the work of the Lord going on in this place."[37] By setting aside rivalries and gathering their adherents, these ministers nurtured a religious fervor that transcended divides between local churches.

If some ministers increasingly accepted interdenominational worship, so, too, did they embrace other forms of collaboration, such as ministerial exchange. To be sure, some pastors continued to reject such cross-pollination. The Piscataqua Association flatly forbade its ministers to preach in other denominations' churches ("except in special cases") or exchange with Baptists under any circumstances.[38] But despite this kind of resistance, collaboration across sectarian lines became increasingly common. Interdenominational exchange was not new; the Plan of Union had united Congregationalists and Presbyterians in such efforts since 1801 (though, because few Presbyterians lived in northern New England, this arrangement was less common there). Ministerial exchange, even between less like-minded ministers, became more typical over time. Job Seamans preached periodically for the New London Congregational society.[39] The *Religious Intelligencer* published guidelines in 1824 for Congregationalists who wished to exchange with ministers of other faiths. If the clergy in question "preach *essentially* the same gospel which the Apostles preached," if the differences in their faiths were "*not* essential," and if "their preaching is calculated to promote the *conviction* and *conversion* of sinners," then such exchanges could be acceptable.[40] With endorsements like this one, interdenominational exchange brought ministers and their flocks in ever closer contact with each other.

Ministers supported each other's efforts not just by preaching together or exchanging but also by worshiping in each other's churches. Just as laypeople mingled freely in different churches without compromising their sectarian identities, the clergy sat in on other ministers' services out of professional courtesy, curiosity, or the simple desire to pray. William Babcock, who frequented Methodist meetings, attended an 1801 service with "some of my Baptist Brethren" and a Congregationalist minister.[41] On a mission to Moose Island, Maine, Ephraim Abbot spent a Sabbath praying with a Baptist congregation rather than seeking out a place to preach.[42] For many ministers, visits to a new church offered a first foray into an unfamiliar spiritual culture. George Freeman, a Congregationalist missionary in Vermont, attended a Freewill Baptist conference in 1825, which he judged "quite interesting." The meeting "partook of many of their peculiarities," he reported, but was nonetheless "mostly solemn."[43] Others were less approving. A Universalist itinerant who attended an 1828 Methodist camp meeting in New Hampshire reported appalling sights: "men . . . under the influence of *spirituous liquor*," preachers "threatening [women] with the excruciating pains of damnation," and much of the audience "frightened almost into insanity." After observing this display, the visitor wondered when "people shall be convinced that God is not a God of confusion, but of peace."[44] Even if they were sometimes shocked at what they saw, ministers who attended other groups' meetings highlighted the many ways in which denominations intersected in the northern frontier.

Cooperation among clergy generally took place in an itinerant context, as traveling clergy relied on one another and on local pastors for support, facilities, and collegiality. Collaborative efforts also united churchgoers in local communities. One common challenge was finding space for meetings, as small congregations in divided towns could rarely afford to build churches. So they joined forces to construct multi-denominational houses in which contributing congregations divided meeting time. The strongest precedent for shared meetinghouses was in Vermont, where laws before 1807 required a two-thirds majority in any town or parish to decide ministerial hiring or church construction. (After 1807, the same rules applied to preexisting parishes or societies.) Such majorities were often multi-denominational coalitions; in Springfield, for example, the meetinghouse proprietors included Universalists, Methodists, Freewill Baptists, regular Baptists, and Congregationalists.[45] Shared meetinghouses gained popularity elsewhere as congregations faced greater economic barriers to church building and maintenance. Baptists and Congregationalists in Meredith, New Hampshire, shared a meetinghouse and formed a society in 1826 to maintain and administer the building.[46] Universalists and Congregationalists shared a church in Alstead, New Hampshire, although the two parties engaged in tense negotiations over how to allot time.[47] Shared meetinghouses could generate conflict as partners wrestled over such agreements. But they also fostered a spirit of compromise.

Meetinghouse societies struck an inclusive chord by emphasizing the members' equal footing and insisting on transparency when allotting meeting days and times. The Weston (Vermont) Society reiterated its goal of "brotherly love and harmony among christians of different denomminations" and ensured that all proprietors would "enjoy the privilege of holding public worship . . . under a teacher of their own order." Toward that end, the society's board of directors consisted of one member elected from each of the town's congregations.[48] When the proprietors of the Baptist meetinghouse in Whiting, Vermont, decided in 1823 to accept contributions from other denominations, they drew up a detailed plan that linked each congregation's use of the house to its subscriptions. The Baptists, not surprisingly, contributed the most; having donated $1,269.23, they were entitled to twenty-seven Sabbaths that year. The Congregationalists, who paid $750.68, claimed sixteen; the Universalists donated $373.84 and reserved eight; and a lone Episcopalian, who contributed $50, was allotted one Sunday in 1823 to hear preaching from a minister of his own order.[49] Not all multi-denominational meetinghouses escaped conflict. In Strafford, Vermont, proprietors divided when the Universalist society lobbied to have its own minister ordained over the town—which, had they succeeded, would have created a Universalist town church and placed the meetinghouse arrangement in jeopardy.[50] In other towns, as Ephraim Abbot and James Turner both witnessed throughout New Hampshire, shifting balances among religious groups tipped meetinghouse control in different directions, provoking bitter battles over resources. But when multiple denominations managed to cooperate, they benefited from the arrangement with partial access to a church, which most agreed was better than none at all.

At least as common as multi-denominational meetinghouses were multi-denominational religious societies and congregations. Societies, which procured preaching and supported worship, had to balance members' sectarian differences when they supplied their pulpits. Because of economic and geographic obstacles to church-founding in northern New England, ecumenical religious societies were a longstanding, if not always common, fixture. A society in Plainfield, New Hampshire, gathered in 1779 and included regular Baptists and Congregationalists who, "Considering our Local situation from any place of Publick worship and our own contiguous situation for that purpose," pledged to "do according to our abilities in preaching and supporting the Gospel Among us."[51] The religious society in Craftsbury, Vermont, agreed to hold Sabbath meetings at which one male member each week would read and comment on chapters of the New Testament. The society's covenant stipulated that any lay sermons or prayers "shall not be selected on any Perticular Principle or denomination" but should appeal broadly to those in attendance, regardless of their religious affiliations.[52] Agreements like this one reflected compromises that allowed spiritually diverse towns to support worship.

Multi-denominational congregations sprouted up in divided towns that otherwise had little hope of hiring preachers. Unlike the societies in Plainfield and Craftsbury, most congregations did not sign formal covenants or divide preaching time; rather, they maintained informal arrangements in which independent churches and societies worshiped together or cooperated to support preaching. In Billymead, Vermont, Congregationalists and Baptists met together peacefully for over a year before (according to a Congregationalist missionary) itinerant Freewill Baptist preachers drove a wedge between them.[53] The arrangement in Bethel was more successful. There, a small Baptist church and a handful of Congregationalists worshiped together most weeks, though the Congregationalists went to churches in neighboring towns for communion days. Congregationalists and Baptists similarly met together in Springfield, Vermont, and Effingham, Maine, alternatively hiring temporary ministers of one denomination or the other. Of the latter congregation, missionary Jonathan Calif reported that "they meet together with considerable apparent friendship."[54] Despite their differences, these congregations found enough common ground to support religious worship jointly until they could arrive at more permanent individual solutions.

Multi-denominational efforts usually united relatively like-minded worshipers (like Congregationalists and Baptists), but in some towns, groups that normally opposed each other nonetheless collaborated to support worship. In Calais, Maine, Jotham Sewall discovered a small church composed of Congregationalists and Methodists, "on the Methodist plan" and under a Methodist preacher.[55] In 1827, Nathan Fisk reported that "all the denominations of Christians" in Levant, Maine, had agreed to settle Baptist minister Royal Spaulding—all except the Universalists, who "Violently opposed" him.[56] Spaulding represented a compromise; given a choice, non-Baptists would not have chosen him as their pastor, regardless of his respectable standing in the community. But for churchgoers in isolated towns, a minister like Spaulding was a palatable alternative to religious disorganization and neglect.

Occasionally, ministers and churchgoers pushed the multi-denominational concept beyond makeshift congregations. In 1823, members of the Congregationalist Northwestern Association and the Fairfield Baptist Association—both based in northwestern Vermont—decided to forge a formal union. They shared the hope that their denominations "may be united in one by believing and practicing alike according to the word of God." They ensured equal representation and pledged not to ask each other "to lay aside any thing which the Bible does require us to practice or to maintain." To do so, they conceded, would "hinder the two denominations from becoming united." But how to unite and still retain their distinctiveness? After extensive discussion, the two associations listed what they held in common: their understandings of the Trinity and the doctrine of atonement, their belief in innate human depravity, and their insistence on congregational autonomy. Then, they examined the issues that divided them, including the question of whether the Old Testament and the Abrahamic covenant were binding (Congregationalists believed they were) and the significance of baptism and the Lord's Supper. These differences posed the most difficult obstacles to union. In general, the participants agreed, the points on which they differed were "mostly of the second degree of importance." But those opposing views "[go] near to placing us on different foundations." Despite their common ground, these points of divergence highlighted the difficulties of maintaining an interdenominational union.[57] But the Congregationalists' and Baptists' extensive efforts toward that end reflected a spirit of cooperation that—though by no means universal—had changed the New England frontier's religious landscape.

Competition and collaboration among northern New England's denominations went hand-in-hand. The town-church legacy set local churches at odds by privileging a few with public support and leaving the others to fend for themselves. But adherents of different faiths sometimes forged enough common ground that they could imagine themselves as limited partners in a larger mission. The experience of itinerancy—with its many physical and spiritual trials—united ministers in the largely neutral missionary field. Even as they competed for audiences, they also identified with each other's daily struggles and offered material and spiritual assistance. Too, the increasingly porous physical boundaries between religious communities allowed the laity and clergy alike to mingle in churches, conference meetings, and revivals, building a familiarity that countered mutual suspicion. Neither enemies nor friends, northern New Englanders worked out shifting alliances that furthered their common evangelical goals.

These alliances took shape within the overlapping religious landscapes that northern New England's denominations had created through the town-church and itinerant systems. Congregationalists, whose covenanted communities revolved, ideally, around settled ministers, looked askance at incursions by itinerants, who crossed parish lines and drew churchgoers off from town parishes. Meanwhile, members of the itinerant movements tried to separate themselves visibly from their neighbors with distinctive dress, social habits, and doctrine: a sort of self-imposed spiritual isolation that members of town parishes derided as aloof and un-Christian. But as these groups planted roots in frontier towns, they each borrowed from the other's patterns of church-building and community formation. Itinerant groups, with increasingly stable churches and a steady supply of trained clergy, reconsidered the usefulness of a settled ministry. And Congregationalists, having witnessed the breakdown of parish lines and town churches, looked to other means of establishing and sustaining spiritual communities. As they did so, both groups rearranged their traditional religious geographies.

Widespread itinerancy, disestablishment, and geographic mobility all challenged the town-church legacy during the late eighteenth and early nineteenth centuries. As parishes divided and subdivided, and backcountry inhabitants filtered in and out of settlements, town churches increasingly failed to secure enough funding to support preaching. But the itinerant denominations did not always enjoy a clear advantage. Even though they extended their reach through a traveling ministry, they came to realize that without local clergy to anchor churches and enforce doctrine, their followers would scatter. Accordingly, they began to assume some of the traits of town churches; they created more local churches and ordained more local ministers. More than that, they adopted the

Congregationalist ideal that the town—neighbors who knew each other and could encourage each other's piety—formed a natural foundation for a church.

During the 1810s and 1820s, denominations and churchgoers increasingly sought to ordain local clergy. The Congregationalists and regular Baptists had always favored settled pulpits, but as more trained preachers entered the field, even the itinerant groups considered anew the advantages of a permanent ministry. The Methodists began to limit circuit preachers' powers in the late 1790s by giving them less authority over stationed ministers. Beginning in the 1820s and 1830s, Methodist conferences increasingly assigned preachers to stations rather than circuits, which not only elevated their authority over circuit riders but also diminished the local lay leadership as ministers supplanted lay exhorters and class leaders.[58] The Universalists, who faced a perpetual ministerial shortage, nonetheless urged infant churches to hire clergy whenever possible. The Rockingham Association suggested that "several societies may employ one man, if necessary, whose labours may be divided among them." Better a partial settlement, it implied, than none at all.[59] If the minister's presence limited lay authority, it also benefited local communities by ensuring regular worship and doctrinal consistency.

The Freewill Baptists—who had originally lauded itinerancy as an ideal rather than a compromise—exemplified the shift to a settled ministry. In 1790, fewer than one third of Freewill Baptist churches had ordained preachers; a decade later, just over half did. But those settlements were not exclusive—most early clergy split their time between two or three churches.[60] By the 1820s, the vast majority of Freewill Baptist churches had ordained ministers. According to an 1821–1822 survey, approximately 80 percent of Freewill Baptist churches in northern New England had settled clergy, most of whom were settled over a single church.[61] These figures correlated with a spike in Freewill Baptist ordinations in northern New England. The church ordained approximately 29 northern New England ministers during the 1780s and 1790s, and 74 in each of the following two decades. In the 1820s, that number nearly doubled to 138.[62] These figures suggest an impulse to match ministers with churches, and a shift from the group's itinerant roots.

The Freewill Baptists articulated this shift as they increasingly voiced doubts about an itinerant ministry. "For ministers to go round preaching and baptizing members," one writer suggested in 1820, "and leaving them without being under the watch and care of any body [or] imbody churches and leave them without regular discipline" was tantamount to "selecting a spot for a garden, fencing it, and dressing it, and sowing it with the choicest seeds, then neglecting to weed it."[63] It was one thing to tally conversions and baptisms, but the work of sustaining churches called for an ongoing presence. To encourage long-term ties among preachers and churchgoers, the General Conference began to regulate itinerants in the early 1830s, requiring them to carry licenses, travel approved circuits, and keep records of their labor. The conference encouraged itinerants to travel between a few needy churches (like Methodist circuit riders did) and abandon the random wanderings of past preachers.[64] Through this new approach, the Freewill Baptists recast itinerancy not as an embodiment of gospel liberty, as they had previously imagined it, but instead as a stopgap alternative to a settled ministry.

The trend toward a settled ministry reflected a new emphasis (for the itinerants) on the local community as a proper basis for a church. In a multi-denominational congregation, churchgoers of different (and sometimes sharply opposing) faiths pooled resources and negotiated disagreements in the interest of communal piety. But even when they gathered in sectarian congregations, believers preferred to plant those churches where they lived, and denominations increasingly supported their efforts to do so. The Universalists urged their followers in 1828 to gather local churches and societies for two reasons: to remove themselves from existing parishes (thereby avoiding paying taxes to support other churches) and to unite scattered Universalists who might not otherwise find each other. The convention asserted that "there are but few towns, if any, in New England where there are no believers in Universal Love." Those believers could find power in numbers. "Let us unite ourselves," proclaimed the convention, "that we may stand the more firm amid the whirlwinds of sectarian excitement."[65] The Rockingham Association agreed. It maintained that a local society "brings into light and action the undeveloped resources of a people, gives to them a public character and stability, inspires them with confidence and hope of success, and urges them to . . . more determined perseverance." A society, in other words, did more than raise funds for preaching—it undergirded a community by uniting its members in godly exertion. Using the language of the town-church ideal, the Rockingham Association imagined each Universalist church and society as "a city set on a hill," a covenanted community that modeled piety for all to see.[66]

Many complied. After an 1830 mission in eastern Maine, Universalist minister J. B. Dods reported that new Universalist societies were forming in half of the fourteen towns he visited, and one additional church was planned. In East and West Machias, Universalists formed a society so they might "pay no more of their money to those who oppressed them" by denying them access to the town meetinghouse, which their taxes had supported. In Cherryfield, Universalists were "taking a decided stand" to separate from the town parish. Most of these infant societies could expect to remain headless for the time being. The Maine Convention of Universalists counted only 31 Universalist preachers in the state that year, and it estimated at least 1,500 Universalists in Maine for every preacher. Churchgoers relied on the strength of their mutual commitments to sustain these nascent communities.[67]

The Freewill Baptists, having embraced the idea of a settled ministry, also heeded the call to organize local churches. Clusters of like-minded believers who had worshiped in scattered communities now aspired to form permanent churches in their own towns. The Freewill Baptists of Calais, Maine, had long worshiped with other congregations. But in 1821, "mindful of our local situation," they gathered "in the midst of our dwelling an habitation for our GOD where his worship . . . might be duly attended."[68] Similarly, the Freewill Baptists in Raymond, New Hampshire, who had worshiped in Candia, decided unanimously in 1824 to "divide by the town line" and form a church of their own.[69] Freewill Baptists around the region also redoubled their efforts at local church-founding. The New Durham Quarterly Meeting, founded with four churches in 1796, boasted thirty by 1830. Likewise, the Farmington Quarterly Meeting in Maine grew from five churches at its 1795 founding to twenty-four in 1830. Much of this growth occurred during the 1810s and 1820s. The Sandwich (New Hampshire) Quarterly Meeting expanded from ten churches in 1812 to twenty-seven in 1830; the Huntington (Vermont) Quarterly Meeting included four churches in 1818 and twelve in 1830; the Exeter (Maine) Quarterly Meeting grew from seven to twenty-three churches between 1824 and 1830; and the Enosburg (Vermont) Quarterly Meeting expanded by two-thirds in just three years after its 1827 founding, from nine to fifteen churches.[70] Each new church planted the Freewill Baptist faith more firmly in its surrounding neighborhood. Citing a shared interest in local communities, these congregations took a page from the town-church legacy and adopted it as their own.

The Freewill Baptists' interest in local churches even shaped their preferences for how and where revivals should take root. They had long relied on large gatherings—especially the yearly meetings—to bolster piety and spark revivals. The concentration of ministers and exhorters, the swirl of activity, and the convergence of interested laity had always made for an intensely prayerful atmosphere. But Freewill Baptists also looked to local churches to foster revivals born of the covenant between church members and their clergy. When the *Religious Magazine* attempted in 1822 to outline the "true signs of a revival of religion in a town," they focused mainly on how the minister and his flock should prepare for an awakening. The minister ought to develop "a deep sense of his responsibility" to God and his followers and "emphatically [preach] repentance." Meanwhile, the churchgoers ought to assume a "general seriousness and tenderness," forego worldly pleasures, retire to secret prayer, confess "their faults to one another," and unite in worship. For the minister who hoped to bring a listless church to revival, the magazine suggested that he first "faithfully examine" his own sins and then urge his audience to do the same.[71] Churches should look not to the spectacle of visiting clergy but instead to the ties between a minister and his flock. By placing the onus for stimulating a revival on the settled minister's shoulders and demanding compliance by the laity, the Freewill Baptists offered a model for a village revival in the Congregationalist tradition.

The itinerant denominations, on balance, held to the itinerant model. They continued to rely heavily on a traveling ministry, and they continued to employ elders who oversaw (and traveled among) clusters of congregations. They also maintained their centralized hierarchies, which allowed leaders to enforce doctrine and discipline and limited congregational autonomy. And they rejected the part of the town-church tradition that united the civil and religious communities. But their drive to organize local churches under settled ministers suggests that they tried to balance a broad, regional perspective with an understanding of religious community that vested neighbors with mutual responsibility for one another's spiritual fate.

Although remnants of the town-church ideal survived among Congregationalists and itinerant groups alike, the itinerant model prevailed as the organizing force of church-gathering and religious expansion. The influence of itinerancy was especially evident in the success of the denominational church: an institution with roots in dissenting congregations and poll parishes, which defined its members by belief alone. As towns fractured into parishes, churches relied on doctrine rather than residence to distinguish insiders from outsiders. Because they judged membership more on religious identity than on geographic community, the faithful looked outward from their home churches to establish long-distance ties with like-minded believers. Using regional activity such as concerts of prayer and broad-based revivals, adherents broke the insular bounds of local churches and formed larger networks of faith. To be sure, the tradition of local autonomy persisted among Congregationalists and (to a slightly lesser extent) regular Baptists. But even in those denominations, individual churches came to rely on regional associations to coordinate missionary and benevolence activity, maintain communication among far-flung ministers, and enforce doctrine among constituent churches. These efforts fostered a regional orientation that undercut the religious geography of the traditional town church.

Because they could rarely match churches with towns, itinerant denominations had long used belief rather than geography to determine membership. As the combined forces of migration and religious pluralism challenged the town church, it, too, came to base membership on common doctrine. Increasingly, layfolks preferred to worship with those who shared their beliefs rather than with all who shared their towns. Asaph Morgan discovered as much when he tried to unite Congregationalists in Goshen, New Hampshire, in 1813. Goshen already boasted a small Congregationalist church, but most of its potential members worshiped elsewhere, largely because of unspecified doctrinal differences. A Congregationalist union had been "a subject of frequent conversation," but Morgan, like others before, failed to bring it about. He hosted a conference "to see if the chh would accept a *creed and covenant* in which some members of a neighboring chh, who reside in this town, could unite." But the opposing sides could not agree on articles of faith and covenant, and Morgan predicted that "the consequence will probably be that [they] *will not* unite."[72] By choosing doctrine over the neighborly ties, Goshen's Congregationalist churchgoers rejected the town-church tradition of their own denomination.

Jonathan Fisher, an orthodox minister who had long defended the town-church tradition, confronted a similar departure from the Congregationalist legacy in 1819, when three men from nearby Castine, Maine, approached him with an unexpected request. Castine had a church of its own under the longtime leadership of William Mason, but the men explained that they "could not conscientiously unite" with that church "as it then stood." They respected Mason "as a man and a neighbor," but they did not believe that "he was acquainted with the religion of the heart." They found much lacking in his liberal religious views, and they doubted that he had experienced conversion. Accordingly, they asked Fisher to help them sever ties with the Castine church so they might unite with his congregation in Blue Hill, to which he agreed. The men also wished Fisher to baptize their children, but "to bring them to Blue Hill was not convenient." Therefore, they invited him to travel to Castine and baptize them there: an unusual move that would breach a sitting minister's territory. Fisher, uneasy at the prospect, consulted Mason, who appeared resigned to the defection but "doubted whether it were consistent with church order." Fisher doubted as much, too, but after preaching in the home of a dissenting family, he went ahead with the baptisms nonetheless. The Castine churchgoers, with Fisher's complicity, challenged not only Mason's authority but also his church's territorial integrity. Fisher shared Mason's misgivings about his own actions, but he thought this situation merited an "exception from the general rule" because Castine's dissenters were, in his view, "born after the spirit." Although he harbored no ill will toward Mason (in fact, the two were friends), Fisher judged that the dissenters' doctrinal misgivings merited violating the town church's bounds. In this case, Fisher allowed, conscience trumped residence.[73]

Churchgoers found other ways to erect doctrinal walls between themselves and those with whom they differed spiritually. Congregationalists echoed regular and Freewill Baptists, who had long discouraged their members from "going to law" with each other, preferring to settle disputes in church rather than in court. Whereas legal action may have been appropriate means to resolve difficulties with worldly neighbors, those who shared a religious community should first address conflicts through church discipline. Congregationalist Nathan Coolidge wrote that "it is not justifiable for Brother to go to law with brother," and his colleague John Griswold observed that "many Churches . . . have a particular article of their own forbidding one Br to go to law with another."[74] In 1822, an ecclesiastical council reprimanded the Church of Christ in Montpelier, Vermont, for failing to discipline a member who had sued another. The plaintiff should have "taken further measures" to resolve the matter "in christian amity," the council found. Not to do so "wound[ed] the cause of Christ and the feelings of the Christian brethren."[75] A church's reluctance to air its disputes in public was nothing new; many sectarian churches forbade legal action between members, and many town churches had long urged members to resolve conflicts internally before seeking legal recourse. But as town churches evolved into denominational churches, their inclination toward privacy assumed a different meaning. No longer part of an effort to include the entire town under the umbrella of a mutual covenant, a church's appeal to keep disputes out of the courts amounted to another sort of barrier that it constructed between members of the church polity and their neighbors.

Even as churches exercised greater vigilance to cut themselves off from unbelieving neighbors, they also reached out to like-minded congregations across town, county, and state lines. The itinerant denominations, which had long used expansive bureaucracies, extended and multiplied their administrative structures in the 1810s and 1820s. The Universalists founded the Franklin Association (1822), the Rockingham Association (1824), the New Hampshire Universal Association (1825), and the Green Mountain Association (1829). Moreover, the existing Universalist associations in Maine reorganized under the new Maine Convention in 1829.[76] The Methodist New England Conference spun off separate annual conferences in Maine (1824), New Hampshire (1829), and Vermont (1829); within each, the number of districts and circuits continued to multiply.[77] The Freewill Baptists, who had organized one yearly meeting and six quarterly meetings by 1810, boasted seven yearly meetings and thirty quarterly meetings two decades later, by which time they had also added another administrative layer—a General Conference—to oversee these bodies.[78] The Baptists also augmented their relatively decentralized network of associations. In Maine, for instance, they added the Eastern Maine Association (1818), the York Association (1818), the Penobscot Association (1826), and the Waldo Association (1828). These associations (along with those that predated them) organized under the Maine Baptist Convention (1824), which Baptists founded to better administer their activities, train new ministers, support churches and missionary activity, and "promote a still greater union in doctrine and church discipline."[79] As with the other religious groups, the Baptists' expansion and centralization of authority reflected a desire to manage more members, ministers, and churches.

The Congregationalists, too, expanded and consolidated their authority by forming associations and conferences that coordinated the activities of far-flung ministers and congregations. Ministerial associations, long a fixture of Congregationalism, brought together clergy who assisted each other in ecclesiastical councils and met periodically to organize exchanges and advise on church matters. During the 1810s and 1820s, many of these associations expanded their powers, enlarged their organizations, and assumed more authority over their member activities. The Cumberland Association in Maine was over three decades old when it reorganized under new articles in 1819. The association imposed strict rules for attending its meetings; it required absent ministers who were not performing missions to pay fines and provide written excuses. It also licensed preachers within its jurisdiction, set educational prerequisites for all preaching candidates (which included training in classical studies and various branches of theology), and created a board of examiners to evaluate preaching candidates in member churches. Although the association stopped short of interfering with congregational affairs, it nonetheless advised societies that wished to gather churches, and it assumed some responsibility (that had heretofore fallen to the churches) for approving ministerial candidates. No longer an informal advisory group, the Cumberland Association echoed the itinerant model by transforming itself into a centralized authority.[80]

Some ministerial associations added another layer of authority by forming Congregational conferences: formal bodies that had greater powers of enforcement and more financial resources to support missions and Bible societies. Congregationalists lauded conferences as a way to extend their reach and connect isolated congregations. The *Religious Intelligencer* observed that by 1826, "nearly all the evangelical congregational churches in Maine are now united on what is called 'the Conference system,'" which members predicted would soon link with similar systems in neighboring states. Conferences, according to the *Intelligencer,* aimed to "bring churches to know each other, and think and act together as churches, in any work of faith, or labor of love." The new system would help Congregationalists in Maine, where churches had historically been "planted in neighboring towns, and for years and generations had little intercourse, little knowledge of each other's concerns, and of course little fellowship of the Spirit." Conferences, by contrast, allowed churches to "associate as sister communities of the faithful" and even "feel as *one body,* having a common interest, and lying under the same obligations."[81] In effect, they created a community writ large by binding formerly self-contained churches into a relationship of interdependence and mutual support.

The Piscataqua Conference of Congregational Churches, which grew out of the Piscataqua Association of Ministers in 1826, exemplified this interconnection. The conference included clergy and lay delegates and offered "all possible encouragement and assistance in advancing vital godliness" among its members. It served as a communications clearinghouse for churches, decided questions on matters such as baptism and the admission of members from other religious traditions, and organized campaigns to provide financial assistance to destitute churches and benevolence societies. Eventually, the conference grew so large that it added a bureaucratic layer, creating five districts in New Hampshire and Maine, each of which gathered for its own annual meeting in addition to uniting for quarterly meetings.[82] Although the Piscataqua Conference and other Congregationalist bodies like it never assumed as much power as corresponding denominational organizations did, they nonetheless mirrored those bodies by consolidating their authority and extending their geographic reach. By doing so, they joined churches under a Congregationalist umbrella, which helped diminish the town parishes' spiritual boundaries.

Even Congregationalists recognized that centralized bodies could manage religious activity and suggest (if not enforce) consistent doctrine. But bureaucracy alone did not a denomination make. Inside the figurative institutional housing lay the spiritual stuff of religious life: worship, revival, and the makings of religious community. Town churches had traditionally contained local spiritual activity. But centralized organizations fostered long-distance connections among believers, forged through common devotion. Adopting some of the itinerant tradition, Congregationalists found new ways to cement those bonds.

One institution that extended religious ties was the monthly concert of prayer: simultaneous meetings in several churches to pray for revival. The ritual dated to eighteenth-century Scotland and found favor among both Scottish and English clergy during the Great Awakening. Concerts of prayer waned during the Revolutionary period but revived in the late eighteenth century, when Connecticut's New Divinity clergy agreed to designate one day each month for the meetings and invited members of every denomination to participate. Eventually the practice migrated to northern New England, where ministers seized on the idea as a way to reverse the dulling effects of dwindling congregations and spiritual isolation.[83] By connecting distant churchgoers, the clergy hoped, they could bolster piety and ignite revival.

Northern New Englanders embraced concerts of prayer, and by the second decade of the nineteenth century, churches around the region had set aside the first Monday of each month for common observance. They designated other days for a Sabbath School concert of prayer and a concert of secret prayer. In 1815, the Maine Missionary Society noted that "the first Monday of every month is extensively observed by Christians of different denominations in the several quarters of the world, as a concert of prayer." Accordingly, the society urged its members to "observe the same, that we may unitedly offer our fervent supplications to the God of all grace . . . especially for the success of Missionary exertions.[84] Some ministers took this suggestion literally; one who led an 1820 concert of prayer in Hallowell used the gathering to "plead the cause of missions" and raise funds for missionary work.[85] But most meetings focused exclusively on prodding souls and preparing for revival. The Church of Christ in Washington, Vermont, underwent an awakening shortly after its members extended their monthly concerts by an hour. [86] The practice also spread to southern New Hampshire, where churches drew large crowds for concerts of prayer beginning around 1816.[87] On an 1817 mission in New Hampshire, Thomas Holt attended six concerts of prayer in as many months.[88] Almost as soon as they were introduced, concerts of prayer took root as a standard element of social worship.

Whereas many complained of dwindling Sabbath attendance, congregations observed the monthly concerts fairly regularly. Among the many appealing features of these meetings was that they did not require a minister's leadership. Accordingly, headless churches could join the endeavor, as did the Second Church at North Yarmouth, Maine, which gathered regularly for the meeting.[89] Despite entreaties to other denominations to participate, the monthly concerts remained largely the province of Congregationalists and Presbyterians. The New Hampshire Baptist Sabbath School Union bemoaned in 1829 that only two of its twenty-seven schools participated in the concerts for Sabbath school prayer.[90] Even so, the concert afforded the chance to establish a connection and sense of community—if only in spirit—with believers beyond one's immediate surroundings. As the Vermont *Adviser* suggested in 1815, "the thought of concert in prayer . . . tends powerfully to excite devotional feelings" and would "awaken in Christians a juster feeling of their duties and obligations."[91] By extending the covenanted community beyond the town, the concert of prayer reinforced among its observers their shared faith and mutual spiritual investment.

Much as concerts of prayer reoriented local churches' sense of spiritual geography, so did changing patterns of revival. To be sure, the town revival persisted, and many awakenings were contained within single churches. But increasingly, Congregationalists experienced the sorts of ecumenical and cluster revivals that had already prevailed in other denominations. An 1816 revival in eastern Maine began when a visiting Baptist preacher sparked some attention in the Blue Hill Baptist Church. From there, according to an observer, the revival "soon spread in every direction: East, West, North, and South, through every part of the town" before progressing to "the adjoining towns, all around us." Both Baptists and Congregationalists joined in the awakening, which many of the area's "oldest christians" called the most "extensive" revival they had ever witnessed.[92] Cluster revivals that spread through neighboring towns and churches emerged more and more frequently in northern New England. An 1819 awakening that began in Bath, New Hampshire, added 104 members to the Congregational church. But it spread farther than that; before long, the Baptists and Methodists, too, were swept up in the work, both in Bath and "in several adjacent towns."[93] Similarly, an 1821 revival that began in Middlebury, Vermont, soon "spread in every direction" until it encompassed "fifteen towns within thirty miles."[94] The following year, an awakening started in a North Yarmouth, Maine, Congregationalist church and spread to Congregationalist, Baptist, and Methodist churches in nearby Woolwich, Palermo, and Sidney.[95] When an awakening caught fire and crossed town lines, its potential seemed nearly limitless.

That revivals spread so commonly from one church or village to the next suggested that formerly strong spiritual boundaries had become permeable. That Congregationalists rejoiced in Methodist and Baptist conversions suggests something more: a conviction that all shared in a common Christian community. An observer of the 1819 Bath revival claimed that "the spirit of discord and alienation [had] not entered" among the several denominations that took part. Indeed, he insisted, they saw themselves as "partakers of the *same* faith, the *same* hope, the *same* baptism." Although they remained members of different churches, a common Protestant identity bound and united their separate communities.[96]

Northern New England's principal denominations created religious networks that focused adherents' attention beyond their local churches to a dispersed community of believers. By providing a template for religious expansion, the itinerant model proved successful. Ironically, the only component of the itinerant system that became less important was itinerancy itself. To be sure, missionaries and circuit preachers continued to traverse the region. Ministerial shortages persisted, and plenty of unchurched towns made up a wide missionary field. But the missionary societies and sectarian conferences that sponsored them did not expand further in search of uncharted spiritual territory. As denominations trained more clergy, who settled in more pulpits, they relied less on ministers who distributed their labors thinly over a wide area.

Furthermore, beginning in the 1820s, many missionary organizations turned their attention from northern New England to other frontiers—especially western New York, Ohio, and the Mississippi Valley—where infant churches and empty pulpits demanded their services.[97] The Methodists organized the Missionary and Bible Society in 1819, which sent most of its missionaries to the Ohio and Mississippi valleys (they maintained a few districts in New England and New York). When the Baptist General Missionary Convention formed in 1814, it focused its missionary operations on foreign missions (and, to a lesser extent, missions to American Indians in the West). Congregationalists focused their efforts in the West beginning in the 1810s. The Connecticut Missionary Society and the Society for Propagating the Gospel, which already had operations underway in New York and Ohio, stepped up these efforts in the late 1810s and 1820s. Whereas the SPG kept missionaries on the ground in Maine at least through the 1820s, the CMS reduced its missionary presence in Vermont after 1816 and withdrew from the state altogether in 1821. Although local missionary societies remained in place, they soon became overshadowed by (and often merged with) national organizations such as the American Home Missionary Society, which concentrated their efforts in the West. By 1830, the gravity of westward migration had tugged missionaries' attention away from northern New England, where the religious landscape seemed settled by comparison.

But despite the growing importance of local churches and the scaling back of missionary operations, the itinerant system nonetheless prevailed as a framework for expanding denominations, organizing churches, maintaining piety, and ensuring doctrinal consistency. By tracing overlapping webs of churches, associations, and conferences, northern New England's denominations established a stable presence and assumed a regional orientation.

The religious culture that emerged in northern New England during the early republic comprised many contradictions. Ministers, denominations, and layfolk who eyed each other disdainfully also relied on each other for resources, audiences, and even a spirit of religious fervor that might overflow from one church into the next. Territorial parishes occupied less and less territory, and as a result, they redefined themselves along doctrinal lines. Town churches, always autonomous, sought authoritative guidance on doctrine and discipline—and when no such guidance was forthcoming, they created institutions to dole it out. Itinerant denominations that had long celebrated their preachers' self-directed wanderings now focused on constructing a bedrock foundation of local congregations with settled clergy. Just as outward-looking sectarian communities glanced inward to shore up their churches, inward-looking town churches turned their gazes outward to constellations of believers. In northern New England's new religious culture, the town-church legacy sustained and grounded local communities, but the itinerant system prevailed as the apparatus of religious expansion and denomination-building. As the respective geographies of town churches and itinerant traditions intersected and overlapped, they took shape around shared spaces where a diverse clergy and laity competed, collaborated, and worshiped with each other.

6 Conclusion

A Place of Paradoxes

To see how northern New England's religious geography had changed by the 1830s, we might leave the backcountry and visit one of the region's new urban centers—Bangor, Maine—as Enoch Pond did in 1832. He found the city (itself once a hinterland settlement) positively humming with activity. "Every thing in the town has the appearance of enterprise and growth and thrift," he reported to his father-in-law—everything from the hundreds of new houses and shops "going up in every direction" to the skyrocketing land prices to the steady traffic of "vessels loading and unloading in the harbor." The town's religious landscape, too, bustled with new growth. Bangor boasted "a society of Baptists, Methodists, and Unitarians—all small." They worshiped in the shadow of a "flourishing" orthodox Congregational church, which had recently grown so large that "a division is absolutely necessary." Pond predicted that the Congregationalists would soon erect a "large and elegant" meetinghouse to house the second society. Having recently arrived from Connecticut to teach at the Bangor Theological Seminary, he saw eastern Maine as a backcountry, and in "these ends of the earth," Pond felt a long way from home. But he was optimistic that Bangor—with its expanding population, "great business and wealth," and promising religious prospects—would soon move beyond this period of frenzied expansion. As it took its place among the leading towns in the state (thanks as much to its Congregationalist seminary as to its commerce), Bangor stood as a beacon of progress in "this extended and destitute country."[1]

Bangor, as Enoch Pond experienced it, was a place of paradoxes. At once a remote outpost and a booming market, a center of both financial risk and great wealth, Bangor seemed to have one foot planted in its hinterland past and the other in a metropolitan future. Its religious environment, too, combined tradition and innovation in unlikely ways. On the one hand, the proliferation of new religious societies reflected the pluralism that had become a trademark of northern New England's religious culture. On the other, the dominant church (or, as of 1833, churches) was neither upstart Baptist nor Methodist but old-line Congregationalist. Sectarian expansion notwithstanding, the gravity of spiritual life and the engine of religious growth in Bangor concentrated in the Standing Order. Such departures from expectations had come to typify northern New England's religious culture by the early 1830s. By that time, the weak town-church establishment had broken down, itinerant sectarianism had spread, and a new religious world had emerged from tensions between each tradition's legacies.

Three paradoxes characterized this world and framed relations among the denominations, clergy, and laity who occupied it. First, the region's religious culture focused on local communities even as it sprawled widely over a vast territory. The town church, which had depended on establishment and post-establishment legal support, wilted under pressure from the itinerant religious groups and fragile backcountry environment. But even though town churches fared poorly, settlers still needed local institutions to anchor their religious communities and sustain spiritual ties. Increasingly, then, the town church gave way to the denominational church, which represented members who shared a geographic community *and* chose to join a particular denomination. Local denominational churches (including those gathered by Congregationalists) held worship and conferences, sponsored benevolent work, and cemented covenant obligations among members. Because they could not command a whole town's resources, they did not have the same territorial basis of authority that town churches once enjoyed, but they did promote the same corporate ethic and the same sense of physical and spiritual geography. Within a self-selected group, who gathered because of shared doctrine as much as shared neighborhood, local congregations provided landmarks around which churchgoers arranged their religious communities.

Still, whereas the town-church ideal had privileged local ties above all others, denominational churches only spoke for a fraction of a town's population. Their grounding, therefore, was never exclusively local. Fledgling churches emerged within networks of scattered institutions tied together by itinerants and denominational governing bodies. A longstanding ministerial shortage meant that many headless churches continued to depend on itinerant labor. Although churches settled ministers when they could, the infrastructure of the itinerant system remained intact, and denominations continued to use their bureaucracies and traveling ministers to engineer expansion. The Congregationalists, too, built itinerancy and centralization into their system by relying more and more on missionaries and conferences. Itinerancy breathed new life into Congregationalism, even as it undercut town churches. The laity looked inward to build up their local congregations, but they also gazed outward toward regional networks of like-minded believers. In both directions, they found religious communities.

These communities were based most of all in shared belief and doctrine, but even as they sought to shelter participants from a world of religious error, northern New England's churches reached out to newcomers from that very same world. These opposite tendencies point to a second paradox in northern New England's emerging religious culture: it simultaneously favored denominational exclusivity and ecumenical openness. Lacking a specific place where a religious community could take root, religious groups used doctrine as an article of membership. Believers joined, unbelievers did not, and errant worshipers faced discipline or excommunication. Rites like baptism and communion suggested their participants' standings within religious communities, and public displays of these rituals visibly distinguished insiders from outsiders. Once formed, a religious community closed ranks, imposing rules for moral and religious conduct on its members, and mediating disputes among its own rather than exposing its divisions to outsiders. If churches could no longer contain members within clearly defined town borders, they could do so within less tangible—but no less real—boundaries.

But if they built these walls too high, denominations risked isolating themselves from untapped pools of potential converts. In a region (like most others in early America) where most inhabitants were unchurched, such exclusivity seemed foolhardy. Accordingly, denominations opened gateways through which outsiders might enter. Some staged camp meetings and large conferences that the general public could attend. Some practiced open communion. Many clergy preached in each other's churches, and most preached in public venues (like fields or schoolhouses) open to all observers. And when revivals broke out, they often drew in members of other religious communities from other towns, whose ministers collaborated to maximize conversions and baptisms. Among the laity, the common practice of attending worship with different congregations and flocking to attend distant meetings further diminished the boundaries that town-church and sectarian communities had built. However much denominations tried to gather their churchgoers and construct religious identities based on strict codes of belief and conduct, the realities of hinterland religion—where preachers could not always meet demand, and communities overlapped—required no small degree of flexibility.

So, too, did the endless negotiations between the clergy and laity, who arrived at different and often competing understandings of religious adherence and community. Their relationships, which ranged from alliance to antagonism, point to the third paradox of northern New England's religious culture: its structure of authority was neither top-down nor bottom-up but rather existed within twin bases of power—the clergy and laity. During the early republic, the clergy (and, by extension, their denominations) claimed more authority over religious life. But the layfolk's authority was just as real. The Congregationalist town-church culture had been essentially democratic, by early republican standards. In these small polities, any adult male church member in good standing could vote, and any parish member who could vote in civil elections could also vote in religious societies. Layfolk decided which ministers to ordain and dismiss, when to levy taxes, and, with their ministers, how to enforce discipline. Most churches fell within accepted Congregationalist doctrine, but each adopted the version thereof that suited the clergy and laity.

At first glance, it might seem that the laity gave up power under the itinerant plan, which concentrated authority within denominational governing bodies. Methodists, Freewill Baptists, and Universalists all employed more centralized means of ordaining ministers, carrying out church discipline, and enforcing correct doctrine. Individual churches enjoyed more or less influence over choosing their own clergy (the Universalists more and the Methodists less), but they exercised rather little authority over doctrine and discipline, which central bodies handled so as to maintain consistency and propriety. From their position atop multilayered hierarchies, denominational leaders also coordinated itinerant efforts that extended their watch into new geographic territory. Even Congregationalists and regular Baptists turned to conferences to orchestrate missionary efforts and decide doctrinal and disciplinary questions. Whereas independent polities suited the town-church ideal, only a centralized effort could maintain a denomination's watch over increasing numbers of churches, parishes, and adherents.

Still, the laity had real sway in the itinerant groups. The growing churchgoing public quickly outpaced expanding numbers of clergy, and as a result, headless communities were more the norm than the exception through the 1820s. And that created an opening for a flourishing lay religious culture. It assumed many forms, from the private religious world of secret prayer to the microcosmic community of the family to local headless churches to regional networks born of migration, correspondence, and a growing print culture. In each case, people's spiritual lives did not necessarily match the directives that denominations handed down. Churchgoers worshiped with different groups, traded one doctrine for another, or abstained entirely. They turned to friends and relatives instead of (or in addition to) clergy for spiritual counsel. Even baptized and converted believers—subject to their denominations' strict doctrinal and moral codes—attended other churches and dabbled in unchurched behaviors. Headless churches and societies oversaw much of spiritual life in their communities. Some denominations—especially the Congregationalists, regular Baptists, and Universalists—treated these lay institutions as churches in a transitional state, waiting for permanent clergy. Others, particularly the Methodists and Freewill Baptists, made headless churches (in the form of class meetings) a part of the denominational system. But whether they were ad hoc or officially sanctioned, headless churches concentrated lay authority in their communities and often chafed against efforts by denominations to gain control.

None of this is to posit the laity and clergy as two monolithic and inherently oppositional blocks of power. They were not. When denominations competed, their adherents and ministers allied against rivals. When they collaborated, the laity and clergy alike forged bonds across sectarian lines. Laypeople acted at once in opposition to, in partnership with, and independently from the clergy. Whatever divisions existed between or within these groups ran across many intersecting lines that divided denominations from each other, churched from unchurched, or a momentarily unpopular movement from its enemies (whose alliance may have been just as fleeting). The paradox of religious authority, then, does not necessarily suggest an antagonistic struggle between the clergy and the laity to overpower each other and control religious affairs. Rather, it points to simultaneous developments in which the religious leadership took strides to manage denominational expansion, even as lay communities claimed ever greater authority over their spiritual lives and communities.

These three paradoxes gave shape to a new religious culture, which cleared new spiritual spaces—elastic spaces, well-suited for expansion—and gave followers the tools to navigate them. We could (as many people did) call northern New England's religious hinterland anarchic—laity dashing to and fro, ministers fighting over pulpits, and a few religious scofflaws writing their own rules—but, in fact, it was very orderly. When denominational governing bodies centralized control, they could extend their reach, secure in their confidence that itinerants on the leading edge of migration would carry out their mandates. As they did so, these itinerants planted local churches that became polestars in denominational constellations. These churches lit the way for migrants who found themselves in unfamiliar places, otherwise lacking communities that could give refuge. A religious landscape that appeared unruly actually channeled migration, sheltered believers, and allowed settlers to arrange their lives around spiritual centers.

What took place in northern New England became part of a wider current that followed migration paths across the country. And everywhere that current flowed, the three paradoxes of northern New England's spiritual settlement—itinerant and settled orientations, doctrinal rigidity and ecumenism, and shared ministerial and lay authority—came along. The religious settlement of the northern hinterland coincided with similar patterns in other places like Kentucky, Tennessee, and the Ohio Valley, where itinerants organized religious territory, communities, and believers.[2] The apparatus of the itinerant system then stretched west, directing new migrants to new churchly communities and clearing their spiritual paths through unfamiliar places. Itinerants followed (and led) settlers into places like the Mississippi Valley and the trans-Mississippi West, which proved hospitable to religious growth precisely because the denominations that succeeded there were able to manage followers who spread out over vast terrain. These movements included some groups that figured into northern New England's story, like the Methodists, and others that did not, like the Mormons.[3] And to many eyes, the landscapes they occupied may have looked every bit as chaotic as northern New England did, but in fact they were every bit as ordered. The denominations that helped guide settlement did so by centralizing authority and overseeing their followers. In this way, they played a crucial role in structuring westward migration.

Like the churches that reached north, churches that spread west secured their places by making their boundaries fluid and permeable, thereby drawing a broad range of believers into their midst. But once believers became converts, these denominations expected them to meet exacting standards of doctrine and comportment. Missionaries and circuit riders in places like the Rocky Mountain West, California, and Oregon sought out new settlers who needed spiritual homes and helped them build communities on foundations of Victorian morality and piety.[4] And, casting farther forward, when Americans flooded new suburbs after World War II, moving into neighborhoods far from their families and friends, a great many of them found guidance and community in the evangelical and nondenominational churches that sprawled across the "crabgrass frontier."[5] Many of these churches are somewhat unspecific on doctrine, but they use preaching, popular culture, and the strength of their own membership to nurture a collective (and usually conservative) Protestant identity. They guard their autonomy and rely on local leadership but nonetheless establish formal, almost denominational, networks of like-minded churches. These churches serve secular as well as spiritual functions that allow churchgoers to manufacture communities where none had existed before, and in doing so, to replace the social networks they left behind.[6] It is no wonder, then, that Americans have flocked to these churches in droves, just as they did to the denominational churches in nineteenth-century frontier outposts.

The "joining" culture that fills pews today harkens back to the voluntarism of the early republic. Churches may have helped Americans forge communities in unsettled places, but church-building has not come from institutional leadership alone. Rather, layfolk have supported religious expansion by assuming responsibilities that paralleled institutional roles: they have taken on missions and other church work; served as exhorters and Sunday school teachers; written for evangelical publications; spearheaded social reform movements for abolition, temperance, and civil rights; and (more recently) packed stadiums with Promise Keepers and festival grounds with Christian music fans. In some denominations, which place unordained leaders in charge of youth and women's ministries, the line between clergy and laity is difficult to discern. But these two groups have not always spoken with one voice. Churchgoers might switch allegiances, reject bits of doctrine, revolt from within to change their denominations, or resist the changes that the clergy might impose. If the churches have provided the wandering layfolk spiritual homes, then the laity have in turn insisted on remodeling those homes to suit their needs.

The religious culture that spans our map today, in other words, has its roots in places like early republican northern New England, where settlers had to negotiate a shifting environment to plant seeds of religious community. They did so by adapting old institutions and inventing new ones, and by relying on believers to trace new religious pathways. They created new networks, which absorbed old outposts. Northern New England's religious culture was at once lawless and meticulously designed. But for those who took part—as for many who observed from its fringes—it provided a spiritual map in a physical wilderness.

Notes

Introduction

1. *A Narrative on the Subject of Missions*, 9; John Maltby to his parents, August 27, 1825, Maltby Family Papers, folder D.

2. Solomon Stevens to Enos Stevens, April 24, 1805; Solomon Stevens to John Johnson, May 12, 1805, both in Stevens Family Papers, box 4, folder 22.

3. William Miller, "Journal of a Mission to the Northern Settlements," November 16, 1802, Connecticut Missionary Society Papers, reel 7.

4. *An Address of the General Association of Connecticut*, 3.

5. Sidney E. Mead, "The American People"; Linenthal and Chidester, eds., *American Sacred Space;* Lane, *Landscapes of the Sacred;* DeRogatis, *Moral Geography*, 111–120; Isaac, *The Transformation of Virginia*, especially chapters 2–4.

6. Nash, *Wilderness and the American Mind*, chapter 2; Butler, *Awash in a Sea of Faith*, chapter 4; Isaac, *The Transformation of Virginia*, chapter 4; DeRogatis, *Moral Geography*, 41–46; Albanese, "Savages, Sinners, and Saved"; Robins, "Vernacular American Landscape"; Schneider, *The Way of the Cross Leads Home.*

7. A classic study of the conflict between a parish-based and itinerant system is Isaac, *The Transformation of Virginia.*

8. See Andrews, *The Methodists and Revolutionary America;* Butler, *Awash in a Sea of Faith;* Hatch, *The Democratization of American Christianity;* Heyrman, *Southern Cross;* Johnson, *A Shopkeeper's Millennium;* Noll, *America's God.* Most studies of early republican "frontier religion" have focused on Baptists and Methodists in the old Southwest; see Boles, *The Great Revival, 1787–1805;* Conkin, *Cane Ridge;* Miyakawa, *Protestants and Pioneers;* Sweet, *Religion in the Development of American Culture.* For treatments of the Second Great Awakening in northern New England specifically, see Jaffee, *People of the Wachusett;* Marini, *Radical Sects of Revolutionary New England;* Roth, *The Democratic Dilemma;* Taylor, *Liberty Men and Great Proprietors.*

9. Linenthal and Chidester, eds., *American Sacred Space;* Lane, "Giving Voice to Place," 57–60.

10. Like Stephen Marini and Jon Butler, I argue that the revival's most prevailing legacy was concentrating ecclesiastical authority in complex organizations that were designed to grow right along with the American frontier. Marini, *Radical Sects of Revolutionary New England*, 6; Butler, *Awash in a Sea of Faith*, chapter 9.

11. Fuller, *Religious Revolutionaries*, 64–75; Sidney E. Mead, "Denominationalism: The Shape of Protestantism in America," in Richey, ed., *Denominationalism*, 68–105; Russell E. Richey, "Denominations and Denominationalism: An American Morphology," in Mullin and Richey, eds., *Reimagining Denominationalism*, especially 80–82, 91.

12. As Joseph Wood points out, the image of the New England village with the town meetinghouse or church at its center has its roots in the early republic. Wood, *The New England Village*, 92–93, 115–116.

13. Hatch, *The Democratization of American Christianity*, 7.

14. Curry, *The First Freedoms,* chapters 6–7; Gaustad, *Faith of Our Fathers,* 110–133, 59–74; Isaac, *The Transformation of Virginia;* Lambert, *The Founding Fathers and the Place of Religion in America,* chapters 8–9; Levy, *The Establishment Clause,* chapters 2–3; Benke and Grenda, eds., *The First Prejudice;* Sehat, *The Myth of American Religious Freedom.*

15. By locating lay cultures at the center of religious history, I join scholars who link, as Catherine Brekus suggests, "individual agency to cultural change." See Brekus, "Introduction," in Brekus, ed., *The Religious History of American Women,* 31–32; Brekus, *Strangers and Pilgrims;* Orsi, *Between Heaven and Earth;* Seeman, *Pious Persuasions.*

16. See Hansen, *A Very Social Time,* especially chapter 6; Gundersen, "Kith and Kin"; Osterud, *Bonds of Community.*

17. Jürgen Habermas and David S. Shields have similarly demonstrated the role of print culture in creating intangible civic and social communities. See Habermas, *The Structural Transformation of the Public Sphere;* Anderson, *Imagined Communities;* Shields, *Civil Tongues and Polite Letters in British America.*

1. No Schism in the Body

1. William Jenks Diary, February 15, 1810, William Jenks Papers, box 4. Jenks's plan was consistent with a Congregationalist ecumenism that, according to Douglas Sweet, emerged in response to pluralism in eighteenth-century New England. See Sweet, "One Glorious Temple of God," 311–320.

2. Sassi, *A Republic of Righteousness,* especially chapter 1.

3. Burg, "The Cambridge Platform"; Cohen, "Puritanism," 584–587; Foster, *The Long Argument,* 146–155.

4. Dewey, Wheelock, and Gilbert, *A True and Concise Narrative of the Origin and Progress of the Church Difficulties in the Vicinity of Dartmouth College,* 15; Committee of the Congregational Church in Hanover, New Hampshire, to the Orange Association of Ministers, 1810, Cornish, New Hampshire, Congregational Church Correspondence.

5. *The Proceedings and Documents Relative to Certain Members Separating from the Church in Wilton,* 99.

6. Thomas Merrill to Samuel Hopkins, April 30, 1834, Autographs of Vermonters.

7. Joel Winch Autobiography, 1802, Joel Winch Papers, folder 2, 71–74. The difference between dismission and expulsion had to do with the standing of the departing church member; dismission was a leave to depart in good standing whereas an expulsion was closer to an excommunication.

8. Meeting minutes, February 10, 1824, Cumberland Association Rules and Proceedings, Congregational Conference–Maine Missionary Society Records, 138.

9. Result of Council Convened at Greenfield, September 1822, from Union Church of Christ Records; meeting minutes, April 4, June 6, October 20, 1825, Congregational Church (Church of Christ) Records, both in Greenfield, New Hampshire, Union Congregational Church Records.

10. Schmidt, *Holy Fairs;* Philip D. Zimmerman, "The Lord's Supper in Early New England: The Setting and the Service," in Benes, ed., *New England Meeting House and Church,* 124–134.

11. Result of Vote, 1806, Wilmington, Vermont, Congregational Church.

12. Stephen Peabody Diary, October 4, 1789, Stephen Peabody Diaries, vol. 3 (1786–1787, 1789–1790).

13. Samuel Goddard Diary, March 20, 1814, Samuel Goddard Diary and Memorandum Books.

14. William Jenks to the Baptist Church in Bath (copy), Letter No. 1158, March 31, 1817, Diary No. 10, William Jenks Papers, box 27.

15. Meeting minutes, August 8, 1813, Bangor, Maine, All Souls Congregational Church Records, vol. 1.

16. Constitution, 1802, Bridgewater, New Hampshire, Church and Society Records.

17. John Eliot to William Jenks, December 9, 1805, William Jenks Papers, box 3.

18. *The Proceedings and Documents Relative to Certain Members Separating from the Church in Wilton,* 11, 49.

19. Committee of the Church of Christ in Wilton to the Church of Christ in Mason, 1823, Livermore Family Papers, box 14, folder 7.

20. Loveland and Wheeler, *From Meetinghouse to Megachurch,* 5–7; Williams, *Houses of God,* 6.

21. Although this trend was most pronounced in Anglican structures, it also applied to Congregationalist churches. Jon Butler refers to this process as the "sacralization" of the landscape; see Butler, *Awash in a Sea of Faith,* 109–116. See also Abbott L. Cummings, "Meeting and Dwelling House: Interrelationships in Early New England," in Benes, ed., *New England Meeting House and Church,* 4–10; Sweeney, "Meetinghouses, Town Houses, and Churches."

22. The term "meetinghouse" connotes the building's combined sacred and secular uses, whereas the term "church" (when referring to a structure) implies solely religious use. Northern New Englanders used the terms interchangeably regardless of whether their church buildings served civil functions. See Sweeney, "Meetinghouses, Town Houses, and Churches"; Walsh, "Holy Time and Sacred Space in Puritan New England."

23. Ephraim Abbot Diary, February 1, March 1, March 8, 1812, octavo volume 1; Ephraim Abbot to Mary Pearson, August 2, 1811, box 1, folder 1; Ephraim Abbot to Mary Pearson, February 7, 1812, box 1, folder 2, all in Ephraim Abbot Papers; Clark, *History of the Congregational Churches in Maine,* vol. 2, 344; Kilby, *Eastport and Passamaquoddy,* 334, 40.

24. *General Petitions, 1788–1792,* vol. 9, *State Papers of Vermont,* 38–39; Loveland and Wheeler, *From Meetinghouse to Megachurch,* 11; *General Petitions, 1797–1799,* vol. 11, *State Papers of Vermont,* 163–164, 89–90; *Laws of Vermont, 1785–1791,* vol. 14, *State Papers of Vermont,* 9–10, 13–14, 46–47; Petition of the Inhabitants of Marlborough, October 2, 1792, Manuscripts of Vermont State Papers, vol. 18, 372.

25. *Laws of New Hampshire, 1784–1792,* vol. 5, 95–96, 287–288; Shivell, *The Steeples of Old New England,* 92–94, 100–102, 277; Remonstrance of the Inhabitants of Milton, June 1820, New Hampshire Petitions.

26. Wood, *The New England Village,* 92–93, 115–116.

27. Sweeney, "Meetinghouses, Town Houses, and Churches," 70.

28. Petition for a Tax on Land to Build a Meeting House, October 11, 1788, *General Petitions, 1788–1792,* 38–39.

29. For an overview of the neoclassical style, see Whiffen and Koeper, *American Architecture, 1607–1976,* chapter 5, especially 101. To be sure, some of these changes reflected the transformation of material culture more broadly, which had begun in the eighteenth century. See Bushman, *The Refinement of America;* Breen, *The Marketplace of Revolution.*

30. Joseph Warren to Thomas Gray, January 22, 1793, Joseph Warren Letters to Thomas Gray.

31. Autobiography of Reverend Ephraim Abbot, n.d., folio 20, Ephraim Abbot Papers, box 2, folder 6.

32. Shivell, *The Steeples of Old New England,* 94, 100, 104–105. See also Wood, *The New England Village,* 127–128, for a more general discussion of meetinghouse construction and remodeling during this period.

33. Loveland and Wheeler, *From Meetinghouse to Megachurch*, 11.

34. Shivell, *The Steeples of Old New England*, 204–205, 11–13, 176.

35. Meeting minutes from November 24, 1817, Montpelier Meeting House Society Records, Montpelier, Vermont, Bethany Congregational Church Records, reel 2.

36. Abigail Abbott to Abiel Livermore, September 28, 1828, Livermore Family Papers, box 2, folder 8.

37. Waldoborough Meetinghouse Plan, 1820, Congregational Conference–Maine Missionary Society Records, ser. 2, box 3, folder 2.

38. "Report on the Meetinghouse," Dover.

39. Perez Chapin to Thomas Pomroy, May 23, 1827, Perez Chapin Missionary Journal, 1827, Cumberland Conference of Churches Records, folder 6.

40. Williamson, *History of the City of Belfast in the State of Maine*, vol. 1, 222–228.

41. Stephen Peabody Diary, June 4, 1805, Stephen Peabody Diaries, vol. 7 (1805–1806).

42. Petition of the Inhabitants of the Northwesterly Part of Wells, October 1797; Remonstrance of the Inhabitants of Wells and Pawlett, October 1797, Manuscripts of Vermont State Papers, vol. 20, 121–122.

43. Remonstrance of the Inhabitants of Milton, June 1820, New Hampshire Petitions.

44. This definition borrows much from Jonathan Sassi's discussion of the southern New England clergy's corporate vision. See Sassi, *A Republic of Righteousness*, chapter 1.

45. Reports of Council, September–October 1826, Washington, Vermont, Church of Christ Register, 24–28.

46. Constitution, 1802, Bridgewater, New Hampshire, Church and Society Records.

47. *Piscataqua Evangelical Magazine*, January–February 1805, 30; May–June 1806, 90–91.

48. "Rules for Due Regulation of the Church," 1824, chapter 1, Montpelier, Vermont, Bethany Congregational Church Records, reel 2, 118–119.

49. *A Book of the Records of the Church of Christ in Stratton*, 2, 5, 8–12, 17; Records of the First Congregational Church of Waldoboro, Congregational Conference–Maine Missionary Society Records, ser. 2, vol. 77, 9–18.

50. Dismissions and recommendations helped churches oversee their parishioners' movements and mitigate the potentially disruptive social effects of migration. See Najar, *Evangelizing the South*, 98–99.

51. Meeting minutes, April 25, 1793–May 26, 1797, Newbury, Vermont, Congregational Church Records.

52. Meeting minutes, April 2, 1829, Bangor, Maine, All Souls Congregational Church Records, vol. 1.

53. Meeting minutes, November 10, 1826, Middlebury, Vermont, Congregational Church Record Book.

54. Meeting minutes, August 1, 1824, Freeport, Maine, First Parish Congregational Church Records, ser. 1, 86. In Maine, courts supported parishes' demands that residents declare membership by making it more difficult to abstain from church membership than to comply with residency requirements.

55. Heyrman, *Commerce and Culture*; Peterson, *The Price of Redemption*.

56. Andrew Culver and Jeduthan Stone to Abiel Flint, April 18, 1807, Aaron Cleveland Correspondence, Connecticut Missionary Society Papers, reel 3.

57. Report on the State of Religion, 1822, Cumberland Conference of Churches Records, folder 1.

58. Result of Council at North Yarmouth, Third Church, May 5, 1814, Cumberland Conference of Churches Records, folder 5.

59. Records of the First Congregational Society of Jericho, Vermont, Vermont Congregational Conference Records, box 2, folder 20, 36–37.

60. Ephraim Abbot to Mary Pearson, July 27, 1813, Ephraim Abbot Papers, box 1, folder 2.

61. Woodman, ed., "Memoir and Journals of Rev. Paul Coffin, D.D.," 390.

62. Meeting minutes, November 13, 1811, Records of the First Congregational Church of Waldoboro, Congregational Conference–Maine Missionary Society Records, ser. 2, vol. 76, 60–61.

63. Stout, *The New England Soul,* 3–10, 41–43, 95–99, 118–122, 72–79.

64. Samuel Goddard, Missionary Report, September 1813, Samuel Goddard Diary and Memorandum Books; F. Burt to Eliphalet Pearson, January 20, 1819, William Jenks Papers, box 6.

65. Result of Council at North Yarmouth, Third Church, May 5, 1814, Cumberland Conference of Churches Records, folder 5.

66. Isaac Hurd Diary, April 30, 1828, Isaac Hurd Papers.

67. Peabody discusses the academy repeatedly throughout his diaries. See, for instance, his entry on June 6, 1793, Stephen Peabody Diaries, vol. 4 (1792–1794).

68. Ephraim Abbot Diary, April 10, 1814, Ephraim Abbot Papers, octavo vol. 2.

69. William Jenks Diary, November 25, 1810, William Jenks Papers, box 4; Annual Report of the Trustees of the Bath Society for Discontinuing and Suppressing Public Vices, May 13, 1817, William Jenks Papers, box 6.

70. Report of Council, March 23, 1815, Freeport, Maine, First Parish Congregational Church Records, ser. 1, 35–37.

71. Eli Moody to Charity Bryant and Sylvia Drake, March 15, 1830, Charity Bryant and Sylvia Drake Papers.

72. Lambert, *Inventing the Great Awakening,* 62–69. For more on preaching and the New England revival tradition, see Crawford, *Seasons of Grace;* Kling, *A Field of Divine Wonders,* 110–143; Stout, *The New England Soul,* 99–101, 79–81, 95–97.

73. Kling, *A Field of Divine Wonders,* 75–111.

74. "Domestic Intelligence," *Religious Intelligencer,* April 26, 1817, 761–762.

75. *The Adviser; or, Vermont Evangelical Magazine,* March 1809, 61.

76. *Religious Intelligencer,* October 9, 1824, 298–299.

77. Rutland County, Vermont, Association of Congregationalist Churches, "Protest against the System of Exciting and Promoting Revivals of Religion Known to Have Been in Operation during the Year Past in Vermont," 1836. Although the manuscript was written in 1836, it recounts an 1830 controversy.

78. William Jenks Diary, October 4, 1810, William Jenks Papers, box 4.

79. Isaac Hurd Diary, October 1, 1822, Isaac Hurd Papers.

80. See Foster, *The Long Argument,* chapter 5.

81. Many of these decisions to reject the halfway covenant resulted from the increasing popularity of New Divinity Congregationalism, which reacted against moderate trends by reintroducing a stricter Calvinist orthodoxy. Meeting minutes, June 19, 1791, Windham Association Minutes, vol. 1, Windham Union Association, Vermont Conference Records, 15–16; meeting minutes, March 13, 1800, Union Church of Christ Records, Greenfield, New Hampshire, Union Congregational Church Records, 64; meeting minutes, September 27, 1808, Records of the First Congregational Church of Waldoboro, Congregational Conference–Maine Missionary Society Records, ser. 2, vol. 77; meeting minutes, January 22, 1810, Freeport, Maine, First Parish Congregational Records, ser. 1, 16; Articles of Faith and Covenant, Bangor, Maine, All Souls Congregational Church Records, vol. 1.

82. "A Detail of Occurrences and Transactions for a Series of Years between the Parish of Dover and Their Minister," Dover, New Hampshire, First Parish Records, vol. 1, 49–50, 69.

83. Petition of the Inhabitants of Hopkinton, December 1, 1799, New Hampshire Petitions; Henry Blake to John Dudley, September 15, 1790, John Dudley Family Papers, box 1, folder 4b.

84. Joseph Warren to Thomas Gray, August 2, 1793, Joseph Warren Letters to Thomas Gray.

85. Underhill, Vermont, Result of an Ecclesiastical Council, November 4, 1812.

86. Examples of Congregationalist salaries include Lathrop Thompson and Calvin Noble, who settled in Chelsea, Vermont, in 1799 and 1807, respectively, for salaries of $334 and $400, each payable in a combination of cash and grain; and John Denison, Joseph Larabee, and Luther Blodgett, each of whom settled in Jericho (in 1808, 1814, and 1819, respectively) and earned salaries of between $300 and $400 annually, payable in a combination of saleable grain, pork, beef cattle, and cash. The Waldoboro Congregational Church typically paid its ministers $500 per year throughout the 1820s. By contrast, the New England Conference of the Methodist Episcopal Church typically paid its ministers less than $100 per year (with married preachers earning more than unmarried preachers). Baptist churches often paid ministers on a periodic basis (foregoing annual contracts), but typical salaries ranged between $100 and $200. See entries on June 3, 1799, and May 11, 1807, Chelsea, Vermont, Voluntary Congregational Society Records; entries on December 20, 1808, May 11, 1814, January 2, 1826, February 27, 1826, Records of the First Congregational Society of Jericho, Vermont, Vermont Congregational Conference Records, box 2, folder 20; Records of the Waldoboro Congregational First Parish, Congregational Conference–Maine Missionary Society Records, ser. 2, vol. 78; Minutes of the New England Conference of the Methodist Episcopal Church, vol. 1 (typed copy), New England Conference of the Methodist Episcopal Church Records; meeting minutes, December 23, 1826, West Shaftsbury Baptist Church Records. For discussions of ministerial salaries, see Fuller, *Religious Revolutionaries,* 65–66.

87. Stephen Peabody Diary, August 25, 1784, Stephen Peabody Diaries, vol. 2 (1784–1786).

88. Thomas Holt Missionary Journal, 1816–1817, William Jenks Papers, box 6, 28–29.

89. Woodman, ed., "Memoir and Journals of Rev. Paul Coffin, D.D.," 252.

90. For more on the New Divinity, see Conforti, *Samuel Hopkins and the New Divinity Movement;* Conkin, *The Uneasy Center,* 101–113; Haroutunian, *Piety versus Moralism,* 62, 67–68; Holifield, *Theology in America,* 135–149; Kling, *A Field of Divine Wonders,*75–109; Valeri, *Law and Providence in Joseph Bellamy's New England,* 140–179. For more on the fragmentation of Congregationalism in the late eighteenth century, see Holifield, *Theology in America,* chapter 6; Noll, *America's God,* 130–137, chapters 13–14.

91. Woodman, ed., "Memoir and Journals of Rev. Paul Coffin, D.D.," 342.

92. Woodman, ed., "Memoir and Journals of Rev. Paul Coffin, D.D.," 401.

93. Stephen Peabody Diary, June 23, 1784, September 22, 1784, December 26, 1786, Stephen Peabody Diaries, vols. 2 (1784–1786), 3 (1786–87, 1789–1790).

94. Joseph Wingate to Paine Wingate, September 27, 1824, Wingate Family Papers.

95. Gibson, *Dialogue Concerning the Doctrines of Atonement between a Calvinist and a Hopkinsian,* 8.

96. Committee of Raynham to Alden Bradford, December 22, 1827, Evangelical Missionary Society in Massachusetts Records, box 2, folder 9.

97. For more on regular Baptist theology, see Conkin, *The Uneasy Center,* 58–59; Hatch, *The Democratization of American Christianity;* Holifield, *Theology in America,* chapter 13; Noll, *America's God,* 149–152.

98. Marini, *Radical Sects of Revolutionary New England,* 5–6.

99. Stephen A. Marini, "Religious Revolution in the District of Maine, 1780–1820," in Clark, Leamon, and Bowden, eds., *Maine in the Early Republic,* 135.

100. McLoughlin, *New England Dissent,* vol. 2, 791, 843, 875.

101. Constitution, Middletown, Vermont, Baptist Church Records.

102. New London, New Hampshire, Baptist Church Records, vol. 1, 41–43; Job Seamans Journal, August 27, 1798, Job Seamans Papers; McLoughlin, *New England Dissent,* vol. 2, 859–860.

103. Joseph Field, Journal of My Missionary Tour, 1805.
104. Alden Bradford, Missionary Report, 1817, Society for Propagating the Gospel Papers, box 1, folder 13. See also Blue Hill, Maine, Town Records, 91–99. Fisher became a missionary shortly after Bradford submitted his report on Blue Hill, at least in part to supplement his dwindling salary.
105. Jacob Abbot to Abiel Abbot, June 22, 1809, Livermore Family Papers, box 13, folder 14; Jacob Abbot to Samuel Abbot, February 5, 1825, Livermore Family Papers, box 14, folder 9.
106. Woodman, ed., "Memoir and Journals of Rev. Paul Coffin, D.D.," 331.
107. Stephen Bemis Journal, April 13, 1797.
108. Solomon Livermore to Anna Livermore, June 9, 1803, Livermore Family Papers, box 2, folder 5.
109. William Jenks Diary, July 20, 1816, William Jenks Papers, box 27.
110. Jacob Abbot to Samuel Abbot, February 2, 1825, Livermore Family Papers, box 14, folder 9; Jacob Abbot to Nehemiah Cram, February 12, 1829, Livermore Family Papers, box 14, folder 15.
111. Asa Lyon, Speech Read in Association, May 28, 1833, Asa Lyon Papers, box 5, folder 55.

2. Zion Travels

1. "Extract of a Letter from the Rev. William Batchelder," *Massachusetts Baptist Missionary Magazine,* September 1805, 137–139.
2. Ibid., 140.
3. Bressler, *The Universalist Movement in America,* 7; Haroutunian, *Piety versus Moralism,* chapter 3.
4. Baptist associations date back to the Philadelphia Association, established in 1707. See Marini, *Radical Sects of Revolutionary New England,* 20, 46.
5. *Minutes of the New Hampshire Association* (Portsmouth: Charles Pierce, 1801), 11; Burrage, *History of the Baptists in Maine,* 85, 106.
6. *Minutes of the Vermont Baptist Association* (Salem: Dodd and Rumsey, 1805), 13; *Minutes of the Woodstock Association* (Windsor, 1789), 4. See, for example, the Articles of Faith and Covenants for the Lincoln and Bowdoinham Associations: *Minutes of the Lincoln Association* (Wiscasset: Babson and Rust, 1806), 2; *Minutes of the Bowdoinham Association* (Portland: Daniel George, 1802), 6.
7. *Minutes of the Vermont Baptist Association,* 1805, 14.
8. These schedules appear in many associations' annual reports. See, for example, *Minutes of the Bowdoinham Association,* 1802, 7; *Minutes of the Lincoln Association,* 1806, 5.
9. *Minutes of the Woodstock Association* (Keene: John Prentiss, 1806), 1; minutes, 1792 annual meeting, Woodstock Association Records, 5.
10. *Minutes of the Vermont Baptist Association* (Salem: Dodd and Rumsey, 1806), 6; *Minutes of the Vermont Baptist Association* (Salem: Dodd and Rumsey, 1807), 5–6.
11. Burrage, *History of the Baptists in Maine,* 114–117.
12. Letter from the Rev. James Murphy, *Massachusetts Baptist Missionary Magazine,* May 1804, 58.
13. Conkin, *The Uneasy Center,* 75–77.
14. Ibid., 63–71; Andrews, *The Methodists and Revolutionary America,* 19–24; Holifield, *Theology in America,* 268–270.
15. Andrews, *The Methodists and Revolutionary America,* 61, 63–72; Conkin, *The Uneasy Center,* 75–80. The Methodist *Discipline* was reprinted and revised several times; see, for ex-

ample, *A Form of Discipline, for the Ministers, Preachers and Members (Now Comprehending the Principles and Doctrines) of the Methodist Episcopal Church in America.*

16. Andrews, *The Methodists and Revolutionary America,* 70–72, 199–207, 208; Heyrman, *Southern Cross,* 101–102.

17. Allen and Pillsbury, *History of Methodism in Maine,* 11–19; Lee, *A Short History of the Methodists in the United States of America,* 195–223; Mudge, *History of the New England Conference of the Methodist Episcopal Church,* 25–26, 32–35, 47–50.

18. Joel Winch Autobiography, 1802, Joel Winch Papers, folder 2, 34–35.

19. Minutes, New England Conference of the Methodist Episcopal Church Records, vol. 1, 75–76, 146–147; vol. 2, 55–56, 67–69, 95–97, 99.

20. Scholars tend to disagree as to whether the origins of Universalism in America lay with individual leaders or a more decentralized movement. See Bressler, *The Universalist Movement in America,* 14–19; Cassara, ed., *Universalism in America,* 6–17; Conkin, *American Originals,* 95–99; Hughes, "The Origins of New England Universalism"; Marini, "The Origins of Universalism"; Marini, *Radical Sects of Revolutionary New England,* 68–74.

21. Bressler, *The Universalist Movement in America,* 15; Holifield, *Theology in America,* 220–227; Marini, "The Origins of Universalism"; Marini, *Radical Sects of Revolutionary New England,* 68.

22. Bressler, *The Universalist Movement in America,* 15–19; Hughes, "The Origins of New England Universalism," 36; Marini, *Radical Sects of Revolutionary New England,* 68–73. The definitive tract that influenced Murray's thinking was Relly, *Union,* first published in Boston in 1779. The tract that held most sway among New England Universalists was Huntingdon, *Calvinism Improved.*

23. Bressler, *The Universalist Movement in America,* 32–33; Marini, *Radical Sects of Revolutionary New England,* 107–109, 22–23.

24. Marini, *Radical Sects of Revolutionary New England,* 124–125; meeting minutes, 1794, 1800, Universalist Church of America General Convention Records, 61–64.

25. Bressler, *The Universalist Movement in America,* 33–34; Conkin, *American Originals,* 100; Marini, *Radical Sects of Revolutionary New England,* 125–127.

26. Conkin, *American Originals,* 100.

27. The spelling of Randel's last name appears variously as Randall and Randel (he himself used different spellings over the course of his life). Most current scholars use Randel, which he used earlier in his adult life. Randel's followers did not consistently identify themselves as "Freewill Baptist" until about 1800. Prior to that, they were known as the Randallites, Freewillers, or Open Communion Baptists. They used the term "freewill" to refer to their central doctrine, and the term "Freewill Baptist" is now commonly used retroactively to refer to the denomination from its founding. The original Articles of Faith no longer exist but are documented in many sources. The story of Randel's conversion and the formation of the Freewill Baptist Church is described in greater detail in Baxter, *History of the Freewill Baptists,* chapter 1; Stewart, *The History of the Freewill Baptists,* vol. 1, chapter 1; and Marini, *Radical Sects of Revolutionary New England,* 64–67, 103.

28. Baxter, *History of the Freewill Baptists,* 2, 21, 55–56; Marini, *Radical Sects of Revolutionary New England,* 40–43, 67; Stewart, *The History of the Freewill Baptists,* vol. 1, 55, 80–81. For more on Alline, see Rawlyk, *Ravished by the Spirit.*

29. John Buzzell, "A Short History of the Church of Christ," *A Religious Magazine,* April 1811, 58–59; Marini, *Radical Sects of Revolutionary New England,* 86–87; Stewart, *The History of the Freewill Baptists,* vol. 1, 59–61.

30. Meeting minutes, June 10, 1783, New Durham, New Hampshire, Freewill Baptist Church Records of Quarterly and Yearly Meetings.

31. Meeting minutes, June 1783, June 1784, March 1785, September 1785, December 1785, New Durham, New Hampshire, Freewill Baptist Church Records of Quarterly and Yearly Meetings.

32. Meeting minutes, June 11, 1791, New Durham, New Hampshire, Freewill Baptist Church Records of Quarterly and Yearly Meetings; Marini, *Radical Sects of Revolutionary New England,* 104–106; Stewart, *The History of the Freewill Baptists,* vol. 1, 65–70.

33. Marini, *Radical Sects of Revolutionary New England,* 117; Stewart, *The History of the Freewill Baptists,* vol. 1, 110–111.

34. Meeting minutes, March 10, 1794, Pittsfield, New Hampshire, Freewill Baptist Church Records.

35. William Smyth Babcock Journal, August 18, 1801, William Smyth Babcock Papers, folder 4.

36. Marini, *Radical Sects of Revolutionary New England,* 119–121; New Durham Quarterly Meeting Records of the Elders' Conference.

37. Burrage, *History of the Baptists in Maine,* 66–74, 90–96; Isaac Case to unknown, December 13, 1816, Isaac Case Papers.

38. Phinehas Pillsbury Diary, vol. 1, 1–4.

39. Circular Letter, August 21, 1827, Rockingham Association Records, 8–9.

40. Meeting minutes, 1802, Universalist Church of America General Convention Records, 90.

41. "Religious Notice," *Christian Intelligencer,* August 16, 1823, 27.

42. Meeting minutes, May 20, 1795, New Durham, New Hampshire, Freewill Baptist Church Records of Quarterly Meetings, vol. 1, 56; preface and meeting minutes, October 23, 1801, New Durham Quarterly Meeting Record of the Elders' Conference, 1, 6.

43. John Buzzell, "A Short History of the Church of Christ, Gathered at New-Durham," *A Religious Magazine,* July 1812, 220.

44. Meeting minutes, May 21, October 22, 1802, New Durham Quarterly Meeting Record of the Elders' Conference, 12–17.

45. Minutes, New England Conference of the Methodist Episcopal Church Records, vol. 1, 143, 162, 176, 188.

46. Ibid., vol. 1, 109.

47. Meeting minutes, 1796, Universalist Church of America General Convention Records, 49.

48. Meeting minutes, 1819, Universalist Church of America General Convention Minutes and Circular Letters, box 1, folder 1, 228.

49. "Sketch of Rev. Mr. Bradley's Tour among a Number of Vacant Churches in New-Hampshire and Vermont, at the Request of the Committee of the Society," *Massachusetts Baptist Missionary Magazine,* January 1806, 173.

50. In 1810, there were 7,014 Methodists in the part of northern New England that fell within the New England Conference (all but Vermont west of the Green Mountains, which was in the New York Conference). That area was served by 52 preachers including 4 presiding elders. In 1821, the same region included 11,872 Methodists who were served by 54 preachers including 5 presiding elders. See minutes, New England Conference of the Methodist Episcopal Church Records, vol. 1, 146–510, 316, 326–328.

51. Benjamin Randel to unknown, n.d., Ephraim Stinchfield Papers, box 1, folder 1.

52. "Extract of a Letter from the Rev. Peter P. Roots," *Massachusetts Baptist Missionary Magazine,* September 1804, 76.

53. "Preface," *A Religious Magazine,* October 1811, 111–112.

54. Circular Letter, August 21, 1827, Rockingham Association Records, 9.

55. William Johns, "The Age of Missions," sermon excerpted in *Vermont Baptist Missionary Magazine,* April 1812, 161–163.

56. Burrage, *History of the Baptists in Maine,* 66–74, 90–96; Isaac Case to unknown, December 13, 1816, Isaac Case Papers; meeting minutes, August 1827, Livermore, Maine, First Baptist Church Records, vol. 2, part 1; Burrage, *History of the Baptists in Maine,* 261–262.

57. Summary of the Order and Discipline of the Church of New Durham as Delivered by Elder Benjamin Randel, August 12, 1801, William Smyth Babcock Papers, box 1, folder 1; Heyrman, *Southern Cross,* 101; Marini, *Radical Sects of Revolutionary New England,* 118.

58. Minutes, New England Conference of the Methodist Episcopal Church Records, vol. 1, 61.

59. *Religious Informer,* October 1820, 146; Minutes, New England Conference of the Methodist Episcopal Church Records, vol. 1, 283; vol. 2, 13, 25; meeting minutes, 1796, Universalist Church of America General Convention Records, 75.

60. For more on the itinerant experience, see Wigger, *Taking Heaven by Storm,* especially chapter 3.

61. "Sketch of Rev. Mr. Bradley's Tour," 174.

62. Jonathan Wallace to Edward Turner, March 6, 1821, Edward Turner Family Papers, box 3, folder 18.

63. W. A. B., Anonymous Diary, 31.

64. Mudge, *History of the New England Conference of the Methodist Episcopal Church,* 52; Minutes, New England Conference of the Methodist Episcopal Church Records, vol. 1, 121, 241.

65. Lee, *A Short History of the Methodists in the United States of America,* 181. At times, the records use the term "supernumerary" to refer to the same classification.

66. "Extract of a Letter from Rev. Mr. Case," *Massachusetts Baptist Missionary Magazine,* May 1805, 102–103.

67. "Religious Intelligence," *Herald of Gospel Liberty,* January 19, 1809, 3.

68. *The Doctrines and Discipline of the Methodist Episcopal Church in America,* 22.

69. Preface, Greene, Maine, Free Baptist Churches Records, vol. 1. Although filed with records from a Freewill Baptist church, this record book is clearly that of a Calvinist Baptist church. Volume 2 of this collection, the record book of the Greene Free Baptist Church, comes from a separate body.

70. Meeting minutes, November 27, 1798, April 5, 1813, Windsor, Vermont, Universalist Society Record Book, 7, 39.

71. Proceedings of the Eastern Association of Universalists, Convened at Turner, Maine, June 1822, printed in *Christian Intelligencer,* September 1822, 24.

72. John Buzzell, "A Short History of the Church of Christ, Gathered at New-Durham," *A Religious Magazine,* January 1811, 12.

73. "Religious Intelligence," *The Christian's Magazine,* 1806, 177–180.

74. Meeting minutes, May 18, 1802, October 19, 1804, New Durham Quarterly Meeting Records of the Elders' Conference, 37–38, 45.

75. Minutes, New England Conference of the Methodist Episcopal Church Records, vol. 1, 180, 242, 250–251.

76. Hall, *Contested Boundaries,* chapter 2; Heyrman, *Southern Cross,* 130–133.

77. See, for example, meeting minutes, May 21, October 22, 1802, New Durham Quarterly Meeting Record of the Elders' Conference, 13–17; minutes, New England Conference of the Methodist Episcopal Church Records, vol. 1, 251; meeting minutes, August 24, 1830, Rockingham Association Records.

78. Meeting minutes, October 23, 1801, New Durham Quarterly Meeting Record of the Elders' Conference, 6–7.

79. Meeting minutes, 1796, Universalist Church of America General Convention Records, 187.

80. Papers Related to the Trial of Leonard Frost, 1829, New England Conference of the Methodist Episcopal Church Records; minutes, New England Conference of the Methodist Episcopal Church Records, vol. 2, 92.

81. Meeting minutes, September 1785, March 1786, New Durham, New Hampshire, Freewill Baptist Church Records of Quarterly and Yearly Meetings.

82. *Minutes of the Leyden Association,* 1803, 6.

83. *Minutes of the Vermont Baptist Association,* 1805, 6.

84. References to the Bath Baptist meetinghouse construction appear in William Jenks Diary, January 1, 3, June 11, 1817, William Jenks Papers, box 27. See also Burrage, *History of the Baptists in Maine,* 147, 50; Shivell, *The Steeples of Old New England,* 329. By contrast, the first Congregationalist churches in those towns had organized in 1767 (Bath) and 1772 (Blue Hill) and had begun construction on their meetinghouses in 1760 (Bath) and 1790 (Blue Hill). See Clark, *History of the Congregational Churches in Maine,* vol. 2, 100–101, 203–204.

85. *A Religious Magazine,* November 1820, 56. In Lewiston, the Freewill Baptist church predated the Congregationalist church, which was organized in 1826. See Clark, *History of the Congregational Churches in Maine,* 268.

86. Russell Streeter to Edward Turner, April 30, 1821, Edward Turner Family Papers, box 3, folder 12. The First (Congregational) Church of Portland organized (as the First Church of Falmouth) in 1727, and its meetinghouse had been built six years earlier. Clark, *History of the Congregational Churches in Maine,* 92–93.

87. An Act to Incorporate the Trustees of the Methodist Episcopal Meetinghouse in Rochester, 1826, and An Act to Incorporate the Trustees of the Methodist Episcopal Meeting House at Lamprey River Village in New Market, 1827, both in *Laws of New Hampshire, 1821–1828,* vol. 9, 508, 634. In Rochester, a class meeting organized in 1807. The Methodists gained a foothold in Newmarket by 1808 and later established their academy there, which may explain why construction on the Congregationalist meetinghouse in nearby Lamprey River Village stalled after it commenced in the early 1810s. Kern, *God, Grace, and Granite,* 16, 22.

88. William Smyth Babcock Journal, August 7, September 9, 1803, William Smyth Babcock Papers, folder 4.

89. Minutes, New England Conference of the Methodist Episcopal Church Records, vol. 1, 69.

90. Royal Clark to Timothy Remick, February 13, 1818, Timothy Remick Papers.

91. F. Burt to Eliphalet Pearson, January 20, 1819, William Jenks Papers, box 6. Stoves in meetinghouses caught on slowly; churches largely declined to install them until after 1815. See Jane C. Nylander, "Toward Comfort and Uniformity in New England Meeting Houses, 1750–1850," in Benes, ed., *New England Meeting House and Church,* 87–89.

92. As J. B. Jackson suggests, the evangelical styles spawned by the Great Awakening reacted against what he calls the "territoriality" of the established parish by diminishing boundaries between sacred and profane space. See J. B. Jackson, "The Order of a Landscape: Reason and Religion in Newtonian America," in D. W. Meinig, ed., *The Interpretation of Ordinary Landscapes,* 156–157.

93. Anonymous, "Prospective Camp-Meeting," *Zion's Herald,* September 5, 1827, 1.

94. Minutes, 1800 Convention, Universalist Church of America General Convention Records, 64.

95. John Buzzell, "A Short History of the Church of Christ, Gathered at New-Durham," *A Religious Magazine,* January 1811, 21.

96. Andrews, *The Methodists and Revolutionary America,* 93; Heyrman, *Southern Cross,* 145–149.

97. Preface, Shoreham, Vermont, Baptist Church Ecclesiastical Records.

98. In likening their surroundings to a wilderness, these ministers drew on two centuries of typology that treated the southern and northern New England frontiers as untamed places, both naturally and spiritually. See Albanese, *Nature Religion in America;* Canup, *Out of the Wilderness;* Carroll, *Puritanism and the Wilderness;* Cherry, *Nature and Religious Imagination;* Lowance, *The Language of Canaan;* Miller, *Nature's Nation;* Nash, *Wilderness and the American Mind;* Slotkin, *Regeneration through Violence.*

99. Circular Letter, 1827, Rockingham Association Records, 7–8.

100. John Buzzell, "A Short History of the Church of Christ, Gathered at New-Durham," *A Religious Magazine,* July 1812, 224–225.

101. W. A. B., Anonymous Diary, 48.

102. *Religious Informer,* April, 1820, 49–50.

103. Epistle from 1819 annual meeting, Universalist Church of America General Convention Minutes and Circular Letters, 227–229.

104. Meeting minutes, 1826, Conference Journals, Maine Conference of the Methodist Episcopal Church Records.

105. Andrews, *The Methodists and Revolutionary America,* 93; meeting minutes, August 4, 1810, Poland, Maine, Poland Circuit of the Methodist Church Quarterly Conference Record Book and Deed of Pew.

106. "Of Meetings for Church Business," *Religious Informer,* May 1820, 69.

107. Meeting minutes, December 1799–September 1800, Mason, New Hampshire, Baptist Church of Christ Records, 36–37.

108. Minutes, November 9, 1821, Andover, Vermont, Baptist Church of Christ Book of Records.

109. Benjamin Randel to Tosier Lord, n.d. (according to accompanying notes, probably ca. 1777–1780), Ephraim Stinchfield Papers, box 1, folder 1; meeting minutes, January 11, 1796, Records of Quarterly Meeting, Ephraim Stinchfield Papers, box 1, folder 3.

110. Andrews, *The Methodists and Revolutionary America,* 93; Stewart, *The History of the Freewill Baptists,* vol. 1, 110–111. The Methodists allowed lawsuits only as a last resort and threatened to expel any member who did not let the arbitration process take its course. See *The Doctrines and Discipline of the Methodist Episcopal Church in America,* 26.

111. Meeting minutes, April 5, 1802, Marlowe, New Hampshire, Baptist Church Records; meeting minutes, August 3, 1811, Clarendon, Vermont, Second Baptist Church Records; meeting minutes, October 13, 1804, Sanford, Maine, Baptist Church Records. Monica Najar has demonstrated that southern Baptists similarly assumed civil functions to police their church members' behavior, even as the Anglican/Episcopalian establishment (and former establishment) handed these functions over to civil authorities. See Najar, *Evangelizing the South,* especially chapter 4.

112. Andrews, *The Methodists and Revolutionary America,* 92–95; Heyrman, *Southern Cross,* 89–94, 137, 59; Schneider, *The Way of the Cross Leads Home,* 78–91.

113. Joel Winch Autobiography, 1802, Joel Winch Papers, folder 2, 26–27, 58–59.

114. Sylvanus Haynes, "A Revival of Religion in Middletown," *Vermont Baptist Missionary Magazine,* June 1811, 12.

115. "Religious Intelligence," *A Religious Magazine,* January 1811, 29.

116. Joel Winch Autobiography, 1802, Joel Winch Papers, folder 2, 61. A. Gregory Schneider argues that the class meeting was the single most important component of the Methodist

society and polity, because it afforded the greatest opportunity to enforce discipline and undergird piety. See Schneider, *The Way of the Cross Leads Home*, 78–82.

117. *The Doctrines and Discipline of the Methodist Episcopal Church in America*, 11; Holifield, *Theology in America*, 269, 76–77; Marini, *Radical Sects of Revolutionary New England*, 108, 17.

118. "Religious Intelligence," *A Religious Magazine*, January 1811, 25–27.

119. William Smyth Babcock, Untitled Sermon, June 15, 1800, octavo 2; Babcock Journal, February 15, 1801, folder 2, both in William Smyth Babcock Papers.

120. 1804 Profession and Covenant of the Christian Church of Langdon, Langdon, New Hampshire, Christian Church Records, box 1, folder 2, 17–18.

121. Peach, ed., "The Reverend Joel Winch," 268.

122. Schneider, *The Way of the Cross Leads Home*, xviii, 82–91.

123. William Smyth Babcock Journal, March 27, 1802, William Smyth Babcock Papers, folder 3.

124. Meeting minutes, August 18, 1802, New Durham, New Hampshire, Freewill Baptist Church Records of Quarterly Meetings, vol. 2, 39–40.

125. Peach, ed., "The Reverend Joel Winch," 22–23.

126. Wentworth, ed., *Journals of Enoch Hayes Place*, vol. 1, 21, 28, 49, 51, 70.

127. William Smyth Babcock Journal, May 17, 1806, William Smyth Babcock Papers, octavo vol. 5.

128. Clark, *The Language of Liberty*, 41–45; Hall, *Contested Boundaries*, 48, 42, 7; Lambert, *Inventing the Great Awakening*, 57, 81; O'Brien, "A Transatlantic Community of Saints," 825–827; Westerkamp, *The Triumph of the Laity*, 189–191.

129. Nordbeck, "Almost Awakened," 23–58; Ricard, "The Northern New England 'New Light' Clergy and 'Declension' Reconsidered," 125–149; Clark, *The Eastern Frontier*, 279–280.

130. Wentworth, ed., *Journals of Enoch Hayes Place*, 60.

131. Richey, "From Quarterly to Camp Meeting," 204, 206, 211.

132. Marini, *Radical Sects of Revolutionary New England*, 120–121.

133. Meeting minutes, n.d., Records of Quarterly Meeting, Ephraim Stinchfield Papers, box 1, folder 3. Although the volume (and many of the minutes contained therein) is cataloged as undated, the dated records it contains are all from the 1790s.

134. Allen and Pillsbury, *History of Methodism in Maine*, 259.

135. The definitive work on Cane Ridge is still Conkin, *Cane Ridge*. See also Eslinger, *Citizens of Zion*.

136. William Smyth Babcock Journal, November 8, 1801, William Smyth Babcock Papers, folder 3.

137. Samuel Train, Jr., to Nabby Binney, February 20, 1802, Fisk Family Papers, box 3, folder 1.

138. William Smyth Babcock Journal, June 29, 1805, William Smyth Babcock Papers, octavo vol. 5.

139. Allen and Pillsbury, *History of Methodism in Maine*, 72; Cole and Baketel, eds., *History of the New Hampshire Conference of the Methodist Episcopal Church*, 268; Kern, *God, Grace, and Granite*, 60.

140. Mudge, *History of the New England Conference of the Methodist Episcopal Church*, 386–391.

141. Joseph Field, "Journal of My Missionary Tour," July 3, 1805.

142. John Flagg to Elmira Flagg, September 17, 1822, Bowers-Flagg Family Papers, box 1, folder 6.

143. Anonymous, "Prospective Camp-Meeting," *Zion's Herald*, September 5, 1827, 1; Moses Springer, "Camp-Meetings," *Zion's Herald*, October 5, 1825, 2. For more on camp meetings

as sacred space, see Robins, "Vernacular American Landscape," 165–191; Weiss, *City in the Woods.*

144. *A Religious Magazine,* June 1822, 249–251.

145. *Religious Informer,* April 1820, 50.

146. Meeting minutes, October 19, 1803, New Durham, New Hampshire, Freewill Baptist Church Records of Quarterly Meetings, vol. 2, 91–92.

147. "Extract of a Letter from the Rev. Stephen Choate," *Massachusetts Baptist Missionary Magazine,* September 1807, 332–338.

148. "Religious Intelligence," *A Religious Magazine,* January 1811, 23–28.

149. Circular Letter, 1827, Rockingham Association Records, 7.

3. Scrambling for the Right

1. This chapter includes material that originally appeared in "Equal Right and Equal Privilege: Separating Church and State in Vermont," *Journal of Church and State* 50 (Winter 2008): 23–48, published by Oxford University Press.

2. Aaron Cleveland to the Connecticut Missionary Society Committee of Missions, May 16, 1808, Connecticut Missionary Society Papers, reel 3.

3. I borrow both the term "legal fiction" and its usage from Edmund Morgan, who applied this concept to popular sovereignty in early modern England and revolutionary America. Morgan argued that popular sovereignty was a necessary fiction that convinced the population to submit to their governments. See Morgan, *Inventing the People,* especially chapter 3. Although this discussion argues that the severing of church-state ties was an incomplete process, for the sake of simplicity it will also use the term "disestablishment" to refer to the laws by which states ended compulsory religious taxation. "Establishment" could include a wide array of state support for religion.

4. Bassett, *Gods of the Hills,* 12; Comstock, *The Congregational Churches of Vermont and Their Ministry,* 8–9; Levy, *The Establishment Clause,* 185. Of the ninety-seven churches that Congregationalists had organized as of 1800, three failed before the close of the eighteenth century, bringing the total to ninety-four.

5. Isaac Backus to "My Dear Friend," June 3, 1796, Isaac Backus Papers; McLoughlin, *New England Dissent,* vol. 2, 791, 794. McLoughlin notes that while the number of Congregationalist churches in Vermont grew from eleven in 1776 to one hundred in 1807, the corresponding number of Baptist churches grew from two to seventy-six.

6. Minutes, New England Conference of the Methodist Episcopal Church Records, vol. 1, 75–76.

7. Bressler, *The Universalist Movement in America,* 33–34; Conkin, *American Originals,* 100; Marini, *Radical Sects of Revolutionary New England,* 125–127.

8. Marini, *Radical Sects of Revolutionary New England,* 119–121; Stewart, *The History of the Freewill Baptists,* vol. 1, 254, 61; New Durham Quarterly Meeting Records of the Elders' Conference.

9. Sherman, Sessions, and Potash, *Freedom and Unity,* 120, 42.

10. Bassett, *Gods of the Hills,* 13.

11. The 1787 version retained a Protestant test for members of the state assembly—so the Constitution permitted at least one such infringement. The Constitution of 1793 eliminated all religious tests. Constitution of Vermont, 1777, *Laws of Vermont, 1777–1780,* ed. Allen Soule, vol. 12, *State Papers of Vermont* (Montpelier, Vt., 1964), chapter 1, article 3; Constitution of Vermont, 1787, *Laws of Vermont, 1785–1791,* ed. John A. Williams, vol. 14, *State Papers of Vermont* (Montpelier, Vt., 1966), chapter 1, article 3; Constitution of Vermont, 1793, *Laws of*

Vermont, 1791–1795, ed. John A. Williams, vol. 15, *State Papers of Vermont* (Montpelier, Vt., 1967), chapter 1, article 3.

12. *Journals and Proceedings of the General Assembly of the State of Vermont, Part II,* vol. 3, *State Papers of Vermont,* 189; An Act to Enable Towns and Parishes to Erect Proper Houses for Public Worship and Support Ministers of the Gospel, 1783, *Laws of Vermont, 1781–1784,* ed. John A. Williams, vol. 13, *State Papers of Vermont* (Montpelier, Vt., 1965), 195; An Act for Supporting Ministers of the Gospel, 1787, *Laws of Vermont, 1785–1791,* 348–350.

13. New Hampshire did not recognize Universalists, Methodists, and Freewill Baptists as denominations until the early nineteenth century, and Massachusetts at first reserved the right of exemption only for regular Baptists, Quakers, and Anglicans. For New Hampshire, see Kinney, *Church and State,* 91–97; McLoughlin, *New England Dissent,* vol. 2, 863–871. For Massachusetts, see McLoughlin, *New England Dissent,* vol. 1, 221–243.

14. Vermont was distinctive for its many multi-denominational religious societies (in towns like Craftsbury and Windsor) and for the number of towns (like Montpelier, where Universalists predominated) in which the first organized church was not Congregationalist. Roth, *The Democratic Dilemma,* 36; DeBoer and DeBoer, "The Formation of Town Churches"; Latham, "Church and State in Thetford."

15. Petition of John Williams, William Deane, et al., February 3, 1787, Manuscripts of Vermont State Papers, vol. 17, 259.

16. Petition of the Baptist Society of Chester, August 31, 1787, Manuscripts of Vermont State Papers, vol. 17, 312; Petition for Postponement of Consideration of a Church Controversy, October 7, 1788, *General Petitions, 1788–1792,* ed. Edward A. Hoyt, vol. 9, *State Papers of Vermont* (Montpelier, Vt., 1955), 65–66.

17. Blood, *A Sermon Preached before the Honorable Legislature of the State of Vermont,* 34–36; Levy, *The Establishment Clause,* 189; McLoughlin, *New England Dissent,* vol. 2, 803.

18. For more on these petitions, see McLoughlin, *New England Dissent,* vol. 2, 803–807. The reason for the timing of this campaign is unclear, but McLoughlin suggests that it might have been a response to the influx of Congregationalist missionaries and their relative success in establishing new churches.

19. Petitions for the Repeal of an Act Supporting Ministers of the Gospel, all October 1794, *General Petitions, 1793–1796,* ed. Allen Soule, vol. 10, *State Papers of Vermont* (Montpelier, Vt., 1958), 90–96.

20. An Act for the Support of the Gospel, 1797, *Laws of the State of Vermont, 1797,* 474–479.

21. "An Address of the Council of Censors to the People of Vermont," October 21, 1799, Council of Censors Transcriptions, 1785–1820, Vermont Constitution Records, box 1, 72. The council proposed to keep the first and last sections of the act, which preserved the right to form voluntary religious societies, repealed all earlier forms of the law, and ensured that preexisting contracts between societies and their ministers would remain valid.

22. Ibid., 70–71.

23. An Act to Repeal a Certain Act, and Parts of an Act, Therein Mentioned, 1807, *Acts and Laws Passed by the Legislature of the State of Vermont, October 1807* (Randolph, Vt.: Sereno Wright, 1807), 22.

24. McLoughlin, *New England Dissent,* vol. 2, 811; Aaron Cleveland to the Connecticut Missionary Society Committee of Missions, May 16, 1808, Connecticut Missionary Society Papers, reel 3.

25. For more on church and state in seventeenth-century New Hampshire, see Kinney, *Church and State,* chapter 1; McLoughlin, *New England Dissent,* vol. 2, 833–836, 842; Farmer, *An Ecclesiastical Register of New-Hampshire,* 7, 11; Turner, *The Ninth State,* 88.

26. Kinney, *Church and State,* 50–54; McLoughlin, *New England Dissent,* vol. 2, 837–838.

27. For a survey of New Hampshire politics during the Revolutionary and early republican periods, see Daniell, *Experiment in Republicanism.*

28. McLoughlin, *New England Dissent,* vol. 2, 844; Bouton, ed., *New Hampshire Provincial and State Papers,* vol. 9, 837–838.

29. Bouton, ed., *New Hampshire Provincial and State Papers,* vol. 9, 853.

30. Ibid., 863–864, 67, 73–74. The constitution also preserved full religious liberty to Protestants in the Declaration of Rights and other provisions that established Protestant tests for officeholders.

31. Meeting minutes, June 2, August 14, 1791, Piscataqua Association Records, vol. 1, 44–47.

32. McLoughlin, *New England Dissent,* vol. 2, 850–851; Turner, *The Ninth State,* 128–129. The definitive biography of William Plumer is Turner, *William Plumer of New Hampshire.*

33. Bouton, ed., *New Hampshire Provincial and State Papers,* vol. 10, 41–42, 108, 13–14, 46; McLoughlin, *New England Dissent,* vol. 2, 851–854; Turner, *The Ninth State,* 129, 422n.

34. Kinney, *Church and State,* 83.

35. Hazen, *The Congregational and Presbyterian Ministry and Churches of New Hampshire,* 66. The figure for Congregationalist churches includes Presbyterian churches under the Plan of Union, but only a handful of these were actually Presbyterian. Hazen notes that as of 1875, no more than twenty churches had been Presbyterian at any time, most of which reverted to Congregationalism. Congregationalists vastly outnumbered Presbyterians during this period. In 1820, John Farmer estimated that Congregationalist communicants outnumbered Presbyterians by about eleven or twelve thousand to one thousand. See Farmer, *An Ecclesiastical Register of New-Hampshire,* 7, 9.

36. Farmer, *An Ecclesiastical Register of New-Hampshire,* 11; Turner, *The Ninth State,* 201.

37. New Durham, New Hampshire, Freewill Baptist Church Records of Quarterly and Yearly Meetings, 1783–1793; New Durham, New Hampshire, Freewill Baptist Church Records of Quarterly Meetings, vol. 1, 1792–1801; Kinney, *Church and State,* 192–194; McLoughlin, *New England Dissent,* vol. 2, 855n.

38. Petition of James Osgood and others, November 5, 1800; Petition of James Wille and others, June 1807, New Hampshire Petitions.

39. Meeting minutes, January 20, 1804, New Durham Quarterly Meeting Records of the Elders' Conference, 35.

40. Kinney, *Church and State,* 88.

41. Jacob Abbot to Abiel Abbot, June 22, 1809, Livermore Family Papers, box 13, folder 14; McLoughlin, *New England Dissent,* vol. 2, 861–862.

42. Petition of Thomas P. Richardson and others, June 10, 1812, New Hampshire Petitions.

43. McLoughlin, *New England Dissent,* vol. 2, 907–908.

44. Petition of the Committee of the Town of Surry, October 11, 1800, New Hampshire Petitions.

45. Petition of Thomas Clark and others, May 20, 1807, New Hampshire Petitions.

46. The sequence of events surrounding Erskine's case are recounted in somewhat more detail in Kinney, *Church and State,* 91–94; McLoughlin, *New England Dissent,* vol. 2, 870–871; and *Decisions of the Superior and Supreme Court of New Hampshire,* 37n.

47. McLoughlin, *New England Dissent,* vol. 2, 870.

48. Universalist Church of America General Convention Records, 88, 108, 110–111, 126–132.

49. See the text of Jeremiah Smith's decision in *Decisions of the Superior and Supreme Court of New Hampshire,* 1–38. This case is also discussed in Kinney, *Church and State,* 95–97; McLoughlin, *New England Dissent,* vol. 2, 863–870; and Turner, *The Ninth State,* 204.

50. *Decisions of the Superior and Supreme Court of New Hampshire,* 20–29.

51. Bressler, *The Universalist Movement in America*, 33–34; Marini, *Radical Sects of Revolutionary New England*, 106–109, 24–27.

52. The operative text in Article 6 reads, "No person of any particular religious sect or denomination shall ever be compelled to pay towards the support of the teacher or teachers of another persuasion, sect, or denomination."

53. *Decisions of the Superior and Supreme Court of New Hampshire*, 12–15, 9.

54. Meeting minutes, October 17, 1804, August 18, 1805, New Durham, New Hampshire, Freewill Baptist Church Records of Quarterly Meetings, vol. 2, 139, 144, 160–161; Petition of the Freewill Baptists, November 1804, New Hampshire Petitions.

55. Petition of the Universalists, June 1805, New Hampshire Petitions; Resolve, June 13, 1805, *Laws of New Hampshire*, vol. 7, 417.

56. Petition of the Methodists, May 11, 1807, New Hampshire Petitions; Resolve, June 15, 1807, *Laws of New Hampshire*, vol. 7, 622.

57. In an 1868 decision, a Superior Court judge found that the matter of recognizing new denominations should have been left to the courts alone, and that the resolutions were probably unconstitutional (and, if not, they carried no legal weight). See McLoughlin, *New England Dissent*, vol. 2, 875, 880.

58. This generalization typically held true, but it belies more complex relationships among political parties and denominations. The Congregationalist clergy tended to support the Federalists but many voiced concern about partisanship in politics and religion, and some liberal Congregationalists had begun to ally with the Republicans by the late 1810s. Republicans often favored liberal toleration policies, but because they had to court the Congregationalist majority to remain politically viable, they only slowly came to favor complete disestablishment. But they also saw the rapidly growing dissenting denominations as a key element of their own political base. See Kaplanoff, "Religion and Righteousness"; Kinney, *Church and State*, 97–108; McLoughlin, "The Bench, the Church, and the Republican Party in New Hampshire"; McLoughlin, *New England Dissent*, vol. 2, 877–893; Turner, *The Ninth State*, 352–357.

59. An Act Authorizing Selectmen to Tax the Ratable Estates of All Ordained Ministers of Every Denomination, 1816, *Laws of New Hampshire*, vol. 8, 582.

60. William P. Strickland, ed., *The Autobiography of Dan Young* (New York: Carlton and Porter, 1860), 279–281, cited in McLoughlin, *New England Dissent*, vol. 2, 897; Turner, *The Ninth State*, 353, 464n66.

61. This progress is outlined in Kinney, *Church and State*, 100–101; McLoughlin, *New England Dissent*, vol. 2, 897–898; and Turner, *The Ninth State*, 353.

62. This debate was also carried out in the partisan newspapers of the time, which featured eyewitness records of the legislative proceedings. The main sources for this discussion are the weekly installments in the *Concord Observer*, a Congregationalist newspaper that covered the debates. This newspaper's transcripts of the House debates closely reflect those found in other contemporary sources, and they echo the series of events sketched out in the House and Senate Journals. Although the actual debates only spanned a few days—from June 22–25, 1819—the *Concord Observer*'s accounts appeared in weekly issues from June 28 through August 23.

63. "Debate," *Concord Observer*, July 26, 1819.

64. Ibid., August 16, August 2, 1819.

65. "New Hampshire Legislature," *Concord Observer*, June 28, 1819.

66. An Act in Amendment of an Act for Regulating Towns and the Choice of Town Officers, Passed February 8, 1791, *Laws of New Hampshire*, vol. 8, 820–821. The term "Toleration Act" actually only applies to the third section of the act, which made all religious societies voluntary, but is typically used to refer to the entire law.

67. *Religious Informer,* August 3, 1819, 14–15; First Christian Toleration Society Record Book, 1820–1838, Alstead, New Hampshire, Universalist Church Records; Isaac Hill, quoted in McLoughlin, *New England Dissent,* vol. 2, 909.

68. Detailed considerations of colonial Massachusetts's treatment of religious dissenters can be found in Curry, *The First Freedoms,* chapter 5; Levy, *The Establishment Clause,* 18–20; and McLoughlin, *New England Dissent,* vol. 1, parts 3–7.

69. A Constitution of Frame of Government for the Commonwealth of Massachusetts, *Acts and Laws of the Commonwealth of Massachusetts, 1780–1781* (Boston: Benjamin Edes and Sons, 1890), 3–30.

70. All Christians could worship as they chose, and all denominations could organize churches, but all Christians were not equal under the law. According to Chapter 5, Article 1, of the 1780 Constitution, all officeholders had to pledge that they owed no allegiance to any "foreign Prince, Person, State, or Potentate . . . in any matter civil, ecclesiastical, or spiritual." The content of this oath effectively made Catholics ineligible for political office.

71. Article 4 in the Declaration of Rights reinforces this corporate-minded purpose of Article 3 by stating that "no man, nor corporation, or association of men, have any other title to obtain advantages, or particular and exclusive privileges, distinct from those of the community." See Neem, "The Elusive Common Good," 387.

72. From the *Boston Gazette,* May 13, 1780, and the (Boston) *Independent Chronicle,* March 21, 1780, quoted in Neem, "The Elusive Common Good," 389–390.

73. Backus and Weston, *A History of New England,* 230.

74. Taylor, *Liberty Men and Great Proprietors,* chapter 3.

75. Woodman, ed., "Memoir and Journals of Rev. Paul Coffin, D.D.," 363, 323.

76. Daniel Little to Peter Thacher, February 17, 1792, Society for Propagating the Gospel Papers, box 3, folder 5.

77. Levi Frisbie, "Journal of a Mission to the County of Lincoln," September 4–8, 1792, Society for Propagating the Gospel Papers, box 2, folder 11. Although the title of this journal refers only to Lincoln County, Frisbie's travels also took him to Kennebec and Franklin counties in the sparsely settled areas north of Augusta.

78. Resolve Directing the Committee on Unappropriated Lands in Lincoln County to Provide a Minister for the Plantations in Said County, 1786, *Acts and Laws of the Commonwealth of Massachusetts, 1786–1787* (Boston: Adams and Nourse, 1893), 341–342. The General Court also attempted periodically to punish towns for not settling and maintaining ministers but to little avail. See Summons of Vassalboro Inhabitants, August 1, 1795, Kennebec Supreme Judicial Court Records, box 9, folder 6; Summons of Sidney Inhabitants, August 1, 1795, Kennebec Supreme Judicial Court Records, box 9, folder 5.

79. John Hancock, "Governor's Message to the General Court," January 28, 1791; Resolve on His Excellency's Message, with the Address of the Society for Propagating the Gospel, 1791, *Acts and Laws of the Commonwealth of Massachusetts, 1790–1791* (Boston: Adams and Nourse, 1894), 563–564, 190–191.

80. See *Frost et al.* v *Cutter,* as discussed in McLoughlin, *New England Dissent,* vol. 1, 642–646.

81. An Act Regulating Parishes and Precincts, and the Officers Thereof, 1786, Resolve Directing the Committee on Unappropriated Lands in Lincoln County, 21–24. A parish was the administrative subdivision that corresponded with a church or society. A parish could have geographic bounds or it could be a solely legal entity.

82. An Act for Incorporating a Number of the Inhabitants of the Towns of New-Gloucester and Gray, in the County of Cumberland, into a Distinct and Separate Religious Society, 1790, *Acts and Laws of the Commonwealth of Massachusetts, 1790–1791,* 18–19.

83. "Fryeburg Baptists Petition," in Baxter, ed., *Documentary History of the State of Maine,* vol. 22, 396–398.

84. For an example of an act of incorporation for a Congregationalist church, see An Act for Incorporating a Religious Society in the Town of Penobscott in the County of Hancock, 1793, *Acts and Laws of the Commonwealth of Massachusetts, 1792–1793* (Boston: Thomas Adams, 1895), 407–408. For examples of acts of incorporation for Baptist churches, see An Act Incorporating a Number of the Inhabitants of the Town of Topsham in the County of Lincoln into a Distinct and Separate Religious Society, 1794; An Act to Incorporate a Number of the Inhabitants of the Towns of Berwick and York, into a Distinct Religious Society, 1795, both in *Acts and Laws of the Commonwealth of Massachusetts, 1794–1795* (Boston: Adams and Larkin, 1896), 54–56, 421–423; An Act to Incorporate a Number of the Inhabitants of Woolwich and Bowdoinham, in the County of Lincoln, into a Society by the Name of the Baptist Society in Woolwich and Bowdoinham, 1797, *Acts and Laws of the Commonwealth of Massachusetts, 1796–1797* (Boston: Wright and Potter, 1897), 352–353.

85. The Act Providing for the Public Worship of God (1800) attempted to expand rights for dissenters by allowing them more latitude in determining how and when to set aside taxes for dissenting ministers or societies, and by clarifying the use of certificates. It remained ambiguous, however, on the question of whether a dissenting society must be incorporated in order to levy taxes. See *Acts and Laws of the Commonwealth of Massachusetts, 1798–1799* (Boston: Wright and Potter, 1897), 495–498.

86. Howe, ed., *Cases on Church and State in the United States,* 29–35; McLoughlin, *New England Dissent,* vol. 1, 650–651; Sassi, *A Republic of Righteousness,* 118.

87. Howe, ed., *Cases on Church and State in the United States,* 31–34; McLoughlin, *New England Dissent,* vol. 2, 1086–1087.

88. An Act Respecting Public Worship and Religious Freedom, 1811, *Laws of the Commonwealth of Massachusetts, 1809–1812,* vol. 5, 387–389.

89. William Jenks, "Diary of Visit to Indians," September 10, 1811, William Jenks Papers, box 4.

90. Banks, *Maine Becomes a State,* 151.

91. Ward Locke, "Autobiography," Ephraim Stinchfield Papers, box 1, folder 4, 23–24, 41–44, 50–51.

92. The original copy of the memorial has been lost, but it was printed in the *Eastern Argus,* January 25, 1820, 2–3. The memorialists represented one of only two non-French and non-Indian Catholic parishes in Maine at the time. See Banks, *Maine Becomes a State,* 156; Perley, *Debates and Journal,* Debates, 92; Journal, 43. Perley's book is divided into separately paginated series; unless otherwise noted, all citations are from the debates (second series).

93. "Constitution of Maine of 1819 to Which Is Prefixed an Address to the People," in Banks, *Maine Becomes a State,* 285.

94. The manuscript record of the convention is brief, but two observers recorded and printed more detailed accounts in local newspapers: an anonymous writer in the *Eastern Argus* and Jeremiah Perley in the *Portland Gazette.* Perley's account was published as a book in 1820 and reprinted in 1894 as *The Debates and Journal of the Constitutional Convention of the State of Maine, 1819–1820.* Both accounts are similar and closely reflect the contents of shorter manuscript minutes, so they are likely reliable renderings of what the delegates said during the convention, though Banks notes that Perley's version was "revised and corrected" by William King, the president of the convention. With this caveat in mind, I have used Perley's book and two manuscript records as the principle sources for this discussion. See Transcript of Proceedings of Maine Constitutional Convention, 26–27, Massachusetts Eastern Lands

Papers, ser. 103x; Religious Issues Folder, Documents of the Constitutional Convention. See also Banks, *Maine Becomes a State,* 394–395n.

95. Transcripts of Proceedings of Maine Constitutional Convention, 27; Perley, *Debates and Journal,* 94.

96. Perley, *Debates and Journal,* 94–95, 96–97, 101, 103.

97. Ibid., 101, 105–107, 111; Mr. Whitman's Motion, Religious Issues Folder, Documents of the Constitutional Convention; Transcripts of Proceedings of Maine Constitutional Convention, 27.

98. Perley, *Debates and Journal,* 104, 108, 107

99. Banks, *Maine Becomes a State,* 162–164; Mr. Knight's motion, Religious Issues Folder, Documents of the Constitutional Convention.

100. Perley, *Debates and Journal,* 115; Mr. Hobbs's Motion, Religious Issues Folder, Documents of the Constitutional Convention; Transcripts of Proceedings of Maine Constitutional Convention, 27.

101. "Constitution of Maine of 1819 to Which Is Prefixed an 'Address to the People,'" in Banks, *Maine Becomes a State,* 281.

102. Elijah Kellogg to Joseph Foxcroft, October 9, 1819, Foxcroft Family Papers, folder 1; Jonathan Fisher, "Journal of Missionary Service, 1819–20," January 30, 1820, Society for Propagating the Gospel Papers, box 2, folder 9.

103. Transcript of Return of Votes, Massachusetts Eastern Lands Papers, ser. 105x. See also Banks, *Maine Becomes a State,* 305–319.

104. Public lands in Vermont (also called glebe lands) had a complicated history. All town charters set aside plots for the first settled minister, but the towns that had been chartered under the Wentworth Grants also included plots to support the Church of England and the Society for the Propagation of the Gospel in Foreign Parts (an Anglican missionary society, not to be confused with the Congregationalist missionary society of a similar name). In 1794, the General Assembly declared that glebe lands were vested in the state and granted them to the towns—a decision declared unconstitutional in 1823, based on the 1819 *Dartmouth College* U.S. Supreme Court case. All glebe lands were supposed to revert to the Episcopal Church, but Vermont contested the Episcopal Church's property claims, and subsequent court decisions produced mixed results. See An Act Directing the Uses of the Rights of Land in This State Heretofore Granted by the British Government as Glebes for the Benefit of the Church of England as by Their Law Established, 1794, *Laws of Vermont, 1791–1795,* 332–333; An Act Empowering the Selectmen in the Several Towns in This State to Take Charge of and Lease out the Lands Granted to the First Settled Minister, and to the Use of the Ministry, 1798, *Laws of Vermont, 1796–1799,* ed. John A. Williams, vol. 16, *State Papers of Vermont* (Montpelier, Vt., 1968), 292–293. Glebe lands are also discussed in Bassett, *Gods of the Hills,* 23, 73; Clarke, "Vermont Lands and the Society for the Propagation of the Gospel"; and McLoughlin, *New England Dissent,* vol. 2, chapter 42.

105. An Act to Provide for the Sale and Distribution of Ministerial and School Lands, 1824, *Public Acts of the State of Maine, 1822–1831,* vol. 3, 968–971.

106. Petition of the Selectmen of Ripton, October 15, 1831, Manuscripts of Vermont State Papers.

107. Petition of Bangs Doane et al., 1828, GY files, box 53, folder 43; Petition of Sundry Inhabitants of Bucksport, 1831, GY files, box 67, folder 26; both in Legislative Archives.

108. Committee of the Baptist Society in Wilton to the Selectmen of Wilton, December 26, 1818, Livermore Family Papers; *Baptist Society in Wilton* v. *The Town of Wilton,* 1822, *Reports of Cases Argued and Determined in the Superior Court of Judicature for the State of New Hampshire,* 508–512. *Bisbee* v. *Evans,* 1826, *Maine Reports,* vol. 4 (Portland: James Adams, Jr., 1828), 374–376.

109. Jacob Bennet et al. to the Selectmen of New Boston, February 1821, New Boston, New Hampshire, First Baptist Society Records, vol. 1.

110. Report on the Petition of William Mann, 1824, Legislative Archives, GY files, box 27, folder 23.

111. Petition of the Selectmen of Ripton, October 15, 1831, Manuscripts of Vermont State Papers, vol. 62, 21.

112. See the many complaints along these lines in petitions such as the following: Report on the Petition of the Selectmen of Sangerville, Legislative Archives, GY files, box 6, folder 28; Report on the Petition of the Selectmen of Athens, 1823, Legislative Archives, GY files, box 19, folder 14; Report on the Petition of Ebenezer Felker et al., 1824, Legislative Archives, GY files, box 26, folder 17; Petition of the Selectmen of Ripton, Manuscripts of Vermont State Papers. Squatting on otherwise unoccupied lands—and especially stripping these lands of valuable timber—was a source of widespread conflict. See Taylor, *Liberty Men and Great Proprietors,* chapters 2–3.

113. See Report on the Petition of the Selectmen of Athens, 1823, Legislative Archives, GY files, box 19, folder 14; Report on the Petition of Jedidiah Sleeper et al., 1824, Legislative Archives, GY files, box 28, folder 29; Petition of the Town of Buckfield, 1831, Legislative Archives, GY files, box 66, folder 19. Given the opportunity in 1830 to allow the ministerial lands to be converted to school funds, the Maine legislature declined, judging it "inexpedient" to do so. See Report to Modify an Act to Provide for the Sale and Distribution of Ministerial Lands, 1830, Legislative Archives, GY files, box 62, folder 17.

114. Kinney, *Church and State,* 109–110; An Act to Authorize Towns to Devote the Proceeds of Funds to Their Original Purposes, 1865, *Laws of the State of New Hampshire, Passed June Session 1865,* 3118.

115. Petition of the Baptists for Use of the Town Meetinghouse, September 29, 1810, Crafts Family Papers, box 9, folder 34.

116. Anonymous, "The Town Meeting: A Comi-tragic Poem," n.d. (typed copy), Crafts Family Papers, box 8, folder 36.

117. An Act in Addition to an Act for the Support of the Gospel, 1814, *Laws Passed by the Legislature of the State of Vermont, 1814,* 112–113.

118. See, for instance, Petition of Henry Smith and William Whitford, October 1, 1816, Manuscripts of Vermont State Papers, vol. 51, 240; Petition of Mary Baker, October 16, 1820, Manuscripts of Vermont State Papers, vol. 54, 2; Petition of the Baptist Church at Brandon, October 12, 1822, Manuscripts of Vermont State Papers, vol. 56, 157; *Journal of the General Assembly of the State of Vermont, 1824* (Bennington, Vt.: Darius Clark, 1824), 154.

119. An Act to Enable Towns and Parishes to Erect Proper Houses for Public Worship and Support Ministers of the Gospel, 1783, *Laws of Vermont, 1781–1784,* 195; An Act for Supporting Ministers of the Gospel, 1787, *Laws of Vermont, 1785–1791,* 348–350.

120. An Act for Regulating Towns and the Support of Town Officers, 1791, *General Petitions,* vol. 8, *State Papers of Vermont* (Montpelier: Secretary of the State of Vermont, 1952), 587; Turner, *The Ninth State,* 89.

121. Article 3 of the Declaration of Rights, A Constitution of Frame of Government for the Commonwealth of Massachusetts, *Acts and Laws of the Commonwealth of Massachusetts, 1780–1781,* 3–30. See also An Act Regulating Parishes and Precincts, and the Officers Thereof, 1786, Resolve Directing the Committee on Unappropriated Lands in Lincoln County, 21–24.

122. Circular Letter, 1828 Annual Meeting, Universalist Church of America General Convention Minutes and Circular Letters, 329–331.

123. An Act for the Support of the Gospel, 1797, *Laws of the State of Vermont, 1797,* 474–475; An Act to Repeal a Certain Act, and Parts of an Act Therein Mentioned, 1807, *Acts and Laws Passed by the Legislature of the State of Vermont, October 1807,* 22; An Act, in Addition to an

Act for the Support of the Gospel, 1814, *Laws Passed by the Legislature of the State of Vermont, 1814*, 112–113.

124. Entries from May 23, 1815; November 20, 1818; and August 14, 1829; all in Middlebury, Vermont, Congregational Church Record Book.

125. "Persecution and Religious Tyranny in All Ages the Same," *New England Missionary Intelligencer*, October 1819, 76–77.

126. *Some Remarks on the "Toleration Act" of 1819*, 7; New Hampshire General Association Report, ca. 1820, 1. Most evidence indicates that these concerns were unjustified. During the 1820s, the number of Congregationalist and Presbyterian churches (most of which were Congregationalist) increased from 160 to 177, and the number of church members from 12,626 to 14,857 (this number also rose slightly in proportion to New Hampshire's population at large). Even though this rate of growth was slower than it had been in the past, Congregationalists still survived that decade and beyond as the most prominent denomination in the state. See Gaustad and Barlow, *New Historical Atlas of Religion in America*, 357–359; Hazen, *The Congregational and Presbyterian Ministry and Churches of New Hampshire*, 66–67.

127. *Some Remarks on the "Toleration Act" of 1819*, 5–6, 17, 10–11, 28, 35. The pamphlet is attributed to William Smith.

128. An Act in Addition to, and in Amendment of an Act Passed July 1, 1819, Entitled An Act in Amendment of An Act Entitled An Act for Regulating Towns and the Choice of Town Officers, Passed February 8, 1791, 1823, *Laws of New Hampshire*, vol. 9, 245.

129. An Act Regulating Towns and the Choice of Town Officers, section 15, 1827, *Laws of New Hampshire*, vol. 9, 617.

130. Papers Concerning Transfer of Church Membership, Lyndeborough, New Hampshire, United Church Records, box 3, folder 7.

131. *Baptist Society in Wilton* v. *The Town of Wilton*, 1822, *Reports of Cases Argued and Determined in the Supreme Court of Judicature for the State of New Hampshire*, 508–512.

132. *Town of Candia* v. *French*, 1835, *New Hampshire Reports*, vol. 8, 133; *Town of Lisbon* v. *Town of Bath*, 1850, *New Hampshire Reports*, vol. 21, 319; *Rice* v. *Wadsworth*, 1853, *New Hampshire Reports*, vol. 27, 104; *Abbot et al.* v. *Town of Dublin*, 1860, *New Hampshire Reports*, vol. 38, 464; Kinney, *Church and State*, 111–112.

133. Not until 1968 did New Hampshire amend Article 6 of its constitution to remove references to public support for religion. See Kinney, *Church and State*, 133–144.

134. Act Concerning Parishes, 1821, *Public Acts of the State of Maine, 1820–1821*, 592–596; An Act in Addition to An Act Entitled "An Act Concerning Parishes," 1825, *Public Acts of the State of Maine, 1822–1831*, 1031–1032.

135. See, for example, *Lord* v. *Chamberlain*, 1822, *Maine Reports*, vol. 2 (Hallowell, Maine: Glazier, 1824), 67–72. This case was based on a dispute that took place prior to 1820, and thus applied Massachusetts law instead of Maine law, but judges continued to use these definitions of territorial and poll parishes in cases where Maine state law applied.

136. *The Inhabitants of Alna* v. *Plummer*, 1824, *Maine Reports*, vol. 3 (Portland: James Adams, Jr., 1826), 88–91. The Supreme Judicial Court confirmed this principle in 1832; see *Ford* v. *Clough et al.*, *Maine Reports*, vol. 8 (Portland: William Hyde, 1834), 334–345. See also *Richardson* v. *Brown*, 1830, which equated the territorial parish with the parochial sense of the word "town." *Maine Reports*, vol. 6 (Portland: G. Hyde, 1831), 355–360. For another example of a town that retained control of its ministerial fund, see Report from the Church in Baldwin, Report on the State of Religion, 1822, Cumberland Conference of Churches Records, folder 1.

137. *Osgood* v. *Bradley*, 1831, *Maine Reports*, vol. 7 (Portland: G. Hyde, 1832), 411–421.

138. Parish membership implied financial obligation and perhaps doctrinal preference, whereas church membership usually indicated that one had experienced conversion and baptism.

139. *Bradford* v. *Cary*, 1828, *Maine Reports*, vol. 5 (Portland: Shirley and Hyde, 1829), 339–345; *Jones* v. *Cary*, 1830, *Maine Reports*, vol. 6, 448–451.

140. *Bradford* v. *Cary*, 342–345; *Jones* v. *Cary*, 450–451.

141. *Bradford* v. *Cary*, 344, 342.

142. *Trustees of the Parsonage Fund in Fryeburg* v. *Ripley*, 1830, *Maine Reports*, vol. 6, 442–447; *Osgood* v. *Bradley*.

143. The 1821 Act Concerning Parishes, the legal foundation of all of this jurisprudence, was never fully repealed. Instead, the legislature modified the law over time to make the act less restrictive; a version of the act remains in effect. For examples of the amended language, see Laws of Maine, Chapter 201 (1850), *Acts and Resolves Passed by the Legislature of the State of Maine*, 1850 (Augusta: William T. Johnson, 1850); Chapter 34 (1858), *Acts and Resolves Passed by the Legislature of the State of Maine*, 1858 (Augusta: Stevens and Sayward, 1858); Chapter 216 (1863), *Acts and Resolves Passed by the Legislature of the State of Maine*, 1863 (Augusta: Stevens and Sayward, 1863); Chapter 44 (1866), *Acts and Resolves Passed by the Legislature of the State of Maine*, 1866 (Augusta: Stevens and Sayward, 1866); Chapter 71 (1867), *Acts and Resolves Passed by the Legislature of the State of Maine*, 1867 (Augusta: Stevens and Sayward, 1867); Chapter 35 (1869), *Acts and Resolves of the Legislature of the State of Maine*, 1869 (Augusta: Sprague, Owen, and Nash, 1869).

144. The idea that we should think of disestablishment as being as much about property as about taxation came in part from a paper by Sarah Barringer Gordon. Gordon, "The Landscape of Belief."

4. 'Tis All on Fire

1. This chapter includes material that originally appeared in "'Scattered as Christians Are in This Part of Our Country': Layfolk's Reading, Writing, and Religious Community in New England's Northern Frontier, 1780–1830," *New England Quarterly* 83:4 (December 2010): 607–640, published by MIT Press Journals.

2. Joanna French Diary, entries from November 1816 to June 1817, French Family Diary. French used the term "stupid" to mean spiritually dull or insensible to matters of religious importance, a common use of this term in the late eighteenth and early nineteenth centuries.

3. Charles E. Clark and James S. Leamon, "Maine in the New Nation," in Clark, Leamon, and Bowden, eds., *Maine in the Early Republic*, 3, 5; Taylor, *Liberty Men and Great Proprietors*, chapter 3; Jaffee, *People of the Wachusett*, especially part 3.

4. This definition of lived religion draws from Robert A. Orsi, "Everyday Miracles in the Study of Lived Religion," in Hall, ed., *Lived Religion in America*, 6–7.

5. For more on popular religious culture, see Hall, "Toward a History of Popular Religion in Early New England," 50–53; Hall, *Worlds of Wonder, Days of Judgment*, 11, 18; Hall, "Introduction," in Hall, ed., *Lived Religion in America*, vii–xiii; Hatch, *The Democratization of American Christianity*, especially 3–16.

6. Matthew 6:6 reads, "But thou, when thou prayest, enter into thy closet, and when thou hast shut the door, pray to thy Father which is in secret; and thy Father which seeth in secret shall reward thee openly."

7. Hambrick-Stowe, *The Practice of Piety*, 156.

8. Niles, *Secret Prayer Explained and Inculcated*, 9.

9. "On the Advantages of Private Prayer," *Christian Observer*, July 1802, 428.

10. Joanna French Diary, June 1, 1817, French Family Diary.

11. Taves, ed., *Religion and Domestic Violence in Early New England,* 10, 104–105.

12. Carroll, *Piety in Humble Life,* 14–18.

13. Sarah Livermore to unknown, February 20, 1814, Livermore Family Papers, box 7, folder 3.

14. This model of conversion and salvation applied more or less in most Protestant faiths, though Calvinist and Arminian denominations differed on the question of who could join the elect and how much individuals could do to effect their own salvation. See Cohen, *God's Caress,* especially part 1; Juster, *Disorderly Women,* chapters 2, 6; Seeman, *Pious Persuasions,* 81–88; LaCelle-Peterson, "'I Got Religion.'"

15. The primary sources for conversion experiences are notoriously flawed. Conversion narratives taken at the time of profession are informative, but the minister's hand is often evident and the subjects of conversion narrated expected sequences of events. In spiritual autobiographies, writers often embellished narratives and adhered to a standard "plot." Diaries and letters, written for confidants, tend to be less self-conscious than other narratives. See Cohen, *God's Caress,* 138–140; Seeman, "Lay Conversion Narratives"; Bercovitch, *The Puritan Origins of the American Self;* Gillespie, "'The Clear Leadings of Providence'"; Shea, *Spiritual Autobiography in Early America;* McCarthy, "A Pocketful of Days," 274–276.

16. Nathaniel Cheever to E. Bond, February 20, 1819, Cheever Family Papers, box 1, folder 7.

17. Elijah Fisk, Jr., to John and Susan Fisk, October 4, 1830, Fisk Family Papers, box 1, folder 9.

18. James Wentworth Autobiography and Diary, 1803–1830, James Jewett Wentworth Diaries, vol. 1.

19. Joel Winch Autobiography, 1802, Joel Winch Papers, folder 2, 47–49, 69.

20. James Wentworth Autobiography and Diary.

21. Sarah Livermore to unknown, March 2, 1817, Livermore Family Papers, box 7, folder 4.

22. Meeting minutes, September 3, 1799, Southwest Harbor (Mt. Desert), Maine, United Church of Christ, Clerk's Records; W. MacLean Journal, August 6, 1800, Society for Propagating the Gospel Records, box 1.

23. Job Seamans Journal, February 10, 1796, Job Seamans Papers.

24. Solomon Bunnel to Asa Lyons, November 20, 1806, Asa Lyons Papers, box 2, folder 240.

25. Nashti Bingham to the Congregational Church of Christ in Cornish, May 31, 1803, Cornish, New Hampshire, Congregational Church Correspondence.

26. Copy of a letter from Elizabeth and Kenelm Winslow to the New Durham Quarterly Meeting, in meeting minutes, September 1790, New Durham, New Hampshire, Freewill Baptist Church Records of Quarterly and Yearly Meetings.

27. Meeting minutes, August 8, 1813; April 11, May 2, December 13, 29, 1819, Bangor, Maine, All Souls Congregational Church Records, vol. 1; meeting minutes, March 14, April 25, 1803; May 4, 1804, New London Church Records, Book 1, Job Seamans Papers.

28. Copies of various certificates, 1800–1801, Chelsea, Vermont, Voluntary Congregational Society Records.

29. William Smyth Babcock Journal, September 8, 1804, William Smyth Babcock Papers, octavo vol. 5.

30. See entries for dismissions and recommendations (throughout), Record Book, 1812–1910, Woolwich, Maine, Baptist Church Records. Most of these certificates concentrate between 1814 and 1832.

31. "Letter from the Rev. James Murphy," *Massachusetts Baptist Missionary Magazine,* May 1804, 57.

32. It is impossible to pin down the exact proportion of northern New England's population that counted itself churched. Church attendance is a suggestive but not completely reliable indicator. I borrow instead Jon Butler's broader definition of church adherence: "a regular or steady attachment to institutional Christianity." According to Butler, adherence in New England during the mid-eighteenth century ranged from under 20 percent to over 67 percent (depending on the location), then declined during the Revolution, stood at about 10 percent in 1810, and rose to between 25 and 30 percent during the 1820s. Randolph Roth's findings for southeastern Vermont bear out Butler's estimates. Roth argues that church membership among adult males in agricultural towns rose from about 12 percent in 1815 to about 26 percent in 1827 (the percentage for women would have been higher than average, as would church adherence in more urban areas). Southeastern Vermont was among the longest-settled and most churched parts of northern New England (in other words, one of the areas most like southern New England), so we can reasonably extrapolate that church adherence in more remote areas would have been lower, as anecdotal evidence suggests. See Bonomi and Eisenstadt, "Church Adherence in the Eighteenth-Century British American Colonies," 253; Butler, *Awash in a Sea of Faith,* 4–5, 191–193, 267, 282–283; Finke and Stark, *The Churching of America, 1776–1990;* Roth, *The Democratic Dilemma,* 82, 187.

33. Meeting minutes, April 14, 1811, Langdon, New Hampshire, Christian Church Records (typescript), box 1, folder 2, 23–24.

34. Meeting minutes, March 17, 1820, Records of the Church of Christ of Sedgwick, Congregational Conference–Maine Missionary Society Records, ser. 2, vol. 66.

35. William Smyth Babcock Journal, September 25, 1802, William Smyth Babcock Papers, folder 4.

36. Stephen Peabody Diary, October 22, 1805, Stephen Peabody Diaries, vol. 7 (1805–1806).

37. Charlotte Cheever to Elizabeth Cheever, September 16, 1829, Cheever-Wheeler Family Papers, box 1, folder 5.

38. Sarah Livermore to unknown, December 1823, Livermore Family Papers, box 7, folder 7.

39. Samuel Goddard Diary, August 17, 1813, Samuel Goddard Diary and Memorandum Books.

40. "Excuses for Not Attending Public Worship, by Exemplary Christians," *Religious Intelligencer,* August 9, 1823, 159.

41. Shalhope, *A Tale of New England,* 40.

42. Meeting minutes, April 4, 1831, Congregational Church (Church of Christ) Records, Greenfield, New Hampshire, Union Congregational Church Records.

43. William Smyth Babcock Journal, January 20, 1802, William Smyth Babcock Papers, folder 3.

44. Jonathan Fisher Journal No. 2, February 5, 1818, Society for Propagating the Gospel Papers, box 2, folder 9.

45. Anonymous letter to Judith Harris, June 21, 1820, Strafford, Vermont, Papers, document box 54.

46. See Gundersen, "The Non-Institutional Church"; Janet Moore Lindman, "Beyond the Meetinghouse: Women and Protestant Spirituality in Early America," in Brekus, ed., *The Religious History of American Women,* 142–160.

47. Griffiths, *Religious Reading;* Hall, *Worlds of Wonder, Days of Judgment,* especially chapter 1; Kelley, "'Pen and Ink Communion.'"

48. See Gilmore, *Reading Becomes a Necessity of Life;* Victor Neuburg, "Chapbooks in America: Reconstructing the Popular Reading of Early America," and David Paul Nord, "A Republican Literature: Magazine Reading and Readers in Late-Eighteenth-Century New York," both in Davidson, ed., *Reading in America,* 81–139.

49. Monaghan, *Learning to Read and Write in Colonial America,* especially chapters 1, 3.

50. These figures derive from William Gilmore's study of the Upper Connecticut River Valley of New Hampshire and Vermont; they represent rough averages based on the trends and fluctuations that Gilmore identifies. Because the region in Gilmore's study exemplifies the northern frontier demographic and socio-economic spectrums, we can extrapolate that similar literacy rates applied throughout the rest of northern New England. See Gilmore, *Reading Becomes a Necessity of Life,* 120–121; Lockridge, *Literacy in Colonial New England,* 38–39; E. Jennifer Monaghan, "Literacy Instruction and Gender in Colonial New England," in Davidson, ed., *Reading in America,* 53–80; Perlmann and Shirley, "When Did New England Women Acquire Literacy?" 50–67, especially 58–59 for a critique of Lockridge's methodology; Perlmann, Siddali, and Whitescarver, "Literacy, Schooling, and Teaching among New England Women."

51. Brown, *The Word in the World,* 1.

52. Ibid., chapter 2; Gilmore, *Reading Becomes a Necessity of Life,* part 2; Nord, *Faith in Reading,* chapters 3, 5; Schantz, "Religious Tracts, Evangelical Reform, and the Market Revolution in Antebellum America."

53. For extensive discussions of how clergy and others in the evangelical publishing enterprise hoped readers would read, see Brown, *The Word in the World,* 115–118; Nord, *Faith in Reading,* chapter 6.

54. Joseph Field, "Journal of My Missionary Tour," June 13–14, 1805.

55. Meeting minutes, June 11, 1811, Greene, Maine, Free Baptist Churches Records, vol. 1.

56. Elijah and Hannah Batchelder and David Hammond to William Jenks, August 1, 1812, William Jenks Papers, box 4.

57. *Religious Informer,* January 1820, 14.

58. Diary, July 10, 1815, March 24, 1816, Member of the First Congregational Church of Loudon, New Hampshire. "Doddridge" refers to Philip Doddridge, whose works were widely read among New England Protestants. "Davis" likely refers to Samuel Davies ("Davis" was a common misspelling of his last name), the Presbyterian minister and Princeton College president whose sermons were standard fare for Protestant readers. Thanks to colleagues who responded to my H-SHEAR and H-AMREL queries to shed light on the likely identity of "Davis."

59. Nathaniel Cheever to E. Bond, February 20, 1819, Cheever Family Papers, box 1, folder 7.

60. W. A. B., Anonymous Diary, ca. 1800, 1–16.

61. Joel Winch Autobiography, 1802, Joel Winch Papers, folder 2, 34, 59. An interesting question—and one that Winch does not answer in his autobiography—is why a subscription library administered by a Congregationalist town church retained a copy of the Methodist *Discipline.*

62. Lindman, "Beyond the Meetinghouse," 143–144; Gillespie, "'The Clear Leadings of Providence,'" 199–200, 216; McCarthy, "A Pocketful of Days," 274–276; Bercovitch, *The Puritan Origins of the American Self;* Dorsey, *Sacred Estrangement;* Shea, *Spiritual Autobiography in Early America.*

63. John Clark Journal, 1774–1842, 53.

64. Stephen Bemis Journal, January 1, 1797, Stephen Bemis Papers.

65. Diary, entries on loose page dated 1818, October 25, 1821, Member of the First Congregational Church of Loudon, New Hampshire; Phinehas Bailey Journal, March 16, 1823, Francis Hopkins Papers, carton 1, folder 1.

66. Diary, July 9, 1815, July 14, 1816, Member of the First Congregational Church of Loudon, New Hampshire.

67. Phinehas Bailey, unbound journal entry, May 8, 1820, Francis Hopkins Papers, carton 1, folder 1.

68. Joanna French Diary, April 7, 1816, French Family Diary.

69. Brekus, *Strangers and Pilgrims,* 48.

70. By the late eighteenth century, Baptists and Separate Congregationalists (like Quakers, Shakers, Christian Connection, and Universal Friends) embraced lay preaching and exhortation out of an anti-establishmentarian impulse. See Brekus, *Strangers and Pilgrims,* 8; Hatch, *The Democratization of American Christianity,* especially 67–101.

71. Meeting minutes, August 21–22, 1801, October 23, 1801, New Durham Quarterly Meeting Records of the Elders' Conference, 3, 6.

72. *A Religious Magazine,* August 1820, 25–26.

73. Meeting minutes, July 29, 1773, Sanford, Maine, Baptist Church Records.

74. Henry Hale Diary, December 15, 1807.

75. The operative Biblical texts are 1 Corinthians 14:34, 1 Timothy 2:12, and Joel 2:28.

76. Articles of Covenant, Londonderry, New Hampshire, Baptist Church of Christ Church Book or Records, 15.

77. William Smyth Babcock Journal, July 12, 1801, William Smyth Babcock Papers, folder 4.

78. Meeting minutes, March 10, 1794, Pittsfield, New Hampshire, Freewill Baptist Church Records; meeting minutes, September 6, 1794, Free Baptist Church Monthly and Yearly Meetings, Ephraim Stinchfield Papers, box 1, folder 6.

79. Wentworth, ed., *Journals of Enoch Hayes Place,* 168.

80. Allen and Pillsbury, *History of Methodism in Maine,* 565–567; Gillespie, "'The Clear Leadings of Providence,'" 214–216; Pillsbury, *History of Methodism in East Maine,* 35–37; Mudge, "A Short Memoir of Mrs. Anna Nickerson," *Methodist Magazine,* August, September 1818, 304–309, 341–343; Newell, *Memoirs of Fanny Newell.*

81. Brekus, *Strangers and Pilgrims,* 119.

82. "New Hampshire Yearly Meeting" and "Meeting at Candia, N.H.," *A Religious Magazine,* August 1821, 113–114; Josiah Phillips to Ephraim Stinchfield, May 20, 1819, Ephraim Stinchfield Papers, box 1, folder 2; Brekus, *Strangers and Pilgrims,* 120, 46–54, 271–298.

83. Juster and Hartigan-O'Connor, "The 'Angel Delusion' of 1806–1811," 394; Taves, *Fits, Trances, and Visions,* 65–75; Winiarski, "Souls Filled with Ravishing Transport." The perception that female visionaries outnumbered their male counterparts reflected an assumed link between visionary behavior and physical and emotional weakness. See Taves, *Fits, Trances, and Visions,* 23, 28–30.

84. W. MacLean Journal, August 9, 1800, Society for Propagating the Gospel Records, box 1.

85. Wentworth, ed., *Journals of Enoch Hayes Place,* 76–79.

86. A detailed account of the Angel Delusion appears in Juster and Hartigan-O'Connor, "The 'Angel Delusion' of 1806–1811."

87. William Smyth Babcock Journal, entries between May and August 1805, William Smyth Babcock Papers, octavo 5. Babcock proposed marriage in 1805, but the union was delayed after the two became entangled in a sexual scandal. Babcock thought best to leave town while the rumors faded, and they finally married in January 1809.

88. Eighteenth- and early nineteenth-century angels were generally characterized as male. Juster and Hartigan-O'Connor, "The 'Angel Delusion' of 1806–1811," 382.

89. William Smyth Babcock Journal; Babcock, "Minutes of Manifestations Made to Elizabeth Babcock by Our Lord Jesus Christ through His Angels," January 5, 1810; both in William Smyth Babcock Papers, folders 4, 1.

90. Babcock may have resumed preaching later. I. D. Stewart notes that his "bark capsized in the Angel Delusion [and] was righted again in 1817." Stewart, *The History of the Freewill Baptists,* vol. 1, 367.

91. Juster and Hartigan-O'Connor, "The 'Angel Delusion' of 1806–1811," 400.

92. Stephen Peabody Diary, November 23, 1785, Stephen Peabody Diaries, vol. 2 (1784–1786).

93. High alcohol consumption had been typical in New England (and British North America generally) since the early seventeenth century; see Rorabaugh, *The Alcoholic Republic;* Salinger, *Taverns and Drinking in Early America;* Thompson, *Rum Punch and Revolution.*

94. Catherine E. Kelly examines a New England social milieu that featured a crowded schedule of cotillions, elegant suppers, sleigh rides, and other pursuits. See Kelly, "'Well Bred Country People,'" 451–479.

95. Carroll, *Piety in Humble Life,* 10–11.

96. Eliza Bryant Diary, entries throughout 1802.

97. Davidson, *Revolution and the Word,* 41. Attacks against novels often took on a gendered tone because most readers and writers of early republican novels were women. Novels preyed on young women, critics insisted: the very people who were most vulnerable to their seductive prose and lurid subjects. The most authoritative work on the subject is Davidson, *Revolution and the Word,* especially chapters 3, 6. See also Brown, *The Word in the World,* 50–51, 95–105; Nord, *Faith in Reading,* 113–122; Kerber, *Women of the Republic,* chapter 8.

98. Meeting minutes, November 20, 1819, Greene, Maine, Free Baptist Churches Records, vol. 1, 100.

99. Committee of the Church in Bath to William Jenks, February 9, 1818, William Jenks Papers, box 6; meeting minutes, December 17, 1819, September 8, 1820, June 20, 1828, Middlebury, Vermont, Congregational Church Record Book.

100. Carroll, *Piety in Humble Life,* 36–37.

101. Nathan Fisk to John and Susan Fisk, October 4, 1830, Fisk Family Papers, box 2, folder 10.

102. Sarah Livermore to unknown, November 1819, Livermore Family Papers, box 7, folder 4.

103. Quoted in *Religious Intelligencer,* November 8, 1823, 367.

104. For definitions of the Puritan culture of discipline and the family's role in enforcing it, see Delbanco, *The Puritan Ordeal,* 224–234; Innes, *Creating the Commonwealth,* 137, 43, 52.

105. Meeting minutes, November 10, 1773, West Shaftsbury, Vermont, Baptist Church Record Book.

106. Circular Letter (copy), 1791, Maine and New Hampshire Freewill Baptist Quarterly Meetings, 139.

107. Meeting minutes, 1817 Annual Convention, Universalist Church of America General Convention Records.

108. Thomas Holt Missionary Journal, January 8, 1818, William Jenks Papers, box 6.

109. Covenant of the Church in Jaffrey, n.d., Jaffrey, New Hampshire, Congregational Church Papers; meeting minutes, May 1, 1804, Union Church of Christ Records, Greenfield, New Hampshire, Union Congregational Church Records, 77; meeting minutes, October 19, 1821, Middlebury, Vermont, Congregational Church Record Book.

110. Ephraim Stinchfield, "The Substance of a Speech Delivered in a Church Meeting Held at Gray," September 8, 1793, Ephraim Stinchfield Papers, box 1, folder 1.

111. Nathan Douglas to Abiel Holmes, October 31, 1817, Society for Propagating the Gospel Papers, box 2, folder 2.

112. Stephen Bemis Journal, January 1, 1797.

113. *An Address by the Ministers of the Original Association of the County of Windham*, 3.
114. Packard, *The Christian's Manual*, 41–43. See also Packard, *Two Discourses on Prayer*.
115. *A Prayerbook for the Use of Families*, xi.
116. See, for example, Enfield, *Prayers for the Use of Families*.
117. "Family Worship," *Religious Intelligencer*, November 8, 1823, 367.
118. Shalhope, *A Tale of New England*, 94.
119. Meeting minutes, July 6, 1805, Chelsea, Vermont, Congregational Church Records.
120. Meeting minutes, September 1, 22, 1826, Bangor, Maine, All Souls Congregational Church Records, vol. 1.
121. The disparity between male and female membership was most pronounced among Congregationalists, but it also held true in dissenting denominations. See Bonomi, *Under the Cope of Heaven*, 111–115; Brekus, *Strangers and Pilgrims*, 138, 274–277; Cowing, "Sex and Preaching in the Great Awakening"; Grossbart, "Seeking Divine Favor"; Heyrman, *Southern Cross*, 215, 311–312n13; Juster, *Disorderly Women*; Ryan, *Cradle of the Middle Class*, 76–83, 257; Sheils, "The Feminization of American Congregationalism."
122. Couples with believing husbands and unconverted wives were less common. Methodists were forbidden to marry "unawakened" spouses through the early 1800s, though this rule was difficult to enforce. See *A Form of Discipline, for the Ministers, Preachers and Members (Now Comprehending the Principles and Doctrines) of the Methodist Episcopal Church in America*, 23–24; Heyrman, *Southern Cross*, 140.
123. Peach, ed., "The Reverend Joel Winch," 91.
124. Carroll, *Piety in Humble Life*, 20.
125. Meeting minutes, October 23, 1817, Bangor, Maine, All Souls Congregational Church Records, vol. 1.
126. George Freeman Journal, November 23, 1825.
127. "Prayer for Unconverted Husbands," *Religious Intelligencer*, October 21, 1826, 331.
128. Unknown to Susan Craige, May 20, 1820, Fisk Family Papers, box 3, folder 2.
129. For more on lay understandings of baptism, see David D. Hall and Anne S. Brown, "Family Strategies and Religious Practice: Baptism and the Lord's Supper in Early New England," in Hall, ed., *Lived Religion in America*, 41–68; Seeman, *Pious Persuasions*, 88–95.
130. Samuel Goddard Diary, February 25, 1813, Samuel Goddard Diary and Memorandum Books.
131. Meeting minutes, August 9, 1826, Cumberland Association Rules and Proceedings (1788–1839), Congregational Conference–Maine Missionary Society Papers, ser. 3, vol. 85, 158–159.
132. Timothy Merritt to Epaphras Kibby, January 11, 1801, Personal Letters Collection.
133. Kilby, *Eastport and Passamaquoddy*, 323.
134. Meeting minutes, August 31, 1825, August 26, 1828, Rockingham Association Records.
135. Kilby, *Eastport and Passamaquoddy*, 328.
136. Jonathan Fisher Journal No. 3, March 10, 1818, Society for Propagating the Gospel Papers, box 2, folder 9.
137. Meeting minutes, July 25, 1795, Goffstown, New Hampshire, Baptist Church Records.
138. Royal Clark to the Baptist Church of Christ in Cornish, December 10, 1817, Timothy Remick Papers.
139. Meeting minutes, November 2, 1793, Manchester, Vermont, Baptist Church Records; meeting minutes, February 14, 1805, Records of the Church of Christ of Sedgwick, Congregational Conference–Maine Missionary Society Records, ser. 2, vol. 66, 50–51; meeting minutes, May 4, 1812, Records of the First Congregational Society of Jericho, Vermont, Vermont Congregational Conference Records, box 2, folder 20, 14.

140. Levi Frisbie, "Journal of a Mission to the County of Lincoln," 1792, Society for Propagating the Gospel Papers, box 2, folder 11.

141. W. A. B., Anonymous Diary, ca. 1800, 21.

142. Meeting minutes, November 21, 1793, Shoreham, Vermont, Baptist Church Ecclesiastical Records.

143. Montpelier, Vermont, Freewill Baptist Church Records, 13–14.

144. Enfield, *Prayers for the Use of Families*, 157–203.

145. Kilby, *Eastport and Passamaquoddy*, 322.

146. Minutes, 1800 annual meeting, Universalist Church of America General Convention Records, 64.

147. Excerpt from Circular Letter, 1827, Rockingham Association Records, 8.

148. Robert Cochran Journal, July 3, 1814, Society for Propagating the Gospel Papers, box 1, folder 20.

149. "Extract of a Letter from the Rev. Stephen Choate," *Massachusetts Baptist Missionary Magazine*, September 1807, 333–334.

150. "Church at Limerick," *A Religious Magazine*, June 1822, 247–248.

151. "Report on the State of Religion," 1822, Cumberland Conference of Churches Records, folder 1.

152. There were two kinds of prayer meetings: a regularly scheduled weekday meeting of churchgoers, usually led by a minister and directly associated with the sponsoring church, and meetings led by the lay societies discussed here.

153. William Smyth Babcock Journal, May 25, 1804, William Smyth Babcock Papers, octavo vol. 5.

154. Articles of Organization, ca. 1816, Shelburne, Vermont, Female Religious Society.

155. Articles of the Female Religious Society in Jericho, Records of the Vermont Cent Society, 1806, Jericho, Vermont, First Congregational Church Records.

156. Meeting minutes, March 23, 1822, Vershire Circuit (Methodist Episcopal Church in Vermont) Records.

157. Ephraim Abbot to Mary Pearson, July 1, 1813, Ephraim Abbot Papers, box 1, folder 2.

158. "Revivals of Religion," *Religious Intelligencer*, June 6, 1818, 11.

159. Diann Smith to Charity Bryant and Sylvia Drake, May 17, 1828, Charity Bryant and Sylvia Drake Papers.

160. Charlotte Cheever to George Cheever, July 16, 1824, Cheever Family Papers, box 2, folder 1.

161. There was precedent for powerful women's prayer societies. Among the notable examples was the Religious Female Society that Sarah Osborn founded in Newport, Rhode Island, during the Great Awakening and helped lead through the 1770s. See Hambrick-Stowe, "The Spiritual Pilgrimmage of Sarah Osborn (1714–1796)"; Norton, "'My Resting Reaping Times.'"

162. For a list of questions class leaders were supposed to ask members, see Schneider, *The Way of the Cross Leads Home*, 80.

163. Heyrman, *Southern Cross*, 166–169; Schneider, *The Way of the Cross Leads Home*, 78–82.

164. Nathan Fisk to Elijah Fisk, August 10, 1817, Fisk Family Papers, box 2, folder 10.

165. William Smyth Babcock Journal, August 18, 1801, William Smyth Babcock Papers, folder 4.

166. Ephraim Abbot to Mary Pearson, August 15, 1811, Ephraim Abbot Papers, box 1, folder 1.

167. Vermont grew from approximately 85,000 inhabitants in 1791 to 217,895 in 1810; New Hampshire grew from 142,018 in 1790 to 244,161 in 1820; and Maine (where the population boom preceded those in New Hampshire and Vermont) grew from 56,321 in 1784 to ap-

proximately 298,335 in 1820. Banks, *Maine Becomes a State*, 5; Charles E. Clark and James S. Leamon, "Maine in the New Nation," in Clark, Leamon, and Bowden, eds., *Maine in the Early Republic*, 2; Sherman, Sessions, and Potash, *Freedom and Unity*, 131–132, 67; Turner, *The Ninth State*, 189–190; Wilson, "Population Trends in North-Western New England, 1790–1930."

168. Putnam, "Vermont Population Trends," 14–16; Stilwell, "Migration from Vermont, 1776–1860," 363–369, 787–789, 96–97, 117–119, 64–65, 72–73.

169. John Sawyer, Journal of Missionary Labor, July 28, 1828, Society for Propagating the Gospel Records, box 1, folder 11. It is possible that the five or six members to whom Sawyer refers were related and migrated as a family, but he does not indicate that this is the case.

170. Livermore, Maine, First Baptist Church Records, vol. 1, 11, 32, 37, 29, 33, 37; Barnstead, New Hampshire, First Free Baptist Church Records; Weathersfield, Vermont, Circuit Record Book. The Weathersfield Circuit counted 519 members at some point between 1822 and 1830.

171. John Clark Journal, 52–55.

172. Joel Winch Autobiography, 1802, Joel Winch Papers, folder 2, 1–2.

173. Nathan Fisk to Elijah Fisk, August 10, 1817; Nathan Fisk to John Fisk, May 26, 1822; both in Fisk Family Papers, box 2, folder 10.

174. Stephen Chapin Journal, 1808, Society for Propagating the Gospel Papers, box 1, folder 17.

175. John Clark Journal, 53–54.

176. Solomon Stevens to Enos Stevens, April 24, 1805; Solomon Stevens to John Johnson, May 12, 1805; both in Stevens Family Papers, box 4, folder 22.

177. Nathan Fisk to John Fisk, March 9, 1817, Fisk Family Papers, box 2, folder 10.

178. Rebecca Brown French to John and Elizabeth Brown, December 25, 1795, in Brown-Groover, "From Concord, Massachusetts to the Wilderness," 36.

179. Jonathan and Clarissa Hovey to Charity Bryant and Sylvia Drake, April 24, 1818, Charity Bryant and Sylvia Drake Papers.

180. For more on social networks, see Gundersen, "Kith and Kin," 100; Hansen, *A Very Social Time*, 1, 137–138; Kelley, "'Well Bred Country People'"; Osterud, *Bonds of Community*, especially part 4. S. Scott Rohrer analyzes the role of religion in American migration patterns from the colonial era through the Civil War in *Wandering Souls*.

181. Rebecca Miller to John Clancy, March 15, 1819, June 16, 1824, John Clancy Letters; Samuel Mosely to Rebecca Miller, October 2, 1822, Weeks Family Papers, box 2, folder 18.

182. Rebecca Miller to John Clancy, July 21, 1821, June 16, 1824, John Clancy Letters.

183. Untraditional but not unprecedented. Pastoral relationships through correspondence became increasingly common in early republican northern New England as the clergy and laity both moved about. See Norton, "'My Resting Reaping Times.'"

184. Clarissa Clark to Maria Phelps, February 6, 1822, Crafts Family Papers, box 3, folder 21.

185. Sarah Watts to Elizabeth Cheever, February 9, 1828, Cheever Family Papers, box 2, folder 5.

186. Elizabeth Cheever to George Cheever, September 13, 1830, December 10, 1828 (postscript to a letter from Charlotte Cheever), Cheever Family Papers, box 3, folder 2; box 2, folder 5.

187. Daniel Skinner to Harvey Leavitt, May 4, 1814, August 26, 1816, Daniel Skinner Correspondence.

188. Nathan Fisk to Elijah Fisk, May 12, 1817, Fisk Family Papers, box 2, folder 10.

189. Betsey Walker to Timothy Remick, n.d., Timothy Remick Papers, 1800–1840 correspondence folder.

190. George Cheever to Charlotte Cheever, October 28, 1824, Cheever Family Papers, box 2, folder 1.

191. Mary Ingalls to Susan Craige, September 10, 1818, Fisk Family Papers, box 3, folder 2.

192. Diann Smith to Charity Bryant and Sylvia Drake, May 2, 1830, Charity Bryant and Sylvia Drake Papers. See note 2 in this chapter for an explanation of the nineteenth-century usage of the term "stupid."

193. Mary Mann to John Fisk, October 9, 1823, Fisk Family Papers, box 3, folder 7.

194. Elijah Fisk to Elijah Fisk, Jr., February 24, 1806, Fisk Family Papers, box 1, folder 1.

195. Anna Weeks to Ebenezer Weeks, July 6, 1807, Weeks Family Papers, box 2, folder 4.

196. Phebe Abbot to Sarah Livermore, May 22, 1816, Livermore Family Papers, box 7, folder 4.

197. Melville Cox to Henry Hilton, May 3, 1821, Personal Letters Collection.

198. Nathaniel Cheever to E. Bond, February 20, 1819, Cheever Family Papers, box 1, folder 7.

199. Nathan Fisk to John and Susan Fisk, October 4, 1830, Fisk Family Papers, box 2, folder 10.

200. Rebecca Miller to John Clancy, January 5, 1819, John Clancy Letters.

201. George Cheever to Charlotte Cheever, April 16, 1824, Cheever Family Papers, box 2, folder 1.

202. Sarah Livermore to unknown, March 2, 1817, Livermore Family Papers, box 7, folder 4.

203. *Religious Informer,* April 1820, 50.

204. Holland Weeks to Ebenezer Weeks, October 24, 1811, Weeks Family Papers, box 2, folder 4. See Holland Weeks, "An Account of the Revivals in Pittsford," *The Adviser; or, Vermont Evangelical Magazine,* October, November, December 1811, 311–317, 345–351, 369–375.

205. Amos Eastman, "An Account of the Late Revival of Religion in Bristol Vermont," *Vermont Baptist Missionary Magazine,* April 1811, 46–47.

206. "Extract of a Letter from a Gentleman in Fairlee, Vermont," *Religious Intelligencer,* February 23, 1822, 620.

207. *Religious Informer,* November 20, 1819, 91.

208. *Massachusetts Baptist Missionary Magazine,* May 1806, 112–115.

209. "Religious Intelligence," *The Christian's Magazine,* 1806, 177.

210. "Minutes of the New England Conference of the Methodist Episcopal Church," vol. 1, New England Conference of the Methodist Episcopal Church Records, 50.

211. "Quarterly Association at Craftsbury," *Universalist Magazine,* March 18, 1828, 150.

212. Nathan Fisk to Elijah Fisk, January 13, 1818, Fisk Family Papers, box 2, folder 10.

213. See various accounts in *Religious Intelligencer,* July 17, 1824, 110–111; October 9, 1824, 298–299; November 13, 1824, 378; November 20, 1824, 394–396; November 27, 1824, 403–405; December 4, 1824, 419–420; February 5, 1825, 569–570.

214. Joseph Carpenter, "Revival of Religion in Ira and Clarendon," *Vermont Baptist Missionary Magazine,* January 1811, 14–16.

215. Asahel Moore to Hebron Vincent, December 10, 1829, Personal Letters Collection.

5. Fairly Missionary Ground

1. Asa Carpenter, "A Journal of Missionary Labors," September 25, 1805; Carpenter to unknown, March 21, 1806; both in Connecticut Missionary Society Papers, reel 2.

2. See, for example, Kling, *A Field of Divine Wonders;* Sassi, *A Republic of Righteousness,* 126; Youngs, *God's Messengers.*

3. Stephen Peabody Diary, July 2, 1793, Stephen Peabody Diaries, vol. 4 (1792–1794).

4. Joseph Warren to Thomas Gray, November 22, 1794, Joseph Warren Letters to Thomas Gray.

5. Meeting minutes, May 3, 4, 1793, Cumberland Association Rules and Proceedings, ser. 3, vol. 85, Congregational Conference–Maine Missionary Society Records, 9–10; meeting minutes, June 15, 1802, Windham Association Minutes, vol. 1, Windham Union Association, Vermont Conference Records, 37.

6. *Collections of the Maine Historical Society,* vol. 4, 250; Alfred Johnson to Peter Thacher, March 23, 1796, Society for Propagating the Gospel Papers, box 3, folder 1.

7. Alden Bradford to Abiel Holmes, April 23, 1807, Society for Propagating the Gospel Papers box 1, folder 13. Bradford was making the request for a missionary assignment on Chadwick's behalf.

8. Alden Bradford to Peter Thacher, May 1800, Society for Propagating the Gospel Papers, box 1, folder 13.

9. DeRogatis, *Moral Geography,* 41–47; Jaffee, *People of the Wachusett,* 3, 200–212.

10. "The General Association of the Pastors of the Consociated Churches of the Colony of Connecticut."

11. Theodore Hinsdale to Jonathan Edwards, June 27, 1793; Noah Meruen to Ezra Stiles, August 19, 1794; both from Incoming Correspondence, Connecticut Missionary Society Papers, reel 13.

12. *An Address of the General Association of Connecticut,* 3.

13. Overviews of the founding of the Committee on Missions and the Connecticut Missionary Society can be found in Ericson, "Missionary Society of Connecticut Papers, 1759–1948," 1–3; DeRogatis, *Moral Geography,* 35–36; and Rohrer, *Keepers of the Covenant,* especially chapter 3, 60–62.

14. The SPG is not to be confused with other organizations with similar names including earlier-established and better-known Anglican and Scottish Presbyterian groups. This organization was founded in Massachusetts with an explicitly Congregationalist mission. For a narrative of the society's founding, see *A Brief Account of the Present State of the Society for Propagating the Gospel among the Indians and Others in North-America; A Brief Account of the Society for Propagating the Gospel among the Indians and Others in North America.*

15. Cary, *To the Members of the Society for Propagating the Gospel,* 2–5.

16. *To All Who Are Desirous of the Spread of the Gospel of Our Lord Jesus Christ,* 7.

17. *An Account of the Massachusetts Society for Promoting Christian Knowledge,* 4, 12. The MSPCK constitution makes brief mention of missionaries, but David Nord asserts that the society did not begin to support missionaries until after 1811. In reality, the society's book agents (typically ministers) were probably indistinguishable from missionaries in terms of their daily contact with frontier residents. See Nord, *Faith in Reading,* 35.

18. Goodykoontz, *Home Missions on the American Frontier,* 138; Constitution of the Hampshire Missionary Society, n.d., Connecticut Missionary Society Papers, reel 13.

19. *The Address and Constitution of the Evangelical Missionary Society,* 3–4, 8.

20. *One Hundred Years of Home Missionary Work in Vermont by the Congregational Churches,* 6; Preface and Constitution, Records of the Maine Missionary Society, Congregational Conference–Maine Missionary Society Records, ser. 1, vol. 1; *The Constitution of the New Hampshire Missionary Society; A Statement of the Affairs of the New-Hampshire Missionary Society;* Enoch Hall to Abel Flint, March 15, 1803, and Ethan Smith to Abel Flint, September 19, 1803, both in Connecticut Missionary Society Papers, reel 13.

21. Meeting minutes, May 7, 1782, June 11, 1783, September 9, 1789, August 14, 1791, May 14, 1800, Piscataqua Association Records, vol. 1.

22. *The Constitution of the Piscataqua Missionary Society,* 4, 7.

23. Committee of the Church of Georgia to the General Association of Connecticut, August 30, 1793; People of Monkton to the General Association of Connecticut, September 14,

1793; Inhabitants of Monkton to the Connecticut Missionary Society, February 25, 1800; all in Incoming Correspondence, Connecticut Missionary Society Papers, reel 13.

24. Committee at Washington Plantation to the Evangelical Missionary Society, January 11, 1811, Evangelical Missionary Society in Massachusetts Records, box 1, folder 2.

25. Inhabitants of Burke to the Connecticut Missionary Society, November 15, 1803, Incoming Correspondence, Connecticut Missionary Society Papers, reel 13.

26. Carter, *Converting the Wasteplaces of Zion,* 120–121; Ericson, "Missionary Society of Connecticut Papers, 1759–1948," 12; "Twentieth Annual Report," *Religious Intelligencer,* February 13, 1819, 593–594; "Twenty-Second Annual Report," *Religious Intelligencer* March 10, 1821, 663–664; Chase, *Jonathan Fisher,* 174; *The Funds and Services of the New Hampshire Missionary Society,* 12–13. Part-time appointments (which included a significant number of missionaries) are not included in these statistics.

27. Because of the decentralized nature of the Congregationalist missionary effort (and its widespread use of part-time missionaries), it is difficult to know exactly how many Congregationalist missionaries were on the ground at any time. As a point of comparison, the Methodists (who maintained the best-documented system of any itinerant denomination) distributed their circuit riders as follows between 1800 and 1820: in Maine, from nine in 1800 to twenty-nine in 1820; in New Hampshire, from one in 1800 to fifteen in 1820; and in Vermont, from twelve in 1804 (the first year the New England Conference included Vermont) to fourteen in 1820. For most of those years, the number of Congregationalist missionaries likely exceeded the number of Methodist itinerants in each state, but whereas the Congregationalist missionaries only traveled for part of the year, the Methodist circuit riders traveled full-time, so the Methodists could expect more weeks of itinerant labor per circuit rider than the Congregationalists could. See "Minutes of the New England Conference of the Methodist Episcopal Church," vol. 1, New England Conference of the Methodist Episcopal Church Records, 35, 77, 308–310.

28. Carroll, *Puritanism and the Wilderness,* 70, 202–204; Heimert, "Puritanism, the Wilderness, and the Frontier," 368–369; Miller, *The New England Mind,* 47; Nash, *Wilderness and the American Mind,* 35; Peterson, *The Price of Redemption,* 120, 68; Slotkin, *Regeneration through Violence,* 99.

29. DeRogatis, *Moral Geography,* 20, 53–58, 62–74; Rohrer, *Keepers of the Covenant,* 104–114.

30. Perkins, "A Narrative of a Tour through the State of Vermont," 46–47.

31. Samuel Mills to Jonathan Edwards, November 20, 1793; William Miller, "Journal of a Mission to the Northern Settlements," September 8, 1802, and post script; both in Connecticut Missionary Society Papers, reel 7.

32. W. MacLean Journal, July 28–August 4, 1800, Society for Propagating the Gospel Records, box 1.

33. Jonathan Fisher, "Journal of Missionary Service," October 30, 1818, January 1, 1819, February 4, 1819, March 11, 1819, April 30, 1819, Society for Propagating the Gospel Papers, box 2, folder 9.

34. Nathan Strong to Samuel Mills, November 9, 1799, Connecticut Missionary Society Papers, reel 7; Kilby, *Eastport and Passamaquoddy,* 332.

35. Jonathan Fisher, "Journal of Missionary Service," March 9–10, 1819, Society for Propagating the Gospel Papers, box 2, folder 9; Jedidiah Bushnell to Nathan Strong, June 2, 1801; Aaron Cleveland to Abiel Flint, April 24, 1807; William Miller, "Journal of a Mission to the Northern Settlements," August 9, 1802; all in Connecticut Missionary Society Papers, reels 2, 3, 7.

36. Kilby, *Eastport and Passamaquoddy,* 330; Perez Chapin, Missionary Journal, March 7–8, 1827, Cumberland Conference of Churches Records, folder 6.

37. Samuel Mills to Jonathan Edwards, January 30, 1794, Connecticut Missionary Society Papers, reel 7.

38. Freeman Parker to the Evangelical Missionary Society, April 7, 1828, Evangelical Missionary Society in Massachusetts Records, box 3, folder 1.

39. Kilby, *Eastport and Passamaquoddy,* 332.

40. Amos Cooke Journal, August 5, 1810, Society for Propagating the Gospel Papers, box 1, folder 24.

41. Perkins, "A Narrative of a Tour through the State of Vermont," 46, 51.

42. Joseph Field, "Journal of My Missionary Tour," July 11, 16, 1805, miscellaneous box 152, folder 3; Stephen Chapin Journal, 1808, "Observations," Society for Propagating the Gospel Papers, box 1, folder 17.

43. "The Village Meeting," *Religious Intelligencer,* February 7, 1824, 573.

44. Jedidiah Bushnell to Nathan Strong, June 2, 1801, Connecticut Missionary Society Papers, reel 2.

45. Job Chadwick to Jedidiah Morse, 1804, Society for Propagating the Gospel Papers, box 1, folder 17.

46. Josiah Hopkins, "Account of Missionary Labours Done for the Connecticut Missionary Society," May 20, 1813, Connecticut Missionary Society Papers, reel 5.

47. DeRogatis, *Moral Geography,* 20, 53–58, 62–74; Roher, *Keepers of the Covenant,* 104–114.

48. Economic stability was usually a prerequisite to supporting a ministry. See Heyrman, *Commerce and Culture;* Peterson, *The Price of Redemption.*

49. John Brewer to Aaron Bancroft, March 12, 1810, Evangelical Missionary Society in Massachusetts Records, box 1, folder 1.

50. Edmund Easton Journal, 1808, post script, Society for Propagating the Gospel Papers, box 2, folder 3.

51. Stephen Chapin Journal, 1808, Society for Propagating the Gospel Papers, box 1, folder 17.

52. Amos J. Cooke Journal, 1810, July 29, 1810, Society for Propagating the Gospel Papers, box 1, folder 24.

53. Silas Bingham to Abel Flint, March 12, 1810; Chauncy Lee, "Journal of a Mission to Vermont," 1808, summary of missionary labor; both in Connecticut Missionary Society Papers, reels 2 and 6.

54. Timothy Rogers to John Foster, March 14, 1825, Evangelical Missionary Society in Massachusetts Records, box 2, folder 1.

55. James Parker to Abel Flint, August 31, 1818; Aaron Cleveland to the Connecticut Missionary Society Committee of Missions, May 16, 1808; both in Connecticut Missionary Society Papers, reels 7, 3.

56. Paul Coffin to Peter Thacher, November 8, 1797, Society for Propagating the Gospel Papers, box 1, folder 22.

57. John Lawton to Abel Flint, August 11, 1818, Connecticut Missionary Society Papers, reel 6.

58. For an example of an EMS missionary assignment, see the Committee of Ellsworth to Nathaniel Thayer, April 8, 1811, Evangelical Missionary Society in Massachusetts Records, box 1, folder 2. For an example of a reference to an SPG missionary assignment, see John Strickland Journal, 1796, Society for Propagating the Gospel Records, box 1, folder 9. For an example of CMS missionary instructions, see Abel Flint to Robert Porter, August 8, 1800, Outgoing Correspondence, Connecticut Missionary Society Papers, reel 14. For a list of Maine Missionary Society stands, see meeting minutes, July 6, 1809, Records of the Trustees

of the Maine Missionary Society, Congregational Conference–Maine Missionary Society Records, ser. 1, vol. 1.

59. Joseph Field, "Journal of My Missionary Tour," 1805; Samuel Goddard Diary, missionary report, September 1816, Samuel Goddard Diary and Memorandum Books.

60. Asa Carpenter Missionary Journal, 1806, summary report, Connecticut Missionary Society Papers, reel 2.

61. John Brewer to Aaron Bancroft, March 12, 1810, Evangelical Missionary Society in Massachusetts Records, box 1, folder 1.

62. "The Inducements to a Missionary Life, and the Qualifications of a Missionary," *Religious Intelligencer,* August 25, 1821, 207.

63. Samuel Brimblecom to Alden Bradford, October 8, 1827, Evangelical Missionary Society in Massachusetts Records, box 2, folder 9.

64. William Miller, "A Journal of a Mission to the Northern Settlements," November 14, 1802, Connecticut Missionary Society Papers, reel 7.

65. Joseph Labaree Missionary Journal, reprinted in *Reports Made to the Vermont Missionary Society,* 4.

66. Jonathan Calif, Missionary Report, November 7, 1818, Society for Propagating the Gospel Papers, box 1, folder 16; Jonathan Fisher, Journal of Missionary Service, 1818–1819, summary report, Society for Propagating the Gospel Papers, box 2, folder 9; Thomas Holt Missionary Journal, 1816, summary, William Jenks Papers, box 5.

67. Abiel Abbot and Daniel Little, Missionary Report to Peter Thacher, November 5, 1791, Society for Propagating the Gospel Papers, box 1.

68. W. MacLean Journal, September 19, 1800, Society for Propagating the Gospel Papers, box 1.

69. Jonathan Fisher Journal No. 1, January 16, 1818, Society for Propagating the Gospel Papers, box 2, folder 9.

70. Robert Cochran Journal, July 31, 1814; Jonathan Calif to Abiel Holmes, April 15, 1819; both in Society for Propagating the Gospel Papers, box 1, folders 20, 16.

71. "An Extract from the Narrative of the Missionary Society of Connecticut," *Piscataqua Evangelical Magazine,* May–June 1805, 118.

72. Stephen Chapin Journal, 1808, "Observations," Society for Propagating the Gospel Papers, box 1, folder 17.

73. Peter Nurse to Nathaniel Thayer, May 21, 1811; Peter Nurse to Nathaniel Thayer, May 17, 1814; Peter Nurse to Samuel Ripley, September 24, 1818; Peter Nurse, answer to the Religious Society in Ellsworth, n.d.; all in Evangelical Missionary Society in Massachusetts Records, box 1, folders 3, 6, 9; box 12, folder 2.

74. David Nord points out that early Bible and tract societies emerged in a localized and decentralized publishing market. See Nord, "The Evangelical Origins of Mass Media in America, 1815–1835," 4–8, 16–17; Nord, *Faith in Reading,* 6–7, 27–28, 30–33.

75. Ephraim Abbot Diary, January 20, 1812, Ephraim Abbot Papers, octavo vol. 1; Kilby, *Eastport and Passamaquoddy,* 323.

76. Samuel Goddard Diary, August 30, 1813, Samuel Goddard Diary and Memorandum Books.

77. Bible and tract societies organized on the state and county levels in every northern New England state during the early nineteenth century. Most eventually affiliated with regional or national tract societies. They were among the few kinds of organizations to welcome membership from nearly any Protestant denomination, though in northern New England they tended to work most closely with Congregationalist missionary societies. See Records of the Vermont Bible Society, Vermont Church Council Records, box 4, folder 1;

Tracts Published by the Lincoln and Kennebec Religious Society; An Account of the Massachusetts Society for Promoting Christian Knowledge. For more on Bible and tract societies, see Brown, *The Word in the World,* 60–65; Nord, "The Evangelical Origins of Mass Media in America, 1815–1835," 4–5, 13–19; Nord, *Faith in Reading;* Smith Rosenberg, *Religion and the Rise of the American City;* and Schantz, "Religious Tracts, Evangelical Reform, and the Market Revolution in Antebellum America," 425–466.

78. Mighill Blood to Jedidiah Morse, April 28, 1807, Society for Propagating the Gospel Papers, box 1, folder 12.

79. Peter Holt, Report of Distribution of Books, 1792, Society for Propagating the Gospel papers, box 2, folder 19; Joseph Field, "Journal of My Missionary Tour," July 26, 1805; Samuel Goddard Diary, February 9, June 19, 1813, Samuel Goddard Diary and Memorandum Books. Of the various kinds of religious media that missionaries distributed, Bibles were the most expensive to produce and most difficult to carry, which is why missionaries and agents distributed relatively few of them and took such care to find appropriate recipients. Nord, "The Evangelical Origins of Mass Media in America, 1815–1835," 6–7, 22.

80. Alpheus Coburn to Nathan Strong, September 19, 1806, Incoming Correspondence, Connecticut Missionary Society Papers, reel 13.

81. Amos Cooke to Abiel Holmes, February 28, 1812, Society for Propagating the Gospel Papers, box 1, folder 24.

82. Silas Bingham Missionary Journal, October 3, 1809, Connecticut Missionary Society Papers, reel 2.

83. "Small Congregations," *Religious Intelligencer,* February 21, 1824, 605.

84. *A Narrative on the Subject of Missions,* 9.

85. Samuel Brimblecom to Alden Bradford, October 8, 1827, Evangelical Missionary Society in Massachusetts Records, box 2, folder 9.

86. Samuel Mills to Jonathan Edwards, November 20, 1793, Connecticut Missionary Society Papers, reel 7.

87. Kilby, *Eastport and Passamaquoddy,* 331.

88. *Reports Made to the Vermont Missionary Society,* 4; "State of Religion in Vermont," *Religious Intelligencer,* October 31, 1818, 343.

89. Curtis Coe to Jedidiah Morse, May 6, 1818, William Jenks Papers, box 6.

90. John Anthony to Abel Flint, June 1, 1801, Incoming Correspondence, Connecticut Missionary Society Papers, reel 13.

91. Union Consociation to the Connecticut Missionary Society, October 21, 1812, Incoming Correspondence, Connecticut Missionary Society Papers, reel 13.

92. Committee of Ellsworth to Nathaniel Thayer, April 8, 1811, Evangelical Missionary Society in Massachusetts Records, box 1, folder 2.

93. See, for example, Nathaniel Dodge to Thomas Underhill, April 20, 1820, Autographs of Vermonters; Cyrus Washburn to Ezra Gannett, December 1, 1826, Evangelical Missionary Society in Massachusetts Records, box 2, folder 9; Samuel Pierson to Alden Bradford, October 10, 1824, Evangelical Missionary Society in Massachusetts Records, box 1, folder 17.

94. Warren seems to have left the church in Jackson around 1827 but requested a new mission to Jackson the following year. See Silas Warren to the Evangelical Missionary Society Executive Committee, n.d., box 9, folder 27; Committee at Washington Plantation to the Evangelical Missionary Society, January 11, 1811, box 1, folder 2; Silas Warren to the Evangelical Missionary Society Trustees, December 9, 1811, box 1, folder 3; Result of Council at Jackson and Washington Plantations (copy), September 17, 1812, in Treasurers' Reports, 1811–1813, box 10, folder 2; Congregational Church and Society in Jackson to the Evangelical Missionary Society Executive Committee, May 7, 1824, box 1, folder 16; Church of Christ in Jackson to

the Evangelical Missionary Society, September 19, 1826, box 2, folder 4; Silas Warren to Alden Bradford, May 19, 1828, box 3, folder 2; all in Evangelical Missionary Society in Massachusetts Records.

95. Committee of Ellsworth to Nathaniel Thayer, January 26, 1811, April 8, 1811, both in box 1, folder 2; Rev. Peter Nurse's Answer to the Religious Society in Ellsworth, n.d., box 13, folder 2; Result of Council at Ellsworth (copy), September 8, 1812, in Treasurers' Reports, 1811–1813, box 10, folder 2; all in Evangelical Missionary Society in Massachusetts Records; Committee of the Town of Ellsworth to William Jenks, May 18, 1812, William Jenks Papers, box 4.

96. Amos Cooke to Abiel Holmes, April 26, 1823, box 1, folder 24; Carleton Hurd to Abiel Holmes, December 10, 1823, box 2, folder 22; both in Society for Propagating the Gospel Papers.

97. See annual meeting minutes from 1812–1817, Records of the Trustees of the Maine Missionary Society, Congregational Conference–Maine Missionary Society Records, ser. 1, vol. 21.

98. The Church in Derby to the Connecticut Missionary Society, January 1, 1813; Luther Leland to the Connecticut Missionary Society, January 5, 1813, both in Incoming Correspondence, Connecticut Missionary Society Papers, reel 14.

99. Cotton Mather Smith, "A Journal and Diary of My Preaching Tour Thro the State of Vermont," August 11, 1793.

100. Mighill Blood to Jedidiah Morse, April 27, 1810, Society for Propagating the Gospel Papers, box 1, folder 12. Lincolnville did not appear to live up to Blood's expectations. Freeman Parker, who visited the town in 1829 for the EMS, reported that no missionary had been there "excepting transiently for a single sabbath or occasional lecture" and claimed that he "found but very few decided and intelligent Congregationalists." Freeman Parker to the Evangelical Missionary Society, April 14, 1829, Evangelical Missionary Society in Massachusetts Records, box 13, folder 7.

101. Elijah Kellogg to Abiel Holmes, August 11, 1818, June 16, 1819, October 2, 1821, Society for Propagating the Gospel Papers, box 3, folder 2.

102. F. Burt to Eliphalet Pearson, January 20, 1819, William Jenks Papers, box 6.

103. F. Parker to the Evangelical Missionary Society, April 29, 1826, Evangelical Missionary Society in Massachusetts Records, box 2, folder 4.

104. Stephen Chapin Journal, 1808, "Observations," Society for Propagating the Gospel Papers, box 1, folder 17.

105. Kilby, *Eastport and Passamaquoddy*, 327.

106. Jedidiah Bushnell to Nathan Strong, June 2, 1801, Connecticut Missionary Society Papers, reel 2.

107. Ephraim Abbot Diary, 1812, Ephraim Abbot Papers, octavo vol. 1.

108. Jonathan Fisher Journal No. 1, January 15, January 18, February 1, 1818, Society for Propagating the Gospel Papers, box 2, folder 9.

109. Chauncy Lee, "Journal of a Mission to Vermont," February 26, 1808, Connecticut Missionary Society Papers, reel 6.

110. Samuel Brimblecom, for example, was dropped by the SPG but retained by the EMS because of his liberal theology. Samuel Brimblecom to Francis Parkman, August 17, 1829; Francis Parkman to Samuel Brimblecom, August 28, 1829; both in Society for Propagating the Gospel Papers, box 1, folder 15; First Unitarian Society in Anson, Maine, to the Evangelical Missionary Society, August 1828; Society of Norridgewock to George Ripley, December 23, 1828; both in Evangelical Missionary Society in Massachusetts Records, box 3, folders 4, 5; Samuel Peirson to Alden Bradford, October 10, 1824, Evangelical Missionary Society in Massachusetts Records, box 1, folder 17.

111. Benjamin Wooster, Account Book and Memoirs, 75–76; Ephraim Abbot, Autobiography, n.d., Ephraim Abbot Papers, box 2, folder 6, 13–14; H. Packard to Alden Bradford, April 3, 1827, Evangelical Missionary Society in Massachusetts Records, box 2, folder 6.

112. Candy Gunther Brown suggests that an evangelical print culture served an important purpose for groups (like Baptists and Congregationalists) that lacked centralized governing bodies, because these groups relied on their periodicals to foster a sense of community that transcended individual congregations. See Brown, *The Word in the World*, 1, 112, 46–47.

113. "Religious Newspapers," *Religious Intelligencer*, October 12, 1822, 317.

114. "Religious Newspapers," *Religious Intelligencer*, September 2, 1826, 216; "Importance of Religious Newspapers," *Religious Intelligencer*, December 1, 1827, 420.

115. Woodman, ed., "Memoir and Journals of Rev. Paul Coffin, D.D.," 346.

116. Ephraim Abbot to Mary Pearson, September 19, 1811, Ephraim Abbot Papers, box 1, folder 1.

117. Justin Parsons to Thomas Merrill, October 19, 1818, Autographs of Vermonters.

118. Alden Bradford to John Eliot, May 22, 1811, Society for Propagating the Gospel Papers, box 1, folder 13.

119. Jonathan Harvey to Abel Flint, April 9, 1811, Connecticut Missionary Society Papers, reel 5.

120. Timothy Hilliard Journal, December 25, 1817, February 15, 1818, William Jenks Papers, box 6.

121. Paul Coffin to Peter Thacher, March 6, 1797, Society for Propagating the Gospel Papers, box 1, folder 22.

122. Amos Cooke Journal, September 2, November 4, 1810, Society for Propagating the Gospel Papers, box 1, folder 24.

123. George Freeman Journal, November 15, December 11, 1825, March 20, 1826.

124. Sewall, *A Memoir of Rev. Jotham Sewall*, 404–407. Sewall also preached (albeit less often) in the other New England states and in the South.

125. Abbot meant by "this country" the region surrounding Eastport. Joseph Field, "Journal of My Missionary Tour," July 16, 1805; Kilby, *Eastport and Passamaquoddy*, 332.

126. Broughton White, "Revival of Religion," *Religious Intelligencer*, August 22, 1818, 187–188.

127. "Plan for the Promotion of Revivals of Religion," *Religious Intelligencer*, June 17, 1820, 45–46.

128. "Revivals of Religion," *Religious Intelligencer*, March 13, 1819, 664; "Means of Extending Revivals of Religion," quoted in *Religious Intelligencer*, September 27, 1823, 271.

129. In New Hampshire and Vermont, Congregationalists prevailed in every county through 1830 (and in most counties as late as 1850). Baptists gained a stronghold in Maine between 1790 and 1830, though subdivisions in these counties by 1850 reveal a more even balance between Congregationalists and Baptists throughout the state. See Gaustad and Barlow, *New Historical Atlas of Religion in America*, 357–359.

6. A City Set on a Hill

1. Samuel Goddard Diary, November 22, December 17, 1816, Samuel Goddard Diary and Memorandum Books.

2. Ibid.

3. William F. Miller, "Journal of a Mission to the Northern Settlements," August 15, 1802, Connecticut Missionary Society Papers, reel 2.

4. Nathan Douglas to Abiel Holmes, November 27, 1823, Society for Propagating the Gospel Papers, box 2, folder 2. The Baptists eventually failed in their takeover. The First Parish sued and won the right to exclude unwanted members, which allowed them to remove the Baptists from their rosters and reclaim the parish's property. See *Lord* v. *Chamberlain* (1822), *Maine Reports,* vol. 2 (Hallowell, Maine: Glazier, 1824), 67–72.

5. Ephraim Abbot to Mary Pearson, March 8, 1813; April 2, 1813; July 1, 1813; and July 27, 1813; all in Ephraim Abbot Papers, box 1, folder 2. Adding to the competition in places like Greenland was the law that granted ministerial and church lands to the society with the first settled minister.

6. Joel Winch, Autobiography, 1802, Joel Winch Papers, folder 2, 36.

7. Samuel Goddard Diary, August 21, 1813, Samuel Goddard Diary and Memorandum Books.

8. Peach, ed., "The Reverend Joel Winch," 85.

9. Thomas Holt Journal, October 11, 1818, William Jenks Papers, box 6.

10. Stephen Chapin Journal, 1808, "Observations," Society for Propagating the Gospel Papers, box 1, folder 17.

11. William F. Miller, "Journal of a Mission to the Northern Settlements," August 21, 1802, Connecticut Missionary Society Papers, reel 7.

12. Ibid., November 14, 1802.

13. Nathan Douglas to Abiel Holmes, November 1, 1820, Society for Propagating the Gospel Papers, box 2, folder 2.

14. Meeting minutes, August 18, 1802, New Durham, New Hampshire, Freewill Baptist Church Records of Quarterly Meetings, vol. 2, 39–40; Peach, ed., "The Reverend Joel Winch," 85.

15. David Pickering to Edward Turner, March 10, 1820, Edward Turner Family Papers, box 3, folder 1.

16. John Turner, Missionary Account, 1818, William Jenks Papers, box 5.

17. Ibid.

18. Ibid.; John Turner to Eliphalet Pearson, December 20, 1819, William Jenks Papers, box 6.

19. Levi Bartlett to Sanborn J. McRuter, 1818 (copy), Dix Family Papers; Levi Bartlett to Ezra Bartlett, December 2, 1818, Bartlett Family Papers, series D, box 1, folder 7.

20. Levi Bartlett to Ezra Bartlett, April 15, 1818, Bartlett Family Papers, series D, box 1, folder 7.

21. William F. Miller, "Journal of a Mission to the Northern Settlements," August 15, 1802, Connecticut Missionary Society Papers, reel 7.

22. William Smyth Babcock, Sermon No. 36 (1800, 1819), William Smyth Babcock Papers, octavo vol. 2. Notes on the manuscript state that he delivered this sermon both in 1800 (location unidentified) and in Barrington, New Hampshire, in 1819.

23. The ecumenical impulse only went so far; multi-denominational organizations, whether by default or design, generally excluded Catholics and non-Christians. Nord, *Faith in Reading,* 154–155.

24. Edward Payson to William Jenks, August 30, 1809, William Jenks Papers, box 4.

25. Phinehas Pillsbury Diary, February 24, 1806, Phinehas Pillsbury Diaries, vol. 1.

26. Asaph Morgan, Missionary Journal, August 26, 1813, Connecticut Missionary Society Papers, reel 7.

27. Samuel Goddard Diary, March 30, 1814, Samuel Goddard Diary and Memorandum Books.

28. Joseph Field, "Journal of My Missionary Tour," September 3, 1805, miscellaneous box 152, folder 3.

29. Thomas Holt Missionary Journal, March 25, 1818, William Jenks Papers, box 6.

30. Circular Letter, August 1829 meeting, Rockingham Association Records, 20–21.

31. Benjamin Chadwick to Jedidiah Morse, September 4, 1804, Society for Propagating the Gospel Papers, box 1, folder 17.

32. Timothy Hilliard Journal, January 12, 1818, William Jenks Papers, box 6.

33. Jotham Sewall, "Journal of Three Months Missionary Labors Performed for the Massachusetts Society for Promoting Christian Knowledge," April 26, 1818, William Jenks Papers, box 2.

34. Original Journal of Elder Job Seamans, September 18, October 2, 1803, Job Seamans Papers.

35. Phinehas Pillsbury Diary, February 19, 1806, Phinehas Pillsbury Diaries, vol. 1.

36. Kilby, *Eastport and Passamaquoddy,* 323.

37. Edmund Easton Journal, August 30, 1808, Society for Propagating the Gospel Papers, box 2, folder 3.

38. Meeting minutes, October 17, 1826, Piscataqua Association Records, vol. 2, 136–137.

39. Original Journal of Elder Job Seamans, June 29, 1817, Job Seamans Papers.

40. "Ministerial Exchanges," *Religious Intelligencer,* November 13, 1824, 377.

41. William Smyth Babcock Journal, June 4, 1801, William Smyth Babcock Papers, folder 4.

42. Kilby, *Eastport and Passamaquoddy,* 333.

43. George Freeman Journal, December 8, 1825.

44. "Camp Meeting," *Trumpet and Universalist Magazine,* September 27, 1828, 50–51.

45. Asaph Morgan, Missionary Journal, August 8, 1813, Connecticut Missionary Society Papers, reel 7.

46. An Act to Incorporate the Proprietors of the Congregational and Baptist Meeting House in Meredith, 1826, *Laws of New Hampshire, 1821–1828,* vol. 9 (Concord, N.H.: Evans Printing Company, 1921), 511–512.

47. Meeting minutes, March 18, April 11, 1823; December 25, 1827; January 11, 1828, Records of the First Christian Toleration Society (1820–1838), Alstead, New Hampshire, Universalist Church Records.

48. Records of the Weston Society for Building a Meetinghouse, 1815, Vermont Records, 3–4.

49. Report of the Committee, January 1823, Whiting, Vermont, Records of the Baptist Meetinghouse.

50. Meeting minutes, December 7–10, 1798, copy of Universal Society Records (1798–1801); Warnings of Meetings (November 5, December 28, 1798, October 27, 1799); D. Burch's legal opinion relative to sharing meetinghouse, September 9, 1801; all in Strafford, Vermont, Meetinghouse Records.

51. Zea, *Order and Dissent,* 14–15.

52. Church Covenant of the Residents of Craftsbury, ca. 1790s, Crafts Family Papers, box 9, folder 31.

53. Jonathan Hovey to Abiel Flint, September 1, 1810, Connecticut Missionary Society Papers, reel 5.

54. Asaph Morgan, Missionary Journal, April 19, August 8, 1813, Connecticut Missionary Society Papers, reel 7; Jonathan Calif to Abiel Holmes, April 15, 1819, Society for Propagating the Gospel Papers, box 1, folder 16.

55. Jotham Sewall, "A Journal of Three Months' Missionary Labors," October 23, 1817, William Jenks Papers, box 6.

56. Nathan Fisk to John and Susan Fisk, March 25, 1827, Fisk Family Papers, box 2, folder 10.

57. Minutes of the proceedings, included under Statement of the Baptists, Minutes, and Articles of Faith, Georgia Vermont, 1823–1825, Asa Lyons Papers, box 4, folder 119. These incomplete records show that the multi-denominational association met for at least two years.

58. Heyrman, *Southern Cross*, 102–103; Schneider, *The Way of the Cross Leads Home*, 200–201.

59. Circular Letter, 1827, Rockingham Association Records, 7.

60. In 1790, of twenty churches, seven had settled ministers; in 1800, there were twenty-eight ordained ministers for fifty-one churches. This figure does not include ruling elders and unordained preachers. See Stewart, *The History of the Freewill Baptists*, vol. 1, 95, 172–173.

61. This informal survey polled quarterly meetings to find out their memberships and leadership. Of the nine northern New England quarterly meetings that responded (out of twelve total), there were 110 settled ministers in 140 pulpits. Among the quarterly meetings' reports were these: the Gorham Quarterly Meeting in Maine had eight settled pulpits and five vacant ones. The Edgcomb (Maine) Quarterly Meeting reported that all fifteen of its churches had settled ordained ministers. Among the twenty churches in the New Durham Quarterly Meeting, two pulpits remained vacant, and of the Strafford Quarterly Meeting's eight churches, only one did. See *A Religious Magazine*, June 1821, 126–127; November 1821, 161–162, 165–166; November 1822, 277–281.

62. By "northern New England ministers," I refer to those clergy who ministered in that region for any length of time. These numbers are approximate because there were a few northern New England ministers for whom the ordination dates are not recorded. See Stewart, *The History of the Freewill Baptists*, vol. 1, 473–479.

63. *A Religious Magazine*, August 1820, 19–20.

64. Bordin, "The Sect to Denomination Process in America," 85.

65. Circular Letter, 1828, Records of the General Convention of Universalists, Universalist Church of America General Convention Minutes and Circular Letters, box 1, folder 1, 329–331.

66. Circular Letter, 1827, Rockingham Association Records, 8–9. The association's language tapped into a long history of church- and community-gathering in British North America and the United States. By paraphrasing John Winthrop's "A Modell of Christian Charity" (1630), the Universalists implied (as Winthrop had) that each covenanted society stood as a public example of a godly people for the non-professing world.

67. "Maine and New-Brunswick," *Trumpet and Universalist Magazine*, February 13, 1830, 131; "Number of Universalists," *Christian Intelligencer and Eastern Chronicle*, August 20, 1830, 134.

68. Copy of a letter to the Marshfield Freewill Baptist Church, November 29, 1823, Records of the Freewill Baptist Church and Society of Calais, Lebanon, New Hampshire, Freewill Baptist Church Records and Minutes.

69. Meeting minutes, August 19, 1824, New Durham, New Hampshire, Freewill Baptist Church Records of Quarterly Meetings.

70. Stewart, *The History of the Freewill Baptists*, vol. 1, 472.

71. "A Question" and "Another Important Question," *A Religious Magazine*, June 1822, 249–251.

72. Asaph Morgan's Missionary Journal, July 21–22, 1813, Connecticut Missionary Society Papers, reel 7.

73. Jonathan Fisher to Abiel Holmes, April 24, 1820, Society for Propagating the Gospel Papers, box 2, folder 9. Calvin Clark corroborates and augments this story in Clark, *History of the Congregational Churches in Maine*, vol. 2, 323–324.

74. Nathan Coolidge to Chester Wright, August 31, 1821; John Griswold to Chester Wright, September 5, 1821; both in Chester Wright Letters.

75. Result of Council, Montpelier, May 1, 1822, Autographs of Vermonters, folder 57.

76. John Brooks, "New Association of Universalists," *Universalist Magazine,* November 2, 1822, 74; meeting minutes, August 21, 1827, Rockingham Association Records, 5; Lemuel Willis, "A New Association of Universalists," *Universalist Magazine,* August 28, 1824, 39; "New Universalist Association," *Trumpet and Universalist Magazine,* September 5, 1829, 38; "Maine Convention," *Trumpet and Universalist Magazine,* July 11, 1829, 6. By this time, northern New England was not the only area of Universalist expansion; the denomination also added associations in New York, Ohio, and Boston.

77. Kern, *God, Grace, and Granite,* 27–29.

78. Bordin, "The Sect to Denomination Process in America," 80; Stewart, *The History of the Freewill Baptists,* vol. 1, 265, 450. Four of the seven yearly meetings were in northern New England (one each in New Hampshire and Vermont, and two in Maine); others were organized in New York, Ohio, and Pennsylvania.

79. Burrage, *History of the Baptists in Maine,* 153, 54, 61, 88–91, 220–222.

80. Meeting minutes, January 12, 1819; July 13, 1821; February 10, August 10, 1824; Cumberland Association Rules and Proceedings, Congregational Conference–Maine Missionary Society Records, ser. 3, vol. 85.

81. "Conference of Churches," *Religious Intelligencer,* September 23, 1826, 270–271, September 30, 1826, 286.

82. Meeting minutes, April 18, September 19, October 17, November 14, 1826; February 20, July 17, September 18, October 16, 1827, Piscataqua Association Records, vol. 2.

83. "History of the Monthly Concert," *Religious Intelligencer,* July 29, 1826, 136–137; *Circular Letters, Containing an Invitation to the Ministers and Churches of Every Christian Denomination in the United States.* For background on the concerts of prayer, see Conforti, *Jonathan Edwards, Religious Tradition, and American Culture,* 16; Kling, *A Field of Divine Wonders;* Rohrer, *Keepers of the Covenant,* 54–57.

84. Meeting minutes, June 28–29, 1815, Records of the Maine Missionary Society, Congregational Conference–Maine Missionary Society Records, ser. 1, vol. 2.

85. Elias Bond to Charlotte Cheever, June 7, 1820, Cheever Family Papers, box 1, folder 8.

86. Meeting minutes, May 12, 1819, and subsequent undated notes, Washington, Vermont, Church of Christ Register, 10–12.

87. According to Joanna French's diary, the towns near Epping, in southeastern New Hampshire, first observed concerts of prayer in 1816; French Family Diary, July 1, 1816, June 2, 1817.

88. Thomas Holt Journal, October 22, 1817, William Jenks Papers, box 6.

89. Report on the State of Religion, December 25, 1822, Cumberland Conference of Churches Records, folder 1.

90. "New Hampshire Baptist Sabbath School Union," *The American Sunday School Magazine,* November 1829, 325.

91. "Concert of Prayer," *The Adviser; or, Vermont Evangelical Magazine,* March–April, 1815, 112–114.

92. Ebezer Pinkham, "Home Intelligence," *Massachusetts Baptist Missionary Magazine,* September 1816, 351–353.

93. David Sutherland, "Bath, N.H.," *Religious Intelligencer,* June 23, 1821, 54–56.

94. "Revivals of Religion," *Religious Intelligencer,* August 25, 1821, 204.

95. "Revivals of Religion," *Religious Intelligencer,* August 3, 1822, 152–153.

96. David Sutherland, "Bath, N.H.," *Religious Intelligencer,* June 23, 1821, 56.

97. For surveys of missionary activities in the 1810s and 1820s, see Elsbree, "The Rise of the Missionary Spirit in New England"; Ericson, *Missionary Society of Connecticut Papers,*

1759–1948; Goodykoontz, *Home Missions on the American Frontier,* chapters 5–6; Oliphant, "The American Missionary Spirit, 1828–1835"; Rohrer, *Keepers of the Covenant;* Smith, *An Historical Sketch of Home Missionary Work in Vermont by the Congregational Churches,* 10.

Conclusion

1. Enoch Pond to John Maltby, June 12, 1832, March 18, 1833, March 4, 1834, Maltby Family Papers, folder C.

2. Eslinger, *Ciizens of Zion;* Heyrman, *Southern Cross;* DeRogatis, *Moral Geography.*

3. Taysom, *Shakers, Mormons, and Religious Worlds.*

4. Maffly-Kipp, *Religion and Society in Frontier California.*

5. The term comes from Jackson, *Crabgrass Frontier.*

6. Thumma, "The Kingdom, the Power, and the Glory."

Bibliography

Primary Sources

Records of Churches, Conferences, and Other Religious Organizations

Alstead, New Hampshire. Universalist Church. Records, 1820–1838. New Hampshire Historical Society, Concord.

Andover, Vermont. Baptist Church of Christ. Book of Records, 1803–1869. University of Vermont Special Collections, Burlington.

Bangor, Maine. All Souls Congregational Church. Records, 1811–1895. Microfilm, RG 4374. Congregational Library and Archives, Boston, Massachusetts. Courtesy First Congregational Church of Bangor.

Barnstead, New Hampshire. First Free Baptist Church. Records, 1803–1846. New Hampshire Historical Society, Concord.

Bridgewater, New Hampshire. Church and Society. Records, 1802–1866. New Hampshire Historical Society, Concord.

Chelsea, Vermont. Congregational Church. Records, 1789–1857. Vermont Historical Society, Barre.

Chelsea, Vermont. Voluntary Congregational Society. Records, 1799–1841. Vermont Historical Society, Barre.

Clarendon, Vermont. Second Baptist Church. Records, 1739–1832. Microfilm, American Baptist Historical Society, Mercer University, Atlanta, Georgia.

Congregational Conference–Maine Missionary Society. Records, 1788–1962. Coll. 1704. Maine Historical Society, Portland.

Connecticut Missionary Society. Papers, 1759–1948. Microfilm, Connecticut Historical Society, Hartford. Courtesy Connecticut Conference Archives, Hartford.

Cornish, New Hampshire. Congregational Church. Correspondence, 1781–1853. New Hampshire Historical Society, Concord.

Cumberland Conference of Churches. Records, 1810–1893. Coll. 1815. Maine Historical Society, Portland.

Dover, New Hampshire. First Parish. Records, 1614–1862. Microfilm, RG 1319. Congregational Library and Archives, Boston, Massachusetts. Courtesy First Parish Church, Dover.

Evangelical Missionary Society in Massachusetts. Records, 1808–1914. bMS 502. Andover-Harvard Theological Library, Cambridge, Massachusetts.

Freeport, Maine. First Parish Congregational Church. Records, 1789–1961. Microfilm, RG 0079. Congregational Library and Archives, Boston, Massachusetts. Courtesy First Parish Church Congregational, Freeport.

Goffstown, New Hampshire. Baptist Church. Records previous to 1820. New Hampshire Historical Society, Concord.

Greene, Maine. Free Baptist Churches. Records, vols. 1–2, 1780–1887. Coll. 1177. Maine Historical Society, Portland.

Greenfield, New Hampshire. Union Congregational Church. Records, 1791–1991. Congregational Library and Archives, Boston, Massachusetts. Courtesy Greenfield Covenant Church.

Jaffrey, New Hampshire. Congregational Church. Papers, 1790–1830. New Hampshire Historical Society, Concord.

Jericho, Vermont. First Congregational Church. Records, 1791–1966. RG 1121. Congregational Library and Archives, Boston, Massachusetts. Courtesy First Congregational Church of Jericho.

Langdon, New Hampshire. Christian Church. Records, 1791–ca. 1930. bMS 210. Andover-Harvard Theological Library, Cambridge, Massachusetts.

Lebanon, New Hampshire. Freewill Baptist Church. Records and Minutes, 1800–1806. Vermont Historical Society, Barre.

Livermore, Maine. First Baptist Church. Records, 1793–1931. American Baptist Historical Society, Mercer University, Atlanta, Georgia.

Londonderry, New Hampshire. Baptist Church of Christ. Church Book or Records, 1749–1843. Microfilm, American Baptist Historical Society, Mercer University, Atlanta, Georgia.

Loudon and Chichester, New Hampshire. Congregational Church. Records, 1780–1782. New Hampshire Historical Society, Concord.

Lyndeborough, New Hampshire. United Church. Records, 1782–1937. bMS 450. Andover-Harvard Theological Library, Cambridge, Massachusetts.

Maine and New Hampshire. Freewill Baptist Quarterly Meetings, 1783–1792. Microfilm, American Baptist Historical Society, Mercer University, Atlanta, Georgia.

Maine Conference of the Methodist Episcopal Church. Records, 1825–1835. Boston University School of Theology Library, Boston, Massachusetts.

Manchester, Vermont. Baptist Church. Records, 1781–1900. American Baptist Historical Society, Mercer University, Atlanta, Georgia.

Marlowe, New Hampshire. Baptist Church. Records, 1777–1807. Microfilm, American Baptist Historical Society, Mercer University, Atlanta, Georgia.

Mason, New Hampshire. Baptist Church of Christ. Records, 1786–1836. American Baptist Historical Society, Mercer University, Atlanta, Georgia.

Middlebury, Vermont. Congregational Church. Record Book, 1790–1853. Henry Sheldon Museum of Vermont History, Middlebury.

Middletown, Vermont. Baptist Church. Records, 1805–1847. University of Vermont Special Collections, Burlington.

Montpelier, Vermont. Bethany Congregational Church. Records, 1808–1959. Microfilm, RG 1371. Congregational Library and Archives, Boston, Massachusetts. Courtesy Bethany Church, UCC, Montpelier.

Montpelier, Vermont. Freewill Baptist Church. Records, 1823–1846. MSS 23–28. Vermont Historical Society, Barre.

New Boston, New Hampshire. First Baptist Society. Records, vol. 1, 1819–1940. Microfilm, American Baptist Historical Society, Mercer University, Atlanta, Georgia.

New Durham, New Hampshire. Freewill Baptist Church. Records of Quarterly and Yearly Meetings, 1783–1793. New Hampshire Historical Society, Concord.

New Durham, New Hampshire. Freewill Baptist Church. Records of Quarterly Meetings, vols. 1–2, 1792–1809. New Hampshire Historical Society, Concord.

New Durham, New Hampshire. Quarterly Meeting. Records of the Elders' Conference, 1801–1813. New Hampshire Historical Society, Concord.

New England Conference of the Methodist Episcopal Church. Records, 1797–1970. Boston University School of Theology Library, Boston, Massachusetts.

New Grantham Circuit. Quarterly Conference. Records, 1813–1872. New Hampshire Records. Boston University School of Theology Library, Boston, Massachusetts.

New Hampshire. General Association. Report, ca. 1820. Congregational Library and Archives, Boston, Massachusetts.

New London, New Hampshire. Baptist Church. Records, 1788–1863. Microfilm, American Baptist Historical Society, Mercer University, Atlanta, Georgia.

Newbury, Vermont. Congregational Church. Records, 1786–1835. Miscellaneous Collections. MSS 347. Vermont Historical Society, Barre.

Piscataqua Association. Records, 1781–1900. RG 1158. Congregational Library and Archives, Boston, Massachusetts.

Pittsfield, New Hampshire. Freewill Baptist Church Records, 1791–1838. New Hampshire Historical Society, Concord.

Poland, Maine. Poland Circuit of the Methodist Church Quarterly Conference. Record Book and Deed of Pew, 1808–1872. Coll. 1218. Maine Historical Society, Portland.

Rockingham Association. Records, 1824–1924. New Hampshire Historical Society, Concord.

Rutland County, Vermont. Association of Congregational Churches. "Protest against the System of Exciting and Promoting Revivals of Religion Known to Have Been in Operation during the Year Past in Vermont." 1836. MS 285.8743. Vermont Historical Society, Barre.

Ryegate, Vermont. Meetinghouse Records, 1806–1826. MSS 24–150. Vermont Historical Society, Barre.

Sanford, Maine. Baptist Church. Records, 1772–1877. American Baptist Historical Society, Mercer University, Atlanta, Georgia.

Shelburne, Vermont. Female Religious Society. Articles of Organization, ca. 1816. Vermont Historical Society, Barre.

Shoreham, Vermont. Baptist Church. Ecclesiastical Records, 1794–1837. Microfilm, American Baptist Historical Society, Mercer University, Atlanta, Georgia.

Society for Propagating the Gospel. Papers, 1791–1875. Phillips Library, Salem, Massachusetts.

Society for Propagating the Gospel. Records, 1752–1948. Massachusetts Historical Society, Boston.

Southwest Harbor (Mt. Desert), Maine. United Church of Christ. Clerk's Records, 1792–1892. Microfilm, RG 1396. Congregationalist Library and Archives, Boston, Massachusetts. Courtesy Southwest Harbor Congregational Church.

Strafford, Vermont. Meetinghouse Records. MSS 25–81. Vermont Historical Society, Barre.

Underhill, Vermont. Result of an Ecclesiastical Council, 1812. MSS-7. Vermont Historical Society, Barre.

Universalist Church of America General Convention. Minutes and Circular Letters, 1793–1869. bMS 163. Andover-Harvard Theological Library, Cambridge, Massachusetts.

Universalist Church of America General Convention. Records, 1793–1818. bMS 143. Andover-Harvard Theological Library, Cambridge, Massachusetts.

Vermont. Church Council. Records, 1812–1874. University of Vermont Special Collections, Burlington.

Vermont. Records. Boston University Theological Library, Boston, Massachusetts.

Vermont Congregational Conference. Records, 1773–1959. University of Vermont Special Collections, Burlington.

Vershire Circuit (Methodist Episcopal Church in Vermont). Records, 1802–1861. AC 802110. Vermont Historical Society, Barre.

Washington, Vermont. Church of Christ. Register, 1800–1863. Vermont Historical Society, Barre.

Weathersfield, Vermont. Circuit Record Book, 1821–1857. Vermont Historical Society, Barre.

West Shaftsbury, Vermont. Baptist Church. Record Book (manuscript copy), 1799–1805. American Baptist Historical Society, Mercer University, Atlanta, Georgia.

Whiting, Vermont. Records of the Baptist Meetinghouse, 1811–1823. Henry Sheldon Museum of Vermont History, Middlebury.

Wilmington, Vermont. Congregational Church. Result of Vote, 1806. MSS-28, 102. Vermont Historical Society, Barre.

Windham Union Association. Vermont Conference. Records, 1775–1931. United Church of Christ. Records. RG 0172. Congregational Library and Archives, Boston, Massachusetts. Courtesy Windham Union Association, Vermont.

Windsor, Vermont. Universalist Society. Record Book, 1798–1861. AC 798357. Vermont Historical Society, Barre.

Woodstock Association. Records, 1786–1812. Vermont Baptist Historical Society Records. Microfilm, American Baptist Historical Society, Mercer University, Atlanta, Georgia.

Woolwich, Maine. Baptist Church. Records, 1797–1840. Microfilm, American Baptist Historical Society, Mercer University, Atlanta, Georgia.

Personal and Family Collections

Abbot, Ephraim. Papers, 1801–1904. American Antiquarian Society, Worcester, Massachusetts.

Autographs of Vermonters. MSS 17. Vermont Historical Society, Barre.

Babcock, William Smyth. Papers, 1757; 1788–1839. American Antiquarian Society, Worcester, Massachusetts.

Backus, Isaac. Papers, 1724–1806. American Baptist Historical Society, Mercer University, Atlanta, Georgia.

Bartlett Family. Papers, 1743–1888. New Hampshire Historical Society, Concord.

Beede, Thomas. Papers, 1779–1904. Massachusetts Historical Society, Boston.

Bemis, Stephen. Journal, 1796–1798. American Antiquarian Society, Worcester, Massachusetts.

Blanchard, Stephen. Papers, 1789–1809. Massachusetts Historical Society, Boston.

Bowers-Flagg Family. Papers, 1756–1930. American Antiquarian Society, Worcester, Massachusetts.

Bryant, Charity, and Sylvia Drake. Papers, 1794–1850. Henry Sheldon Museum of Vermont History, Middlebury.

Bryant, Eliza. Diary, 1801–1803. Coll. 1398. Maine Historical Society, Portland.

Case, Isaac. Papers, 1761–1852. American Baptist Historical Society, Mercer University, Atlanta, Georgia.

Cheever Family. Papers, 1800–1900. American Antiquarian Society, Worcester, Massachusetts.

Cheever-Wheeler Family. Papers, 1773–1979. American Antiquarian Society. Worcester, Massachusetts.

Clancy, John. Letters, 1816–1840. Henry Sheldon Museum of Vermont History, Middlebury.

Clark, John. Journal, 1774–1842. MSS-7. Vermont Historical Society, Barre.

Crafts Family. Papers, 1782–1908. University of Vermont Special Collections, Burlington.

Dix Family. Papers, 1818–1822. Massachusetts Historical Society, Boston.

Dudley, John, Family. Papers, 1728–1853. New Hampshire Historical Society, Concord.

Field, Joseph. Journal of My Missionary Tour, 1805. Miscellaneous Collections, box 152, folder 3. Coll. S-5886. Maine Historical Society, Portland.

Fisk Family. Papers, 1782–1911. New Hampshire Historical Society, Concord.

Foxcroft Family. Papers, 1732–1829. American Antiquarian Society, Worcester, Massachusetts.

Freeman, George. Journal, 1825–1826. Vermont Historical Society, Barre.
French Family. Diary, 1815–1817. New Hampshire Historical Society, Concord.
Goddard, Samuel. Diary and Memorandum Books, 1813–1821. MSS 20–47. Vermont Historical Society, Barre.
Hale, Henry. Diary, 1806–1818. Coll. S-1583. Maine Historical Society, Portland.
Hopkins, Francis. Papers, 1843–1923. University of Vermont Special Collections, Burlington.
Hurd, Isaac. Papers, 1807–1831. New Hampshire Historical Society, Concord.
Jenks, William. Papers, 1802–1879. Massachusetts Historical Society, Boston.
Livermore Family. Papers, 1787–1883. New Hampshire Historical Society, Concord.
Lyons, Asa. Papers, 1754–1840. University of Vermont Special Collections, Burlington.
Maltby Family. Papers, 1811–1843. Connecticut Historical Society, Hartford.
Member of the First Congregational Church of Loudon, New Hampshire. Diary, 1815–1822. New Hampshire Historical Society, Concord.
Peabody, Elizabeth Palmer. Letter and Commonplace Book, 1821–1832. Microfilm, Massachusetts Historical Society, Boston.
Peabody, Stephen. Diaries, 1767–1814. American Antiquarian Society, Worcester, Massachusetts.
Personal Letters. Collection. Boston University School of Theology Library, Boston, Massachusetts.
Pillsbury, Phinehas. Diaries, 1803–1858. Coll. 1440. Maine Historical Society, Portland.
Remick, Timothy. Papers. RG 1325. American Baptist Historical Society, Mercer University, Atlanta, Georgia.
Seamans, Job. Papers, 1748–1830. Microfilm, American Baptist Historical Society, Mercer University, Atlanta, Georgia.
Skinner, Daniel. Correspondence. MSS 25–36. Vermont Historical Society, Barre.
Smith, Cotton Mather. "A Journal and Diary of My Preaching Tour Thro the State of Vermont," 1793. Misc. file 1419. Vermont Historical Society, Barre.
Stevens Family. Papers, 1732–1901. University of Vermont Special Collections, Burlington.
Stinchfield, Ephraim. Papers, 1777–1830. Coll. 44. Maine Historical Society, Portland.
Turner, Edward. Family Papers, 1711–1873. bMS 513. Andover-Harvard Theological Library, Cambridge, Massachusetts.
W. A. B. Anonymous Diary, ca. 1800. RG 1498. American Baptist Historical Society, Mercer University, Atlanta, Georgia.
Warren, Joseph. Letters to Thomas Gray, 1792–1810. Massachusetts Historical Society, Boston.
Weeks Family. Papers, 1764–1900. Henry Sheldon Museum of Vermont History, Middlebury.
Wentworth, James Jewett. Diaries, 1803–1832. New Hampshire Historical Society, Concord.
Whitelaw, James. Papers. Vermont Historical Society, Barre.
Winch, Joel. Papers, 1780–1849. MS-25198. Vermont Historical Society, Barre.
Wingate Family. Papers, 1769–1897. New Hampshire Historical Society, Concord.
Wright, Chester. Letters, 1821–1824. MSS 28–147.Vermont Historical Society, Barre.
Wooster, Benjamin. Account Book and Memoirs, 1816–1851. University of Vermont Special Collections, Burlington.

Manuscript Town, County, and State Records

Blue Hill, Maine. Town Records, 1767–1892. American Antiquarian Society, Worcester, Massachusetts.
Documents of the Constitutional Convention. Maine State Archives, Augusta.
Executive Council. Reports. Maine State Archives, Augusta.

Kennebec Supreme Judicial Court. Records. Maine State Archives, Augusta.
Legislative Archives. Maine State Archives, Augusta.
Manuscript Journal of the House, November 1800. New Hampshire Division of Archives and Records Management, Concord.
Manuscript Journal of the Senate, 1797–1800. New Hampshire Division of Archives and Records Management, Concord.
Manuscripts of Vermont State Papers. Vermont State Archives, Montpelier.
Massachusetts Eastern Lands. Papers. RG EA14. Massachusetts State Archives, Boston.
New Hampshire Petitions. New Hampshire Division of Archives and Records Management, Concord.
Strafford, Vermont. Papers, 1795–1851. Vermont Historical Society, Barre.
Vermont Constitution. Records. Vermont State Archives, Montpelier.
York County Case Files. Manuscript Records. Maine State Archives, Augusta.
York County Supreme Judicial Court. Records. Maine State Archives, Augusta.

Books, Pamphlets, and Broadsides

An Account of the Massachusetts Society for Promoting Christian Knowledge. Cambridge, Mass.: William Hilliard, 1806.
The Address and Constitution of the Evangelical Missionary Society. Cambridge, Mass.: William Hilliard, 1807.
An Address by the Ministers of the Original Association of the County of Windham, to the Heads of Families in Their Respective Societies, on the Duty of Family Religion, with Several Forms of Prayer Annexed. Windham, Conn.: John Byrne, 1803.
An Address of the General Association of Connecticut to the District Associations on the Subject of a Missionary Society, Together with Summaries and Extracts of Late European Publications on Missions to the Heathen. Norwich, Conn.: Thomas Hubbard, 1797.
Backus, Isaac, and David Weston. *A History of New England with Particular Attention to the Denomination of Christians Called Baptists, vol. 2.* Newton, Mass.: Backus Historical Society, 1871.
Blood, Caleb. *A Sermon Preached before the Honorable Legislature of the State of Vermont, Convened at Rutland, October 11th, 1792, Being the Day of General Election.* Rutland, Vt.: Anthony Haswell, 1792.
A Book of the Records of the Church of Christ in Stratton. Published Transcription. Barre, Vt.: Vermont Historical Society Collections, n.d.
A Brief Account of the Present State of the Society for Propagating the Gospel among the Indians and Others in North America, with a Sketch of the Manner in Which They Mean to Pursue the Object of Their Institution. Boston: Thomas Adams, 1790.
A Brief Account of the Present State of the Society for Propagating the Gospel among the Indians and Others in North-America, with a Sketch of the Manner in Which They Mean to Pursue the Objects of Their Institution. Boston: Thomas Adams, 1791.
A Brief Account of the Society for Propagating the Gospel among the Indians and Others in North America. Boston: n.p., 1798.
Carroll, Betsey. *Piety in Humble Life; or, Life and Recollections of Betsey Carroll.* St. Albans, Vt.: Messenger Steam Print, 1871.
Cary, Richard. *To the Members of the Society for Propagating the Gospel.* Boston: Hall, 1789.
Circular Letters, Containing an Invitation to the Ministers and Churches of Every Christian Denomination in the United States, to Unite in Their Endeavours to Carry into Execution the "Humble Attempt" of President Edwards, to Promote Explicit Agreement and Visible

Union of God's People, in Extraordinary Prayer, for the Revival of Religion and Advancement of Christ's Kingdom on Earth. Concord, N.H.: George Hough, 1798.

Circular Letters from the Woodstock and Stonington Baptist Associations, to Their Respective Churches. Newburyport, Mass.: E. W. Allen, 1806.

Colman, Benjamin. *An Argument for and Persuasive unto the Great and Important Duty of Family Worship, with Rules and Directions for the Due Performance of It.* Boston: Gamaliel Rogers, 1728.

The Constitution of the New Hampshire Missionary Society, Together with an Address to All Christian People. Concord, N.H.: George Hough, 1801.

The Constitution of the Piscataqua Missionary Society, Together with an Address. Portsmouth, N.H.: Samuel Nutting, 1803.

Dewey, Benoni, James Wheelock, and Benjamin Gilbert. *A True and Concise Narrative of the Origin and Progress of the Church Difficulties in the Vicinity of Dartmouth College, in Hanover.* Hanover, N.H.: Charles Spear, 1815.

The Doctrines and Discipline of the Methodist Episcopal Church in America, Revised and Approved at the General Conference Held at Baltimore, in the State of Maryland, in November, 1792, in Which Thomas Coke, and Francis Asbury, Presided, to Which Are Added, the Minutes of the General Conference Held at Baltimore, October 20th, 1796. Ninth ed. Philadelphia: Henry Tuckniss, 1797.

Edwards, Jonathan. *An Account of the Life of the Late Reverend Mr. David Brainerd, Minister of the Gospel, Missionary to the Indians, from the Honourable Society in Scotland, for the Propagation of Christian Knowledge, and Pastor of a Church of Christian Indians in New-Jersey.* Boston: D. Henchman, 1749. Reprint Worcester, Mass.: Leonard Worcester, 1793.

Enfield, William. *Prayers for the Use of Families: A New Edition with Additions, Consisting of Prayers for Congregations, When Destitute of a Minister.* Boston: Belknap and Hall, 1794.

Farmer, John. *An Ecclesiastical Register of New-Hampshire.* Concord, N.H.: Hill and Moore, 1821.

A Form of Discipline, for the Ministers, Preachers and Members (Now Comprehending the Principles and Doctrines) of the Methodist Episcopal Church in America, Considered and Approved at a Conference Held at Baltimore, in the State of Maryland, on Monday the 27th of December, 1784: In Which Thomas Coke, and Francis Asbury, Presided: Arranged under Proper Heads, and Methodised in a More Acceptable and Easy Manner. Sixth ed. Philadelphia: R. Aitken and Son, 1790.

The Funds and Services of the New Hampshire Missionary Society, Being a Continuation of the Statement of Their Affairs. Concord, N.H.: George Hough, 1806.

"The General Association of the Pastors of the Consociated Churches of the Colony of Connecticut, Convened by Delegation at Mansfield, June 22, 1774." Broadside. Norwich, Conn.: Robertsons and Trumbull, 1774.

Gibson, William. *Dialogue Concerning the Doctrines of Atonement between a Calvinist and a Hopkinsian, Wherein a Number of the Arguments on Both Sides of the Question Are Endeavoured to Be Candidly Examined, That the Truth May Appear.* Windsor, Vt.: Alden Spooner, 1803.

Huntingdon, Joseph. *Calvinism Improved.* New London, Conn.: Samuel Green, 1796.

Lee, Jesse. *A Short History of the Methodists in the United States of America, Beginning in 1766 and Continued Till 1809, to Which Is Prefixed a Brief Account of Their Rise in England.* Baltimore: Magill and Clime, 1810.

Mather, Cotton. *Family-Religion, Excited and Assisted.* Boston: Bartholomew Green, 1707.

Minutes of the Bowdoinham Association. Various editions, 1790–1807.

Minutes of the First Fifteen Annual Meetings of the General Convention of Ministers in the State of Vermont, 1795–1810. Montpelier: Polands' Steam Printing Establishment, 1877.

Minutes of the Leyden Association, Holden at Guilford. Greenfield, Vt.: John Denio 1803.

Minutes of the Lincoln Association. Various editions, 1805–1807.

Minutes of the New Hampshire Association. Various editions, 1801–1807.

Minutes of the Vermont Baptist Association. Various editions, 1802–1807.

Minutes of the Woodstock Association. Various editions, 1789–1807.

A Narrative on the Subject of Missions: And a Statement of the Funds of the Connecticut Missionary Society. Hartford: Hudson and Goodwin, 1802.

Newell, Fanny. *Memoirs of Fanny Newell, Written by Herself, and Published at Her Particular Request, and the Desire of Numerous Friends.* Hallowell, Maine: Glazier, 1824.

Niles, Nathaniel. *Secret Prayer Explained and Inculcated, in Four Discourses, on Matthew 6:6.* Boston: John Kneeland, 1773.

Packard, Hezekiah. *The Christian's Manual.* Amherst, N.H.: Samuel Preston, 1801.

———. *Two Discourses on Prayer, Particularly on Family Worship, Preached in Wiscasset, February 12, 1804.* Wiscasset, Maine: Babson and Rust, 1804.

A Prayerbook for the Use of Families; Prepared by the Association of Ministers, on the Piscataqua-River, and Recommended by Them as an Assistant to the Social Devotions of Families. Portsmouth, N.H.: Charles Pierce, 1799.

The Proceedings and Documents Relative to Certain Members Separating from the Church in Wilton. Concord, N.H.: Isaac Hill, 1824.

Proceedings of the General Convention of the Universalian Churches. N.p.: n.p., 1808.

Relly, James. *Union; or, a Treatise on the Consanguinity and Affinity between Christ and His Church.* London: n.p., 1759.

Report of the Trustees of the Maine Missionary Society, June 21, 1818. N.p.: n.p., n.d.

"Report on the Meetinghouse." Dover, 1824. Broadsides Collection, New Hampshire Historical Society, Concord.

Reports Made to the Vermont Missionary Society, September 10, 1818. Middlebury, Vt.: n.p., 1818.

Some Remarks on the "Toleration Act" of 1819, Addressed to the Hon. John Taylor Gilman, by a Friend to the "Public Worship of the Deity." Exeter, N.H.: Samuel T. Moses, 1823.

A Statement of the Affair of the New-Hampshire Missionary Society, Together with an Address to the Public. Concord, N.H.: George Hough, 1803.

To All Who Are Desirous of the Spread of the Gospel of Our Lord Jesus Christ. Boston: n.p., 1799.

Tracts Published by the Lincoln and Kennebec Religious Society. Wiscasset, Maine: Babson and Rust, 1804.

Trustees of the Missionary Society of Connecticut. *A Summary of Christian Doctrine and Practice, Designed Especially for the Use of the People in the New Settlements of the United States of America.* Hartford: Hudson and Goodwin, 1804.

Documentary Editions and Collections

Baxter, James Phinney, ed. *Documentary History of the State of Maine.* Vol. 22. Portland: Fred L. Tower Company, 1916.

Cram, Jacob. *Journal of a Missionary Tour in 1808, Through the New Settlements of Northern New Hampshire and Vermont.* Rochester, N.Y.: Genesee Press of Rochester, 1909.

Howe, Mark deWolfe, ed. *Cases on Church and State in the United States.* Cambridge, Mass.: Harvard University Press, 1952.

Peach, Arthur Wallace, ed. "The Reverend Joel Winch, Pioneer Minister: Selections from His Diaries." *Proceedings of the Vermont Historical Society*, new ser., 9 (1941): 235–270; new ser., 10 (1942): 21–35, 83–103.

Perkins, Nathan. "A Narrative of a Tour through the State of Vermont from April 27 to June 12, 1789." *Vermont Quarterly* 19 (1951): 43–52.

Perley, Jeremiah. *The Debates and Journal of the Constitutional Convention of the State of Maine, 1819–1820*. Augusta: Maine Farmer's Almanac Press, 1894.

Thrift, Minton. *Memoir of the Reverend Jesse Lee with Extracts from His Journals*. New York: N. Bangs and T. Mason, 1823. Reprint New York: Arno Press, 1969.

Wentworth, William Edgar, ed. *Journals of Enoch Hayes Place*. Vol. 1 (1810–1849). Boston: New England Historic Genealogical Society and the New Hampshire Society of Genealogists, 1998.

Woodman, Cyrus, ed. "Memoir and Journals of Rev. Paul Coffin, D.D., of Buxton, Me." *Collections of the Maine Historical Society* 4 (1856): 239–406.

Government Documents

Acts and Laws of the Commonwealth of Massachusetts. Boston, 1890–1898.

Acts and Laws Passed by the Legislature of the State of Vermont, October 1807. Randolph, Vt.: Sereno Wright, 1807.

Acts and Laws Passed by the Legislature of the State of Vermont, 1812. Danville, Vt.: Ebenezer Eaton, 1812.

Acts and Resolves of Massachusetts. Boston: various publishers, 1889.

Acts and Resolves Passed by the Legislature of the State of Maine. Augusta: various publishers, 1850–1869.

Bouton, Nathaniel, ed. *New Hampshire Provincial and State Papers*, vols. 9–10. Concord, N.H.: Edward A. Jenks, 1867, 1877.

A Constitution and Form of Government for the State of Massachusetts-Bay. Boston: J. Gill, 1778.

Decisions of the Superior and Supreme Court of New Hampshire, from 1802 to 1809, and from 1813 to 1816, Selected from the Manuscript Records of the Late Jeremiah Smith. Boston: Little, Brown, 1879.

General Petitions. Vols. 8–11, *State Papers of Vermont*. Montpelier, Vt.: various publishers, 1952–1962.

Journal of the Honorable Senate of the State of New-Hampshire (June Session, 1819). Concord, N.H.: Hill and Moore, 1819.

Journal of the House of Representatives of the State of New-Hampshire (June Session, 1819). Concord, N.H.: Hill and Moore, 1819.

Journals and Proceedings of the General Assembly of the State of Vermont, Part II, Vol. 3, *State Papers of Vermont*. Bellows Falls, Vt.: P. H. Gobie Press, 1925.

Journals of the General Assembly of the State of Vermont, 1803–1824. Windsor, Vt.: various publishers, 1804–1824.

Laws of New Hampshire. Vols. 5–9. Concord, N.H.: Evans Printing Company, 1916–1921.

Laws of the Commonwealth of Massachusetts, 1809–1812. Vol. 5. Boston: Adams, Rhoads, 1812.

Laws of the Commonwealth of Massachusetts, 1815–1818. Boston: Russell, Cutler, 1818.

Laws of the State of New Hampshire, Passed June Session 1865. Concord, N.H.: George E. Jenks, 1865.

Laws of the State of Maine. Hallowell: Glazer, Masters, 1830.

Laws of the State of Vermont, 1797. Rutland, Vt.: Josiah Fay, 1798.

Laws of the State of Vermont (October Session, 1821): Public Acts. N.p.: n.p., 1821.
Laws of Vermont. Vols. 12–16, *State Papers of Vermont.* Montpelier, Vt.: various publishers, 1964–1968.
Laws of Vermont, 1827. Burlington, Vt.: D. Clark, 1827.
Laws Passed by the Legislature of the State of Vermont, 1813–1819. Rutland, Vt.: various publishers, 1813–1819.
Maine Reports. Vols. 1–9. Hallowell and Portland: various publishers, 1822–1834.
The New Hampshire Reports. Vols. 8–38. Orford, N.H.: Equity Publishing, 1838–1860.
Private and Special Laws of the State of Maine. Vol. 2. Augusta: William R. Smith and Company, 1842.
Public Acts of the State of Maine. Vols. 1–3. Portland: various publishers, 1821–1831.
Public Laws of the State of Maine. Vols. 1–2. Brunswick: J. Griffin, 1821.
Reports of Cases Argued and Determined in the Superior Court of Judicature for the State of New Hampshire, 1819–1823. Exeter, N.H.: various publishers,1819–1824.
Resolves of the State of Maine (1820–1828). Vol. 1. Portland: Thomas Todd, 1828.
Special Laws of the State of Maine (1820–28). Vol. 1. Augusta: Sprague, Owen, and Nash, 1874.

Periodicals

The Adviser; or, Vermont Evangelical Magazine (Middlebury). 1809–1815.
The American Sunday School Magazine (Philadelphia). 1824–1830.
Christian Herald (Portsmouth, N.H.). 1818–1825.
Christian Intelligencer (Portland, Maine). 1821–1827.
Christian Intelligencer and Eastern Chronicle (Gardiner, Maine). 1827–1834.
Christian Monitor (Hallowell, Maine). 1814–1818.
Christian Observer (Boston). 1802–1866.
Christian Repository (Woodstock, Vt.). 1820–1825.
The Christian's Magazine, Reviewer, and Religious Intelligencer (Portsmouth, N.H.). 1805–1808.
Concord (New Hampshire) Observer. 1819–1822.
Connecticut Evangelical Magazine (Hartford). 1800–1807.
Eastern Argus (Portland, Maine). 1803–1863.
Evangelical Monitor (Woodstock, Vt.). 1821–1824.
Herald of Gospel Liberty (Portsmouth, N.H.). 1808–1930.
Massachusetts Baptist Missionary Magazine (Boston). 1803–1816.
Methodist Magazine (New York). 1818–1828.
New England Missionary Intelligencer (Concord, N.Y.). 1819.
New England Observer (Keene, N.H.). 1826.
New Hampshire Chronicle (Dover). 1830–1832.
New Hampshire Gazette (Portsmouth). 1793–1847.
New Hampshire Patriot (Concord). 1809–1819.
Piscataqua Evangelical Magazine (Amherst, N.H.). 1805–1808.
Religious Informer (Enfield, N.H.). 1819–1821, 1823–1825.
Religious Intelligencer (New Haven, Conn.). 1816–1837.
A Religious Magazine (Portland, Maine). 1811–1822.
Trumpet and Universalist Magazine (Boston). 1828–1851.
Universalist Magazine (Boston). 1819–1828.
Vermont Baptist Missionary Magazine (Rutland). 1811–1812.
Vermont Chronicle and the Windham Advertiser (Westminster). 1796.
Zion's Herald (Boston). 1823–1841.

Secondary Sources

Albanese, Catherine L. *Nature Religion in America from the Algonkian Indians to the New Age*. Chicago: University of Chicago Press, 1990.

———. "Savages, Sinners, and Saved: Davy Crockett, Camp Meetings, and the Wild Frontier." *American Quarterly* 33 (1981): 482–501.

Allen, Stephen, and W. H. Pillsbury. *History of Methodism in Maine*. Augusta: Charles E. Nash, 1887.

Anderson, Benedict. *Imagined Communities: Reflections on the Origins and Spread of Nationalism*. London: Verso, 1983.

Andrews, Dee E. *The Methodists and Revolutionary America, 1760–1800: The Shaping of an Evangelical Culture*. Princeton, N.J.: Princeton University Press, 2000.

Banks, Ronald F. *Maine Becomes a State: The Movement to Separate Maine from Massachusetts, 1785–1820*. Middletown, Conn.: Wesleyan University Press, 1970.

Bassett, T. D. Seymour. *Gods of the Hills: Piety and Society in Nineteenth-Century Vermont*. Montpelier: Vermont Historical Society, 2000.

Baxter, Norman Allen. *History of the Freewill Baptists: A Study in New England Separatism*. Rochester, N.Y.: American Baptist Historical Society, 1957.

Beeman, Richard, Stephen Botein, and Edward C. Carter II, eds. *Beyond Confederation: Origins of the Constitution and American National Identity*. Chapel Hill: University of North Carolina Press, 1987.

Benes, Peter, ed. *Itinerancy in New England and New York: The Dublin Seminar for New England Folklife Annual Proceedings*. Boston: Boston University Press, 1986.

———, ed. *New England Meeting House and Church: 1630–1850*. Boston: Boston University Press, 1979.

Beneke, Chris, and Christopher S. Grenda, eds. *The First Prejudice: Religious Tolerance and Intolerance in Early America*. Philadelphia: University of Pennsylvania Press, 2011.

Bercovitch, Sacvan. *The Puritan Origins of the American Self*. New Haven, Conn.: Yale University Press, 1975.

Boles, John B. *The Great Revival, 1787–1805*. Lexington: University Press of Kentucky, 1972.

———."Turner, the Frontier, and the Study of Religion in America." *Journal of the Early Republic* 13 (1993): 205–216.

Bonomi, Patricia U., and Peter R. Eisenstadt. "Church Adherence in the Eighteenth-Century British American Colonies." *William and Mary Quarterly*, 3rd ser., 39 (1982): 245–286.

Bordin, Ruth B. "The Sect to Denomination Process in America: The Freewill Baptist Experience." *Church History* 34 (1965): 77–94.

Brauer, Jerald C. "Regionalism and Religion in America." *Church History* 54 (1985): 366–378.

Breen, T. H. *The Marketplace of Revolution: How Consumer Politics Shaped American Independence*. New York: Oxford University Press, 2005.

Brekus, Catherine A., ed. *The Religious History of American Women: Reimagining the Past*. Chapel Hill: University of North Carolina Press, 2007.

———. *Strangers and Pilgrims: Female Preaching in America, 1740–1845*. Chapel Hill: University of North Carolina Press, 1998.

Bressler, Ann Lee. *The Universalist Movement in America, 1770–1880*. New York: Oxford University Press, 2001.

Brown, Candy Gunther. *The Word in the World: Evangelical Writing, Publishing, and Reading in America, 1789–1880*. Chapel Hill: University of North Carolina Press, 2004.

Brown-Groover, Mary-Agnes. "From Concord, Massachusetts to the Wilderness: The Brown Family Letters, 1792–1852." *New England Historical and Genealogical Register* 131 (1977): 28–39, 113–120, 200–206.

Burg, B. R. "The Cambridge Platform: A Reassertion of Ecclesiastical Authority." *Church History* 43 (1974): 470–487.
Burrage, Henry S. *History of the Baptists in Maine*. Portland: Marks Printing House, 1904.
Bushman, Richard L. *The Refinement of America: Persons, Houses, Cities*. New York: Vintage Books, 1993.
Butler, Jon. *Awash in a Sea of Faith: Christianizing the American People*. Cambridge, Mass.: Harvard University Press, 1990.
Canup, John. *Out of the Wilderness: The Emergence of an American Identity in Colonial New England*. Middletown, Conn.: Wesleyan University Press, 1990.
Carroll, Peter N. *Puritanism and the Wilderness: The Intellectual Significance of the New England Frontier*. New York: Columbia University Press, 1969.
Carter, Michael D. *Converting the Wasteplaces of Zion: The Maine Missionary Society (1807–1862)*. Wolfeboro, N.H.: Longwood Academic, 1990.
Cassara, Ernest, ed. *Universalism in America: A Documentary History*. Boston: Beacon Press, 1971.
Chase, Mary Ellen. *Jonathan Fisher: Maine Parson, 1768–1847*. New York: Macmillan, 1948.
Cherry, Conrad. *Nature and Religious Imagination from Edwards to Bushnell*. Philadelphia: Fortress Press, 1980.
Clark, Calvin M. *History of the Congregational Churches in Maine*. Vol. 2. Portland: Congregational Christian Conference of Maine, 1935.
Clark, Charles E. *The Eastern Frontier: The Settlement of Northern New England, 1610–1763*. Hanover, N.H.: University Press of New England, 1983.
Clark, Charles E., James S. Leamon, and Karen Bowden, eds. *Maine in the Early Republic: From Revolution to Statehood*. Hanover, N.H.: University Press of New England, 1988.
Clark, J. C. D. *The Language of Liberty, 1660–1832: Political Discourse and Social Dynamics in the Anglo-American World*. Cambridge: Cambridge University Press, 1994.
Clarke, L. D. "Vermont Lands and the Society for the Propagation of the Gospel." *New England Quarterly* 3 (1930): 279–286.
Cohen, Charles Lloyd. *God's Caress: The Psychology of Puritan Religious Experience*. New York: Oxford University Press, 1986.
———. "Puritanism." In *Encyclopedia of the North American Colonies*, edited by Jacob Ernest Cook et al., 577–593. New York: C. Scribner's Sons, 1993.
Cole, Otis, and Oliver S. Baketel, eds. *History of the New Hampshire Conference of the Methodist Episcopal Church*. New York: Methodist Book Concern, 1929.
Comstock, John M. *The Congregational Churches of Vermont and Their Ministry, 1762–1942*. St. Johnsbury, Vt.: Cowles Press, 1942.
Conforti, Joseph. *Imagining New England: Explorations of Regional Identity from the Pilgrims to the Mid-Twentieth Century*. Chapel Hill: University of North Carolina Press, 2001.
———. *Jonathan Edwards, Religious Tradition, and American Culture*. Chapel Hill: University of North Carolina Press, 1995.
———. *Samuel Hopkins and the New Divinity Movement: Calvinism, the Congregational Ministry, and Reform in New England between the Great Awakenings*. Grand Rapids, Mich.: Christian University Press, 1981.
Conkin, Paul K. *American Originals: Homemade Varieties of American Christianity*. Chapel Hill: University of North Carolina Press, 1997.
———. *Cane Ridge: America's Pentecost*. Madison: University of Wisconsin Press, 1990.
———. *The Uneasy Center: Reformed Christianity in Antebellum America*. Chapel Hill: University of North Carolina Press, 1995.
Cowing, Cedric B. *The Saving Remnant: Religion and the Settling of New England*. Urbana: University of Illinois Press, 1995.

———. "Sex and Preaching in the Great Awakening." *American Quarterly* 20 (1968): 624–644.

Crawford, Michael J. *Seasons of Grace: Colonial New England's Revival Tradition in Its British Context.* New York: Oxford University Press, 1991.

Curry, Thomas J. *The First Freedoms: Church and State in America to the Passage of the First Amendment.* New York: Oxford University Press, 1986.

Cushing, John D. "Notes on Disestablishment in Massachusetts, 1780–1833." *William and Mary Quarterly,* 3rd ser., 26 (1969): 169–190.

Daniell, Jere R. *Experiment in Republicanism: New Hampshire Politics and the American Revolution, 1741–1794.* Cambridge, Mass.: Harvard University Press, 1970.

Davidson, Cathy N., ed. *Reading in America: Literature and Social History.* Baltimore: Johns Hopkins University Press, 1989.

———. *Revolution and the Word: The Rise of the Novel in America.* New York: Oxford University Press, 1986.

DeBoer, John C., and Clara Merritt DeBoer. "The Formation of Town Churches: Church, Town, and State in Early Vermont." *Vermont History* 64 (1996): 69–88.

Delbanco, Andrew. *The Puritan Ordeal.* Cambridge, Mass.: Harvard University Press, 1989.

DeRogatis, Amy. *Moral Geography: Maps, Missionaries, and the American Frontier.* New York: Columbia University Press, 2003.

Dorsey, Peter. *Sacred Estrangement.* University Park: Pennsylvania State University Press, 1993.

Doyle, William. *The Vermont Political Tradition and Those Who Helped Make It.* Montpelier, Vt.: Northlight Studio Press, 1984.

Elsbree, Oliver Wendell. "The Rise of the Missionary Spirit in New England, 1790–1815." *New England Quarterly* 1 (1928): 295–322.

Ericson, Jack T. "Missionary Society of Connecticut Papers, 1759–1948: A Guide to the Microfilm Edition." Typescript. Glen Rock, N.J.: Microfilming Corporation of America, 1976.

Eslinger, Ellen. *Citizens of Zion: The Social Origins of Camp Meeting Revivalism.* Knoxville: University of Tennessee Press, 1999.

Finke, Roger, and Rodney Stark. *The Churching of America, 1776–1990: Winners and Losers in Our Religious Economy.* New Brunswick, N.J.: Rutgers University Press, 1992.

Foster, Charles I. *An Errand of Mercy: The Evangelical United Front, 1790–1837.* Chapel Hill: University of North Carolina Press, 1960.

Foster, Stephen. *The Long Argument: English Puritanism and the Shaping of New England Culture, 1570–1700.* Chapel Hill: University of North Carolina Press, 1991.

Frederic, Paul B. "We're Out of Here! Leaving Nineteenth-Century Rural Northern New England: Diaspora from the Town of Industry, Maine." Paper presented at the Washburn Humanities Seminar, Livermore, Maine, June 2–4, 2005.

Fuller, Robert C. *Religious Revolutionaries: The Rebels Who Shaped American Religion.* New York: Palgrave Macmillan, 2004.

———. *Spiritual, but Not Religious: Understanding Unchurched America.* New York: Oxford University Press, 2001.

Gaustad, Edwin S. *Faith of Our Fathers: Religion and the New Nation.* San Francisco: Harper and Row, 1987.

Gaustad, Edwin Scott, and Philip L. Barlow. *New Historical Atlas of Religion in America.* New York: Oxford University Press, 2001.

Gillespie, Joanna Bowen. "'The Clear Leadings of Providence': Pious Memoirs and the Problems of Self-Realization for Women in the Early Nineteenth Century." *Journal of the Early Republic* 5 (1985): 197–221.

Gilmore, William J. *Reading Becomes a Necessity of Life: Material and Cultural Life in Rural New England, 1780–1835.* Knoxville: University of Tennessee Press, 1989.

Goodykoontz, Colin Brummitt. *Home Missions on the American Frontier, with Particular Reference to the American Home Missionary Society.* Caldwell, Idaho: Caxton Printers, 1939.

Gordon, Sarah Barringer. "The Landscape of Belief: Disestablishment and Property." Paper presented at the Society for Historians of the Early American Republic, Baltimore, July 20, 2012.

Gribbin, William. "Vermont's Universalist Controversy of 1824." *Vermont History* 41 (1973): 82–94.

Griffiths, Paul J. *Religious Reading: The Place of Reading in the Practice of Religion.* New York: Oxford University Press, 1999.

Grossbart, Stephen R. "Seeking Divine Favor: Conversion and Church Admission in Eastern Connecticut, 1711–1832." *William and Mary Quarterly,* 3rd ser., 46 (1989): 696–740.

Gundersen, Joan R. "Kith and Kin: Women's Networks in Colonial Virginia." In *The Devil's Lane: Sex and Race in the Early South,* edited by Catherine Clinton and Michele Gillespie, 90–108. New York: Oxford University Press, 1997.

———. "The Non-Institutional Church: The Religious Role of Women in Eighteenth-Century Virginia." *The Historical Magazine of the Protestant Episcopal Church* 51 (1982): 347–357.

Habermas, Jürgen. *The Structural Transformation of the Public Sphere: An Inquiry into a Category of Bourgeois Society.* Cambridge, Mass.: MIT Press, 1991.

Hall, David D., ed. *Lived Religion in America: Toward a History of a Practice.* Princeton, N.J.: Princeton University Press, 1997.

———. "Toward a History of Popular Religion in Early New England." *William and Mary Quarterly,* 3rd ser., 41 (1984): 49–55.

———. *Worlds of Wonder, Days of Judgment: Popular Religious Belief in Early New England.* New York: Knopf, 1989.

Hall, Timothy D. *Contested Boundaries: Itinerancy and the Shaping of the Colonial American Religious World.* Durham, N.C.: Duke University Press, 1994.

Hambrick-Stowe, Charles E. *The Practice of Piety: Puritan Devotional Disciplines in Seventeenth-Century New England.* Chapel Hill: University of North Carolina Press, 1982.

———. "The Spiritual Pilgrimage of Sarah Osborn (1714–1796)." *Church History* 61 (1992): 408–421.

Handy, Robert T. "American Methodism and Its Historical Frontier: Interpreting Methodism on the Western Frontier, between Romanticism and Realism." *Methodist History* 23 (1984): 44–53.

Hansen, Karen V. *A Very Social Time: Crafting Community in Antebellum New England.* Berkeley: University of California Press, 1994.

Haroutunian, Joseph. *Piety versus Moralism: The Passing of the New England Theology.* New York: Henry Holt, 1932.

Hatch, Nathan O. *The Democratization of American Christianity.* New Haven, Conn.: Yale University Press, 1989.

———. "The Puzzle of American Methodism." *Church History* 63 (1994): 175–189.

Hatch, Nathan O., and John H. Wigger, eds. *Methodism and the Shaping of American Culture.* Nashville: Kingswood Books, 2001.

Hazen, Henry A. *The Congregational and Presbyterian Ministry and Churches of New Hampshire.* Boston: Alfred Mudge and Son, 1875.

Heimert, Alan. "Puritanism, the Wilderness, and the Frontier." *New England Quarterly* 26 (1953): 361–382.

Heitzenrater, Richard P. "At Full Liberty: Doctrinal Standards in Early American Methodism." *Quarterly Review* 5 (1985): 6–27.

Heyrman, Christine Leigh. *Commerce and Culture: The Maritime Communities of Colonial Massachusetts, 1690–1750*. New York: Norton, 1984.

———. *Southern Cross: The Beginnings of the Bible Belt*. Chapel Hill: University of North Carolina Press, 1997.

Hill, Samuel S. "Religion and Region in America." *Annals of the American Academy of Political and Social Science* 480 (1985): 132–141.

History of Coos County, New Hampshire. Syracuse: W. A. Fergusson, 1888.

Holifield, E. Brooks. *Theology in America: Christian Thought from the Age of the Puritans to the Civil War*. New Haven, Conn.: Yale University Press, 2003.

Hughes, Peter. "Early New England Universalism: A Family Religion." *Journal of Unitarian Universalist History* 26 (1999): 93–113.

———. "The Origins of New England Universalism: A Religion without a Founder." *Journal of Unitarian Universalist History* 24 (1997): 31–63.

Innes, Stephen. *Creating the Commonwealth: The Economic Culture of Puritan New England*. New York: Norton, 1995.

Isaac, Rhys. *The Transformation of Virginia, 1740–1790*. New York: Norton, 1982.

Jackson, Kenneth T. *Crabgrass Frontier: The Suburbanization of the United States*. New York: Oxford University Press, 1987.

Jaffee, David. *People of the Wachusett: Greater New England in History and Memory, 1630–1860*. Ithaca, N.Y.: Cornell University Press, 1999.

Johnson, Paul E. *A Shopkeeper's Millennium: Society and Revivals in Rochester, New York, 1815–1837*. New York: Hill and Wang, 1978.

Juster, Susan. *Disorderly Women: Sexual Politics and Evangelicalism in Revolutionary New England*. Ithaca, N.Y.: Cornell University Press, 1994.

Juster, Susan, and Ellen Hartigan-O'Connor. "The 'Angel Delusion' of 1806–1811: Frustration and Fantasy in Northern New England." *Journal of the Early Republic* 22 (2002): 375–404.

Kaplanoff, Mark D. "Religion and Righteousness: A Study of Federalist Rhetoric in the New Hampshire Election of 1800." *Historical New Hampshire* 23 (1968): 3–20.

Kelley, Mary. "'Pen and Ink Communion': Evangelical Reading and Writing in Antebellum America." *New England Quarterly* 84 (2011): 555–587.

Kelly, Catherine E. "'Well Bred Country People': Sociability, Social Networks, and the Creation of a Provincial Middle Class, 1820–1860." *Journal of the Early Republic* 19 (1999): 451–479.

Kerber, Linda K. *Women of the Republic: Intellect and Ideology in Revolutionary America*. Chapel Hill: University of North Carolina Press, 1980.

Kern, Charles W. *God, Grace, and Granite: The History of Methodism in New Hampshire, 1768–1988*. Canaan, N.H.: Phoenix Publishing, 1988.

Kilby, William Henry. *Eastport and Passamaquoddy: A Collection of Historical and Biographical Sketches*. Eastport, Maine: Edward E. Shead, 1888.

Kinney, Charles B., Jr. *Church and State: The Struggle for Separation in New Hampshire*. New York: Teachers College of Columbia University, 1955.

Kling, David W. *A Field of Divine Wonders: The New Divinity and Village Revivals in Northwestern Connecticut, 1792–1822*. University Park: Pennsylvania State University Press, 1993.

Kruman, Marc W. *Between Authority and Liberty: State Constitution Making in Revolutionary America*. Chapel Hill: University of North Carolina Press, 1997.

LaCelle-Peterson, Kristina Marie. "'I Got Religion': Men, Women, and Theology in Evangelical Conversion Narratives in the Early Republic." Ph.D. dissertation, Drew University, 2001.

Lacey, Barbara E. "The World of Hannah Heaton: The Autobiography of an Eighteenth-Century Connecticut Farm Woman." *William and Mary Quarterly,* 3rd ser., 45 (1988): 280–304.

Lambert, Frank. *The Founding Fathers and the Place of Religion in America.* Princeton, N.J.: Princeton University Press, 2003.

———. *Inventing the Great Awakening.* Princeton, N.J.: Princeton University Press, 1999.

Lane, Belden C. "Giving Voice to Place: Three Models for Understanding American Sacred Space." *Religion and American Culture* 11 (2001): 53–81.

———. *Landscapes of the Sacred: Geography and Narrative in American Spirituality.* Baltimore: Johns Hopkins University Press, 2001.

Latham, Charles, Jr. "Church and State in Thetford." *Vermont History News* 45 (1994): 61–64.

Leavelle, Tracy Neal. "Geographies of Encounter: Religion and Contested Spaces in Colonial America." *American Quarterly* 56 (2004): 913–943.

Levy, Leonard W. *The Establishment Clause: Religion and the First Amendment.* New York: Macmillan, 1986.

Lindman, Janet Moore. "Beyond the Meetinghouse: Gender and Religion in Early America." Paper presented at Women and American Religion: Reimagining the Past, Chicago, October 8–10, 2003.

———. *Bodies of Belief: Baptist Community in Early America.* Philadelphia: University of Pennsylvania Press, 2008.

Linenthal, Edward T., and David Chidester, eds. *American Sacred Space.* Bloomington: Indiana University Press, 1995.

Lippy, Charles. *Being Religious, American Style: A History of Popular Religiosity in the United States.* Westport, Conn.: Greenwood Press, 1994.

———. "The 1780 Massachusetts Constitution: Religious Establishment or Civil Religion?" *Journal of Church and State* 20 (1978): 533–549.

Lockridge, Kenneth. *Literacy in Colonial New England: An Enquiry into the Social Context of Literacy in the Early Modern West.* New York: Norton, 1974.

Loveland, Anne C., and Otis B. Wheeler. *From Meetinghouse to Megachurch: A Material and Cultural History.* Columbia: University of Missouri Press, 2003.

Lowance, Mason I. *The Language of Canaan: Metaphor and Symbol in New England from the Puritans to the Transcendentalists.* Cambridge, Mass.: Harvard University Press, 1980.

Ludlum, David M. *Social Ferment in Vermont, 1791–1850.* New York: Columbia University Press, 1939.

Lyerly, Cynthia Lynn. *Methodism and the Southern Mind, 1770–1810.* New York: Oxford University Press, 1998.

MacDonald, Edith Fox. *Rebellion in the Mountains: The Story of Universalism and Unitarianism in Vermont.* Concord, N.H.: New Hampshire Vermont District of the Unitarian Universalist Association, 1976.

Maffly-Kipp, Laurie F. *Religion and Society in Frontier California.* New Haven, Conn.: Yale University Press, 1994.

Marini, Stephen A. "The Origins of Universalism: Daughter of the New Light." *Journal of Unitarian Universalist History* 24 (1997): 64–75.

———. *Radical Sects of Revolutionary New England.* Cambridge, Mass.: Harvard University Press, 1982.

Mathews, Donald G. "The Second Great Awakening as an Organizing Process, 1780–1830: An Hypothesis." *American Quarterly* 21 (1969): 23–43.

McCarthy, Molly. "A Pocketful of Days: Pocket Diaries and Daily Record Keeping among Nineteenth-Century New England Women." *New England Quarterly* 73 (2000): 274–296.

McClymond, Michael J., ed. *Embodying the Spirit: New Perspectives on North American Revivalism.* Baltimore: Johns Hopkins University Press, 2004.

McLoughlin, William G. "The Bench, the Church, and the Republican Party in New Hampshire, 1790–1820." *Historical New Hampshire* 20 (1965): 3–31.

———. *New England Dissent, 1630–1883: The Baptists and the Separation of Church and State.* 2 vols. Cambridge, Mass.: Harvard University Press, 1971.

Mead, Sidney E. "The American People: Their Space, Time, and Religion." *Journal of Religion* 34 (1954): 244–255.

———. *The Lively Experiment: The Shaping of Christianity in America.* New York: Harper and Row, 1963.

Meinig, D. W., ed. *The Interpretation of Ordinary Landscapes: Geographical Essays.* New York: Oxford University Press, 1979.

Merill, Geirgia Drew, ed. *History of Carroll County, New Hampshire.* Boston: W. A. Fergusson, 1889.

Miller, Perry. *Nature's Nation.* Cambridge, Mass.: Belknap Press of Harvard University Press, 1967.

———. *The New England Mind: From Colony to Province.* Cambridge, Mass.: Belknap Press of Harvard University Press, 1953.

Miyakawa, T. Scott. *Protestants and Pioneers: Individualism and Conformity on the American Frontier.* Chicago: University of Chicago Press, 1964.

Monaghan, E. Jennifer. *Learning to Read and Write in Colonial America.* Amherst: University of Massachusetts Press, 2005.

Morgan, Edmund S. *Inventing the People: The Rise of Popular Sovereignty in England and America.* New York: Norton, 1988.

Mudge, James. *History of the New England Conference of the Methodist Episcopal Church, 1796–1910.* Boston: New England Conference, 1910.

Mullin, Robert Bruce, and Russell E. Richey, eds. *Reimagining Denominationalism: Interpretive Essays.* New York: Oxford University Press, 1994.

Murphy, Andrew R. *Conscience and Community: Revisiting Toleration and Religious Dissent in Early Modern England and North America.* University Park: Pennsylvania State University Press, 2001.

Musgrove, Richard W. *History of the Town of Bristol, Grafton County, New Hampshire.* Vol. 1. Somersworth: New Hampshire Publishing Company, 1976.

Najar, Monica. *Evangelizing the South: A Social History of Church and State in Early America.* New York: Oxford University Press, 2008.

Nartonis, David K. "The 'New Divinity' Movement and Its Impact on New Hampshire's Town Churches, 1769–1849." *Historical New Hampshire* 55 (2000): 25–40.

Nash, Roderick. *Wilderness and the American Mind.* New Haven, Conn.: Yale University Press, 1967.

Neem, Johann N. "The Elusive Common Good: Religion and Civil Society in Massachusetts, 1780–1833." *Journal of the Early Republic* 24 (2004): 381–417.

Newton, W. M. "Old Weston Circuit: The Early Days of Methodism in Windsor and Bennington, Vt." n.d. MSS 23–87. Vermont Historical Society, Barre.

Nobles, Gregory H. *American Frontiers: Cultural Encounters and Continental Conquest.* New York: Hill and Wang, 1997.

Noll, Mark A. *America's God: From Jonathan Edwards to Abraham Lincoln.* New York: Oxford University Press, 2002.

Noll, Mark A., David W. Bebbington, and George A. Rawlyk, eds. *Evangelicalism: Comparative Studies of Popular Protestantism in North America, the British Isles, and Beyond, 1700–1990.* New York: Oxford University Press, 1994.

Nord, David Paul. “The Evangelical Origins of Mass Media in America, 1815–1835.” *Journalism Monographs*, no. 88 (1984): 1–31.

———. *Faith in Reading: Religious Publishing and the Birth of Mass Media in America*. New York: Oxford University Press, 2004.

Nordbeck, Elizabeth C. “Almost Awakened: The Great Revival in New Hampshire and Maine, 1727–1748.” *Historical New Hampshire* 35 (1980): 23–58.

Norton, Mary Beth. “‘My Resting Reaping Times’: Sarah Osborn’s Defense of Her ‘Unfeminine’ Activities.” *Signs* 2 (1976): 512–529.

O’Brien, Susan. “A Transatlantic Community of Saints: The Great Awakening and the First Evangelical Network, 1735–1755.” *American Historical Review* 91 (1986): 811–832

Oliphant, J. Orin. “The American Missionary Spirit, 1828–1835.” *Church History* 7 (1938): 125–137.

One Hundred Years of Home Missionary Work in Vermont by the Congregational Churches. N.p.: Vermont Domestic Missionary Society, 1901.

Orsi, Robert A. *Between Heaven and Earth: The Religious Worlds People Make and the Scholars Who Study Them*. Princeton, N.J.: Princeton University Press, 2005.

Osterud, Nancy Grey. *Bonds of Community: The Lives of Farm Women in Nineteenth-Century New York*. Ithaca, N.Y.: Cornell University Press, 1991.

Pearson, Samuel C., Jr. “From Church to Denomination: American Congregationalism in the Nineteenth Century.” *Church History* 38 (1969): 67–87.

Perlmann, Joel, and Dennis Shirley. “When Did New England Women Acquire Literacy?” *William and Mary Quarterly*, 3rd ser., 48 (1991): 50–67.

Perlmann, Joel, Silvana R. Siddali, and Kevin Whitescarver. “Literacy, Schooling, and Teaching among New England Woman, 1730–1820.” *History of Education Quarterly* 37 (1997): 117–139.

Peters, Ronald M., Jr. *The Massachusetts Constitution of 1780: A Social Compact*. Amherst: University of Massachusetts Press, 1978.

Peterson, Mark A. *The Price of Redemption: The Spiritual Economy of Puritan New England*. Stanford, Calif.: Stanford University Press, 1997.

Pillsbury, W. H. *History of Methodism in East Maine*. Augusta: Charles E. Nash, 1887.

Potash, P. Jeffrey. *Vermont’s Burned-over District: Patterns of Community Development and Religious Activity, 1761–1850*. Brooklyn: Carlson, 1991.

Putnam, Herbert E. “Vermont Population Trends: 1790 to 1930 as Revealed in the Census Reports.” *Proceedings of the Vermont Historical Society*, new ser., 9 (1941): 14–26.

Rawlyk, George. *Ravished by the Spirit: Religious Revivals, Baptists, and Henry Alline*. Kingston, Ontario: McGill-Queen’s University Press, 1984.

Ricard, Laura Broderick. “The Northern New England ‘New Light’ Clergy and ‘Declension’ Reconsidered.” *Historical New Hampshire* 42 (1987): 125–149.

Richey, Russell E., ed. *Denominationalism*. Nashville: Abingdon, 1977.

———. “From Quarterly to Camp Meeting: A Reconsideration of Early American Methodism.” *Methodist History* 23 (1988): 199–213.

Robins, Roger. “Vernacular American Landscape: Methodists, Camp Meetings, and Social Respectability.” *Religion and American Culture* 4 (1994): 165–191.

Roeber, A. G. *Palatines, Liberty, and Property: German Lutherans in Colonial British America*. Baltimore: Johns Hopkins University Press, 1998.

Rohrer, James R. *Keepers of the Covenant: Frontier Missions and the Decline of Congregationalism*. New York: Oxford University Press, 1995.

Rohrer, S. Scott. *Wandering Souls: Protestant Migrations in America, 1630–1865*. Chapel Hill: University of North Carolina Press, 2010.

Rorabaugh, W. J. *The Alcoholic Republic: An American Tradition*. New York: Oxford University Press, 1981.

Roth, Randolph A. *The Democratic Dilemma: Religion, Reform, and the Social Order in the Connecticut River Valley of Vermont, 1791–1850*. Cambridge: Cambridge University Press, 1987.

Rothenberg, Winifred Barr. *From Market-Places to a Market Economy: The Transformation of Rural Massachusetts, 1750–1850*. Chicago: University of Chicago Press, 1992.

Ryan, Mary P. *Cradle of the Middle Class: The Family in Oneida County, New York, 1790–1865*. Cambridge: Cambridge University Press, 1981.

Salinger, Sharon V. *Taverns and Drinking in Early America*. Baltimore: Johns Hopkins University Press, 2004.

Sassi, Jonathan D. *A Republic of Righteousness: The Public Christianity of the Post-Revolutionary New England Clergy*. New York: Oxford University Press, 2001.

Scales, John. *History of Strafford County, Hew Hampshire, and Representative Citizens*. Chicago: Richmond-Arnold Publishing, 1914.

Schantz, Mark S. "Religious Tracts, Evangelical Reform, and the Market Revolution in Antebellum America." *Journal of the Early Republic* 17 (1997): 425–466.

Schmidt, Leigh Eric. *Hearing Things: Religion, Illusion, and the American Enlightenment*. Cambridge, Mass.: Harvard University Press, 2000.

———. *Holy Fairs: Scottish Communions and American Revivals in the Early Modern Period*. Princeton, N.J.: Princeton University Press, 1989.

Schneider, A. Gregory. *The Way of the Cross Leads Home: The Domestication of American Methodism*. Bloomington: Indiana University Press, 1993.

Seeman, Erik R. "Lay Conversion Narratives: Investigating Ministerial Intervention." *New England Quarterly* 71 (1998): 629–634.

———. *Pious Persuasions: Laity and Clergy in Eighteenth-Century New England*. Baltimore: Johns Hopkins University Press, 1999.

Sehat, David. *The Myth of American Religious Freedom*. New York: Oxford University Press, 2011.

Sewall, Jotham. *A Memoir of Rev. Jotham Sewall of Chesterville, Maine, by His Son*. Boston: Tappan and Whittemore, 1853.

Shalhope, Robert E. *A Tale of New England: The Diaries of Hiram Harwood, Vermont Farmer, 1810–1837*. Baltimore: Johns Hopkins University Press, 2003.

Shea, Daniel B., Jr. *Spiritual Autobiography in Early America*. Princeton, N.J.: Princeton University Press, 1968.

Sheils, Richard D. "The Feminization of American Congregationalism, 1730–1835." *American Quarterly* 33 (1981): 46–62.

Sherman, Michael, Gene Sessions, and P. Jeffrey Potash. *Freedom and Unity: A History of Vermont*. Barre: Vermont Historical Society, 2004.

Shields David S. *Civil Tongues and Polite Letters in British America*. Chapel Hill: University of North Carolina Press, 1997.

Shivell, Kirk. *The Steeples of Old New England: How the Yankees Reached for Heaven*. Marina Del Rey, Calif.: Lighthouse Press, 1998.

Slotkin, Richard. *Regeneration through Violence: The Mythology of the American Frontier, 1600–1860*. Middletown, Conn.: Wesleyan University Press, 1973.

Smith, C. S. *An Historical Sketch of Home Missionary Work in Vermont by the Congregational Churches*. Montpelier: Watchman Publishing, 1893.

Smith Rosenberg, Carroll. *Religion and the Rise of the American City: The New York City Mission Movement, 1812–1870*. Ithaca, N.Y.: Cornell University Press, 1970.

Stewart, I. D. *The History of the Freewill Baptists for Half a Century, with an Introductory Chapter, vol. 1.* Dover: Freewill Baptist Printing Establishment, 1862.

Stilwell, Lewis B. "Migration from Vermont, 1776–1860." *Proceedings of the Vermont Historical Society,* new ser., 5 (1937): 63–246.

Stout, Harry S. *The New England Soul: Preaching and Religious Culture in Colonial New England.* New York: Oxford University Press, 1986.

Sweeney, Kevin M. "Meetinghouses, Town Houses, and Churches: Changing Perceptions of Sacred and Secular Space in Southern New England, 1720–1850." *Winterthur Portfolio* 28 (1993): 59–93.

Sweet, Douglas H. "One Glorious Temple of God: Eighteenth-Century Accommodations to Changing Reality in New England." In *Studies in Eighteenth-Century Culture,* vol. 11, edited by Harry C. Payne, 311–320. Madison: University of Wisconsin Press, 1982.

Sweet, William Warren. *Religion in the Development of American Culture, 1765–1840.* New York: Charles Scribner's Sons, 1952.

Taves, Ann. *Fits, Trances, and Visions: Experiencing Religion and Explaining Experience from Wesley to James.* Princeton, N.J.: Princeton University Press, 1999.

———, ed. *Religion and Domestic Violence in Early New England: The Memoirs of Abigail Abbot Bailey.* Bloomington: Indiana University Press, 1989.

Taylor, Alan. *Liberty Men and Great Proprietors: The Revolutionary Settlement in the Maine Frontier, 1760–1820.* Chapel Hill: University of North Carolina Press, 1990.

Taysom, Stephen C. *Shakers, Mormons, and Religious Worlds: Conflicting Visions, Contested Boundaries.* Bloomington: Indiana University Press, 2010.

Thompson, Peter. *Rum Punch and Revolution: Taverngoing and Public Life in Eighteenth-Century Philadelphia.* Philadelphia: University of Pennsylvania Press, 1998.

Thumma, Scott. "The Kingdom, the Power, and the Glory: Megachurches in Modern American Society." Ph.D. dissertation, Emory University, 1996.

Turner, Lynn Warren. *The Ninth State: New Hampshire's Formative Years.* Chapel Hill: University of North Carolina Press, 1983.

———. *William Plumer of New Hampshire, 1759–1850.* Chapel Hill: University of North Carolina Press, 1962.

Ulrich, Laurel Thatcher. *A Midwife's Tale: The Life of Martha Ballard, Based on Her Diary, 1785–1812.* New York: Vintage Books, 1990.

Valeri, Mark. *Law and Providence in Joseph Bellamy's New England: The Origins of the New Divinity in Revolutionary America.* New York: Oxford University Press, 1994.

Vorpahl, Ben Merchant. "Presbyterianism and the Frontier Hypothesis: Tradition and Modification in the American Garden." *Journal of Presbyterian History* 45 (1967): 180–192.

Walsh, James P. "Holy Time and Sacred Space in Puritan New England." *American Quarterly* 32 (1980): 79–95.

Ward, Donal. "Religious Enthusiasm in Vermont, 1761–1847." Ph.D. dissertation, University of Notre Dame, 1980.

Weiss, Ellen. *City in the Woods: The Life and Design of an American Camp Meeting on Martha's Vineyard.* New York: Oxford University Press, 1987.

Westerkamp, Marilyn J. *The Triumph of the Laity: Scots-Irish Piety and the Great Awakening, 1625–1760.* New York: Oxford University Press, 1988.

Whiffen, Marcus, and Frederick Koeper. *American Architecture, 1607–1976.* Cambridge, Mass.: MIT Press, 1981.

White, Richard. *The Middle Ground: Indians, Empires, and Republics in the Great Lakes Region, 1650–1815.* Cambridge: Cambridge University Press, 1991.

Wigger, John H. *Taking Heaven by Storm: Methodism and the Rise of Popular Christianity.* New York: Oxford University Press, 1998.

Williams, Peter W. *Houses of God: Region, Religion, and Architecture in the United States.* Urbana: University of Illinois Press, 1997.

Williamson, Joseph. *History of the City of Belfast in the State of Maine: From Its Settlement in 1770 to 1875.* Vol. 1. Portland: Loring, Short, and Harmon, 1877.

Wilson, Harold F. "Population Trends in North-Western New England, 1790–1930." *New England Quarterly* 7 (1934): 276–306.

Winiarski, Douglas L. "Souls Filled with Ravishing Transport: Heavenly Visions and the Radical Awakening in New England." *William and Mary Quarterly,* 3rd ser., 61 (2004): 3–46.

Wood, Joseph S. *The New England Village.* Baltimore: Johns Hopkins University Press, 1997.

Youngs, J. William T., Jr. *God's Messengers: Religious Leadership in Colonial New England, 1700–1750.* Baltimore: Johns Hopkins University Press, 1976.

Zea, Philip. *Order and Dissent: A History of the Meriden Parish in Plainfield and the Separation of Church and State in New Hampshire.* Meriden, N.H.: n.p., 1980.

Zelinsky, Wilbur. "An Approach to the Religious Geography of the United States: Patterns of Church Membership in 1952." *Annals of the Association of American Geographers* 51 (1961): 139–193.

Index

Italicized page numbers refer to figures, maps, and tables.

SHELBY M. BALIK is Assistant Professor of American History at Metropolitan State University of Denver.

www.ingramcontent.com/pod-product-compliance
Lightning Source LLC
LaVergne TN
LVHW010352080826
844660LV00004B/256

* 9 7 8 0 2 5 3 0 1 2 1 0 4 *